Knowledge and Space

MW00824144

Volume 9

Series editor
Peter Meusburger, Department of Geography, Heidelberg University, Heidelberg, Germany

Knowledge and Space

This book series entitled "Knowledge and Space" is dedicated to topics dealing with the production, dissemination, spatial distribution, and application of knowledge. Recent work on the spatial dimension of knowledge, education, and science; learning organizations; and creative milieus has underlined the importance of spatial disparities and local contexts in the creation, legitimation, diffusion, and application of new knowledge. These studies have shown that spatial disparities in knowledge and creativity are not short-term transitional events but rather a fundamental structural element of society and the economy.

The volumes in the series on Knowledge and Space cover a broad range of topics relevant to all disciplines in the humanities and social sciences focusing on knowledge, intellectual capital, and human capital: clashes of knowledge; milieus of creativity; geographies of science; cultural memories; knowledge and the economy; learning organizations; knowledge and power; ethnic and cultural dimensions of knowledge; knowledge and action; and mobilities of knowledge. These topics are analyzed and discussed by scholars from a range of disciplines, schools of thought, and academic cultures.

Knowledge and Space is the outcome of an agreement concluded by the Klaus Tschira Foundation and Springer in 2006.

More information about this series at http://www.springer.com/series/7568

Peter Meusburger • Benno Werlen
Laura Suarsana

Editors

Knowledge and Action

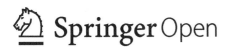

Klaus Tschira Stiftung
Gemeinnützige GmbH

Editors
Peter Meusburger
Department of Geography
Heidelberg University
Heidelberg, Germany

Benno Werlen
Department of Geography
Friedrich Schiller University Jena
Jena, Germany

Laura Suarsana
Department of Geography
Heidelberg University
Heidelberg, Germany

ISSN 1877-9220
Knowledge and Space
ISBN 978-3-319-83087-2   ISBN 978-3-319-44588-5   (eBook)
DOI 10.1007/978-3-319-44588-5

Printed on acid-free paper

This Springer imprint is published by Springer Nature
The registered company is Springer International Publishing AG
The registered company address is: Gewerbestrasse 11, 6330 Cham, Switzerland

Acknowledgements

The editors thank the Klaus Tschira Stiftung for funding the symposia and book series on Knowledge and Space. The staff of the Klaus Tschira Stiftung and Studio Villa Bosch always contributes a great deal to the success of the symposia.

Together with all the authors in this volume, we are especially grateful to David Antal for his tireless dedication to quality as technical editor of the chapters. We are also indebted to Patricia Callow for her assistance on the editing of Chaps. 9 and 15. Volker Schniepp at the Department of Geography at Heidelberg University has been an enormous support in getting the figures and maps to meet the high standards of publication. We also thank the students of Heidelberg University's Department of Geography who helped organize the 9th symposium and prepare this publication, especially Heike Dennhard, Helen Dorn, Maike Frank, Andreas Kalström, Claudia Kämper, Frederike Kempter, Nathalie Krabler, Laura Krauß, Julia Lekander, Pia Liepe, Anna Mateja Schmidt, Veronika Walz, Florence Wieder and Angela Zissmann.

Contents

Contributors

Ariane Berthoin Antal Research Group Science Policy Studies, WZB Berlin Social Science Center, Berlin, Germany

Huib Ernste Department of Human Geography, Radboud University, Nijmegen, The Netherlands

Renato Frey Center for Cognitive and Decision Sciences (CDS), Department of Psychology, University of Basel, Basel, Switzerland

Victor J. Friedman Department of Sociology and Anthropology/Department of Behavioral Sciences, Max Stern Academic College of Emek Yezreel, Jezreel Valley, Israel

Joachim Funke Department of Psychology, Heidelberg University, Heidelberg, Germany

Peter Gärdenfors Department of Philosophy, Lund University Cognitive Science, Lund, Sweden

Peter M. Gollwitzer Department of Psychology, New York University, New York, NY, USA
Department of Psychology, University of Konstanz, Konstanz, Germany

Ralph Hertwig Center of Adaptive Rationality (ARC), Max Planck Institute for Human Development in Berlin, Berlin, Germany

Annette Hieber German Center for Research on Aging, Heidelberg University, Heidelberg, Germany

Anand Krishna Institute for Psychology, University of Würzburg, Würzburg, Germany

Peter Meusburger Department of Geography, Heidelberg University, Heidelberg, Germany

Heidrun Mollenkopf German Center for Research on Aging, Heidelberg University, Heidelberg, Germany

Gunnar Olsson Department of Social and Economic Geography, University of Uppsala, Uppsala, Sweden

Richard Peet Graduate School of Geography, Clark University, Worcester, MA, USA

Tilman Reitz Institute of Sociology, Friedrich Schiller University Jena, Jena, Germany

Nico Stehr Karl Mannheim Professor for Cultural Studies, Zeppelin University, Friedrichshafen, Germany

Fritz Strack Institute for Psychology, University of Würzburg, Würzburg, Germany

Laura Suarsana Department of Geography, Heidelberg University, Heidelberg, Germany

Hans-Werner Wahl Institute of Psychology, Heidelberg University, Heidelberg, Germany

Benno Werlen Department of Geography, Friedrich Schiller University Jena, Jena, Germany

Thomas Widlok African Studies Institute, University of Cologne, Cologne, Germany

Department of Anthropology and Development Studies, Radboud University, Nijmegen, The Netherlands

Frank Wieber School of Health Professions, Institute for Health Sciences, ZHAW Zurich University of Applied Sciences, Winterthur, Switzerland

Department of Psychology, University of Konstanz, Konstanz, Germany

Chapter 1
Knowledge, Action, and Space: An Introduction

Peter Meusburger and Benno Werlen

> *The present epoch will perhaps be above all the epoch of space.*
>
> *Michel Foucault (1984/2002, p. 229).*

Open and Contested Research Questions

This book starts from the widely accepted premise that parts of knowledge can be defined as ability, aptitude, or "capacity for social action" (Stehr, 1994, p. 95)[1] and that the production and dissemination of knowledge are always embedded in specific environments (spatial context, spatial relations, and power structures). That point of departure makes it evident that the mutual relations between knowledge, action, and space are central research issues in disciplines dealing with human existence. For instance, acting under conditions of uncertainty, people must rely on experience gained in various situations and environments. To achieve their goals, they have to gather new information, acquire new knowledge, and develop new skills in order to cope with unexpected situations and unfamiliar challenges. Knowledge, experience, and information-processing are the foremost resources determining how aims of actions are set; how situations, opportunities, and risks are assessed; and how constellations, cues, and patterns are interpreted. They are the primary foundations for evaluating locations and spatial configurations, solving

---

[1] The close relationship between knowledge and power is evident by the very fact that they have the same etymological roots. The word *power* derives from the Latin *potere* (to be able). The Latin noun *potentia* denotes an ability, capacity, or aptitude to affect outcomes, to make something possible. It can therefore be translated as both knowledge and power (see also Avelino & Rotmans, 2009, p. 550; Meusburger, 2015c, p. 31; Moldaschl & Stehr, 2010, p. 9; Schönrich, 2005, p. 383). Most authors define action as goal-directed human activity that should be differentiated from pure behavior. Action is that part of behavior that occurs intentionally (see the Chap. 6 by Joachim Funke in this volume). Knowledge has an impact on action *and* behavior.

P. Meusburger (✉)
Department of Geography, Heidelberg University, Heidelberg, Germany
e-mail: peter.meusburger@uni-heidelberg.de

B. Werlen
Department of Geography, Friedrich Schiller University Jena, Jena, Germany

© The Author(s) 2017
P. Meusburger et al. (eds.), *Knowledge and Action*, Knowledge and Space 9,
DOI 10.1007/978-3-319-44588-5_1

problems, and enabling individual actors and social systems to appropriate space. Knowledge, learning, and information-processing can be regarded as links between action and space or action and environment (for details see Meusburger, 2003). Conversely, the spatial dimension plays a key role in the acquisition of knowledge and the implementation of actions. Scholars broadly agree on several points:

- Commitment and willful intent alone do not guarantee goal attainment.
- Goal-setting (is a given goal desirable and feasible?) and goal-striving (how is the goal being pursued?) are affected by knowledge, skills, experience, and the search for new information.
- Experience rests upon former actions in specific settings.
- There are manifold relationships between knowledge, power, and action,
- Learning processes are embedded in, and to some extent shaped by, the social and material environment.
- Settings and locations have a fundamental significance in the search for and access to rare or valuable information, the acquisition and distribution of knowledge, and the successful implementation of actions.

However, the devil is in the details. Relationships between knowledge, action, and space are very complex, some of them are still not fully understood. Some theoretical approaches focus on very simple problems (laboratory experiments) or work with a number of black boxes or questionable premises. Studying the interrelations of knowledge and action, one is apt to raise the following questions: To what extent is knowledge a precondition for action? How much knowledge is necessary for action? To what extent do various types of knowledge influence aspirations, attention, evaluation of situations, search for alternatives, implementation of intentions, decision-making, and problem-solving? How do bidirectional connections between knowledge and action function? How do different representations of knowledge shape action? Are knowledge, skills, experience, and educational achievement useful categories or should they be replaced by broader terms such as "reflective system" or "cognitive capacities"? How rational is human behavior? What categories of rationality should be distinguished? Does irrational behavior reflect a lack of appropriate information or is it rather affected by the impulsive system and orientation knowledge? How do deliberative, rational thought and impulsive affect interact and influence action? Why do people occasionally act against their knowledge? What are the social functions of knowledge? In which way can action research profit from interventions of arts and aesthetics?

Some of the most pressing questions in the study of the interrelations of action and space are: Which concepts of space and place are appropriate for analyzing relations between knowledge, action, and space? At what level of aggregation (individual, organization, spatial units)[2] can relations between knowledge, action,

---

[2] A social system's ability to act competently and achieve its goals depends not only on the knowledge of individual actors but also on their integration in organizations (institutions), the way organizations process information and share knowledge, interact with external social environment, and structure the way decisions are taken.

and space be documented by which indicators and empirical methods? How much are the spatial conditions of actions exposed to historical transformation? What exactly is the role and importance of spatial representations for the construction of sociocultural realities in the past, present and future? How does the digital revolution change the historically established society–space relations? What are the spatial implications for the formation of knowledge? Is the term *environment* an abstract category, a social macrophenomenon, a local cluster of individual factors of influence, or a localized culture? How can one measure an environment's impact on action and knowledge production (Meusburger, 2015a)?

These and other questions indicate that relations between knowledge, action, and space are not as simple as some people might assume or as some decision and risk models or traditional rational choice theories suggest. The questions simultaneously underscore the urgent need to explore the interdependencies of knowledge, action, and space from different disciplinary angles, scales of analysis,[3] time dimensions,[4] and ontologies.

The main ambition of this book is to contribute to the clarification of the linkages between knowledge, action and space beyond the well-established models. To redeem this claim it is first necessary to overcome the problematic legacy of *homo oeconomicus* and traditional rational choice theories and discuss some of the reasons why the spatial dimension was neglected or played only a marginal role in action-centered social theories. If we want to deepen the insights into the relations between action, knowledge and space, then the spatial dimension needs as much theoretical inquiry as the relations between knowledge and action (see the chapters by Werlen (Chap. 2), Ernste (Chap. 3), Olsson (Chap. 4), Gardenförs (Chap. 12), and Berthoin Antal and Friedman (Chap. 13) in this volume).

The Neglected Spatial Dimension in Modern Social Theory

Until the first decade of this century, one of the key shortcomings of modern social theory was the nearly total neglect of the spatial dimension of agency (Giddens, 1984), communication, social actions (Werlen, 1993b), and social relations. Systematic social theories and action theories in particular have so far widely ignored the spatial dimension of the social. This blindness for the spatial is embedded in more general features of modern social theory that have important implications not only in the field of theory, but consequently also for current societal problem constellations.

---

[3] Each scale of analysis yields certain insights that other scales cannot deliver.

[4] Often the question of whether actors possess the knowledge necessary to solve a problem and of which impact on decision-making and actions is due to superior or earlier knowledge or ignorance can be answered only after events or actions have taken place and unintended consequences have surfaced. Time lags between knowledge acquisition (e.g., research) and successful action (e.g., innovations) can amount to many years or even decades.

According to Giddens (1984), one of the chief reasons for the underrepresenta-tion of spatial issues in social theory is the overemphasis on time. Time, not space, has been pivotal for philosophy (Hegel, Bergson), the social sciences (Marx, Spencer, Durkheim), biology (Darwin), and history. Time—the sequential ordering of events—is obviously central in action theory. The implementation of action plans and intentions lies in the future, whereas the present situation of actions has resulted from actions of the past. Another notable reason that space aspects have not figured greatly in social theory is that the spatial dimension refers first to the ordering of physical objects and artifacts. It is thus allied somewhat more closely to immediate visual experience and is therefore less "abstract" than is the case with the temporal order. But the main explanation for the relative neglect of the spatial dimension pertaining to social realities in the action-centered perspective certainly stems from emphasis on the subjective meaning of action. The theory of social action as formu-lated by Weber (1912/1988, 1913, 1922/1980) implied that the embodied actor and the physical world were largely left out of the biologistic and functionalist tenden-cies in the social sciences (Werlen & Weingarten, 2003, pp. 205–207). This exclu-sion essentially arrested the development of concepts that could have integrated the spatial dimension and avoided the pitfall of biologistic or materialistic reductionism.

However, when the spatial dimension is taken into account, the word *space* is often not understood as a theory-dependent term but rather as a given fact. The social sciences commonly refer to notions of geographic space that are considered rather traditional or outdated in current social and cultural geography because they conceptualize space as a material object, a container, or projection plane of material and immaterial social life. Although lack of a systematic theoretical reformulation of *space* in a more sociotheoretical compatible way is detectable in the work of Pierre Bourdieu as well as in substantial parts of Giddens' (1984) theory of struc-turation, it is primarily found in social and cultural studies after a shift toward acceptance of the spatial dimension occurred. Exponents of this "spatial turn" claim to have overcome the spatial ignorance identified in their fields and disciplines of study. Their assertion is often unconvincing, however, because space continues to be thought of as a material object or container, with little progress toward a conception of space that is firmly grounded in social theory in a manner compatible with action.

The continuing overemphasis on the container or geographical earth-space in cultural studies and the social sciences leaves the spatial turn incomplete, inflexible, and myopic. These limitations also underlie fields of research and social policies in which it is not apparent at first glance, especially when "nature" is taken into account. An especially prominent example is the sustainability research based on the World Commission on Environment and Development (1987), known as the Brundtland report (Gäbler, 2015; Werlen, 2015), and on purportedly environmental policies derived from it. Casting the environment as a container space conceived in terms of Newton's mechanics, the recommendations for environmental policies are the product of a mechanical world view. They advertise the idea that it could suffice to turn some screws of the world machine to, say, decrease the global temperature by 2.0° Celsius, as propagated by the COP 21.[5]

Reconceptualization of the spatial dimension is imperative in the study of the interrelation of knowledge and space. When focusing on the role of places, spaces, spatial settings, environments, milieus, and fields of communication for cognitive processes, learning, knowledge production, and action, one must be careful to use the appropriate concepts of place and space in order to avoid implicit determinism and reductionism. When the concept of space as used in the natural sciences becomes a primary category of social research, it has major and problematic implications. In keeping with Newton's theoretical construction of space as a container, the two most relevant ones are the underlying spatial determinism and the likelihood that values, norms, and other nonmaterial entities will be reduced to earth-spatially positioned material objects. The morphing from immaterial to material or physical form will certainly not improve the results of social sciences and social politics, for all it does is falsify the real nature of sociocultural realities. Social research needs to find its own conceptualization of the spatial dimension of societal realities, including the generation of knowledge (for details see Schwan, 2003; Steiner, 2003; Weichhart, 2003, pp. 19–39).

For decades, unfortunately, subject-oriented action theory neglected the link between action and space, that is, the knowledge, competence, experience, skills, and learning processes of individuals, social systems, and institutions. Vague allusions to cognitive processes and reflective systems or ascriptions of meaning and value to material objects do little to explain why actions succeed or fail, why goals are achieved or missed, why some agents are competitive and others not, or why interactions with and adaptations to the environment vary so greatly in the spatial dimension. The focus should be more on different preconditions and outcomes of cognitive processes. To what extent do different levels of knowledge, educational achievement, occupational skills, experience, and scientific and technological standards influence the results of cognitive processes—from perception and situation analysis to decision-making and acting.

Material artifacts and spatial configurations acquire a social or symbolic meaning only through symbolic appropriation, through processes of learning, evaluating, interpreting, and using them. The results of such ascriptions, evaluations, and interpretations range from knowledgeable to ignorant, depending on the degree of experience brought to these processes, and the results change over time. It is therefore crucial to take into account the social, spatial, and cultural disparities of knowledge, competence, and experience as well as the level of research and technology when analyzing relations between space and action.

Geodeterminism emerges when the learning and evaluation processes between space (as a material object) and action are skipped. For instance, a geodeterminist would argue that a mountain range is a natural border; a specific terrain or a gorge, an optimal location for a fortification. A social geographer would argue that it is not

---

[5] Conference of the Parties (COP 21) held in Paris, 15–16 April 2016, was part of the cycle of major UN conferences on climate change.

the terrain, gorge, or mountain pass itself that has induced people over the centuries to build one fortress after the other at the same place. It is rather the result of knowledge accumulation and experience over many generations that led to the firm conviction or knowledge that a specific place is an ideal location for a fortress given the available transportation and military technologies. As soon as hitherto existing technologies are disrupted or political territories are expanded, the situation will be evaluated differently and people will conclude that other locations are more suitable.

In human geography the adventurous sense of reconceptualizing space and spatiality suffuses the publications of Belina (2013), Gregory (1994, 1998), Harvey (2005), Lippuner (2005), Lippuner & Lossau (2004), Massey (1985, 1999a, 1999b, 2005), Paasi (1991), Schmid (2005), Soja (1985), Tuan (1977), Weichhart (1996, 1999, 2003), and Werlen (1987, 1993a, 1993b, 1995, 1997, 2010a, 2010b, 2013, 2015), to name just a few. Geographies of knowledge, education, and science (Freytag, Jahnke, & Kramer, 2015; Jöns, 2008; Livingstone, 1995, 2000, 2002, 2003; Meusburger, 1998, 2000, 2008, 2009, 2015a) and creativity studies (Amabile, Conti, Coon, Lazenby, & Herron, 1996; Amabile, Goldfarb, & Brackfield, 1990; Csikszentmihalyi, 1988, 1999; Hennessey & Amabile, 1988; Meusburger, 2009; Sternberg & Lubart, 1999) contributed to that discussion by documenting how educational achievement, occupational skills, research, and creative processes influence actions of individuals and social systems, how research and creative processes are the result of interactions between agents and their environment, and why various spatial disparities of socioeconomic structures persist for long periods.

The Problematic Legacy of Homo Oeconomicus and Rational Choice Theories

Taking the spatial dimension into account first requires a critical review of the classical models used in social sciences, especially the model of economic actions based on the concept of *homo oeconomicus*. The claims about its general validity and applicability are inherently linked to the alienation of space. The concept of *homo oeconomicus* and the assumptions that traditional rational choice theorists make about the human decision-maker and some other premises have been criticized by many authors as empirically unfounded and psychologically unrealistic (Buskens, 2015; Flache & Dijkstra, 2015; Gigerenzer & Gaissmaier, 2015; Green & Shapiro, 1994; Goldthorpe, 2000; Haselton et al., 2009; Hertwig & Herzog, 2009; Samuels & Stich, 2015). Theories of bounded rationality, behavioral economics, evolutionary economics, new theories of the firm, the strategic management approach, and nonrational theories have been divested of many unrealistic premises; nevertheless, some theoretical concepts of decision-making used in economics and partly also in social sciences[6] still carry the detrimental legacy of *homo oeconomicus*

---

[6] For an overview of the large variety of rational choice models, see Wittek, Snijders, & Nee (2013).

and traditional rational choice theories. We do not repeat here the extensive critique of that model but rather focus on those aspects for which the lack of sensitivity to the spatial dimension of human existence and sociocultural realities is playing an important role, at least from a geographer's point of view. In the geography of knowledge (Meusburger, 1998, 2015a, 2017), one critique is that many theoretical concepts of decision-making ignore—

- social and spatial disparities of knowledge;
- the impact that environments, spatial contexts, and spatial relations have on the generation and diffusion of knowledge;
- the selective mobility of different categories and levels of knowledge; and
- power structures in space. The enduring persistence of national and global urban hierarchies is due mainly to relations between knowledge and power, the spatial concentration of power, the vertical division of labor, and selected migration.

Mutual relations between knowledge and power have been intensely discussed elsewhere (Gregory, 1998; Meusburger, 1998, 2000, 2015c; Meusburger, Gregory, & Suarsana, 2015) and need not be repeated here. They are neatly summarized by Foucault (1980):

- The exercise of power perpetually creates knowledge and, conversely, knowledge constantly induces effects of power. (p. 52)
- Knowledge and power are integrated with one another, and there is no point in dreaming of a time when knowledge will cease to depend on power. (p. 52)
- It is not possible for power to be exercised without knowledge, it is impossible for knowledge not to engender power. (p. 52)

It is also criticized that some scholars do not distinguish between knowledge and information,[7] and that the costs and time needed to acquire the knowledge, expertise, and the advanced levels of educational achievement necessary to solve complex problems are neglected or underestimated.

From a geographer's point of view, the ideal-type premises of homogeneous space and ubiquity of knowledge are the most critical shortcomings, the assumptions farthest from empirically verifiable realities. Unequal spatial and social distribution of various categories of knowledge and skills can be traced to early human history, at least to the time when the first scripts were developed (5500 BC). Spatial and social inequalities of knowledge, spatial concentrations of power (Meusburger, 1998, 2000; 2008; 2015c) and hierarchically structured urban systems are a constitutive element of highly differentiated societies that are based on horizontal and vertical division of labor. In a knowledge society, the range of knowledge gaps, knowledge asymmetries, and spatial disparities of knowledge is larger than ever and is constantly growing.[8] With respect to the assumption that knowledge is spatially

---

[7] For detailed discussion see vol. 10 in the series on Knowledge and Space.

[8] This statement contradicts the popular view that anybody in the digital age has access to the knowledge available worldwide. The Internet offers access to information, not to knowledge. Whether available information is understood, accepted, and assimilated into a person's existing knowledge base depends on complex psychological processes (Meusburger, 2017).

ubiquitous, the rational choice model is so remote from the empirical facts that its heuristic value tends toward zero if the spatial dimension is taken seriously. The wide dissemination and use of the premise that space is homogenous certainly has to do with the exclusion of spatial and cultural constellations. Unfortunately, it has ecologically and culturally problematic consequences as well.

Even within the rules of social modeling, the rational choice model does not meet applicable standards. Models may idealize empirical reality only if their heuristic value is not undermined (see Werlen 1993a; 1993b, pp. 43–51). If the model strays too far from empirical reality, it can no longer help detect that reality's regularities or properties. "Without *knowledge*, or beliefs that correspond to reality, thinking is an empty shell" (Baron 2008, p. 15, italics in the source).

The premise that knowledge is ubiquitous is sometimes justified by the impact of the Internet. The Internet facilitates the spatial distribution of easily understandable information and routine knowledge but certainly does not have deeper balancing effects on spatial disparities when it comes to the spatial distribution of jobs that need advanced scientific, technical, and expert knowledge. Such jobs are not as mobile as some authors may assume, they tend to concentrate in certain places or areas (Malecki, 2000; Meusburger, 2000, 2017). Different categories of knowledge travel at different speeds and very selectively.[9] The individual has limited cognitive capacities and only a minute and constantly diminishing share of all knowledge worldwide (see the Chap. 7 by Stehr in this volume). Even if the individual possesses the cognitive capacities to specialize in a certain field, it takes years and incurs great cost for that person to acquire such knowledge, educational achievement, and expertise.

For decades, traditional rational choice theory and instrumental rational action models focused on a peculiarly rational and omniscient type of person who has or easily gains access to all the knowledge, skills, and expertise needed in order to make rational decisions and achieve his or her goals.[10] Most adherents of these theories have ignored or suppressed the fact that people differ in their cognitive capacities, level of knowledge, professional experience, and skills, not to mention their level of education.[11] A number of authors writing about rational choice theory

---

[9] Mobilities of knowledge are the topic of volume 10 in this series.

[10] "Neoclassical economics typically employs the assumption of perfect rationality…Rational actors never fail to find the action that maximizes their utility, even if this requires unlimited capacities to process and memorize all information available and to have unlimited foresight of the consequences of all available courses of actions in a distant future" (Flache & Dijkstra, 2015, p. 907). Empirical evidence shows that people have limited and unequal information-processing and computational capabilities. These findings have led to various models of bounded rationality (Simon, 1956, 1982, 1990).

[11] Professionals, scientists, engineers, and other experts must study many years to acquire the task-related or goal-relevant knowledge they need for their problem-solving and decision-making. Much of this knowledge and expertise can be learned only in specific institutions of higher education. It is therefore difficult to understand why differences in the level of educational achievement play but a marginal role in action theory and rational choice theories.

(e.g., Buskens, 2015; Radner, 2015) simply altogether avoid using categories such as knowledge, skills, expertise, and educational achievement.

Another weakness of traditional rational choice theory is the fact that rationality—conventionally understood to be a method of thinking and logical consistency—has little explanatory power. The concept of rational behavior focuses on a person's strategic choice of the best means to achieve a certain goal, but it does not include consideration of the goal's reasonableness and attainability or of the resources needed in order to pursue the goal.

> [F]ormal logic is concerned with the rules for drawing conclusions from evidence with certainty. That is, it is concerned only with inference. It says nothing about how evidence is, or should be, obtained. Formal logic, therefore, cannot be a complete theory of thinking. (Baron, 2008, p. 81)

In decision-making and goal-oriented social action, formal logic must be combined with knowledge, expertise, skills, and the newest information. Because actors differ in their levels of information, knowledge, skills, experience, and educational achievement, they arrive at very different decisions if they follow the principle of rational decision-making. What seems rational to an agent who has little expertise and relies on public information might be irrational to an actor with great expertise or to a stock broker with insider knowledge. "[A] given act may appear rational at the time it is undertaken; yet when a different goal is activated to which that act was detrimental it may appear irrational and one might come to regret it" (Kruglanski & Orehek, 2009, p. 647). High levels of knowledge, skill, expertise, and early access to important information help people come to decisions that are apt to achieve the desired goal. Gaps in expertise, skills, educational achievement, and information usually restrict goal attainment.[12]

> Like any goal-directed activity, thinking can be done well or badly. Thinking that is done well is thinking of the sort that achieves its goals. When we criticize people's thinking, we are trying to help them achieve their own goals. When we try to think well, it is because we want to achieve our goals. (Baron, 2008, p. 29)

Max Weber (1922/1980), who first made rationality a key concept in modernistic thinking, was interested in the fact that rationality created a culture of objectification (*Versachlichung*) and relegated myths, superstition, and unjustified beliefs to the background. He used the term specifically in the sense of economic rationality that denotes the strategic choice of the best means to reach a given goal. However, Weber's concept of rationality was later extended to fields where it was not appropriate. Max Weber never asserted that rationality alone will help define expedient and achievable goals, that rational agents are capable of recognizing the value and the utility of their goals, or that rational behavior will trigger creativity and innovation.

Aspects of space and spatial contexts did not play a particular role in the debates mentioned above, but they were highlighted by debates around nonrational theories. Since the late 1990s, nonrational theories, concepts of ecological rationality, geographies of science, and other fields of social geography have developed a growing sensitivity for the significance of spatial contexts, spatial relations, environments,

---

[12] This observation is even more relevant for social systems than for individual decision-makers.

and contact fields for learning processes, knowledge production, decision-making, and innovation. They have emphasized that learning processes are intrinsically interwoven with conceptions of space (see the Chap. 12 by Gardenförs in this volume).

Recent Developments in Decision-Making Theories and Geographies of Science: Improvements in the Understanding of Relations Between Knowledge, Action, and Space

In proposing to use theories of heuristics[13] and nonrational tools, Gigerenzer and his collaborators have introduced a concept they call *ecological rationality* (Gigerenzer & Gaissmaier, 2011; 2015; Gigerenzer & Selten, 2001; Goldstein & Gigerenzer, 2002; Samuels & Stich, 2015; Todd, Gigerenzer, & ABC Research Group, 2012). Unlike rational choice theories, heuristic theories of decision-making are concerned with psychological realism relating to the capacities and limitations of actual humans and emphasize the importance of a specific context, frame, or environment and focus on the performance of actors in the external physical and social world (Buskens, 2015, p. 903; Gigerenzer & Gaissmaier, 2015, pp. 911–912; Hertwig & Herzog, 2009; Lindenberg, 2013; Todd & Gigerenzer, 2000).

> In a world where not all risks are known and where optimization is not feasible, 'nonrational' tools such as heuristics are needed…[N]onrational theories apply to 'decision-making under uncertainty,' where not all alternatives, consequences, and probabilities are known or knowable…Rational theories, in contrast, are tailored to situations where all risks are known. (Gigerenzer & Gaissmaier, 2015, p. 911)

> The study of the ecological rationality of heuristics,[14] or strategies in general, is a framework to study performance in the external world: A heuristic is ecologically rational to the degree that it is adapted to the structure of the environment. Heuristics are 'domain-specific' rather than 'domain-general'; that is, they work in a class of environments in which they are ecologically rational. Heuristics provide not a universal rational calculus but a set of domain-specific mechanisms…, and have been referred to collectively as the 'adaptive toolbox'. (Gigerenzer & Gaissmaier, 2015, p. 912)

---

[13] "A heuristic is not per se rational or irrational; rather, its rationality depends on the match between the architecture of the tool and the structure of the environment in which it is employed" (Hertwig & Herzog, 2009, p. 668). "An inferential or judgmental strategy is ecologically rational if it is accurate and efficient on the sorts of tasks that were important in the environments in which we evolved" (Samuels & Stich, 2015, p. 722).

[14] "A heuristic is a strategy that ignores part of the information, with the goal of making decisions more accurately, quickly, and frugally (i.e., with fewer pieces of information) compared to more complex methods" (Gigerenzer & Gaissmaier, 2015, p. 913). "A heuristic is ecologically rational to the degree that it is adapted to the structure of the environment. Heuristics are 'domain-specific' rather than 'domain-general'; that is, they work in a class of environments in which they are ecologically rational. Heuristics provide not a universal rational calculus but a set of domain-specific mechanisms" (Gigerenzer & Gaissmaier, 2015, p. 912).

The heuristic approach to decision-making and the concept of ecological ratio-nality are very similar to concepts used by geographies of knowledge and science (Livingstone, 1995, 2000, 2002, 2003; Meusburger, 1998, 2015a, 2015b, 2015c). They not only respect the view that human cognitive abilities are unequal because of different experience and learning processes, but—like the geography of knowl-edge—also take the environment's information structure and knowledge milieu into account. They accept that both the formulation of goals and the processes of information-processing, learning, research, and decision-making can be somewhat shaped by their social environment (Flache & Dijkstra, 2015, pp. 908, 911; Meusburger, 2015a).

Depending on the prior knowledge and experience of actors, a physical and social environment can play the role of an external storage space of information that may trigger associations and send cues to the informed agent. People, pictures, traces, patterns, institutions, and written sources can help overcome the limitations of human memories and cognitive capacities, including the time and effort needed to acquire specific forms of knowledge and expertise (Baron, 2008, p. 15). Structures and dynamics of environments also affect how people seek out information (Navarro, Newell, & Schulze, 2016, p. 45) and which kind of bias they must cope with in their search (Fiedler & Wänke, 2009).

Two categories—recognition-based heuristics[15] and one-clever-cue heuris-tics[16]—closely resemble a concept used in the geography of knowledge, prior knowledge. The term *Vorwissen* (translated in this chapter as prior knowledge) draws on the hermeneutic circle and Gadamer's (1960/1999) term *Vorverständnis* (prior understanding, pp. 250, 275).[17]

Prior knowledge accrues through learning and experience, includes intuition and latent subconscious experience, and is domain specific. Optimal search for possibilities, evidence, new goals, and "actively open-minded thinking" (Baron 2008, p. 63, italics in the original) need a superior level of prior knowledge. Prior knowledge determines whether and how available information is perceived, ana-lyzed, and evaluated by an actor and whether it enters and broadens that person's body of knowledge.[18] Prior knowledge helps one select the most meaningful cues and has an impact on how patterns and cues are interpreted. Bushmen (San) in the

---

[15] The goal of recognition-based heuristics is to "make inferences about a criterion that is not directly accessible to the decision-maker, based on recognition retrieved from memory" (Gigerenzer & Gaissmaier, 2015, p. 914).

[16] One-clever-cue heuristics looks for only one 'clever' cue and bases its decision on that cue alone (Gigerenzer & Gaissmaier, 2015, p. 914).

[17] *Prior knowledge* and *prior understanding* are synonymous in the hermeneutic method. The method entails a paradox in the sense that what is to be understood somehow has to have been understood beforehand. Gadamer also calls it positive prejudgment (hence the terms *Vorwissen* and *Vorverständnis*). To have prior knowledge or prior understanding of something, one has to have already understood individual parts or aspects of it. This requisite is also called the hermeneu-tic circle. Philosophers preceding Gadamer also thought about this circle.

[18] The concept of prior knowledge plays an important role in the communication of various catego-ries of knowledge (for details see Meusburger, 2017).

Kalahari are able to sleuth animals like nobody else. Experienced doctors can diagnose a disease by interpreting a few signs (students of medicine may not have this ability yet). Geographers who are specialists in a certain field of knowledge may draw path-breaking conclusions from a thematic map, whereas other persons will glean no information at all from the same map. Local people living in the Alps may have acquired enough knowledge from previous generations or from personal experience to recognize from scant, subtle indications which places may be endangered by avalanches; most tourists will not be able to evaluate these risks. Many culturally transmitted bodies of knowledge are learned through observation of[19] important environmental cues. In fact, observing and interpreting cues and spatial configurations is a long-standing heuristic device of geography.

Humans are susceptible to social influence and to the type of information that is available in their environment. Geographies of knowledge and science have illustrated how learning processes, research, and scientific careers can be influenced by the local availability of role models, resources, specific thought styles,[20] face-to-face contacts to prominent scholars, institutional logics, and organizational rules. The interrelationships of these factors and others constitute the knowledge environment of a place (for details see Meusburger, 2008, 2015a; Meusburger & Schuch, 2012). An extreme example of the impact that different informational environments have on decision-making and acting is given by Gregory (2015, pp. 113–114). Describing World War I battlefields at the western front and the differences between a *paper war* and a *trench war*,[21] he illustrates the insurmountable gulf between the experienced knowledge of the infantry in the muddy trenches of the battlefield and the abstract knowledge of the staff officers surrounding the map table in a comfortable room and planning the movements of their soldiers for the next days.

Scientific evidence from cognitive psychology (see the Chap. 6 by Funke in this volume), sociology (Stehr, 1994, 2005), social geography (Meusburger, 2015a, 2015c; Werlen, 1993b, pp. 8–11), and other research fields shows that there is no direct if–then relation between knowledge and action. There are a number of intervening variables—many of them related to the environment or place of action— that may modify, weaken, or strengthen the relations between knowledge and action. The concurrence and coaction of these variables at a certain place or in a specific area build a spatial context, social environment, or knowledge milieu that may affect decision-making and action. As pointed out by Fiedler and Wänke (2009, p. 699), properties of the environment can constrain or enhance the input to cognitive processes. These two researchers illustrate that error and bias may often originate in the information environment, in selective accessibility to information; that observations

---

[19] Learning by observing "includes all cases in which we learn about our environment from observation alone, without intentional experimentation" (Baron, 2008, p. 14).

[20] "The greater the difference between two thought styles, the more inhibited will be the communication of ideas" (Fleck, 1935/1979, p. 109).

[21] "Trench war is an environment that can never be known abstractly or from the outside. Onlookers could never understand a reality that must be crawled through and lived in. This life, in turn, equips the inhabitant with a knowledge that is difficult to generalize or explain" (Leed, 1981, p. 79).

can be influenced by environmental sampling; and that agents—in their capacity as available sources of information—may lack first-hand experience, overdo some risks, and neglect others. In brief, "cognitive processes are fed with an environmental input that is itself often biased and highly selective" (p. 700).

Talent, motivation, and wealth of ideas are not the only characteristics determining how successfully a scholar's research and academic career develops (Meusburger, 2015a). What we academics call creative is never the result of individual action alone. Learning processes and actions are situated in environments, organizational structures, and spatial relations. We cannot study scientific creativity by isolating scholars and their works from the social and historical milieu in which their actions are carried out. The key issue is the interaction with the environment. It is well known from creativity studies that a stimulating environment and a talented individual must come together and interact before a creative process can occur (for details see Amabile et al., 1990, 1996; Csikszentmihalyi, 1988, 1999; Hennessey & Amabile, 1988; Meusburger, 2009; Sternberg & Lubart, 1999).

An environment's impacts on action must not be regarded deterministically. An environment should not be thought of as an independent variable that directly influences all relevant actors through a direct cause-and-effect relation (if A, then B). It depends on processes of evaluation based on learning, knowledge, and experience whether spatial structures, physical space, or social environments have an impact on human action.

> A knowledge environment is a locally available potential or a local range of resources. It stands for incentives, challenges, stimulations, opportunities, and support networks that can be used, overlooked, or ignored. A knowledge environment can operate as it should only if the actors involved use the local resources and interact with each other. The outcomes of human interactions and experiences in life are always indeterminate. No one can predict the results of appropriation and interaction, whether and how often the local potential for integrating diverse viewpoints and knowledge bases will be activated, and how the relationships between creative agents will develop. Therefore, a knowledge environment's significance and effect can be analyzed only after events have taken place, after the scientific careers and research results associated with that environment have become evident. (Meusburger, 2015a, pp. 266–267)

Collective Action

Organizations, institutions, and other power structures are an environment's most efficient elements for enhancing or impeding the conversion of a person's knowledge into action. Without the support of institutions, most decision-makers cannot reach their goals (Meusburger, 1999, 2015a; Werlen, 1995, pp. 40–49). When studying the relations of knowledge and action in social systems, organizations, or institutions, one must take additional aspects into account (some of them are discussed in the Chap. 11 by Reitz; others, in volumes 6 and 7 of this series). As Goldman (2004) states, epistemic organizations need nodal points where information converges and theoretical conclusions are arrived at. But any organization has at least two problems to cope with. First, the knowledge and experience necessary for solving a problem or making the right decisions to achieve a certain goal may be available somewhere in an organization, but it may not reach the people authorized to act on it. Second, the nodal points or authorized decision-makers may not have the prior knowledge, experience, and intuition necessary to understand and evaluate the importance of information that has been forwarded to them. Those who decide often not understand those who know. And those who know are often experts in narrow domains only or are not close to those in power.

Weber's (1922/1980) ideal bureaucracy rested on the principles of meritocracy and the absence of nepotism and incompetence. In that system the hierarchy of decision-making corresponded to a hierarchy of competence. High-ranking decision-makers were expected to have broader expertise and more experience than their subordinates; the superiors would at least be able to understand, evaluate, and embrace the information forwarded to them. In large and complex organizations, it happens quite frequently that line managers (immediate superiors) have achieved their position because of merits other than broad knowledge and expertise in a certain domain. In some political systems, ideological reliability and loyalty to a political party, ethnic group, or powerful network counts for more than expertise does when it comes to promotion to a high post. Even if managers understand the relevance and urgency of information, they may fail to draw the necessary practical consequences because they are indebted to a political party or a powerful person or are under pressure from their social environment.

Organization theory, especially the research field following the tradition of Mintzberg (1979), and the geography of knowledge have an abiding interest in the organization and coordination of social systems in space and in the spatial concentration of jobs involving high levels of educational achievement and decision-making. Originally, region meant a space that was organized, coordinated, controlled, and influenced by a power center or a social system's authority (for details see Berthoin Antal, Meusburger, & Suarsana, 2014; Gottmann, 1980; Meusburger et al., 2015). Organization theory and the geography of knowledge have documented how the structure of a social system—the centralization or decentralization of decision-making authority, skills, and competence within an organization—varies with the complexity of its tasks and the uncertainty of its environment. In summary, a number of research fields have underlined the importance of an environment or spatial context and its possible impact on individual and collective action, but their strands of argumentation have seldom coalesced.

Aims, Claims, and Content of this Volume

A main intention of this volume is to raise awareness of important research issues that various disciplines have brought into the field of knowledge, action, and space to define research gaps and misunderstandings and, if possible, to build bridges between diverse theoretical approaches. For this purpose we editors have selected a broad range of topics and various scales of analysis. More than a dozen disciplines do research on knowledge, learning, education, innovation, and creativity. Even a glance at the definitions and concepts of knowledge used in different disciplines[22] documents the necessity of looking beyond the fence of one's own subject and avoiding monodisciplinary lists of references. Even if some of the approaches initially seem mutually incompatible, a synopsis of the relevant research from a variety disciplines can help improve the understanding of the links between knowledge, action, and space and can prompt new research questions.

This volume brings together a broad range of theoretical approaches delving into knowledge, action, and space from different angles. Some of the contributors discuss knowledge as a social construct based on collective action, on socially embedded and guiding social action. Others look at knowledge as an individual capacity to act. The breadth of studies ranges from the role of knowledge in individual action to its role in collective action, from knowledge and action in the hunter–gatherer society to knowledge production in financial capitalism. The discussion of concepts and theories of knowledge touches on topics such as semantic knowledge and its organization into domains, asymmetrical knowledge and the polarization of knowledge and nonknowledge, knowledge and collective action,[23] situated problem-solving, spatial dispersion of knowledge, knowledge and planning, and expertise as a link between knowledge and practical action.

In the chapter following this introduction, Benno Werlen describes the long path geographers had to follow before they arrived at concepts of space suitable for issues of social geography. Until the late 1990s, the theoretical concepts in many fields of human geography diverted attention from the key role that the social dimension plays in the construction of meaningful geographical realities.[24]

Werlen identifies the reasons for the current failure of the spatial turn in the social sciences and offers an action-centered approach to developing a constructivist geography for the digital age. His contribution includes a specific, action-related, and action-compatible theory of space that can also take account of different concepts of space for different types of action. In this conceptualization of space, the spatial dimension of action and society is related to the corporeality of the actors and to the necessity of overcoming distances between actors and the physical elements of situations and means of action. Because the actor's body is simultaneously

---

[22] For an overview of different concepts and definitions of knowledge, see Abel (2008), Meusburger (2015c), Stehr (1994, 2005), Stehr and Meja (2005), and Reitz (Chap. 11 in this volume). Reitz distinguishes between knowledge as a systematic set of applicable recipes, knowledge as an organized body of theoretical statements, and knowledge as a developed capacity for situated problem-solving.

[23] The role of knowledge in organizations was the focus of volume 6 in this series (Berthoin Antal et al., 2014) and will be discussed in volumes 11 and 13 as well.

[24] The hitherto most convincing theoretical way to integrate the spatial dimension into the field of action research is also the narrowest and is of only limited use in social and cultural studies—that is, embedding metric space in locational decision-making theory applied to action models based on rational choice.

the key criterion for distinguishing between direct and mediated experiences and between face-to-face and mediated communication, the three main foci of this book—action, knowledge, and space—are conceptualized in a new framework, the socially constructed relations of space.

The geographer Huib Ernste illustrates in his chapter that the divorce of rationality and reason during the philosophical development of modernity led to recognition of different types of rationality, each with its own logics of deliberation and argumentation. Poststructuralists emphasize that each rationality contains multiple paradigms, each establishing its own set of principles, institutions, and lines of conflict that need to be taken into account. He demonstrates how these views are intricately involved in late-modern geographical theories of action and in language-pragmatic approaches[25] in geography.

Proponents of poststructuralist approaches emphasize the structural aspects of discourse, especially power structures. Laclau and Mouffe (1985), by contrast, try to retain and restore the possibility of deliberative interventions in these discursive structures by inverting Foucault's power/knowledge equation. Ernste explores the extent to which this inversion reinstates responsible and rational spatial decisions and actions as a focus of research in human geography. In his view rationality could be reconstituted as a culturally contingent phenomenon, and critical geographical analysis could again contribute to concrete problem-solving, albeit in a culturally much more informed and embedded way than hitherto. Ernste also discusses geographical action theory as put forward by Werlen (1987, 1993a, 1993b, 1995, 1997, 2010a, 2010b, 2013, 2015; see also Werlen's Chap. 2 in this volume) in the phenomenological tradition of Schütz (1932). According to that school of thought, the internal mental intentionality directed to outer objects is what ascribes meanings to these objects, as people do through their everyday place-making and everyday spatially differentiated actions. Ernste interprets this geographic action theory as the subjectivist version of what Schatzki, Knorr-Cetina, and Savigny (2001) and Reckwitz (2002) designated as the mentalist paradigm in social theory. This approach contrasts with the objectivist version of mentalism, which stems from classical structuralism.

Ernste shows that the advent of poststructuralist thinking ushered in a great reluctance to conceptualize human behavior as conscious rational actions and that the term *action* is generally avoided in most poststructuralist literature. Talking about practice instead of action indeed amounts to a novel picture of human agency and rationality (Reckwitz, 2008, p. 98). In contrast to Benno Werlen, with his subjective, meaning-oriented approach to geographical action theory, and unlike Zierhofer (2002), who advocated the language-pragmatic approach in geography, poststructuralist thinkers do not tend to place structures inside the mind or in pragmatic procedures of interaction but rather "outside" both—in chains of signs, in symbols, discourse, or text.

---

[25] Pragmatics is "a branch of linguistics dealing with language in its situational context, including the knowledge and beliefs of the speaker and the relationship and interaction between speaker and listener" ("Pragmatics," 2010).

Ideologies of urban and regional planning have a powerful effect on human actions. But to what extent can social behavior be influenced or even determined by planning concepts? How can one explain the gap between intention and behavior? The geographer Gunnar Olsson describes the ideology of social engineering that predominated in Sweden in the 1950s and early 1960s, principles intended to forge a happy marriage between scientific knowledge and political action. As the affinities between totalitarian thinking and social engineering are impossible to deny, Olsson starts his narrative with the role that central place theory and location theory played in Nazi Germany. Christaller (1933) and Lösch (1943/1954) were seeking a scientific method to colonize or settle a given area, especially how a set of hierarchically nested and hexagonally distributed centers *should* be tied together into a functional whole.

In the thought style of location theory, regional science, positivist thinking, spatial models, and social engineering, it is necessary to describe the functioning of society by mathematical calculations. In the 1950s and 1960s politically anchored experts took it as their mission to turn Sweden into a People's Home, a state of rationality in which the maximizing principles of utilitarian ethics were institutionalized. Their intention was to capture the power of social relations in a net of scientific laws (e.g., the social gravity model) and to acquire the means for understanding the world and for changing it as well. The history of the social gravity model in regional science and of quantitative geography provides an excellent example of the ups and downs of theoretical concepts. At first the model was treated as a formulation of great explanatory power; subsequent generations have come to see it as an expression of autocorrelation. To demonstrate power-and-knowledge relations in the form of a self-referential presentation, Olsson discusses the sculpture *Mappa Mundi Universalis*, conceived and designed by himself and Ole Michael Jensen and exhibited in the Museum Gustavianum in Uppsala, Sweden.

A Marxist view on relations between knowledge, action, and space is presented by the geographer Richard Peet. Viewing knowledge production from a global scale, he analyzes the role of expertise[26] in financial institutions, which are now the dominant economic institutions in capitalist societies. Following Marx and Gramsci, he states that knowledge production serves a class interest and that class forces lead, direct, and control the production of knowledge. What matters in the making of history are the broad social and cultural trends in thought, imagination, and comprehension, such as political-economic-cultural ideas.

He calls the production of sophisticated, but inimical, knowledge in the financial system perverse expertise. In this expertise some of the world's finest minds, such as professional economists, do the intellectual and practical modeling and are well paid and respected for doing so. But they accumulate knowledge in order to continue augmenting the incomes of already wealthy people, the capitalist class. In Peet's view, critical mass reaction to financial crisis or the pending world environmental catastrophe is prevented by hegemonic control over imaginaries by a combi-

---

[26] Peet (Chap. 5) defines expertise as high-quality, specialized, theoretical, and practical knowledge and regards it as the junction of knowledge and action.

nation of perverse expertise and mass social unconsciousness. The elites practice perverse expertise, and the masses lose their capacity to think rationally and respond unconsciously. Peet's conclusion is that the intersecting economic and environmental crises will continue *ad infinitum* because the existing hegemonic knowledge cannot guide effective social action. Although investor confidence is presented by the business media as a neutral, technical, and necessary factor—in everyone's best long-term interest—it is actually a committed, financial capitalist interest based on utterly biased knowledge. An instructive example is the global bond market. The interest paid on sovereign bonds is determined by the risk of default, with experts employing formulae stemming from long experience measured statistically—apparently scientific and necessary. Yet it is actually a few thousand experts representing the interests of accumulated capital who tell governments how to run their economies.

The next seven chapters focus on the microscale of analysis and discuss concepts, definitions, and research results from philosophy, psychology, and sociology. Psychologist Joachim Funke starts his contribution with three questions: How much knowledge is necessary for action? Is action possible without knowledge? Why do people sometimes act against their knowledge? He discusses some of the standard views on the relation between knowledge and action, specifically, the theory of planned behavior, the theory of unconscious thought, and the option-generation framework. He illustrates the delicate relation between knowledge and action with an example from problem-solving research. In Funke's understanding, problem-solving means the intentional generation of knowledge for action instead of simple trial-and-error behavior. His studies on the MicroDYN approach, which was used in the 2012 cycle of the worldwide PISA study, demonstrate the existence of a clear connection between the generation of knowledge and action (i.e., application of that knowledge). From the angle of a problem-solving approach, the connection between knowledge and action is a classical means–end relation. It is not possible to act *without* knowledge, but people can act *against* their knowledge.

Nico Stehr, a sociologist of science, offers a sociological critique of the prevalent argument that the increasing polarization of knowledge and nonknowledge (or ignorance) has become a distinguishing feature of modernity. He acknowledges that significant asymmetries of knowledge exist and that knowledge gaps are growing, but he rejects the interpretation that nonknowledge is the opposite of knowledge. Seeking to avoid that either–or polarity as an arbitrary, theoretically and empirically unproductive antithesis, he posits knowledge instead as a context-dependent anthropological constant representing a continuum. In his view there is only less or more knowledge, and there are only those who know something and those who know something else. The practical problem is always to know how much or how little one knows in a given situation. From his perspective the key sociological question is how to address the issue of knowledge asymmetry and knowledge gaps in various spheres of modern society, such as the economy, politics, the life world, and governance. He argues that nonknowledge has, in different societal institutions, its own functional meaning. There are myriad convincing references to the virtues and advantages of ignorance, a lack or asymmetry of knowledge, and nontransparent situations.

The psychologists Ralph Hertwig and Renato Frey address the question of how different representations of knowledge shape human actions. Before choosing to act, people often try to acquire knowledge about a given situation, opportunities and risks, and possible consequences of their actions. In some cases they can draw on convenient descriptions of actions and their consequences—such as a medicine's accompanying information on possible side effects and their probabilities. People thereby make decisions from description. In everyday life, however, there are usually no actuarial tables of risks to consult. Instead, people make such decisions in the twilight of their sampled—and often limited—experience.

Recent research in psychology has demonstrated that decisions from description and decisions from experience can lead to substantially different choices, especially where rare events are involved. Studies on modern behavioral decision-making have commonly focused on decisions from description. The observations stemming from this research suggest that humans overestimate and overrate rare events. To improve the understanding of how people make decisions with incomplete and uncertain information and how people respond to rare events that have severe consequences, Hertwig and Frey recommend study of the psychology and rationality of people's decisions from experience. They find that people relying on knowledge from experience behave as though rare events are attributed less impact than they deserve, relative to their objective probabilities. These two researchers review the literature on this gap between description and experience and consider its potential causes and explanations, arguing that research on description-based behavior should not be played off against research on experience-based behavior, that the contrast between the two types is enlightening. These observations are not contradictory; they describe how the mind functions in two different informational environments.

In recent years many psychologists have proposed that action (social behavior) is affected by two interacting systems—the reflective system and the impulsive system—that are operating according to different principles (for an overview of the literature, see Smith & DeCoster, 2000; Strack & Deutsch, 2004, 2007). "The reflective system generates behavioral decisions that are based on knowledge about facts and values, whereas the impulsive system elicits behavior through associative links and motivational orientations" (Strack & Deutsch, 2004, p. 220). The psychologists Anand Krishna and Fritz Strack focus in their chapter on the striking duality of (a) actions planned with reflective, deliberate thought and (b) actions caused by spontaneous impulses. First separately evaluating the characteristics of reflective and impulsive styles of thinking, Krishna and Strack find that the reflective system operates according to propositional principles; it is flexible, it requires effort and motivation, and its operation is typically conscious. The impulsive system operates according to associative principles; it is inflexible, effortless, always active, and capable of operating unconsciously.

Building on existing theories of rational thought as well as impulse, impulse control, and implicit attitudes, the authors propose an integrative model of thinking and action—the reflective-impulsive model (RIM)—to show when which system of thought will be active and under what circumstances they will influence behavior. The rational and rule-based reflective system is slow and driven by working memory capacities and arousal, which set limits for its ability to process information. The impulsive system can be thought of as long-term memory and therefore has functionally unlimited capacity.

In their RIM model Krishna and Strack describe how the reflective and impulsive systems interact during the process of thought. When the reflective system operates, it operates in parallel with the impulsive system, not in place of it. When a reflective operation begins, perceptual input has already activated several associative elements. The purpose of the RIM is to provide an answer to the central question of how the two mental processes are linked to behavior and especially how they interact through behavioral schemata.

The psychologists Frank Wieber and Peter M. Gollwitzer examine the role that spontaneous and strategic planning have in turning an individual's knowledge into action. They point out that knowing which goal one intends to pursue and committing oneself to that goal are only the first step toward successful goal attainment. Planning when, where, and how to act with implementation intentions[27] has proven to be an effective self-regulation strategy for reducing the intention–behavior gap. The authors introduce specific if–then plans for when, where, and how to act, and they discuss how such implementation intentions support goal attainment.

They highlight the importance that the accessibility of goal-relevant knowledge has for spontaneously formed implementation intentions. As for *strategically* formed implementation intentions, they point to the importance of systematically selecting goal-relevant knowledge and translating it into implementation intentions by using the self-regulation strategy called Mental Contrasting with Implementation Intentions. The authors discuss the interplay of automatic and reflective processes and suggest that strategically planning the automatic activation of goal-relevant knowledge can support reflective decision-making and goal-directed actions through use of context-sensitive reminders. Goal systems are introduced as a conceptual framework because they address the question of how goals can increase the accessibility of knowledge about when, where, and how to pursue the goal.

The authors discuss a recent experimental study suggesting that such strategic planning is very useful in unstructured situational contexts that require identification and selection of appropriate goal-relevant knowledge. They further suggest that strategic planning is less useful in structured situational contexts that prompt goal-directed actions without requiring any knowledge about advantageous opportunities to act and about potential obstacles. One of their main findings is that combining mental contrasting and implementation intentions in order to extend planning has proven more effective than either mental contrasting or implementation intentions alone.

Two chapters present a philosophical perspective on knowledge and action. Philosopher Tilman Reitz gives an overview of the broad range of philosophical

---

[27] Implementation intentions refer to specific plans in which individuals and groups can, by using an if–then format, specify when, where, and how they intend to act.

positions on the essence of knowledge. He argues that the social sciences largely lack a well-considered definition of knowledge, whereas philosophical debates about such a definition usually fail to include discussion of the social constitution of knowledge. In his view both approaches have overlooked or repressed a theoretical challenge: the spatial dispersion of social knowledge. He presents a concept of knowledge that is both philosophically transparent and empirically helpful for understanding basic structures of the knowledge society. Following a pragmatic epistemology, he is interested in the question of which understanding of knowledge makes sense in what kind of everyday circumstances. In his view the nature of knowledge also depends on its social organization. Do people talk about the knowledge of individuals, of collectives, or rather of knowledge incorporated in a set of rules? He is interested in changes in the organization and dispersion of epistemic practices and in delocalized and resituated knowledge in the digital information age, when new information technologies will have huge practical and epistemic effects. Encoded information or data can be automatically processed without the intervention of human agents. Stock market programs buy and sell shares, police software identifies dangerous persons, and semantic tools browse scientific data bases. Such operations involve neither beliefs nor truth and justification; no emotion, prejudice, or thought style interferes with them. But they trigger a number of new problems and new research questions.

The philosopher Peter Gardenförs, in support of his central hypothesis that semantic knowledge is organized into domains, presents a model of domain-oriented language acquisition. He defines a domain as a set of integral dimensions separable from all other dimensions. *Basic domains* are cognitively irreducible representational spaces or fields of conceptual potential. The author proposes conceptual spaces as appropriate tools for modeling the semantics of natural language. A conceptual space is defined by a number of perception-based quality dimensions that represent perceived similarity.

He offers linguistic evidence for the hypothesis that it becomes easier to learn new words within in a domain once it has been established. During the first formative years of life, a child acquires semantic knowledge prior to syntactic knowledge. Once the child has learned a word designating a color, for instance, other color words will be learned soon after. It is easier to explain to a 4-year-old the meaning of the color term *mauve* than to explain abstract monetary terms like *inflation* that are not yet within the child's semantic reach. The author explains why grasping a new domain is a cognitively much more difficult step than adding new terms to an already established domain.

A central hypothesis of Gardenförs's chapter is that many of these domains are closely connected to the development of intersubjectivity. The author defines intersubjectivity as "the sharing and representing of others' mentality." If somebody shares the emotions, attention, desires, intentions, beliefs, and knowledge of others, the exchange of knowledge is relatively unproblematic.

Ariane Berthoin Antal and Victor Friedman—both experts on organizational learning with an interest in artistic intervention—investigate the relationship between physical space and processes of creative thinking and action. They point out that the importance of bodily ways of knowing has long been obvious to artists and neuroscientists but that organizational researchers misplaced corporeality for many years and have only recently begun to retrieve it by drawing on notions of aesthetics. The aesthetic approach to studying human behavior can reveal the roles the body plays in reading a context. The authors argue that connecting aesthetic approaches to the analysis of the construction of social space enriches the understanding of the relational processes of generating shared meaning and agreeing on how to behave in the current situation. They stress that people use all their senses to seek cues to make sense of and orient their behavior and that the body thereby also participates in deciding and signaling to others which rules of the game to adopt for the situation at hand (Edenius & Yakhlef, 2007).

This study was set in a region characterized by chronic socioeconomic underdevelopment and deep intergroup divisions, especially between Jews and Palestinian Arabs. Berthoin Antal and Friedman were interested in promoting a process in which people could (a) bring up problems, ideas, and visions, (b) meet others with whom to learn and to collaborate on issues of common concern, (c) work together to create innovative, viable projects and enterprises to meet human and economic needs, and (d) create and enact shared visions of regional development that promotes inclusiveness and interdependence rather than competition and divisiveness. In a series of videorecorded action experiments[28] conducted in a fine-arts studio, the two researchers asked the participants to think about how they would use the space of the studio to combine processes of social entrepreneurship, conflict engagement, and the arts in ways that would connect the college with the community and contribute to regional development.

The analysis of the video recordings illustrates how physical space becomes a part of social space by entering human perception and then being acted upon and shaped by people. The authors identified seven distinct configurations[29] of social space that changed over time as the participants engaged in the task. One of the striking outcomes of their video analysis was that commonalities existed across the sessions in terms of the knowledge-production processes. The fundamental structural similarity of the configurations allows the authors to formulate key insights into the relationships between space, action, and knowledge generation. The study confirms the value of separating visual from verbal analysis.

The final two chapters investigate knowledge (cognitive capacities, rationality) and mobility in space. Thomas Widlok—a social anthropologist—studies the relationship between rationality and action in a hunter–gatherer society. The prime cognitive challenge in this context is human practical reasoning about movement: the

---

[28] By the term *action experiments* they mean having participants develop and actively try out ideas together in a given space, recording the process, then analyzing it as a basis for ensuing steps.

[29] They use the term *configuration* in four senses: (a) the participants' positions in the room and relative to each other during a specific period of time, (b) the observable interactions of the participants among each other and with materials in the room, (c) the observable application of behavioral rules, and (d) the creation of shared meaning (to the extent it can be inferred from the group's observable behavior and outputs). The seven configurations they identified were Orientation, Meeting Mode, Expansion, Creation, Reflection, Exhibition, and Rehearsal.

decision to go or to stay. Based on ethnographic work with various groups of mobile hunters and gatherers in southern Africa and Australia, the chapter presents an investigation of rationality and action from the standpoint of human mobility in space. It begins with a critical assessment of probabilistic rational choice models of mobility and decision-making and suggests that more promising approaches are informed by work on the pragmatics of dialogues and on abductive reasoning. Rationality in that view is no longer a purely mental phenomenon, for it is distributed across social practice and is partially contained in features of the environment that western philosophy has long dismissed as irrelevant for understanding human rationality.

The psychologists Heidrun Mollenkopf, Annette Hieber, and Hans-Werner Wahl document that relations between intention and action (mobility in space) are not immutable in the course of a person's life cycle. Age, mental and physical handicaps, personal resources, environmental conditions, and other factors can separate actions from intentions. The authors study this issue by interviewing older adults about their out-of-home mobility three times over 10 years. They analyze the subjective meaning of mobility over time; perceived changes in mobility and perceived reasons for such change; the course of satisfaction in various mobility domains and with life in general; and interindividual variation. Perceived changes point to experiences of major loss in the array of mobility and decreasing satisfaction with mobility possibilities, out-of-home leisure activities, and travel. At the same time, the authors find that satisfaction with public transport is increasing among older adults. The findings of this study confirm that out-of-home mobility remains of utmost importance when people move from late midlife into old age.

Conclusion

The chapters in this volume illustrate the enormous breadth of the implications that the spatial dimension has for action, the production and dissemination of knowledge, the application and understanding of knowledge, and the generation of sociocultural and economic realities. They also reveal the large number of open or contested research questions to be answered by future research. For obvious reasons, action theory figures prominently in our introduction, but the work presented in the following pages indicates how many more theoretical concepts of various disciplines could contribute to improve the understanding of the relations between knowledge and space on various scales of analysis.

From a geographical point of view, certain key questions are not discussed in this volume: How are epistemic authority and competencies construed and evaluated in nonwestern or acephalous societies in which individuality and rationality are secondary to collective values? In which way will new digital technologies change the organization and coordination of decision-making in complex organizations? To what extent will new digital technologies change communication, interaction, supervision, knowledge storage, and social-spatial relations? Will these changes mainly support and strengthen existing power structures or alter them substantially?

Taking into account how deeply rooted the spatial dimension is in human existence with its manifold facets, we can imagine how deep the social changes will be upon implementation of changes in social-spatial relations through digitalization and with the subsequent changes in the form of communication, interaction, and knowledge storage. It is therefore vitally important to include space in social theory in general and in action theory in particular. It looks as though Foucault's (1984/2002) prediction quoted at the outset of this introduction is likely to be confirmed, possibly even beyond the issues he raised.

References

Abel, G. (2008). Forms of knowledge: Problems, projects, perspectives. In P. Meusburger, M. Welker, & E. Wunder (Eds.), *Clashes of knowledge: Orthodoxies and heterodoxies in science and religion* (pp. 11–33). Knowledge and Space: Vol. 1. Dordrecht: Springer. doi:10.1007/978-1-4020-5555-3_1

Amabile, T. M., Conti, R., Coon, H., Lazenby, J., & Herron, M. (1996). Assessing the work environment for creativity. *The Academy of Management Journal, 39,* 1154–1184. doi:10.2307/256995

Amabile, T. M., Goldfarb, P., & Brackfield, S. (1990). Social influences on creativity: Evaluation, co-action, and surveillance. *Creativity Research Journal, 3,* 6–21.

Avelino, F., & Rotmans, J. (2009). Power in transition: An interdisciplinary framework to study power in relation to structural change. *European Journal of Social Theory, 12,* 543–569. doi:10.1177/1368431009349830

Baron, J. (2008). *Thinking and deciding* (4th ed.). Cambridge: Cambridge University Press.

Belina, B. (2013). *Raum. Zu den Grundlagen eines historisch-geographischen Materialismus* [Space: On the foundations of historical-geographical materialism]. Münster: Westfälisches Dampfboot.

Berthoin Antal, A., Meusburger, P., & Suarsana, L. (Eds.). (2014). *Learning organizations: Extending the field.* Knowledge and Space: Vol. 6. Dordrecht: Springer. doi:10.1007/978-94-007-7220-5

Buskens, V. (2015). Rational choice theory in sociology. In D. Wright (Editor-in-chief), *International encyclopedia of the social & behavioral sciences* (2nd ed., Vol. 19, pp. 901–906). Oxford: Elsevier. http://dx.doi.org/10.1016/B978-0-08-097086-8.32177-8

Christaller, W. (1933). *Die zentralen Orte in Süddeutschland. Eine ökonomisch-geographische Untersuchung über die Gesetzmäßigkeit der Verbreitung und Entwicklung der Siedlungen mit städtischer Funktion* [Central places in southern Germany: An economic-geographical study of the inherent laws of the distribution and development of settlements with urban function]. Jena: Gustav Fischer.

Csikszentmihalyi, M. (1988). Society, culture, and person: A systems view of creativity. In R. J. Sternberg (Ed.), *The nature of creativity* (pp. 325–339). Cambridge, MA: Cambridge University Press.

Csikszentmihalyi, M. (1999). Implications of a systems perspective for the study of creativity. In R. J. Sternberg (Ed.), *Handbook of creativity* (pp. 313–335). New York: Cambridge University Press.

Edenius, M., & Yakhlef, A. (2007). Space, vision and organizational learning: The interplay of incorporating and inscribing practices. *Management Learning, 38,* 193–210. doi:10.1177/1350507607075775

Fiedler, K., & Wänke, M. (2009). The cognitive-ecological approach to rationality in social psychology. *Social Cognition, 27,* 699–732.

Flache, A., & Dijkstra, J. (2015). Rationality in society. In D. Wright (Editor-in-chief), *International encyclopedia of the social & behavioral sciences* (2nd ed., Vol. 19, pp. 907–912). Oxford: Elsevier. http://dx.doi.org/10.1016/B978-0-08-097086-8.32124-9

Fleck, L. (1979). *Genesis and development of a scientific fact* (T. J. Trenn & R. K. Merton, Eds.; F. Bradley & T. J. Trenn, Trans. ; with a Foreword by T. S. Kuhn). Chicago: University of Chicago Press. (Original work published in 1935). Retrieved from http://www.evolocus.com/Textbooks/Fleck1979.pdf

Foucault, M. (1980). *Power/Knowledge: Selected interviews & other writings, 1972–1977* (C. Gordon, Ed.; C. Gordon, L. Marschall, J. Mepham, & K. Soper, Trans.). New York: Pantheon Books.

Foucault, M. (2002). Of other spaces (J. Miskowiec, Trans.). In N. Mirzoeff (Ed.), *The visual culture reader* (2nd ed., pp. 229–236). London: Routledge. (Original work published 1984)

Freytag, T., Jahnke, H., & Kramer, C. (2015). *Bildungsgeographie* [Geography of education]. Darmstadt: Wissenschaftliche Buchgesellschaft.

Gadamer, H.-G. (1999). *Truth and method* (2nd rev. ed.) (J. Weinsheimer & D. G. Marshall, Trans.). New York: Continuum. (Original work published in 1960)

Gäbler, K. (2015). *Gesellschaftlicher Klimawandel. Eine Sozialgeographie der ökologischen Transformation* [Societal climate change: A social geography of ecological transformation]. Sozialgeographische Bibliothek: Vol. 17. Stuttgart: Franz Steiner.

Giddens, A. (1984). *The constitution of society: Outline of the theory of structuration.* Cambridge: Polity Press.

Gigerenzer, G., & Gaissmaier, W. (2011). Heuristic decision making. *Annual Review of Psychology, 62,* 451–482. doi:10.1146/annurev-psych-120709-145346

Gigerenzer, G., & Gaissmaier, W. (2015). Decision making: Nonrational theories. In D. Wright (Editor-in-chief), *International encyclopedia of the social & behavioral sciences* (2nd ed., Vol. 5, pp. 911–916). Oxford: Elsevier. http://dx.doi.org/10.1016/B978-0-08-097086-8.26017-0

Gigerenzer, G., & Selten, R. (Eds.). (2001). *Bounded rationality: The adaptive toolbox.* Cambridge, MA: MIT Press.

Goldman, A. (2004). Group knowledge vs. group rationality: Two approaches to social epistemology. *Episteme: A Journal of Social Epistemology, 1,* 11–22. doi:http://dx.doi.org/10.3366/epi.2004.1.1.11

Goldstein, D. G., & Gigerenzer, G. (2002). Models of ecological rationality: The recognition heuristic. *Psychological Review, 109,* 75–90. http://dx.doi.org/10.1037/0033-295X.109.1.75

Goldthorpe, J. H. (2000). *On sociology: Numbers, narratives, and the integration of research and theory.* Oxford: Oxford University Press.

Gottmann, J. (1980). Organizing and reorganizing space. In J. Gottmann (Ed.), *Centre and periphery: Spatial variation in politics* (pp. 217–224). Beverly Hills: Sage.

Green, D. P., & Shapiro, I. (1994). *Pathologies of rational choice theory: A critique of applications in political science.* New Haven: Yale University Press.

Gregory, D. (1994). *Geographical imaginations.* Oxford: Basil Blackwell.

Gregory, D. (1998). Power, knowledge and geography. *Geographische Zeitschrift, 86,* 70–93. http://www.jstor.org/stable/27818804

Gregory, D. (2015). Gabriel's map: Cartography and corpography in modern war. In P. Meusburger, D. Gregory, & L. Suarsana (Eds.), *Geographies of knowledge and power* (pp. 89–121). Knowledge and Space: Vol. 7. Dordrecht: Springer. doi:10.1007/978-94-017-9960-7_4

Harvey, D. (2005). Space as a key word. In D. Harvey, *Spaces of neoliberalization: Towards a theory of uneven geographical development* (pp. 93–115). Hettner-Lecture: Vol. 8. Stuttgart: Franz Steiner.

Haselton, M. G., Bryant, G. A., Wilke, A., Frederick, D. A., Galperin, A., Frankenhuis, W. E., & Moore, T. (2009). Adaptive rationality: An evolutionary perspective on cognitive bias [Special issue]. *Social Cognition, 27,* 733–763. doi:10.1521/soco.2009.27.5.733

Hennessey, B. A., & Amabile, T. M. (1988). The conditions of creativity. In R. J. Sternberg (Ed.), *The nature of creativity* (pp. 11–38). Cambridge: Cambridge University Press.

Hertwig, R., & Herzog, S. M. (2009). Fast and frugal heuristics: Tools of social rationality. *Social Cognition, 27,* 661–698.

Jöns, H. (2008). Academic travel from Cambridge University and the formation of centres of knowledge, 1885–1954. *Journal of Historical Geography, 34,* 338–362. doi:10.1016/j.jhg.2007.11.006

Kruglanski, A. W., & Orehek, E. (2009). Toward a relativity theory of rationality. *Social Cognition, 27,* 639–660.

Laclau, E., & Mouffe, C. (1985). *Hegemony and socialist strategy: Towards a radical democratic politics.* London: Verso.

Leed, E. (1981). *No Man's Land: Combat and identity in World War I.* Cambridge, UK: Cambridge University Press.

Lindenberg, S. (2013). Social rationality, self-regulation, and well-being. In R. Wittek, T. A. B. Snijders, & V. Nee (Eds.), *Handbook of rational choice social research* (pp. 72–112). Stanford: Stanford University Press.

Lippuner, R. (2005). *Raum, Systeme, Praktiken. Zum Verhältnis von Alltag, Wissenschaft und Geographie* [Space, systems, practices: On the relation between everyday life, science, and geography]. Sozialgeographische Bibliothek: Vol. 2. Stuttgart: Franz Steiner.

Lippuner, R., & Lossau, J. (2004). In der Raumfalle. Eine Kritik des spatial turn in den Sozialwissenschaften [Caught in the space trap: A critique of the spatial turn in the social sciences]. In G. Mein & M. Riegler-Ladich (Eds.), *Soziale Räume und kulturelle Praktiken. Über den strategischen Gebrauch von Medien* (pp. 47–63). Bielefeld: transcript.

Livingstone, D. N. (1995). The spaces of knowledge: Contributions towards a historical geography of science. *Environment and Planning D: Society and Space, 13,* 5–34. doi:10.1068/d130005

Livingstone, D. N. (2000). Making space for science. *Erdkunde, 54,* 285–296. doi:10.3112/erdkunde.2000.04.01

Livingstone, D. N. (2002). Knowledge, space and the geographies of science. In D. N. Livingstone, *Science, space and hermeneutics* (pp. 7–40). Hettner-Lecture: Vol. 5. Heidelberg: University Department of Geography.

Livingstone, D. N. (2003). *Putting science in its place: Geographies of scientific knowledge.* Chicago: University of Chicago Press.

Lösch, A. (1954). *The economics of location* (W. H. Woglom & W. F. Stolper, Trans.) (2nd rev. ed.). New Haven: Yale University Press. (Original work published 1940, 2nd ed. 1943)

Malecki, E. J. (2000). Knowledge and regional competitiveness. *Erdkunde, 54,* 334–351. http://www.jstor.org/stable/25647317

Massey, D. (1985). New directions in space. In D. Gregory & J. Urry (Eds.), *Social relations and spatial structures* (pp. 9–19). New York: St. Martin's Press.

Massey, D. (1999a). Imagining globalisation: Power-geometries of time-space. In D. Massey, *Power-geometries and the politics of space-time* (pp. 9–23). Hettner-Lecture: Vol. 2. Heidelberg: Heidelberg University, Department of Geography.

Massey, D. (1999b). Philosophy and politics of spatiality: Some considerations. In D. Massey, *Power-geometries and the politics of space-time* (pp. 27–42). Hettner-Lecture: Vol. 2. Heidelberg: Heidelberg University, Department of Geography.

Massey, D. (2005). *For space.* London: Sage.

Meusburger, P. (1998). *Bildungsgeographie. Wissen und Ausbildung in der räumlichen Dimension* [Geography of education: Knowledge and education in the spatial dimension]. Heidelberg: Spektrum Akademischer Verlag.

Meusburger, P. (1999). Subjekt—Organisation—Region. Fragen an die subjektzentrierte Handlungstheorie [Subject–organization–region: Questions on subject-centered action theory]. In P. Meusburger (Ed.), *Handlungszentrierte Sozialgeographie. Benno Werlens Entwurf in kritischer Diskussion* (pp. 95–132). Erdkundliches Wissen: Vol. 130. Stuttgart: Franz Steiner.

Meusburger, P. (2000). The spatial concentration of knowledge: Some theoretical considerations. *Erdkunde, 54,* 352–364. http://www.jstor.org/stable/25647318

Meusburger, P. (2003). "Wissen" als Erklärungsvariable in den Mensch-Umwelt-Beziehungen ["Knowledge" as explanatory variable in agent-environment relations]. In P. Meusburger & T. Schwan (Eds.), *Humanökologie. Ansätze zur Überwindung der Natur-Kultur-Dichotomie* (pp. 287–307). Erdkundliches Wissen: Vol. 135. Stuttgart: Franz Steiner.

Meusburger, P. (2008). The nexus of knowledge and space. In P. Meusburger, M. Welker, & E. Wunder (Eds.), *Clashes of knowledge: Orthodoxies and heterodoxies in science and religion* (pp. 35–90). Knowledge and Space: Vol. 1. Dordrecht: Springer. doi:10.1007/978-1-4020-5555-3_2

Meusburger, P. (2009). Milieus of creativity: The role of places, environments, and spatial contexts. In P. Meusburger, J. Funke, & E. Wunder (Eds.), *Milieus of creativity. An interdisciplinary approach to spatiality of creativity* (pp. 97–153). Knowledge and Space: Vol. 2. Dordrecht: Springer. doi:10.1007/978-1-4020-9877-2_7

Meusburger, P. (2015a). Knowledge environments in universities. *Hungarian Geographical Bulletin, 64,* 265–279. doi:10.15201/hungeobull.64.4.1

Meusburger, P. (2015b). Knowledge, Geography of. In J. D. Wright (Editor-in-chief), *International encyclopedia of the social & behavioral sciences* (2nd ed., Vol. 13, pp. 91–97). Oxford: Elsevier. http://dx.doi.org/10.1016/B978-0-08-097086-8.72126-X

Meusburger, P. (2015c). Relations between knowledge and power: An overview of research questions and concepts. In P. Meusburger, D. Gregory, & L. Suarsana (Eds.), *Geographies of knowledge and power* (pp. 19–74). Knowledge and Space: Vol. 7. Dordrecht: Springer. doi:10.1007/978-94-017-9960-7_2

Meusburger, P. (2017). Spatial mobility of knowledge: Communicating different categories of knowledge. In H. Jöns, P. Meusburger, & M. Heffernan (Eds.), *Mobilities of Knowledge* (pp. 23–50). Knowledge and Space: Vol. 10. Dordrecht: Springer. doi:10.1007/978-3-319-44654-7_2

Meusburger, P., Gregory, D., & Suarsana, L. (Eds.). (2015). *Geographies of knowledge and power.* Knowledge and Space: Vol. 7. Dordrecht: Springer. doi:10.1007/978-94-017-9960-7

Meusburger, P., & Schuch, T. (Eds.). (2012). *Wissenschaftsatlas of Heidelberg University: Spatio-temporal relations of academic knowledge production.* Knittlingen: Bibliotheca Palatina.

Mintzberg, H. (1979). *The structuring of organizations: A synthesis of the research.* Englewood Cliffs: Prentice Hall.

Moldaschl, M., & Stehr, N. (2010). Eine kurze Geschichte der Wissensökonomie [A brief history of the economics of knowledge]. In M. Moldaschl & N. Stehr (Eds.), *Wissensökonomie und Innovation. Beiträge zur Ökonomie der Wissensgesellschaft* (pp. 9–74). Marburg: Metropolis.

Navarro, D. J., Newell, B. R., & Schulze, C. (2016). Learning and choosing in an uncertain world: An investigation of the explore–exploit dilemma in static and dynamic environments. *Cognitive Psychology, 85,* 43–77. http://dx.doi.org/10.1016/j.cogpsych.2016.01.001

Paasi, A. (1991). Deconstructing regions: Notes on the scales of social life. *Environment and Planning A, 23,* 239–256. doi:10.1068/a230239

Pragmatics. (2010). *Random House Kernerman Webster's College Dictionary.* Retrieved June 2, 2016, from http://www.thefreedictionary.com/pragmatics

Radner, R. (2015). Decision and choice: Bounded rationality. In D. Wright (Editor-in-chief), *International encyclopedia of the social & behavioral sciences* (2nd ed., Vol. 5, pp. 879–885). Oxford: Elsevier. http://dx.doi.org/10.1016/B978-0-08-097086 -8.43028-X

Reckwitz, A. (2002). Toward a theory of social practices: A development in culturalist theorizing. *European Journal of Social Theory, 5,* 234–263. doi:10.1177/13684310222225432

Reckwitz, A. (2008). Grundelemente einer Theorie sozialer Praktiken [Principles of a theory of social practices]. In A. Reckwitz (Ed.), *Unscharfe Grenzen: Perspektiven der Kultursoziologie* (pp. 97–130). Bielefeld: Transcript.

Samuels, R., & Stich, S. P. (2015). Irrationality: Philosophical aspects. In D. Wright (Editor-in-chief), *International encyclopedia of the social & behavioral sciences* (2nd ed., Vol. 12, pp. 719–723). Oxford: Elsevier. http://dx.doi.org/10.1016/B978-0-08-097086 -8.63039-8

Schatzki, T., Knorr-Cetina, K., & Savigny, E., von (2001). *The practice turn in contemporary theory*. London: Routledge.

Schmid, C. (2005). *Stadt, Raum und Gesellschaft: Henri Lefebvre und die Theorie der Produktion des Raumes* [City, space, and society: Henri Lefebvre and the theory of the production of space]. Sozialgeographische Bibliothek: Vol. 1. Stuttgart: Franz Steiner.

Schönrich, G. (2005). Machtausübung und die Sicht der Akteure. Ein Beitrag zur Theorie der Macht [The exercise of power and the view of the actors: On the theory of power]. In G. Melville (Ed.), *Das Sichtbare und das Unsichtbare der Macht. Institutionelle Prozesse in Antike, Mittelalter und Neuzeit* (pp. 383–409). Cologne: Böhlau.

Schütz, A. (1932). *Der sinnhafte Aufbau der sozialen Welt: Eine Einführung in die verstehende Soziologie* [The phenomenology of the social world: An introduction to interpretive sociology]. Vienna: Springer.

Schwan, T. (2003). Clash of imaginations. Erfahrungswissenschaftliches Menschenbild versus postmoderne Konstruktionen [Clash of imaginations—Experience-based idea of man versus postmodern constructions]. In P. Meusburger & T. Schwan (Eds.), *Humanökologie: Ansätze zur Überwindung der Natur-Kultur-Dichotomie* (pp. 161–173). Erdkundliches Wissen: Vol. 135. Stuttgart: Franz Steiner.

Simon, H. A. (1956). Rational choice and the structure of environments. *Psychological Review, 63,* 129–138.

Simon, H. A. (1982). *Models of bounded rationality*. Cambridge, MA: MIT Press.

Simon, H. A. (1990). Invariants of human behavior. *Annual Review of Psychology, 41,* 1–19. doi:10.1146/annurev.ps.41.020190.000245

Smith, E. R., & DeCoster, J. (2000). Dual process models in social and cognitive psychology: Conceptual integration and links to underlying memory systems. *Personality and Social Psychology Review, 4,* 108–131. doi:10.1207/S15327957PSPR0402_01

Soja, E. (1985). The spatiality of social life: Towards a transformative retheorisation. In D. Gregory & J. Urry (Eds.), *Social relations and spatial structures* (pp. 90–127). London: Macmillan.

Stehr, N. (1994). *Knowledge societies*. London: Sage.

Stehr, N. (2005). *Knowledge politics: Governing the consequences of science and technology*. Boulder, CO: Paradigm Publishers.

Stehr, N., & Meja, V. (Eds.). (2005). *Society and knowledge: Contemporary perspectives in the sociology of knowledge and science* (2nd ed.). New Brunswick: Transaction Books.

Steiner, D. (2003). Humanökologie: Von hart zu weich. Mit Spurensuche bei und mit Peter Weichhart [Human ecology—From hard to soft: Seeking traces with Peter Weichhart]. In P. Meusburger & T. Schwan (Eds.), *Humanökologie: Ansätze zur Überwindung der Natur-Kultur-Dichotomie* (pp. 45–80). Erdkundliches Wissen: Vol. 135. Stuttgart: Franz Steiner.

Sternberg, R. E., & Lubart, T. I. (1999). The concept of creativity: Prospects and paradigms. In R. J. Sternberg (Ed.), *Handbook of creativity* (pp. 3–15). New York: Cambridge University Press.

Strack, F., & Deutsch, R. (2004). Reflective and impulsive determinants of social behavior. *Personality and Social Psychology Review, 8,* 220–247. doi:10.1207/s15327957pspr0803_1

Strack, F., & Deutsch, R. (2007). The role of impulse in social behavior. In A. W. Kruglanski & E. T. Higgins (Eds.), *Social psychology: Handbook of basic principles.* (Rev. & exp. 2nd ed., pp. 408–431). New York: Guilford Press.

Todd, P. M., & Gigerenzer, G. (2000). Précis of simple heuristics that make us smart. *Behavioral and Brain Sciences, 23,* 727–780.

Todd, P. M., Gigerenzer, G., & the ABC Research Group (2012). *Ecological rationality: Intelligence in the world*. New York: Oxford University Press.

Tuan, Y. F. (1977). *Space and place: The perspective of experience*. Chicago: University of Chicago Press.

Weber, M. (1913). Über einige Kategorien der verstehenden Soziologie [Some categories of interpretive sociology]. *Logos: Internationale Zeitschrift für Philosophie der Kultur, 4*, 253–294.

Weber, M. (1980). *Wirtschaft und Gesellschaft: Grundriss der verstehenden Soziologie* [Economy and society: An outline of interpretive sociology] (5th ed.). Tübingen: Mohr & Siebeck. (Original work published 1922)

Weber, M. (1988). Geschäftsbericht und Diskussionsreden auf den deutschen soziologischen Tagungen (1910) [Annual report and discussions at German sociological conferences (1910)]. In Marianne Weber (Ed.), *Gesammelte Aufsätze zur Soziologie und Sozialpolitik* (2nd ed., pp. 431–491). Tübingen: Mohr. (Original work published 1912)

Weichhart, P. (1996). Die Region—Chimäre, Artefakt oder Strukturprinzip sozialer Systeme? [The region—Chimera, artifact, or structural principle of social systems]. In G. Brunn (Ed.), *Region und Regionsbildung in Europa: Konzeptionen der Forschung und empirische Befunde* (pp. 25–43). Schriftenreihe des Instituts für Europäische Regionalforschung: Vol. 1. Baden-Baden: Nomos.

Weichhart, P. (1999). Die Räume zwischen den Welten und die Welt der Räume. Zur Konzeption eines Schlüsselbegriffs der Geographie [The spaces between the worlds and the world of spaces: On the inception of a key concept of geography]. In P. Meusburger (Ed.), *Handlungszentrierte Sozialgeographie: Benno Werlens Entwurf in kritischer Diskussion* (pp. 67–94). Erdkundliches Wissen: Vol. 130. Stuttgart: Franz Steiner.

Weichhart, P. (2003). Gesellschaftlicher Metabolismus und Action Settings. Die Verknüpfung von Sach- und Sozialstrukturen im alltagsweltlichen Handeln [Social metabolism and action settings: The link between technical and social structures in everyday action]. In P. Meusburger & T. Schwan (Eds.), *Humanökologie: Ansätze zur Überwindung der Natur-Kultur-Dichotomie* (pp. 15–44). Erdkundliches Wissen: Vol. 135. Stuttgart: Franz Steiner.

Werlen, B. (1987). *Gesellschaft, Handlung und Raum: Grundlagen handlungstheoretischer Sozialgeographie* (3rd ed.) [Society, action and space: Principles of an action-oriented social geography] (3rd ed.). Erdkundliches Wissen: Vol. 89. Stuttgart: Franz Steiner.

Werlen, B. (1993a). Handlungs- und Raummodelle in sozialgeographischer Forschung und Praxis [Action and space models in social geographical research]. *Geographische Rundschau, 45*, 724–729.

Werlen, B. (1993b). *Society, action and space: An alternative human geography* (G. Walls, Trans.). London: Routledge.

Werlen, B. (1995). *Sozialgeographie alltäglicher Regionalisierungen: Bd. 1. Zur Ontologie von Gesellschaft und Raum* [Social geography of everyday regionalizations: Vol. 1. On the ontology of society and space]. Erdkundliches Wissen: Vol. 116. Stuttgart: Franz Steiner.

Werlen, B. (1997). *Sozialgeographie alltäglicher Regionalisierungen: Bd. 2. Globalisierung, Region und Regionalisierung* [Social geography of everyday regionalizations: Vol. 2. Globalization, region and regionalization]. Erdkundliches Wissen: Vol. 119. Stuttgart: Franz Steiner.

Werlen, B. (2010a). *Gesellschaftliche Räumlichkeit: Bd. 1. Orte der Geographie* [Social spatiality: Vol. 1. Places of geography]. Stuttgart: Franz Steiner.

Werlen, B. (2010b). *Gesellschaftliche Räumlichkeit: Bd. 2. Konstruktion geographischer Wirklichkeiten* [Social spatiality: Vol. 2. Construction of geographical realities]. Stuttgart: Franz Steiner.

Werlen, B. (2013). Gesellschaft und Raum: Gesellschaftliche Raumverhältnisse. Grundlagen und Perspektiven einer sozialwissenschaftlichen Geographie [Society and space: Society–space relationships—Principles and perspectives of a social science geography]. *Erwägen-Wissen-Ethik. Forum für Erwägungskultur, 24*, 3–16.

Werlen, B. (2015). From local to global sustainability: Transdisciplinary integrated research in the Digital Age. In B. Werlen (Ed.), *Global sustainability: Cultural perspectives and challenges for transdisciplinary integrated research* (pp. 3–16). New York: Springer.

Werlen, B., & Weingarten, M. (2003). Zum forschungsintegrativen Gehalt der (Sozial) Geographie [About the integrative substance of (social) geography]. In P. Meusburger & T. Schwan (Eds.), *Humanökologie. Ansätze zur Überwindung der Natur-Kultur-Dichotomie* (pp. 197–216). Erdkundliches Wissen: Vol. 135. Stuttgart: Franz Steiner.

Wittek, R., Snijders, T. A. B., & Nee, V. (Eds.). (2013). *Handbook of rational choice social research*. Stanford: Stanford University Press.

World Commission on Environment and Development. (1987). *Our common future*. Oxford: Oxford University Press.

Zierhofer, W. (2002). Speech acts and space(s): Language pragmatics and the discursive constitution of the social. *Environment and Planning A, 34,* 1355–1372. doi:10.1068/a34198

Chapter 2
Action, Knowledge, and Social Relations of Space

Benno Werlen

Contrary to still well-established understanding, geographical conditions of human actions are to be seen from a sociogeographical point of view, that is, primarily as a social product and only secondarily as a biophysical condition. This ontological status of the age of anthropocene means that geographical social transformations are highly important for all forms of geography-making, which, in turn, are fundamental to social change and transformations. In other words, the constitutive processes of geographical realities are fundamental to a wide range of formative processes of social and cultural realities.

To grasp geographical realities as understandable realities, it is necessary to let go of most received geographical notions, from traditional regionalistic ones and colonial interpretations to present geographical concepts formulated in the aftermath of the spatial turn of the social sciences, cultural studies, and the humanities. But this change in perspective is not only scientifically crucial. It is even more so with respect to everyday practices, especially political actions. With the steady weakening of all-encompassing forms of national territorialization through the Digital Revolution and with the formation of supranational communities, the dominance of the nation-state in nearly all domains of social life is at stake. Just as the territorial organization of social life replaced feudal logic, the territorial principle itself is now at risk in many senses.

It is little different when it comes to the interrelation of knowledge and spatial conditions. The Digital Revolution—the end of distance for a wide range of human activities, and accelerated social change—is establishing what I call "new social relations of space." By that I mean, as elaborated on in this chapter, a new way of relating to preset and spatially distant circumstances that are relevant to one's action. And social relations of space have a strong impact on the production, dissemination, and incorporation of knowledge and information. Of course, I do not mean that

B. Werlen (✉)
Department of Geography, Friedrich Schiller University Jena, Jena, Germany
e-mail: benno.werlen@uni-jena.de

© The Author(s) 2017
P. Meusburger et al. (eds.), *Knowledge and Action*, Knowledge and Space 9,
DOI 10.1007/978-3-319-44588-5_2

supranational trends and globalizations are effacing the local and regional. Globalization also accentuates places and regions as distinctive forums of human action. In one way or another all human actions remain regionally and locally contextualized. But to grasp the social significance of spatial constellations, scientific research has to proceed from social actions and practices to the regional and spatial realm and not vice versa.

The Relevance of the Spatial Dimension and the Spatial Turn

From the perspective of geography-making, which begins with the premises that all socially and culturally relevant geographies are constructed realities, the spatial conditions and spatial relations of individual actions are fundamental to the formation and structuration of social realities. A prime example is the current globalization affecting various aspects of everyday life. Systematic social theories have largely ignored the spatial dimension of social life. The reasons for this omission are profound and require thorough reconstruction of the underlying modes of thought. Without such analysis, one runs the risk of importing the traditional spatial perspective into the social sciences and cultural studies. The fact that such uncritical adoption of the conventional spatial perspective is neither productive nor insightful is exemplified by the "spatial," or "geographical," turn in the social sciences, cultural studies, and the humanities (see Döring & Thielmann, 2008; Foucault, 1999; Levy, 1999; Günzel, 2009; Schlögel, 2002; Soja, 1989; Warf & Arias, 2008).

The absence of the spatial dimension in social and cultural theorizing contrasts with the spatial obsession characteristic of early studies in human geography, a field that emerged in the late nineteenth century as a space-centered science applying to the study of human individuals and societies. This orientation and the way of thinking underlying it have significant ramifications for geography as an academic discipline and entail problematic political implications.

Traditional human geography's rather simplistic focus on space and distance as determining dimensions of behavior results in an emphasis on the individual as part of the human species and neglects his or her capacity to perform social actions, which is fundamental for the meaningful construction of social and cultural realities. Arrival at this perspective needed a theoretical and not always successful debate lasting more than a century. The insights it has contributed greatly help the current debate about the spatial turn in the social and cultural sciences, identify its implications (some of which are problematic), and detect its shortcomings on the background of the history of geographical research.

Observed from the current theoretical debates, the first turn from human geography to social geography as of the early twentieth century was theoretically uninformed about social science and showed that merely integrating the social dimension into a space-centered perspective was insufficient for adequately theorizing about social action and societal dynamics. What was required instead was a reformulation and restructuring of theoretical categories and classifications in order to move from a society-oriented spatial science to a space- and place-oriented social science. This requirement applied to the social sciences and geography alike.

Social science's traditional geographical or spatial descriptions of the world, such as "space is a relational order or arrangement of living organisms and social goods, of living organisms and things that have a social meaning" (Löw, 2001, p. 157, my translation), insufficiently distinguish between the ontological status of physical, subjective, and sociocultural conditions. Such postulations are intended to reestablish a sociology of space and are not too distant from the Chicago School of sociology in the 1920s. However, all they appear to do is help create "ontological slums" (Hard, 1998, p. 250). In fact, sociologies of space that draw on the above ontological premises revert to the state of geography prior to its overhaul by the social sciences.

The challenge of integrating the spatial dimension into the social science perspective—and vice versa—results most of all from ignoring the fact that geographical "space" is a theoretical concept. Rectifying this lapse requires one to adapt the concept's use to an ontological focus of study. It is not possible to apply just any theory and its specific vocabulary to just any context.

Inadequate adaptation of the theoretical term *space* yields contradictions, as Bourdieu's shows in his work on social space. According to Bourdieu (1985), geographical space is not a condition of the social world. But he claims that the social sphere can be located *in* geographical space. The included containerization of social reality contradicts the theory of the social production and construction of reality (Berger & Luckmann, 1966; Giddens, 1984; Schütz, 1932, 1981). That way the social is just part of a material, pregiven space preceding all social praxis. Consequently, the containerization of the social implies the transformation the social into a materiel fact. As already implied, similar problems of reducing the social dimension to geographical space are also evident in the Chicago School's theory of urban sociology, which adapted Warming's ecology—his botanic geography (1895) and geography of "plant communities" (1909)—to urban development. Park (1952) and his disciples (Park, Burgess, & McKenzie, 1925) even went so far as to say that social distance can be measured in spatial distance. Even Giddens's (1984) theory of structuration is, to a certain extent, prone to similar shortcomings when it takes the Newtonian container space of Hägerstrand's (1970) time geography as a basis for the social analysis of routines in everyday life. Similar contradictions are detectable when geographical space is included in theories of history, as in Braudel's (1949) concept of the *longue durée* (long term), which—unlike "event" or "economic cycle" is thought to be spatially determined. In an outline of social history, Koselleck (2000) vehemently argued against the reification of time but remained silent on the reification of space.

The Gaps in Social Theory

Geographical conditions and spatial relations of human action—in short, spatiality—are central to the shaping, or more precisely, the generation of social life and social relationships. Solving the "problem of space" in social theory is therefore a key task despite (or perhaps because of) its significant challenges. Globalization and acceleration affect the conditions and circumstances under which everyday actions are performed. It is against this backdrop that the problem of space in social theory—and its solution—are of utmost importance, not least because of its sociopolitical relevance. Spatial configurations or arrangements of material objects are by no means merely "data...that has to be taken into account" (Weber, 1922/1980, p. 3). They are key conditions for the performance of social actions, hence, for the generation of social realities, and are consequently vital to research in the social sciences.

Space (or the spatial dimension) has an epistemic relevance that differs from the one attributed to it by Max Weber, the founder of the interpretative, action-centered social theory. To Weber (1924/1988), "purely geographic aspects" (p. 462) (i.e., physical features such as climate and terrain) shall not be part of the realm that is accessible via *Verstehen* (i.e., the "interpretive" inquiry into social phenomena). For this reason they ought to be excluded from the problems examined by interpretive sociology specifically and interpretive social sciences more generally (see, for example, Giddens, 1979, p. 202). Without exaggeration, this alignment of interpretative social theoretical thinking—and consequently of social policies—is arguably one of the core reasons for the emergence of modern societies' extreme ecological problems. The exclusion of the geographical aspects of action-centered social theory is pivotal in the current situation, as is the exclusion of meaningful social reality through excessive biologization of the social dimension in both functionalist thinking (Durkheim, 1893, 1957; Parsons, 1952, 1961) and ecological reasoning from its outset in Haeckel (1866) to the Brundtland report (World Commission on Environment and Development, 1987) and subsequent UN environmental policies.

Unlike Max Weber's position (its basic fostering of meaning-oriented modern social theory as opposed to the biological-reductionist and functionalist versions of social theory of his time), my argument in this chapter is that the generation of sociocultural realities always points to specific spatial relations and, hence, to specific society–spatiality relationships and society–nature relationships. This proposition ought not be mistaken as an attempt to revive environmental or geographical determinism—quite the opposite. However, failure to recognize the relevance of societies' spatial relations may bring about profound political and ecological conflicts.

The words *space* and *nature* refer to each other (Werlen, 2000, pp. 40–90). To avoid unnecessary, highly problematic confusion, one must first clearly differentiate them. A spatial constellation of material or natural things and objects is not the same as a physical space. This type of equating is reminiscent of geography as a nascent scientific discipline. Conceiving of space and nature as one, as a single unit, results in a geo- or space-focused environmental policy (with its attendant concepts of sustainability), which is still fashionable in current environmental research programs and policies. That kind of policy posits the earth sciences as the bodies of knowledge most competent for addressing the resulting problems, so they are tasked with the development of solutions to sustainability problems. Such an approach, however, overlooks the point that sustainability problems ultimately arise from human actions, not from space or nature. It is time, therefore, to reassess disciplinary competence and authority.

Notions of space are important not only for the biophysical realm but also for the manner in which one conceptualizes the social dimension. As a kind of "deep ontology" (Werlen, 1995, p. 2), they also influence the way social realities are constituted and perceived, especially with respect to sociopolitical debates. The implications of such a deep ontological linkage between space and society is most evident in Heidegger's (1933/2000) scathing critique of the work of neo-Kantian philosopher Richard Hönigswald. By arguing for liberal society, wrote Heidegger, Hönigswald would make himself a "servant of an indifferent, universal world culture" (p. 132) and would distract from the "historical rootedness and ethnic [*völkisch*] tradition of the origin in soil and blood" (p. 132, my translation) and thereby compromise the German population. In brief, anyone rejecting the notion of spatial rootedness in the sense of the biologically determined nexus of blood and soil, geographical origin, and tradition was an enemy of the biologically justified soil-bound society, the population. In keeping with the assumed deep ontological unity of equating not only space and nature but also space and society, such heretics are to be kept out, expelled, or exterminated. Such a biologically determined space–society combination is characteristic of ethnic nationalism that is still a common foundation of highly problematic political reasoning and comes very close to that other biological typification of the socioculture: racism.

This example semantically illustrates the meaning of the statement that space has profound implications for what is meant by society, and vice versa. In other words, space and society are discursively constructed images that are influence each other. This relationship certainly holds also for constellations unrelated to ethnic ideas. However, the significance of the mutually referential relationship between society and space has thus far been largely neglected, the reason being that sociology and geography have had their specific blind spots for a long time—and to a certain extent still do. Sociology used to offer an only insufficiently reflexive concept of spatial reference (see Bourdieu, 1985; Giddens, 1979, 1984, 1993), and geography's understanding of society long remained undertheorized. The nexus of space and social theory is still mostly rather superficial. It does not seriously take account of the deep implications that concepts of space have for the generation of society and that the relevance of social realities has for the theoretical conceptualization of space in the history of science, particularly the history of geography.

This is the basis on which ontological slums are flourishing. They result mainly from reified everyday concepts being reproduced in a nonreflexive way at the scientific level as meaningful spaces or biomaterial social worlds. The implications of such "slum" reproduction in scientific (dis)guise should be examined in the spirit of science's noblest task: critical doubt. One promising way to approach it is to reconstruct the historical development of geography as an academic discipline in its sociocultural context.

Social Conditions of Scientific Research and the History of Space

Historically, geographers have conceived of space as a three-dimensional earth space, also called geographical space (Werlen, 1993a; 2000). It has been the primary focus of their research. In the mid-nineteenth century, at the beginning of geography as an academic discipline, their foremost task was to classify all manner of phenomena on the earth's surface on the basis of a metric (discrete) concept of space as defined by cartographic coordinates. To produce such "measuring of the world" (Kehlmann, 2007) and the associated spatial-cartographic conception of the world to derive scientific descriptions was customary practice in academic geography at that time. That approach assigned a particular area or space to material objects and immaterial phenomena, laying the groundwork for the further development of geography as a spatial science.

Academic geography moved from being a descriptive and classificatory discipline concerned with nature and the Earth in a biophysical sense to a methodologically inclusive endeavor aimed at discovering causal relationships. That is, scholarly geography changed in its focus (which was established by Alexander von Humboldt and Carl Ritter) from the cartography of objects and a description of the Earth's surface (choro*graphy*) to a causal and integrative geography, or spatial science (choro*logy*). In this approach, space was thought of as a container. It thus represented a specific form of the theoretical concept of space developed by Isaac Newton for mechanics and later transferred to biology by Ernst Haeckel, who referred to it as lebensraum.

One of the most important historical conditions of this development in geography was prepared by Isaac Newton (1687) in *Philosophiae Naturalis Principia Mathematica*, the conceptualization of space as absolute. In *Opticks* Newton (1704/1952) defined space as a three-dimensional container space, containing everything material as an object and "God's Sensorium" (p. 125). With the underlying mechanical view of the natural world, Newton conceives of this container as material and absolute and as having a causal effect on everything contained in it. This definition of the absolute container space constitutes the basis of mechanics and the beginnings of the modern *natural* sciences. Despite being intended for modeling three-dimensional material—but not ideal, immaterial phenomena—this concept of space came to be applied far beyond the realm of mechanics. It became the foundation for an all-encompassing mechanistic world view and provided the rationale for positing universal laws of nature that claim validity for all parts of reality, including consciousness, society, and culture.

In the first development and conceptualization of ecology, Haeckel (1866) gave space a connotation similar to that in Newton (1704/1952). Space appeared to be a container or, more precisely, a container for all forms of life (Weingarten, 2009), as a lebensraum, a living space. At the same time, the lebensraum is also thought of as a sort of antagonist that every life form must contend with if it wishes to survive. The availability of a lebensraum was thus considered a necessary condition for the existence of all life forms and was at the same time a key evolutionary selection mechanism. In other words, the lebensraum in Haeckel's conceptualization and beyond had a causal effect in the sense that it distinguished successful from unsuccessful life forms and selected the former. From this reified and causally productive "authority" lebensraum one can derive a normative principle for life forms. It holds that only the fittest species will survive in a specific lebensraum. More important, the underlying tenor is that these fitting species will not only be able to survive but are the only ones that *should* survive. It is obvious at this point that a premise assuming a nexus of life and space (or blood and soil) also serves as a basis for ideas of racial hygiene and the legitimation of spatial hygiene or ethnic cleansing.

Trained as a zoologist, the founder of academic human geography Friedrich Ratzel (1891, 1897) conceived of space much as his teacher Ernst Haeckel had: as the determining life container of *anthropos*, or humanity. Thus, the human lebensraum was seen as the cause that determines a population's characteristics ("races" and "peoples"), and it became a determining frame for political processes—or, further, an agent of human history. According to this logic, cultures (social and economic forms) are the result of biological—that is, spatially determined—life forms. Natural conditions become natural spatial relations. These biologically interpreted spatial relations determine life and, hence, the specific features of cultures and societies.

Such a reduction of the social dimension to the biological level conceptually and methodologically disregards the interpretive dimensions of social actions and the relevance of interpretive patterns in dealing with natural conditions. The premise of lebensraum and the biologistic reduction it implies are the foundation on which the research program of an early human geography is built. It aims to prove spatial determinism as environmental determinism of cultures, societies, and economies. The geographical world view is thus from the outset a mechanistic world view established by Newton, then transferred by Haeckel to biology and by Ratzel to the field of geographical research.

As for methodology, academic geography morphed at the end of nineteenth century into a causalistic science. It aimed to show empirically the natural space's determining effect on human actions and subsequently offered corresponding geographical explanations for the observed forms of cultural and economic realities. Geography's adaptation of the mechanistic world view as an ideal for scientific inquiry not only enhanced the discipline's scientific reputation and its political influence but thenceforth also served as the point of reference for the formation of the social science perspective on geography. In the context of traditional regional geography, for example, Max Weber (1924/1988) identified the relevance of the geographical point of view as establishing "in any given case which of the specific components of cultural phenomena are attributable to climatic or similar, purely geographic aspects" (p. 462).

Politically, the alleged proof that cultures and societies are environmentally deterministic is connected to the normative claim of identifying the correct spatial expanse of nations by identifying their natural boundaries and uncovering the "commandments of the soil" (Ratzel, 1891, p. 48; my translation). In this way, "geographical facts" (Hettner, 1927, p. 267; my translation) are understood as the actual constitutive aspects that are to be uncovered as the true forces shaping social and cultural realities. Alfred Hettner, one of the important representatives of causal geography in the first half of the twentieth century and the leading figure of regional geography, pithily summarized this program: "By passing over human volition, we ascribe the geographic facts of humans to the environmental conditions present in their respective countries" (p. 267; my translation).

Understanding space as a fact that precedes all human actions opens the door to a line of reasoning that culminates in the idea that the structuring and organization of cultures and societies could be influenced through spatial planning. Geopolitics thus becomes a key concern for politics. Denying human individuals the possibility of making their own decisions and shaping social reality are the key anti-Enlightenment views in the geopolitical world view, especially in its National Socialist hue.

To sum up, the elements of the space–society combination discussed thus far are, first, a substantialist container space; second, a biological concept of life; and third (as a merger of the previous two), a concept of lebensraum as something that determines life forms located in it. Notions of the social dimension as being somehow determined by such a lebensraum imply a naturalistic or biologistic reductionism, that is, a reduction of the social dimension to the biological category "life." The notion of society thus turns into a biologistic one, so it is frequently replaced by "population." The constitution of subjective meanings on basis of the stock of knowledge at hand, subjective interpretations, and symbolic appropriations are *not* considered subjects of scholarly research in general or of the dominant mainstream geographical research in particular. As a result, the interpretative social and cultural sciences can be removed from the catalogue of scientific disciplines; biology and traditional geography are then sufficient for researching societies and social phenomena.

For sociocultural realities to be suitably investigated and characterized, one may invert the space–society combination, recast it as a society–space logic so as to put society first and consider the spatial dimension as an element of social realities but not as its determinant. Attempts to avoid the geodeterministic logic within the space–society paradigm—particularly those efforts made within geography's spatial scientific program (Bartels, 1968; Bunge, 1962; Harvey, 1969)—have been unsuccessful. The spatial turn in sociology resulted in a "sociology of space" (Simmel, 1903) that delved primarily into the research on the "constitution of space" (Löw, 2008, p. 25) and the structuration of spaces instead of the structuration of society. Such a line of inquiry is consistent with the spatial scientific approach in traditional geography and, consequently, becomes trapped in these outdated concepts of space—despite rhetoric that seems to suggest otherwise (Lippuner & Lossau, 2004). To be fair, Lefebvre (1974)—a key reference in the sociology of space—bypassed these problems. Yet his notions of perceived, conceived, and lived spaces call into question spatial practice in spatial terminology (Schmid, 2005, p. 18) instead of helping one regard space an abstract, conceptual element of social practice.

From the preceding discussion it can be concluded that spatial scientific attempts to approach the social dimension ultimately leads to naturalistic reduction of meaningful sociocultural realities. Even more recent attempts to establish a society-oriented spatial science or a spatioscientific sociology end up reducing the social dimension to the geographical space. And because the three-dimensional geographical space permits only the localization of three-dimensional material facts, this procedure leads (at least implicitly) to a reification of nonmaterial established facts. A nonreductionist inclusion of the geospatial dimension in an interpretative analysis of socioculturally constructed realities requires one to differentiate the various dimensions of human action by their ontological status. Only then can the ontological slum be avoided. Perhaps more precisely, only then can the ontological swamp be drained of the sewage of geospatial reductionisms.

Different Spaces for Different Worlds

A sufficiently detailed ontological differentiation is essential in order to give due consideration to both society and space. The flawed arguments put forward by spatially ignorant social sciences and socially ignorant geography are to be avoided, and human geography is to be reconstructed as an interpretative, constructivist, and socioscientific geography, such as a social geography. Such ontological differentiations should make it possible to overcome the kind of reductionism that spatializes social and cultural aspects and to develop alternative approaches.

Social practices can be seen as being composed of three ontologically different dimensions: the corporeal (biophysical), the mental (cognitive), and the sociocultural (Popper, 1972; Schütz, 1981). Subjecting these dimensions to the same kind of analytical procedure would therefore seem improper. Accordingly, social practices can first be distinguished into physical conditions and thought content. The former are characterized by their material substance, which has a spatial extent and can be described in terms of height, width, and depth. The physical realities refer to all material conditions and states, including actors' bodies, and exist independently of the subjects' thought content. The mental dimension refers to a person's knowledge and experience. It includes not only the reflexive (or discursive) but also the unconscious and the practical (or tacit) consciousness and related states of mind and forms of knowledge. The practical (or tacit) consciousness describes those elements of knowledge that subjects competently draw on when acting but that they cannot verbalize (at least not easily).

Concerning the distinction between the physical and the mental world, action- and practice-centered approaches stress that the meaning of material objects depends on subjects' constitution of meaning on the basis of the stock of knowledge at hand. According to Schütz (1981, p. 92), the human body is the epitome of mediation between these two worlds. The body simultaneously is the center of immediate experience, the medium of actions, and a field of expression of subjective meaning. Furthermore, the mental world cannot be analyzed in isolation from the sociocultural world; the former is always—through socialization processes—embedded into the latter. Individuals are initiated into the sociocultural world through socialization or their action (Berger & Luckmann, 1966).

Ontologically, the sociocultural world is identical with neither the physical nor the mental world. Neither is it merely a combination of the two. The sociocultural world includes the intersubjectively accepted and applicable social norms and cultural values and the institutionalized patterns of action in the economic, legal, religious, and other realms. The meanings of these norms, values, and societal action patterns transcend the mental world of individual subjects and are therefore assigned a separate ontological standing.

Action, Knowledge, and Space—Space, Knowledge, and Action

Any definition of space has to take into account that the word has different meanings, depending on the meaning and situation of the action under consideration. Depending on the type of action, both the formal and the classificatory aspect acquire a specific connotation. That is, both aspects are contingent on the specific interests pursued by the actor.

The nomenclature of the spatial dimension changes with the model of action: instrumentally rational action, norm-oriented action, and meaning-oriented action. The shift of the spatial dimension's nomenclature occurs or, more precisely, is necessary because relations with the body change depending on the orientation (or model) of action gives an overview of the characteristic attributes of each dimension (see Table 2.1).

Table 2.1 The characteristic attributes of action and space

Attributes	Formal	Classificatory/relational	Examples
Instrumentally rational	Metric	Classificatory calculation	Land market, real estate
Norm oriented	Metric and body centered	Classificatory-relational prescription	Nation-state, front and back region
Meaning oriented	Body centered	Relational signification	Motherland, homeland

From Werlen (2013, p. 9)

In the instrumentally rational model both orientation and classification are closely related to what Max Weber called "disenchantment of the world" (Weber, 1922/1980, p. 308). Giddens (1990) characterized this pithily as "emptying of space" (p. 18) and "emptying of time" (p. 18). Such disenchantment and emptying of formerly stable and invariable meanings convey the formalization of the interpretation of reality. This formalization builds upon the metrization of spatial expanse and thus facilitates classification and calculation. Formalization and metrization (e.g., longitude and latitude) are the basis of modern cartographic representations of the earth's surface and their use as an orientation for action. If the spatial dimension is included in the course of action in the instrumentally rational model, it is only as purely formal aspects of action; substantively, however, the spatial dimension is no longer tied to specific actions in a general, invariable way.

With regard to norm-oriented day-to-day activities, spatially bound prescriptions—the relation between norm orientation and spatial expanse—are key. When relating to the physical world, actors apply, hypothetically, a classificatory criterion and a relational criterion to orient their actions. Using the classificatory criterion, they apply specific criteria (e.g., park) to categorize (e.g., public/private) the circumstances that are relevant to their actions. Using the relational criterion, actors attribute a relation to these categories (e.g., accessible/inaccessible) according to certain social or legal norms and cultural values.

Of particular societal relevance are relations with normative-prescriptive spatial connotations, such as permitted/prohibited or, "You are allowed to do activity X here but not there." Such attributions result from processes of territorialization based on clearly measurable delineations. Control over people and the means of violence are organized via action-related territorialization, with the human body being the pivotal element. The combination of norm, body, and spatial context is exemplified by the modern nation-state with its territorially bound law and jurisdiction.

The spatial connotation of understanding rests on a distinctive focus on the body as the central element of interaction and communication. The significance of the body (*Körper*) for the spatial connotations becomes obvious as soon as the body is understood as the "particularly suitable link" (Schütz, 1981, p. 41, my translation) between the subjective and the extended, spatial physical world. From this perspective one can understand the body as a kind of a "functional link" (Werlen, 1993b, p. 75), switching element, or mediator for subjective biographical knowledge and symbolic appropriation of physical elements of contexts of action. Assuming that the meaning of the circumstances deemed relevant to someone's actions depends on the person's available knowledge, then the way meaning is attributed arguably depends on that hitherto acquired knowledge.

A decisive factor bearing on the formation of the knowledge stock is the bodily relation in the sense of presence/absence, in other words, the relation between direct and mediated experiences of the world. The significance of copresence—the sharing of corporeality in the here and now—is based on the direct experience of the world through one's senses. The significance lies in having seen something with one's own eyes and having heard something with one's own ears and having gained the attendant intimate knowledge. This *relationship between the physical senses and the world* contrasts with mediated ways of acquiring information and knowledge, which are characterized by a much lower level of intimacy.

The distinction between direct and mediated forms of knowledge acquisition underlies the generation of meanings and the production of significative relations to the world. In much the same way as prescriptions are the basis for territorialization in the norm-oriented model of action, emotive relations are the basis for classificatory significations as emotional/symbolic relations to specific places. They are expressed in regions of meaning attached to material entities and described by words such as *homeland*, *sacred site*, *landmark*, and *image*. In this form they frequently become unquestioned elements of social communication.

Hypothetically, the more these relations are based on immediate experience (intimate knowledge) and bodily everyday practice, the more they elude reflexive control and become linked to hypostatization and reification, eventually eliminating the difference between nomenclature (signification) and the named objects and circumstances (materiality). The represented meaning and the vehicle of representation become one and the same despite all existing ontological differences. As a result, *homeland* does not register as the expression of emotional, symbolic classification of a clearly delineated section of the world through which embodied experiences are represented. Instead, *homeland* "is" also experience, much like *sacred site* "is" itself the sacred. The more the basis for the signification is mediated—for example, via advertising's instrumentally rational, conceptualized images of places—the more they are hypothetically subject to reflexive control. In both cases these relations become elements of communication and can orient normative-political action (e.g., nationalism, regionalism) as well as instrumentally rational consumptive action and productive action (e.g., tourism, place image, place reputation).

Accordingly, physical objects in a certain constellation or arrangement as a situation of action can only carry or convey meaning, but they can never be the meaning. Physical objects are the media of symbolization; they are always mere vehicles that transport meaning. Hence, there can be a spatial order of vehicles but not of meanings. A distinction must be drawn between symbolic space and the spatial arrangement of symbolizing vehicles. Meanings are always located on the side of the subject and never on the side of the object. Meanings are attributed, and the practice of attributing meaning is a way of establishing relations and bonds.

The distinction between three different models of action (instrumentally rational action, norm-oriented action, and meaning-oriented action) and their corresponding terminologically defined appropriation of spatially expansive physical objects hint at the meaning that relations and bonds in these realms of everyday practice may have. At the same time, they illustrate that the relations to space are dependent on the type of action undertaken. Subscribing to this view implies conceptualizing social geography as an investigation of different forms of everyday action-related geography-making, of geographical practices.

Incorporation of the World and the Construction of Geographical Realities

From a world view, a geographical imagination that puts the cognizing, knowing, and acting subject at the center results in a dynamization of the geographical perspective on and understanding of the world. The focus shifts from the question of where objects and people are located in space to the question of scholarly examination of forms of everyday geography-making. In short, attention turns to the interpretation of meaningful constructions of geographical realities, including the meaningful appropriation of objects, places, and spaces.

For this purpose a quite substantial part of geographical terminology needs to be redefined. One, if not the, key word is *regionalization*. From traditional to spatial scientific geography as well as in Giddens's (1984) theory of structuration, regionalization referred to the subdivision of given spaces (in whatever way it was determined). From the subject-centered new perspective, however, "regionalization" is understood to denote an everyday practice of establishing ties to the world in a specific manner. By emphasizing the spatial and temporal aspects of these specific relations, one can call them "world relationship" (*Weltbeziehung*, Werlen, 1996, p. 112) or "world-binding" (*Weltbindung*, Werlen, 1997, p. 215), the act of defining, shaping, or establishing one's own ties to the world. I would now like to call that act of geography-making "world incorporation." World incorporation refers to the social mastering of spatial and temporal relations in order to monitor and control one's own actions and those of others. It refers to the way subjects relate to the world; it constitutes one's relations to the world.

In the context of everyday regionalizations, space is a conceptual tool and a medium for action with which the various forms of world incorporation are implemented. The constraining and enabling component of power is particularly important in this respect. Its various manifestations are reflected in the varying degrees of capability and spatial range of world incorporation. Hence, in the subject-centered reconceptualization of geography, the space-centered question of power over space is replaced by the question of the efficacy of the available spatioconceptual media that are used to exercise power over and surveillance of practices.

The capability of shaping—which is inherent in social practices and does not exist outside them—is characterized, on the one hand, by the spatial and temporal range of one's actions. In this sense power is reflected in the transformative capacity of human action. On the other hand, this capability also depends on the ability to integrate absent subjects and objects into the realization of one's own aims and objectives. In the sense used by Giddens (1984), capability can be understood as consisting of resources and rules of action. According to him, the capability of monitoring and controlling the access to and the appropriation and use of natural resources and the world of material objects can be conceptualized as meaning that one has allocative resources at one's disposal. This capability exists in all forms of societal organization and relates to control over material resources, material artifacts used in the transformation of these resources, and material goods produced in this transformation.

Within the frame of world incorporation, the terminological means with which access to allocative resources is granted is the notion of measured extension as metric space divested of all other symbolic attributions. This notion of space is the one implicit in cost calculations having to do with the distance and scale of transport at the beginning of the production line (e.g., shipping raw materials to the factory) and at its end (e.g., distributing to various retailers the goods produced from those raw materials). In combination with the notion of standardized metric time, it is possible to calculate the parameters for acting over distance. Such calculations facilitate planning of economic activities in both production (including work processes and commodity flows) and capital accumulation (Harvey, 1982) via world incorporation processes in global contexts.

The capability of acquiring and maintaining control and governance over actors—even in one's physical absence—is called authoritative resource. Such a capability of controlling and governing is based on direct or indirect access to the bodies of those being monitored, controlled, or governed, or on direct or indirect access to body-related ways of authorizing or preventing actions and of maintaining those actions over time.

World incorporation via authoritative resources is represented in the term *territory*, which prescriptively connects normative tenets to spatial expanse. These normative tenets (and their legal enforcement strategies) can be called upon in cases where human bodies enter or use the territory. The property rights connected to these normative prescriptions authorize or prevent access by others and facilitate maximum control over people and over the use of areas and material artifacts (means of production). Therefore, the resource-related aspects of incorporating the world refer to economic, social, political, juridical, and other dimensions. Authoritative resources are usually superimposed onto allocative resources, but the mobilization of authoritative resources always requires allocative resources (e.g., to ensure that one's own actions prevail).

However, the structuration of human action and, hence, of all forms of world incorporation does not rely on resources alone. According to Giddens (1984), rules are the second important aspect. They include specific semantic and moral rules that can form powerful interpretive schemes and can regulate courses of action in a value-specific manner. Actors use these interpretive schemes to interpret (in line with the rules) and symbolically organize practice-specific realms of reality. Interpretive schemes are the most comprehensive form of the structuration of human action and, consequently, of the constitution of society or sociocultural realities.

Rule-specific aspects are key for types of action oriented to intersubjective understanding. These aspects underlie all types of symbolic relations to the world. The vocabulary used for such emotionally charged, significative classifications of relations to places and objects includes *sacred site* and *homeland*.

Regionalizations and Regions of Meaningful Geographical Realities

The programmatic research areas concerning meaningful geographical realities are derived from the three already mentioned types of action theories: instrumentally rational, normative, and meaning oriented. Depending on research interests, empirical investigations might focus on socioeconomic aspects (consumptive-productive types of world incorporation), sociopolitical aspects (political-normative types of world incorporation), or sociocultural aspects (informative-significative types of world incorporation). Everyday actions feature all three dimensions simultaneously. In addition, each of these dimensions is interpreted differently by different subjects; that is, it is idiosyncratically relevant to one's actions (see Table 2.2). Therefore, geography turns into everyday geograph*ies*.

Research on the economic type of world incorporation revolves around three main questions: (a) How do producers bring under their control the raw material used in the production process and the labor force? In other words, how do they relate to the world (or bind the world to themselves)? (b) How do consumers decide what to buy? That is, under which conditions and with which medium or resources do they make which decisions? (c) What is the relationship between the productive and consumptive types of world incorporation?

Production-related types of world incorporation involve, first, deciding on a site or location at which to produce. Such decisions are typically made by drawing on the locational focus of production-related activities and commodity flows that are directly mediated by the body. Decisions on where to produce and on the corresponding arrangements generated as a result of such decisions are elements of economic world incorporation. They are always tied to allocative resources and the notion of metric space. The analytical lens of world incorporation (everyday actions yielding multiple everyday geographies) enables one to describe systematically the establishing of global relations pertaining to productive types of world incorporation, especially in times of digital or virtual capitalism, when capital accumulation no longer requires activities involving the body or other matter. In addition, the perspective of world incorporation makes it possible to analyze the varying capabilities of control over resources, material goods, means of production, and the resulting power and power relations.

Table 2.2 Types of world incorporation

Main types	Subtypes
Productive-consumptive	Geographies of production
	Geographies of consumption
Normative-political	Geographies of normative appropriation
	Geographies of political control
Significative-informative	Geographies of information
	Geographies of symbolic appropriation

From Werlen (1997, p. 274)

Consumption decisions largely depend on available financial means (i.e., allocative resources) and lifestyle (traditional or individual). The relevance of consumption decisions is expanding along with people's increasing reflexivity with regard to consumption decisions and intensifying globalization. Consumption decisions reflect subjectively constituted cultural and life worlds because late-modern lifestyles are largely shaped by *subjective* decisions. (In traditional ways of life, by contrast, collective constraints are the dominant factor determining the course of actions). Accordingly, consumption is embedded in the processes through which people develop their subjectivity. This embeddedness also leads to the continuing dissipation of the territorial logic in both the economic and the cultural realm. Against this backdrop it becomes clear why geoscience-based environmental policy-making is doomed to fail. What is needed instead in this context is a practice-centered ecocritique and ecopolicies. Because the local and the global are interwoven, lifestyle-specific consumption for the purpose of moving toward moral and ethical consumption and global sustainability is becoming negotiable in public discourse (Werlen, 2012, 2015).

Research on social and political types of world incorporation currently focuses on geographies of normative appropriation and political control. Prescriptive-normative appropriations prevent or facilitate access to spatial contexts of action. At the same time, they serve to socially regulate types of action within these spatial contexts. In addition to formal political regionalizations such as the nation-state, federal states and counties, important informal normative regionalizations with respect to age, social status, role, and gender are regulating access to and exclusion from certain spatial contexts of everyday life. Goffman's (1959) distinction between front and back region also belongs to this category. His approach usefully highlights the relevance of both the reference point of interaction and the setting for the way interactions are performed.

Thus far, I have informally described negotiated regionalizations. They have to be distinguished from formal, legally recognized, institutionally established, and bureaucratically organized regionalizations. Such formal regionalizations make command and power over others possible in absentia, meaning that physical copresence of the rulers and the ruled is not required for power to be exercised. At the same time, formal regionalizations play a key role in identifying and categorizing classes of rights (e.g., constitutional, administrative, and criminal law; contract, tort, and property law). Research on formal regionalizations also encompasses the relation between public and private space, including surveillance and its legitimacy in public areas.

From the action- and practice-centered perspective proposed here, regionalist, nationalist, or ethnic movements can be seen as forces of everyday geography-making that oppose existing forms of authoritative control. A practice-centered perspective suggests that command and power over territories is actually command and power over subjects. This interpretation highlights the difference between a practice-centered and a traditional geopolitical perspective: The former focuses on subjects and their different way of *making* geography (and power); the latter, on the way that power *over* space supposedly translates into power *of* space. The fact that regionalist and nationalist movements usually follow the traditional geographical and geopolitical logic exposes their Janus-faced character in the light of modernity: claiming the right to *self*-determination within a spatial-material logic when there is actually no self.

Informative-significative types of world incorporation or regionalizations are also closely tied to the corporeality of subjects. In the absence of the physical body, communication media serve as extensions of the body. Significative regionalizations (in the form of symbolic appropriations) are the most comprehensive and arguably the most powerful processes in the construction of meaningful geographical realities.

Research on the geographies of information focuses on the preconditions and processes of acquiring information and knowledge. With respect to the sender, research has to clarify the preconditions for generating and linguistically steering the potential appropriation of information via different information media. In historical order the starting points include the dissemination of information through writing (e.g., books and other print media), the electronic (radio, TV), and digital media (internet-based communication). Of particular interest are the globalizing consequences of the production and use of these media and the resulting tensions between the unfamiliar and familiar, between mediated information and unmediated experience. The implications of those consequences are observable in the context of cultural integration, for example.

Symbolic appropriations (and the symbolic geography-making that they stand for), the production of symbolic structures of spatially locatable phenomena and objects, are key dimensions of cultural representation. Hypothetically, one can assume that such symbolic appropriations are relevant in communication and as media for social integration and regulation (of economic actions). Attributing meaning to material contexts of action through the use of particular terms reflecting the relevant notion of space is always done via practices and usually in the form of routines used to manage standard situations.

Action and practice-centered geographical research should also inquire into the stock of knowledge-based interpretive schemes, rules of interpretation, skills, moral rules, and emotional dispositions that substantiate the different types of appropriations conducted as classificatory significations. Clarification of the following questions is required, too: Which subject-related geographies of symbolic appropriation are being produced in which communicative contexts? What do the symbolizations represent and with what consequences? How are the symbolizations enforced? A further important area of research is the empirical identification of the transformative potential that symbolic appropriations of places and material contexts of action can have for economic and political practices. The reconstruction of the processes constituting everyday "mythologies" (Barthes, 1957) and of their underlying reification techniques ("chosification" p. 112) are particularly important in this context, not least because they have been in the focus of traditional geographical research.

The six main types of world incorporation—the ways of defining, shaping, or establishing one's own ties to the world—are connected in manifold ways. Consumptive actions, for example, belong primarily to the economic field and are linked to allocative resources. However, they are also embedded in normative standards and might have a strong cultural-symbolic and/or lifestyle-related connotation. Particularly with globalization processes, the traditional combinations of a given type of action in only one field or type of resource—which have long been deeply ingrained, not least because of the unchallenged hegemony of nation-state institutions—are not only questioned but put into a new "order."

Social Relations of Space

Processes of world incorporation are both structured and structuring; they are in the focus of practice-centered geographical research. This perspective makes it possible to reformulate the question about the relationship between society and space: Given that the spatiality of actors derives from their corporeality and necessitates world incorporation, what significance does that spatiality have for the generation of societality? How has this basic challenge of spatiality been coped with over the course of history?

These questions broaden the horizon of social science geography and draw attention to two issues: (a) the process of relating social action to the implications of corporeality, and (b) the relevance of these relations for the generation of social realities. In a nutshell, it highlights just how essential society–space relationships are for societality. Research on these relationships should therefore be the macroanalytic complement to the microanalytic level of subjective world incorporation processes in geographical social science research. Together they form the core of social science geography and are an extension of theories of society and of culture.

As the spatial turn in the social and cultural sciences suggests, the concept of society–space relationships takes account of the fact that it is insufficient to include the spatial aspect in social theory as a kind of spatialization of the social dimension. What is needed instead is a reconceptualization of social theory as a theory that refers to the geographical shaping of social realities without relapsing into materialistic or spatial reductionism. It must systematically take into account the implications that the corporeality of the actors and the material basis of many social institutions have for the subsequent spatiality of the social dimension for communication, interactions, socialization, learning situations, and care-giving.

A first important step for highlighting the relevance of spatiality was the contrasting of social relations and spatial structures (Gregory & Urry, 1985). It focused on pointing out the spatial manifestations of social reality with respect to the spatial structure of settlements and transport networks, the spatiotemporal paths of social reproduction, and social inequalities in the sense of regional disparities, for instance. Focusing on society–space relationships reverses the perspective: Research efforts are no longer directed to the spatial structures of societal relationships but rather to the significance that spatial relationships have for the meaningful construction of sociocultural and geographical realities.

With spatiality being understood as describing actors' corporeality, this new perspective raises the question about the role that this spatiality and the ways of coping with it play in co-determining the shaping of sociocultural realities. In this context the ways in which people act over distance are profoundly important. Distance is understood in both a social and the physical sense. According to Tönnies (1887/2001), it is regarded as a core element of the difference between community and society. Consequently, the concept of society–space relationships includes consideration of the ways to cope with one's spatiality and, hence, with spatial distanciation as constituent of society.

The Times They Are a-Changing: From Territorial to Digital Social Realities

As noted in this chapter's introduction, the expression *social relations of space* refers to the historically and socially established ways of relating to given and spatially distant circumstances relevant to one's action. Social relations of space (spatial relations) are determined by the means and tools available for coping with spatiality for the purpose of creating social realities. Accordingly, the dominant spatial relations can be identified best by examining the available means and tools. Social relations of space are in this sense grounded in the sociohistorically created conditions, means, tools, and media of acting over distance, that is, in the forms and options for coping with the everyday world's spatiality with respect to all forms of social practice, social interaction, and communication. Therefore, social relations of space are evident in the current and historical possibilities and impossibilities of the sociogeographical conditions of social coexistence. Because the aforementioned ways of incorporating the world on the basis of terminological media are embedded in the historical development of the technological media of acting over distance, the analysis has to complemented by a diachronic perspective.

The scope of daily geographical practices is limited by the manifestation of the social relations of space in each form of world incorporation. The media for mastering spatiality have advanced in revolutionary steps. The Neolithic Revolution and Industrial Revolution were, in this sense, also revolutions of society–space relations. Another reconfiguration of these society–space relations is taking place as the Digital Revolution. Each of these revolutions can (hypothetically) be characterized by a distinctive range of options for the formation of societality.

Social relations of space determine the *modi operandi* (for acting over distance), based on which the corporeal social practices that construct sociocultural realities can take place. The historically available means, tools, and media are therefore constitutive of all forms of societality. I contend that these means, tools, and media are constitutive of social realities in much the same way as the Marxian relations of production are.

Social relations of space are, however, distinct from relations of production and modes of production. According to Marx (1867, p. 792, 1847/1983, p. 130), societal history progressed from primitive society to slave society (or ancient slave society) to feudal society, bourgeois society, and, finally, communist society. Marx assumed these different societal formations to emerge as the result of changing relations of production. That is, he considered social change to be determined by the respective relations of production. If his analysis can be considered as almost accurate for the period of industrial revolution, it can certainly not be seen as an all-encompassing formula for explaining the social world and its transformation. However, societies can also be classified according to the dominant mode of production and economic sector into agrarian, industrial, service, or information societies. By contrast, society–space relationships focus on the technological media for coping with distance and time. After the Neolithic Revolution they included the wheel; script (cuneiform); plant and animal breeding; irrigation; and storage capacities for food, seed, and water. The Industrial Revolution brought changes in the form of mechanics, metrization, mechanical drivetrain, and electricity, for instance. In the course of the Digital Revolution, numerical data storage and telecommunication in real time have become new technological media for coping with distance and time.

Modern nation-states can thus be viewed as the manifestations of thinking in terms of actions that expand linear reach, territorialization, clearly measurable territorial scope of social norms (state borders), bureaucracy, and communication via the medium of text (as opposed to orality) produced by printing technologies. The key question is, then, what the dissolution of the territorial nexus means for societality in the Digital Age. Further social science research would usefully investigate how to move beyond "methodological nationalism" (Beck & Sznaider, 2006, p. 3) or, more precisely, ontological nationalism, if the differentiation between methodological and ontological is used systematically (Werlen, 1987, p. 78, 1993b, p. 40). Such research would need to take account of the fact that geographical and social realities are based on specific *modi operandi* concerning the manifold ways in which people are coping with their spatiality.

These *modi operandi* are always imposed upon actors and formally specify the possibilities (or impossibilities) of acting over distance. In other words, *modi operandi* can be understood as sets of rules governing the ways in which the available means, tools, and media can (or cannot) be used by actors. A specific *modus operandi* therefore allows for a specific spatial and temporal reach of people's actions and, by implication, also for particular forms of societality, socialization, and communication. For example, pre-Neolithic tribal societies characterized by the primacy of the present and of orality (which, in turn, requires bodily copresence) arguably operate in the synchronic/present mode. By contrast, nation-state forms of societality draw on analog written communication and the availability of the past and therefore operate in the diachronic/distanced mode. I conjecture that the hitherto undetermined societality of the Digital Age—based on numeric digitality—will take the synchronic/distanced modus.

Implications: From Space to Action and from Action to the Spatiality of Action

The approach suggested in this chapter opens up an alternative perspective on many current societal issues, including the global financial crisis, global migration, and sociocultural integration. They can be understood as consequences of the at least potential, continuing, spatiotemporal disembedding of social, cultural, and economic realities in the course of the Digital Revolution. The spatial ties of social practices are at least selective and no longer of the same encompassing nature as those in the predigital age. They are the result of practices of appropriation and socially produced spatiality rather than a quasi-natural condition.

The aforementioned societal issues can be interpreted as manifestations of the mismatch between the spatiotemporal shaping of societality and the logics of control governing that societality. In other words, the above societal issues arise when society–space relationships have changed or are in the process of changing to a new *modus operandi* while politics is still operating according to the logics established in the previous *modus operandi*. The increasing disintegration becomes evident in the continued use of territorial strategies (e.g., territorial wars or national financial policy) to dispel problematic consequences of a-territorial networks with fluid place-bound nodes (e.g., terrorism or digital financial capitalism).

Analyzing sociocultural realities from the geographical perspective outlined in this chapter emancipates the spatial from the temporal dimension. Hägerstrand's (1970) time geography has shown that the time required to perform corporeal actions correlates with spatial order. In other words, new society–space relationships always imply new society–time relationships, and society–space relationships therefore also represent space–time relationships.

Including actors' corporeality and the physical conditions of actions in the analytical perspective means that time no longer takes precedence over space. The acceleration of social life is thus an expression of the altered conditions of coping with spatiality and ultimately leads to action in global contexts in quasi simultaneity. The space–time relationships are at the basis of a reconceptualization of social theory.

In order to understand the significance of the revolution in the spatial and temporal conditions of the social dimension—or of globalization and acceleration (Rosa, 2013) with regard to the circumstances relevant to everyday action—they are to be thought of as two sides of the same coin. Whereas globalization denotes the spatial reach of one's action in real time, acceleration refers to its consequences for the frequency of decisions in social interaction. Thinking of globalization and acceleration as two sides of the same coin enables one to track the societal consequences of reshaping society–space relationships.

This geographical perspective opens up new approaches to issues of sustainability and the analysis of human practices according to ecological criteria. The notion of life and society being literally contained in biological habitats can be overcome with the concept of world incorporation. The a priori container space that was conventionally assumed to exist independently of human experience and social practice—from Haeckel and the ecopolicies based on his ideas to the UN sustainability policies à la the Brundtland Report (World Commission on Environment and Development, 1987)—no longer has to be the criterion for survival or extinction and for calculations of so-called carrying capacity. Focusing on world incorporation means turning the perspective upside down: Human action is privileged above habitat (Earth), so sustainability politics and ecopolitics can be rid of biologistic thinking, which usually puts them in the vicinity of traditional geopolitics. This accounting for society–space relationships makes it possible for an original approach without naturalistic reductionisms to be developed (Becker & Jahn, 2006) with ecological practices (Gäbler, 2015) rather than ecotopes at its center. Such reorientation is a consequence of the geographical turn from space to practice.

Conclusions

The scientific investigation into the shaping of spatial relations in a society can be seen as an important thematic field for holistic study of social, cultural, economic, and political matters, research that is generated by a spatially grounded perspective without ensnarement in natural or spatial determinism. With the recognition of the importance of society's spatiality, sociospatial conditions will identifiably become a part of the social sphere. For example, they will indicate the fundamental conditions for establishing social relations over distance, which are currently enabling many social actors to sustainably shape socialization and power without being physically copresent.

The dissolution of former principles of sociospatial conditions and the revolutionary establishment of new ones are resulting in new social arrangements and issues. As an already apparent reaction to this situation, there is a new (and highly problematic) tendency to address these changes by relying on well-known structural principles and established interpretational frameworks, such as the increasing nationalization of European or global issues. Yet continued deterioration in spatiotemporal conditions limits the potential success of such territorial solutions. In essence they can, hypothetically, be seen as attempts to illustrate how conventional conceptions of the world, regarded as the all-embracing, ingrained, and only possible interpretation, are eventually adapted to newly established spatiotemporal constellations. However, these constellations lay the claim for applying national or territorial logics of societal coexistence to increasingly deterritorialized living conditions rather than simply territorially regulating them.

One of the most important contemporary tasks in social and cultural studies is the establishment of and elaboration on new conceptions of the world that bring about not only the sociocultural spheres but also the attendant political and everyday frameworks. This endeavor, however, also implies the uncoupling from traditional and trusted conventions. Thus, the first and foremost goal is to dismantle and discard ideas and understandings of container space and to spatialize social and cultural realities as the basic principles of world conceptualizations that have been all-encompassing for several centuries. It is not to promote practice-centered views and illustrate how actors relate to the world with and within the conventions of their actions.

Relating to this shift in perception, other urgent issues such as sustainability and the evaluation of human activities involving ecological questions will also have to be renegotiated. Besides the consideration of social issues, the matter of decontainerization will be essential to this process. In this respect, the nomenclature and concepts of space and place and of nature and landscape cannot be regarded as logically separable or independent.

References

Bartels, D. (1968). *Zur wissenschaftstheoretischen Grundlegung einer Geographie des Menschen* [On the epistemological foundation of a geography of men]. Wiesbaden: Steiner.

Barthes, R. (1957). *Mythologies* [Mythologies]. Paris: Seuil.

Beck, U., & Sznaider, N. (2006). Unpacking cosmopolitanism for the social sciences: A research agenda. *British Journal of Sociology, 57,* 1–23.

Becker, E., & Jahn, T. (Eds.). (2006). *Soziale Ökologie: Grundzüge einer Wissenschaft von den gesellschaftlichen Naturverhältnissen* [Social ecology: Outline of a science of social nature-relations]. Frankfurt am Main: Campus-Verlag.

Berger, P. L., & Luckmann, T. (1966). *The social construction of reality.* Garden City, NY: Doubleday.

Bourdieu, P. (1985). *Sozialer Raum und "Klassen": Leçon sur la leçon. Zwei Vorlesungen* [Social space and "classes": Two lectures]. Frankfurt am Main: Suhrkamp.

Braudel, F. (1949). *La Méditerranée et le monde méditerranéen à l'époque de Philippe II* [The Mediterranean and the Mediterranean world in the age of Philip II]. Paris: Colin.

Bunge, W. (1962). *Theoretical geography.* Lund: Gleerup.

Döring, J., & Thielmann, T. (Eds.). (2008). *Spatial Turn: Das Raumparadigma in den Kultur- und Sozialwissenschaften* [Spatial turn: The space paradigm in cultural and social sciences]. Bielefeld: Transcript.

Durkheim, E. (1893). *De la division social du travail.* [The division of labor in society]. Paris: Félix Alcan.

Durkheim, E. (1957). *Professional ethics and civic morals.* London: Routledge/Kegan Paul.

Foucault, M. (1999). Andere Räume [Of other spaces]. In J. Engelmann (Ed.), *Michel Foucault: Botschaften der Macht: Der Foucault Reader* (pp. 145–160). Stuttgart: Deutsche Verlags-Anstalt.

Gäbler, K. (2015). *Gesellschaftlicher Klimawandel: Eine Sozialgeographie der ökologischen Transformation* [Social climate change: A social geography of the ecologic transformation]. Sozialgeographische Bibliothek: Vol. 17. Stuttgart: Franz Steiner.

Giddens, A. (1979). *Central problems in social theory: Action, structure and contradiction in social analysis.* London: MacMillan.

Giddens, A. (1984). *The constitution of society: Outline of the theory of structuration.* Cambridge: Polity Press.

Giddens, A. (1990). *The consequences of modernity.* Stanford: Stanford University Press.

Giddens, A. (1993). Preface. In B. Werlen, *Society, action and space: An alternative human geography* (pp. xii–xvi). London: Routledge.

Goffman, E. (1959). *The presentation of self in everyday life.* New York: Doubleday.

Gregory, D., & Urry, J. (Eds.). (1985). *Social relations and spatial structures.* London: MacMillan.

Günzel, S. (2009). (Ed.). *Raumwissenschaften* [Spatial sciences]. Frankfurt am Main: Suhrkamp.

Haeckel, E. (1866). *Generelle Morphologie der Organismen* [General morphology of organisms]. Berlin: Reimer.

Hägerstrand, T. (1970). What about people in regional science? *Papers in Regional Science, 24,* 7–24.

Hard, G. (1998). Eine Sozialgeographie alltäglicher Regionalisierungen [Social geography of everyday regionalizations]. *Erdkunde, 52,* 250–253.

Harvey, D. (1969). *Explanation in geography*. London: Edward Arnold.

Harvey, D. (1982). *The limits to capital*. Oxford: Basil Blackwell.

Heidegger, M. (Ed.). (2000). *Gesamtausgabe: Vol. 16. Reden und andere Zeugnisse eines Lebensweges: 1910–1976* [Complete edition: Vol. 16. Lectures and other testimonies of a life path: 1910–1976]. Frankfurt am Main: Klostermann. (Original work published 1933)

Hettner, A. (1927). *Die Geographie: Ihre Geschichte, ihr Wesen und ihre Methoden* [Geography: Its history, nature, and methods]. Breslau: Ferdinand Hirt.

Kehlmann, D. (2007). *Measuring the world*. London: Quercus.

Koselleck, R. (2000). *Zeitschichten: Studien zur Historik* [Layers of time: Studies on history]. Frankfurt am Main: Suhrkamp.

Lefebvre, H. (1974). *La production de l'espace* [The production of space]. Paris: Édition Anthropos.

Levy, J. (1999). *Le tournant géographique* [The geographical turn]. Paris: Belin.

Lippuner, R., & Lossau, J. (2004). In der Raumfalle: Eine Kritik des spatial turn in den Sozialwissenschaften [Caught in the space trap: A critique of the spatial turn in the social sciences]. In G. Mein & M. Riegler-Ladich (Eds.), *Soziale Räume und kulturelle Praktiken: Über den strategischen Gebrauch von Medien* (pp. 47–64). Bielefeld: Transcript.

Löw, M. (2001). *Raumsoziologie* [Sociology of space]. Frankfurt am Main: Suhrkamp.

Löw, M. (2008). The constitution of space: The structuration of spaces through the simultaneity of effect and perception. *European Journal of Social Theory, 11,* 25–49.

Marx, K. (1867). *Das Kapital: Kritik der politischen Ökonomie. Erster Band: Buch I. Der Produktionsprocess des Kapitals* [Capital: A critique of political economy: Vol. I, Book I. The process of capitalist production]. Hamburg: Meissner.

Marx, K. (1983). Das Elend der Philosophie: Antwort auf Proudhons "Philosophie des Elends" [The poverty of philosophy: Response to Proudhon's "Philosophy of Poverty"]. In Institut für Marxismus-Leninismus bei ZK der SED (Ed.), *Karl Marx. Friedrich Engels* (pp. 63–182). Marx-Engels-Werke: Vol. 4. Berlin: Dietz. (Original work published 1847)

Newton, I. (1687). *Philosophiae naturalis principia mathematica*. London: Joseph Streater.

Newton, I. (1952). *Opticks: Or, a treatise of the reflexions, refractions, inflexions and colours of light*. New York: Dover. (Original work published 1704)

Park, R. E. (1952). *Human communities: The city and human ecology*. New York: Free Press.

Park, R. E., Burgess, E. W., & McKenzie, R. D. (1925). *The city*. Chicago: University of Chicago Press.

Parsons, T. (1952). *The social system*. London: Free Press.

Parsons, T. (1961). *Theories of societies. Foundations of modern sociological theory: Vol. 2.* New York: Free Press of Glencoe.

Popper, K. (1972). *Objective knowledge: An evolutionary approach*. Oxford, UK: Clarendon Press.

Ratzel, F. (1891). *Anthropo-Geographie: Zweiter Teil. Die geographische Verbreitung des Menschen* [Anthropo-geography: Second part. The geographical distribution of mankind]. Stuttgart: J. Engelhorn.

Ratzel, F. (1897). *Politische Geographie: Geographie der Staaten, des Verkehrs und des Krieges* [Political geography: Geography of states, transport, and war]. Munich: Oldenbourg.

Rosa, H. (2013). *Social acceleration: A new theory of modernity* (J. Trejo-Mathys, Trans.). New York: Columbia University Press.

Schlögel, K. (2002). Kartenlesen, Raumdenken: Von einer Erneuerung der Geschichtsschreibung [Map reading, spatial thinking: Of a renewal of historiography]. *Merkur. Deutsche Zeitschrift für europäisches Denken, 636,* 308–318.

Schmid, C. (2005). *Stadt, Raum und Gesellschaft: Henri Lefebvre und die Theorie der Produktion des Raumes* [City, space, and society: Henri Lefebvre and the theory of the production of space]. Sozialgeographische Bibliothek: Vol 1. Stuttgart: Franz Steiner.

Schütz, A. (1932). *Der sinnhafte Aufbau der sozialen Welt: Eine Einführung in die verstehende Soziologie* [The phenomenology of the social world: An introduction to interpretive sociology]. Vienna: Springer.

Schütz, A. (1981). *Theorie der Lebensformen* [Theory of life forms]. Frankfurt am Main: Suhrkamp.

Simmel, G. (1903). Soziologie des Raumes [Sociology of space]. *Jahrbuch für Gesetzgebung, Verwaltung und Volkswirtschaft im Deutschen Reich, 27*(1), 27–71.

Soja, E. W. (1989). *Postmodern geographies: The reassertion of space in critical social theory.* London: Verso.

Tönnies, F. (2001). *Community and civil society* (J. Harris & M. Hollis, Trans.; J. Harris, Ed.). Cambridge: Cambridge University Press. (Original work published 1887)

Warf, B., & Arias, S. (2008). *The spatial turn: Interdisciplinary perspective.* Routledge studies in human geography: Vol. 26. London: Routledge.

Warming, E. (1895). *Lehrbuch der Ökologischen Pflanzengeographie. Eine Einführung in die Kenntnis der Pflanzenvereine* [Textbook of ecological botanic geography: An introduction to the knowledge of horticultural associations]. Berlin: Gebrüder Borntraeger.

Warming, E. (1909). *Oecology of plants: An introduction to the study of plant communities.* Oxford: Clarendon Press.

Weber, M. (1980). *Wirtschaft und Gesellschaft: Grundriss der verstehenden Soziologie* (5th ed.) [Economy and society: An outline of interpretive sociology]. Tübingen: Mohr & Siebeck. (Original work published 1922)

Weber, M. (1988). Geschäftsbericht und Diskussionsreden auf den deutschen soziologischen Tagungen (1910) [Annual report and discussion speeches at the German sociologic conferences (1910)]. In M. Weber (Ed.), *Gesammelte Aufsätze zur Soziologie und Sozialpolitik* (pp. 431–491). Tübingen: Mohr & Siebeck. (Original Work published 1924)

Weingarten, M. (2009). Biologie/Ökologie [Biology/ecology]. In S. Günzel (Ed.), *Raumwissenschaften* (pp. 77–92). Frankfurt am Main: Suhrkamp.

Werlen, B. (1987). *Gesellschaft, Handlung und Raum: Grundlagen handlungstheoretischer Sozialgeographie* [Society, action and space: Principles of social geography based on action theory] (3rd ed.). Erdkundliches Wissen: Vol. 89. Stuttgart: Franz Steiner.

Werlen, B. (1993a). Gibt es eine Geographie ohne Raum? Zum Verhältnis von traditioneller Geographie und zeitgenössischen Gesellschaften [Is there a geography without space? On the relationship between traditional geography and contemporary societies]. *Erdkunde, 47,* 241–255.

Werlen, B. (1993b). *Society, action, and space: An alternative human geography* (G. Walls, Trans.). London: Routledge.

Werlen, B. (1995). *Sozialgeographie alltäglicher Regionalisierungen: Bd. 1. Zur Ontologie von Gesellschaft und Raum* [Social geography of everyday regionalizations: Vol. 1. On the ontology of society and space]. Erdkundliches Wissen: Vol. 116. Stuttgart: Franz Steiner.

Werlen, B. (1996). Die Geographie globalisierter Lebenswelten [The geography of globalized life worlds]. *Österreichische Zeitschrift für Soziologie, 21,* 97–128.

Werlen, B. (1997). *Sozialgeographie alltäglicher Regionalisierungen. Bd. 2: Globalisierung, Region und Regionalisierung* [Social geography of everyday regionalizations: Vol. 2. Globalization, region, and regionalization]. Erdkundliches Wissen: Vol. 119. Stuttgart: Franz Steiner.

Werlen, B. (2000). *Sozialgeographie.* [Social geography]. Bern: Paul Haupt.

Werlen, B. (2012). True global understanding and pertinent sustainability policies. In I. Scheunemann & L. Oosterbeek (Eds.), *A new paradigm of sustainability* (pp. 163–172). Rio de Janeiro: IBIO.

Werlen, B. (2013). Gesellschaft und Raum: Gesellschaftliche Raumverhältnisse. Grundlagen und Perspektiven einer sozialwissenschaftlichen Geographie [Society and space: Society–space relationships. Principles and perspectives of a social science geography]. *Erwägen-Wissen-Ethik. Forum für Erwägungskultur, 24,* 3–16.

Werlen, B. (2015). From local to global sustainability: Transdisciplinary integrated research in the Digital Age. In B. Werlen (Ed.), *Global sustainability: Cultural perspectives and challenges for transdisciplinary integrated research* (pp. 3–16). New York/London: Springer.

World Commission on Environment and Development. (1987). *Our common future.* Oxford: Oxford University Press.

Chapter 3
Rationality and Discursive Articulation in Place-Making

Huib Ernste

Late-Modern Action-Theoretic Approaches and "Rational" Interventions

Rationality is the ability to design, follow, and have knowledge about a systematic procedure for the redemption of validity claims. In classical philosophy the term denotes the ability of the mind in terms of reason (*nous, intellectus, Vernunft*) and rationality (*logos, ratio, Verstand*) (Mittelstraß, 1995, p. 470). The *logos* provides the argumentation for the views one holds. Logos is the capacity not just for making statements but also for providing their proofs, and a statement is proven by being derived as a conclusion from premises (Welsch, 1999). But these premises themselves cannot be secured through argumentation. It is here that reason comes in. Traditionally, reason is therefore conceived of as the faculty capable of guaranteeing these first premises, by intuition (Plato) or induction (Aristotle). One could say that reason provides the specificity of the situation at hand, the context from which rationality is supposed to draw its conclusions.

It was the paradigmatically modern philosopher Immanuel Kant who, with his Copernican turn, stated that it is actually the other way around, that rationality provides the constitutive categories and principles of cognition and that reason provides only regulative ideas, through which one experiences particularities as parts of a destined whole.[1] In modernity, therefore, rationality is regarded as the most important ability, and reason can ultimately be done away with (Feyerabend, 1987). Seen in this way, rationality autonomously establishes its own principles, methods, and

[1] In Kant's terminology the idea of a *soul* prescribes us to link particular psychological appearances to a whole; the idea of a *world* prescribes us to connect all our singular observations to a unity called world; and, finally, the idea of *God* urges us to see things as result of a causal chain. Together these ideas create a systematic unity in our perception (Störig, 1989, p. 404).

H. Ernste (✉)
Department of Human Geography, Radboud University, Nijmegen, The Netherlands
e-mail: h.ernste@fm.ru.nl

© The Author(s) 2017   57
P. Meusburger et al. (eds.), *Knowledge and Action*, Knowledge and Space 9,
DOI 10.1007/978-3-319-44588-5_3

perspectives. In modernity it is also recognized that there is not just one single type of rationality but different types, which cannot be reduced to each other. Each type determines its own principles. Developing Kant's ideas about theoretical, practical, and aesthetic rationality further, Habermas (1984) paradigmatically distinguished between cognitive, moral, and aesthetic rationality. Habermas built not only on Kant's work but also on that of Max Weber, who first made rationality a key concept in modernistic thinking and used the term specifically in the sense of purposive rationality or economic rationality, the meaning it is also often has in colloquial language. It thereby denotes the strategic choice of the best means to reach a certain goal. In this way rational decision-making became of central interest and positioned rationality and action theory as core concepts in high modernity. Weber elaborated the role of rationality for individual everyday actions and called attention to the tendency toward disenchantment, that is, toward continuous differentiation and rationalization.

Rationalization in this sense designates a historical drive toward a world in which "one can, in principle, master all things by calculation" (Weber, 1919/1946, p. 136), by rational decision-making. This process of rationalization was not limited to the economic sphere but was extended with its own rational logics also to law and administration, the social and political spheres, and other domains. As a prerequisite, a peculiarly rational and intellectual type of personality or person of vocation was presupposed. Modern scientific and technological knowledge slowly pushed back the germinating grounds of human knowledge, such as religion and metaphysics, and created a culture of "objectification" (*Versachlichung*). At the same time, there was a loss of substantive-value rationality, the emergence of a polytheism of value fragmentation, and the related tensions between these two developments, in other words, rationality without reason in practice.

It is in this framework that one must also situate geographical action theory as put forward by Benno Werlen (Chap. 2, in this volume or 1987, 1995, 1997) in the phenomenological tradition of Alfred Schütz (1932). According to this school of thought, the internal mental intentionality directed to outer objects is what ascribes meanings to these objects, as people do through their everyday place-making and everyday spatially differentiated actions. This geographic action theory can be interpreted as the subjectivist version of what Schatzki, Knorr-Cetina, and Savigny (2001) and Reckwitz (2002) designated as the mentalist paradigm in social theory. This approach contrasts with the objectivist version of mentalism, which stems from classical structuralism as exemplified by de Saussure (1916/1972) in linguistics, Lévy-Strauss (1969) in anthropology, Althusser (1965/2005) and Emerson (1984) in Marxist economics, and Piaget (1970) in psychology. One could also add the more contemporary version of psychological structuralism (Lacan, 2002); behaviorist psychology (Skinner, 1938; Watson, 1913); and cognitive psychology (e.g., Broadbent, 1987), including cognitive linguistics (Fauconnier, 1999). The approach diverges from behavioral geography (Golledge & Stimson, 1996) as well, for which human behavior is an effect of structures in the unconscious mind in relation to structured situations and is thus part of the objectivist mentalist tradition.

In geographic action theory, on the other hand, the assumption is that the active mind is in charge. In this case, however, the sources of spatial structurations are not unconscious cognitive structures in hard-wired reaction to external structures but rather the sequence of intentional acts as conscious decisions. The aim of analysis from the angle of this social phenomenology is to describe the voluntarist subjective act, mental interpretations of agents and subjective logics, and rationalities of decision-making and behavior. This intentional goal-oriented kind of geographic action is thus clearly related to the late-modern project based on Weber's ideas of rationalization as a purely subjective mental process and individual rational interventions in the surrounding world. Even in Schütz's (1932) version of social phenomenology or Mead's (1934) social behaviorist approach, in which meanings are grounded in social relations, the individual subjective mind is still the seat of judgment and rational choice. Mental structures and mental activities, therefore, are treated as an incontestable "center" of social and spatial structuration (Reckwitz, 2002, p. 247).

Habermas's (1984) stance on rationalization differs in this sense from Werlen's approach in that Habermas partly decenters rationalization from the individual subject to the pragmatics of social interaction. "In speech acts, the agents refer to a non-subjective realm of semantic propositions and of pragmatic rules concerning the use of signs" (Reckwitz, 2002, p. 249). For geography, this language-pragmatics approach was detailed by Zierhofer (2002) and Schlottmann (2007). This approach can be seen as a critique of the pure mentalist program but does not reject it entirely, for there are still interacting agents endowed with minds (Reckwitz, 2002, p. 249). In that sense one can speak of a further development in action theory or of late-modernist views on rational action and intervention, where agency is partly decentered from the individual actor to external pragmatic procedures of interaction[2] and structural relationships within whose framework these interactions occur. Reckwitz (2002, p. 249) and Moebius (2008, p. 67) call these intersubjective performative approaches *intersubjectivism*. A third stream of social theory in their systematics is based on poststructuralist thinking.

Poststructuralist Theories of Practice and "Critical" Interventions

With the advent of poststructuralist thinking, there has been great reluctance to conceptualize human behavior as conscious rational actions, and in most poststructuralist literature the term *action* is generally avoided. Systematic content analysis would probably reveal a shift in the discursive use of the term even in those poststructuralist writings that do not explicitly address this change in conceptualization. Foucault's early work, for example, shows a preference for the term *practice* rather than the

---

[2] This understanding of rationality is not restricted to purposive economic rationality; it is refigured as a *praxial* (pragmatic) form of rationality and rational critique (Schrag, 1992, p. 57–59).

term *action*. In a seminal paper on this change, Schatzki et al. (2001) even coined the expression *practice turn*. Talking about practice instead of action indeed amounts to a novel picture of human agency and rationality (Reckwitz, 2008, p. 98) and opens up a certain way of seeing and analyzing social phenomena, which inevitably also imply a certain political and ethical dimension. For lack of a better word, Reckwitz, writing about theories of practice, describes this poststructuralist endeavor as *textualism*. In contrast to Benno Werlen, with his subjective mentalist approach of geographical action theory, and to Zierhofer (2002), who advocated the language-pragmatics approach in geography, poststructuralist thinkers do not tend to place structures inside the mind or in pragmatic procedures of interaction but rather "outside" it—in chains of signs, in symbols, discourse, or text. The subject is thereby decentered even further, that is, into discourses about sign systems. These discourses are seen not as mere representations of mental qualities behind them but as a sequence of external events from which symbolic structures are manifested. In a similar way, but with different arguments, Geertz's (1973) symbolic anthropology and Luhmann's (2002/2013) constructivist theory of social systems also focus on the structural aspects of society outside the subject. What all these textualist approaches have in common is their critical perspective on the essentialization of a universal and fixed principle of rationality and their celebration of the contextually and historically dependent logics of structuration and discursive meanings. But that is then their only critical thrust, and one could ask whether it spells the end of critical rational deliberations or what will be next? To a certain degree the view of poststructuralist thinkers is not that different from the late-modernist view of action theory or from language pragmatics. The poststructuralists proceed along the same line, only going a bit further. They, too, advocate a plurality of kinds of rationality, and list a wide range of possible frames for action but do not describe them as types of rationality but rather as systems of meanings and logics of structurations of power. Furthermore, poststructuralists emphasize that there is no single standard version of a given rationality, that each rationality contains multiple paradigms, each establishing its own set of principles, institutions, and lines of conflict that need to be taken into account.

In this context it is important to be aware that relationships between different players within this language game are described only in terms of power relations, which make it difficult to imagine some kind of metarationality regulating this plurality of differences. The relational sense in which Foucault and most of his poststructuralist followers use the concept of power makes clear that power is everywhere and that it is not an attribute of individuals. Yet that understanding subsumes almost all relational issues under the highly ambiguous concept of power, reducing it to a merely descriptive term and sapping most of its critical potential. Both late-modern and poststructuralist approaches thus lack of a metanarrative.

However, what started as a reconceptualization of human actions as practices—a change that began in early poststructuralist approaches in order to counterbalance the mentalist roots of action-theoretic approaches—ultimately overstated structuralist effects of discursive systems of meaning and obscured rationality's critical potential to solve struggles of difference. Full-fledged theories of practice as discussed by Schatzki et al. (2001) and Reckwitz (2002) are bids to find a real balance between body and mind, things and knowledge, discourse and language pragmatics, structure and process, and the agent and the individual.

Current theories of practice constitute an effort to reformulate the Aristotelian conception of phronesis, which implies that practice is seen as the basis and purpose of theoretical knowledge (Flyvbjerg, 2001). That conception also implies an escape from the dualism of the subjective and objective (Bernstein, 1971; Stern, 2003, p. 185). Schatzki is seen as one of the leading thinkers in this approach, and he bases his practice theory on a new societal social ontology in which the dualism of ontological individualism and holism is overcome (Schatzki, 2006). He calls his new ontology *site ontology*, defining *site* as a type of context in which human coexistence takes place and which also includes the social entities themselves. Social events can thus be understood only through an analysis of this site. The close relationship between this concept of site and the geographic concept of place (Tuan, 2001) is evident:

> Practice theory places practices at the center of the socio-human sciences instead of traditional structures, systems, events, actions. None of the practices can be reduced to a sum of its elements, which are of a complex character: they are mental and material, factual and relational, human and material, individual and supra-individual, etc. This conception also overcomes the dualism action/structure,…Each practice then operates in a typical regime, according to particular scenarios, it has its inherent normativity, etc. (Višňovský, 2009, p. 391)

Because these particular practices are interlinked and intertwined, there arises the issue of how one can rationally deal with this host of situations. With this question in mind, it is worthwhile to explore some of discourse theory's new developments that may be able to offer important answers.

Discursive Articulations and the Return of "Rational" Interventions

In a review of different theoretical approaches to analyzing the restructuring of space and place in urban regions in Hungary and England, Varró (2010) shows the genealogy of what she called a "Politics of Space Approach" (p. 59) based on application of discourse theory to the analysis of spatial change. Focusing chiefly on discourse theory, she refers to the work of Laclau and Mouffe (1985; see also Andersen, 2003). Laclau and Mouffe draw on Gramsci's (1992) concept of hegemony, which denoted the capacity of the ruling class to eliminate oppositional forces by incorporating them into a collective will based on a shared system of meanings (values, attitudes, beliefs, and morality). "Laclau and Mouffe acknowledge, and carry forward, Gramsci's proposition to see collective will as formed through the articulation of various identities, i.e., processes where identities are 'brought together' and mutually modify each other" (Varró, 2010, p. 46). But they disapprove of Gramsci's (1992) class reductionism and the assumed dominance of economic relations in the making of space. Social and spatial identities are thus fundamentally "unfixed" (p. 88) and are only partially fixed through hegemonic practices of articulation. Discourse becomes "an attempt to dominate the field of discursivity, to arrest the flow of differences, to construct a centre" (Laclau & Mouffe, 1985, p. 112). Discourse can therefore be seen as the totality of an act of performance, including linguistic and nonlinguistic elements (Laclau & Mouffe, 1987). This inclusiveness brings in an element of political, strategic, or deliberative interaction and thus opens room for the process of rational deliberation, though Laclau and Mouffe (1985, 1987) refrain from using the qualification *rational* for this inherently political process of radical democracy. Jessop (1990) and Howarth (2004, p. 271) have criticized Laclau and Mouffe (1985, 1987) for not illustrating how such a radical democracy can be characterized and institutionalized. Mouffe (2005) does not get much further than stating that the crucial issue for democratic politics is not the eradication of conflict via consensus but rather the legitimation of a multiplicity of opinions, attributions of meaning, and identities—in short, the legitimation of conflict or a consensus on difference. His observation seems to imply that the potential hostility and *antagonism* of political forces is turned into *agonism*, where opponents are seen not as enemies to be destroyed but as legitimate adversaries whose ideas can be countered (Mouffe, 2005). As Jacob Torfing (1999) observed,

> post-structuralist insights might help to sustain an *agonistic democracy* that is capable of transforming enemies into adversaries....the nomadization and hybridization of identity might contribute to the dissolution of antagonistic frontiers (Mouffe, 1994, pp. 110–111). Nomadization refers to the attempt to undercut the allegiance of a specific identity to a certain place or a certain property, and thereby to show that all identities are constructed in and through hegemonic power struggles. This will tend to denaturalize social and political identities and make them more negotiable. Hybridization refers to the attempt to make people realize that their identity is multiple in the sense of constituting an over-determined ensemble of identifications. (p. 255)

In Laclau and Mouffe's thinking this idea of an agonistic democracy is also extended to their own normative claim for radical democratization, as the very nature of the process of radical democratization is itself part of an agonistic debate and depends on a contingent, but at least largely shared, symbolic space (Mouffe, 2005, p. 121). This extension, however, still does not explain how such a political debate or deliberation takes place and what the radical democratic politics look like in action, not just as a starting point or outcome. At this juncture the interactionist outlook seems to be more useful. In general it is clear how the different traditions of social theory, ranging from mentalist and interactionist to textualist points of view, each address different complementary aspects of the political praxis put forward by Laclau and Mouffe (1985).

To develop this approach to praxis theory further, it is essential to rethink concepts of reason and rationality so as to create space for pluralistic forms of rationality and for transversal reflections (Welsch, 1999), even for rational interventions. This space seems to have been obscured thus far by the concepts used by Laclau and Mouffe (1985), which were inspired mainly by Marxist and poststructuralist thinking, and by some misinterpretation of the original concept of rationality in this context. Varró (2010) noted a similar misunderstanding with respect to the concept of discourse between critical realist thinkers and discourse theorists.

In the de-essentialized and dynamic, but nevertheless highly structuralist and imprisoning, interpretation of discourses and practices reminiscent of early Foucault (1972) and the practice turn (Schatzki et al., 2001; Višňovský, 2009), there seems little space for rationality or reason in the traditional modernist sense. In this framework, politics—and thus also spatial politics—seems to be defined primarily as authority and power and seems to deal only with the effects of power relations and not with the structure of the deliberations that take place in the framework of these relations.

As part of the misunderstanding of rationality, rationality is seen only as a foundational universal concept, for it was forwarded by enlightenment at a time when reason had actually been expelled from the view of the human being's abilities to deliberate about the world. However, Welsch (1997, 1999) prompted the question of how to differentiate and judge the various systems of meaning and logics, or the various forms of rationality involved, without some all-embracing perspective. Distinctions and judgments based on any one of these types or paradigms of rationality would necessarily misrepresent the others. Welsch suggested that there must be a different type of functioning that underlies human reflective capacity. It is this type of reflection that he reintroduced as reason, enhancing rationality—or better, enhancing rationali*ties*. In a seminal book written in the Anglo-Saxon tradition, Schrag (1992) took up and endorsed this very specific kind of reason. Both scholars called it *transversal reason* (Schrag, 1992, p. 148; Welsch, 1997, p. 315). Because transversal reason relates geographic realities and geographic differences to each other, it is crucial for the geographic perspective as well. As the reflexive ability to recognize and clarify the differences as well as the relationships between the various forms of rationality, transversal reason is actually a necessary condition for the theory of plurality and difference.

Related to the current situation of plurality and hybridity, this kind of transversal reason is not a new invention but rather a skill that is increasingly used consciously or unconsciously in everyday practice and that is becoming more and more an inner constituent of people's reasoning and life designs. The present age is not one seemingly bereft of rationality but rather one in which reason and rationality are reunited as a mental and reflective activity operating at every step of rational deliberation on discursive articulations.

> Reason and rationality are not two separate faculties, and in a sense are not faculties at all, but rather signify different layers and functional modes of our reflective activity. 'Reason' refers to the basic mechanism, 'rationality' to the various concrete, object-directed [or place related] versions of this activity. (Welsch, 1999, Pt. III, sec. 5, par. 2)

From this standpoint geography is primarily about developing these skills of reason and rational deliberation in a situation characterized by social and geographical diversity. The latest advances in social theory and in their operationalization in human geography—possible to outline only very tentatively in this chapter—yield a research program on human geography that combines several schools of thought with that discipline's political commitment to create a knowledge base and reflective skills for subsequent rational interventions.

Conclusion

To conclude this chapter, I offer a summary of the main steps in my argumentation. First, I have tried to show that rationality was separated from reason during the philosophical development of modernity and that it assumed a universal and fixed principle of rationality. In late-modern times this discernment led to recognition of different types of rationality, each with its own logics of deliberation and argumentation. Second, I have shown how these views are intricately involved in late-modern geographical theories of action and in language-pragmatic approaches in geography. At the same time, I have pointed out the mentalistic inheritances of this approach. Third, I have noted that proponents of poststructuralist theories, in a quest to emphasize the structural aspects of discourses, seem to have totally done away with rational deliberations. However, advocates of full-fledged theories of practice do not go that far and really seek a middle road. Fourth, I have tried to show that newer forms of discourse theory in the tradition of Laclau and Mouffe (1985) seem to offer this space for a real theory of practice and seem to reopen an opportunity for reflective political deliberations in the different fashions of discursive articulation. Finally, I argued that combining Laclau and Mouffe's discursive approach with new forms of rationalization that include transversal reason (Schrag, 1992; Welsch, 1997) might result in a framework for a rational approach to the politics of space as a core business for human geographers.

References

Althusser, L. (2005). Contradiction and overdetermination. In L. Althusser, *For Marx* (pp. 87–128; B. Brewster, Trans.). London: Verso. (Original work published 1965)

Andersen, N. Å. (2003). *Discursive analytical strategies: Understanding Foucault, Koselleck, Laclau, Luhmann*. Bristol: Policy Press.

Bernstein, R. J. (1971). *Praxis and action: Contemporary philosophies of human activity.* Philadelphia: University of Pennsylvania Press.

Broadbent, D. E. (1987). *Perception and communication.* Oxford: Oxford University Press.

de Saussure, F. (1972). *Course in general linguistics* (W. Baskin, Trans.). Chicago: Open Court. (Original work published 1916)

Emerson, M. (1984). Althusser on overdetermination and structural causation. *Philosophy Today, 28*, 203–214. doi:10.5840/philtoday198428319

Fauconnier, G. (1999). Methods and generalizations. In T. Janssen & G. Redeker (Eds.), *Cognitive linguistics: Foundations, scope, and methodology* (pp. 95–127). The Hague: Mouton De Gruyter.

Feyerabend, P. (1987). *Farewell to reason.* London: Verso.

Flyvbjerg, B. (2001). *Making social sciences matter: Why social inquiry fails and how it can succeed again* (S. Sampson, Trans.). Cambridge: Cambridge University Press.

Foucault, M. (1972). *The archaeology of knowledge and the discourse on language* (A. M. Sheridan Smith, Trans.). New York: Pantheon.

Geertz, C. (1973). *The interpretation of cultures.* New York: Basic Books.

Golledge, R. G., & Stimson, R. J. (1996). *Spatial behavior: A geographic perspective.* New York: Guilford Press.

Gramsci, A. (1992). *Prison notebooks* (J. A. Buttigieg, Ed. & Trans.). New York: Columbia University Press. (Italian original written 1929–1935, published after World War II)

Habermas, J. (1984). The *theory of communicative action: Vol. 1. Reason and the rationalization of society* (T. McCarthy, Trans.). Boston: Beacon Press.

Howarth, D. (2004). Hegemony, political subjectivity, and radical democracy. In S. Critchley & O. Marchart (Eds.), *Laclau: A critical reader* (pp. 256–276). London: Routledge.

Jessop, B. (1990). *State theory: Putting the capitalist state in its place.* Cambridge: Polity.

Lacan, J. (2002). *Écrits: The first complete edition in English* (B. Fink, Trans.). New York: Norton.

Laclau, E., & Mouffe, C. (1985). *Hegemony and socialist strategy: Towards a radical democratic politics.* London: Verso.

Laclau, E., & Mouffe, C. (1987). Post-Marxism without apologies. *New Left Review, 166,* 79–106.

Lévy-Strauss, C. (1969). *The elementary structures of kinship* (2nd ed., R. Needham, Ed.; H. Bell, Trans.). Boston: Beacon Press.

Luhmann, N. (2013). *Introduction to systems theory* (Dirk Baecker, Ed.; P. Gilgen, Trans.). Cambridge: Polity Press. (Original work published 2002)

Mead, G. H. (1934). *Mind, self, and society from the standpoint of a social behaviorist.* Chicago: University of Chicago Press.

Mittelstraß, J. (Ed.). (1995). *Enzyklopädie Philosophie und Wissenschaftstheorie* [Encyclopedia of philosophy and the theory of science], Vol. 3. Stuttgart: Metzler.

Moebius, S. (2008). Handlung und Praxis: Konturen einer poststrukturalistischen Praxistheorie [Action and practice: Contours of a poststructuralist theory of practice]. In S. Moebius & A. Reckwitz (Eds.), *Poststrukturalistische Sozialwissenschaften* (pp. 58–74). Frankfurt am Main: Suhrkamp.

Mouffe, C. (1994). For a politics of nomadic identity. In G. Robertson, M. Mash, L. Tickner, J. Bird, B. Curtis, & T. Putnam (Eds.), *Travellers' tales: Narratives of home and displacement* (pp. 105–113). London: Routledge.

Mouffe, C. (2005). *On the political.* London: Routledge.

Piaget, J. (1970). *Structuralism* (C. Maschler, Trans.). New York: Harper & Row.

Reckwitz, A. (2002). Toward a theory of social practices: A development in culturalist theorizing. *European Journal of Social Theory, 5,* 234–263. doi:10.1177/13684310222225432

Reckwitz, A. (2008). Grundelemente einer Theorie sozialer Praktiken [Principles of a theory of social practices]. In A. Reckwitz (Ed.), *Unscharfe Grenzen: Perspektiven der Kultursoziologie* (pp. 97–130). Bielefeld: Transcript.

Schatzki, T., Knorr-Cetina, K., & Savigny, E. von. (2001). *The practice turn in contemporary theory.* London: Routledge.

Schatzki, T. (2006). On organizations as they happen. *Organization Studies, 27,* 1863–1873. doi:10.1177/0170840606071942

Schlottmann, A. (2007). Wie aus Worten Orte werden: Gehalt und Grenzen sprechakttheoretischer Sozialgeographie [How words turn into places: Content and limitations of speech-act-theoretical social geography]. *Geographische Zeitschrift, 95*(1–2), 5–23.

Schrag, C. O. (1992). *The resources of rationality.* Bloomington: Indiana University Press.

Schütz, A. (1932). *Der sinnhafte Aufbau der sozialen Welt: Eine Einleitung in die verstehende Soziologie* [The meaningful construction of the social world: An introduction to interpretive sociology]. Vienna: Springer.

Skinner, B. F. (1938). *The behavior of organisms.* New York: Appleton-Century-Crofts.

Stern, D. G. (2003). The practical turn. In S. Turner & P. A. Roth (Eds.), *The Blackwell guide to the philosophy of the social sciences* (pp. 185–206). Cambridge: Blackwell.

Störig, H. J. (1989). *Kleine Weltgeschichte der Philosophie* [Brief world history of philosophy]. Frankfurt am Main: Fischer.

Torfing, J. (1999). *New theories of discourse: Laclau, Mouffe and Žižek.* Oxford: Blackwell.

Tuan, Y.-F. (2001). *Space and place: The perspective of experience* (New ed.). Minneapolis: University of Minnesota Press.

Varró, K. (2010). *After resurgent regions, resurgent cities? Contesting state geographies in Hungary and England.* Doctoral dissertation, Radboud University, Nijmegen, The Netherlands.

Višňovský, E. (2009). The "practice turn" in the contemporary socio-human sciences. *Human Affairs, 19,* 378–396. doi:10.2478/v10023-009-0051-7

Watson, J. B. (1913). Psychology as the behaviorist views it. *Psychological Review, 20,* 158–177. doi:http://dx.doi.org/10.1037/h0074428

Weber, M. (1946). Science as a vocation. In H. H. Gerth & C. Wright Mills (Eds. & Trans.), *From Max Weber: Essays in sociology* (pp. 129–156). Oxford: Oxford University Press. (Original work published 1919)

Welsch, W. (1997). *Unsere postmoderne Moderne* [Our postmodern modernity]. Berlin: Akademie Verlag.

Welsch, W. (1999). *Reason: Traditional and contemporary or Why should we still speak of reason after all?* Retrieved from http://sammelpunkt.philo.at:8080/199/1/reason.htm

Werlen, B. (1987). *Gesellschaft, Handlung und Raum: Grundlagen handlungstheoretischer Sozialgeographie* (3rd ed.) [Society, action and space: Basics of an action-oriented social geography]. Stuttgart: Franz Steiner.

Werlen, B. (1995). *Sozialgeographie alltäglicher Regionalisierungen. Bd. 1: Zur Ontologie von Gesellschaft und Raum* [Social geography of everyday regionalizations. Vol. 1: On the ontology of society and space]. Erdkundliches Wissen: Vol. 116. Stuttgart: Franz Steiner.

Werlen, B. (1997). *Sozialgeographie alltäglicher Regionalisierungen. Bd. 2: Globalisierung, Region und Regionalisierung* [Social geography of everyday regionalizations. Vol. 2: Globalization, region and regionalization]. Erdkundliches Wissen: Vol. 119. Stuttgart: Franz Steiner.

Zierhofer, W. (2002). Speech acts and space(s): Language pragmatics and the discursive constitution of the social. *Environment and Planning A, 34,* 1355–1372. doi:10.1068/a34198

Chapter 4
Thought-in-Action/Action-in-Thought

Gunnar Olsson

An entire volume devoted to the theme of knowledge and action! What a gift and what a wonderful opportunity to return once again to the Olsson Laboratory of Epistemology and Ontology, to the company of the twin sisters of rhetoric and dialectics, to the mutating banana flies that by now have been with me for more than half a century. And what a fascinating, non-ending, and interesting adventure those years have been, from beginning to end an attempt to understand how we understand, every day steeped in the hope of catching a glimpse of how we become whatever we become.[1]

But wait! What is it to be interesting, and where do I go to find it? As so often before, the answer lies in the word itself, for the English term *inter-esting* stems from the Latin *inter esse*, literally *in-between-being*. To be interesting is, consequently, to dwell in the razor-sharp limit between categories, to explore the trenches of the no-man's land of the excluded middle. Now, if I am courageous enough to enter that crater-strewn wasteland, and if I am curious enough to keep my eyes and ears open, then I will eventually encounter a troupe of traveling magicians who to great applause are performing their magic tricks of ontological transformations, an antiphony of voices, some divine some other human. As the angels keep chanting

---

[1] In what follows I will draw freely on the history of my own works, occasionally even quoting without quotation marks. In addition to the texts listed toward the end of this chapter, there is much to learn from *GO: On the Geographies of Gunnar Olsson*, a remarkable anthology edited by Christian Abrahamsson and Martin Gren (2012). It contains not only a representative selection of facsimile reproductions of some of my own articles from 1967 to 2010 but also some brilliant illuminations set off by a long list of first-rate pyrotechnists: Christian Abrahamsson, Trevor Barnes, Alessandra Bonazzi, Michael Dear, Marcus Doel, Franco Farinelli, Reginald Golledge, Martin Gren, Jette Hansen-Møller, David Jansson, Gunnael Jensson, Ole Michael Jensen, Tom Mels, Chris Philo, Michael Watts. And I who always fancied myself as a Wittgensteinian solipsist! Stand corrected, identity crisis in the making, Paulus Gunnarius on the road to Damascus.

G. Olsson (✉)
Department of Social and Economic Geography, University of Uppsala, Uppsala, Sweden
e-mail: Gunnar.Olsson@kultgeog.uu.se

© The Author(s) 2017
P. Meusburger et al. (eds.), *Knowledge and Action*, Knowledge and Space 9,
DOI 10.1007/978-3-319-44588-5_4

their wor(l)ds of "Let there be—and there was," the plebeians respond that "*Verum factum*—the true is the made," indeed that to them something is true because they have made it themselves. And in that perspective both Jahweh and Giambattista Vico come out as what they really are—expert jugglers of worlds which from one viewpoint are and from another are not, true creativity in both cases nothing but a speech act through which the powerful can claim that something is something else and be believed when they do so. Knowledge is by definition an exercise in translation.

"What, then, is truth?" asked Nietzsche in his essay *On Truth and Lie*, immediately replying that truth is

> a mobile army of metaphors, metonyms, and anthropomorphisms—in short, a sum of human relations, which have been enhanced, transposed, and embellished poetically and rhetorically, and which after long use seem firm, canonical, and obligatory to a people: truths are illusions about which one has forgotten that this is what they are; metaphors which are worn out and without sensuous power. (Penguin edition, 1976, pp. 46–47)

Whereas the self-declared LORD created the world by uttering it—light and darkness, mountains and rivers, you and me, everything flowing out of his mouth—the humpbacked Vico was a Neapolitan professor of rhetoric it is not only to American pragmatists that meaning lies in practice and the paradigm of informative truth in the finger-pointing index of $a = b$. The Kantian *as-if* at work. Yet we must never forget that although words may well change people, to things they do nothing.

What follows will be structured as a retracing of routes taken, essentially a collage of vistas glimpsed in the distance. Nothing new, merely a dose of coherence dashed into a cocktail which to the aficionados has been a source of intoxicating enlightenment, to the doubters a drug of impure ingredients and frightening side-effects. The recommended antidote is a product of the Nicomachean Pharmacy, delivery a mouse-click away:

> It is the mark of an educated man to look for precision in each class of things just so far as the nature of the subject admits; it is evidently equally foolish to accept probable reasoning from a mathematician and to demand from a rhetorician scientific proofs.
>
> Now each man judges well the things he knows, and of these he is a good judge. And so the man who has been educated in a subject is a good judge of that subject, and the man who has received an all-round education is a good judge in general. Hence a young man is not a proper hearer of lectures on political science; for he is inexperienced in the actions that occur in life, but its discussions start from these and are about these; and, further, since he tends to follow his passions, his study will be in vain and unprofitable, because the end is not knowledge but action. And it makes no difference whether he is young in years or youthful in character; the defect does not depend on time, but on his living, and pursuing each successive object, as passion directs.
>
> [These] remarks about the student, the sort of treatment to be expected, and the purpose of the inquiry, may be taken as our preface. (Aristotle, trans. 1941, Book 1, Chapter 3, 1094b and 1095a)

***

Beware though, for the fact that the young man is young does not mean that he is a *tabula rasa*. On the contrary, because like everyone else he is a product of his own upbringing: a palimpsest of impressions, layers upon layers of indicatives and imperatives; a ceaselessly over-painted canvas onto which the world is casting whatever it is casting; a self-referential story composed in a mixed code of genetics and socialization, its nonachievable purpose to make us obedient and predictable, to turn you and me into exchangeable, yet unique, pieces in the ongoing game of one against many, us versus them. It is these traces of the taken-for-granted that function as an invisible map of the invisible, a library of the unconscious, a nontouchable guide that leads me through the unknown, rewards and punishments distributed along the way. And as the explorer now moves on, (s)he gradually realizes not only that the first-person singular is the linguistic shifter par excellence but that this same *I* is the cartographers' fix-point of fix-points. Little wonder, therefore, that the world refuses to sit still, for when pushed to the interesting limit of in-between-being I discover that I am one with my own map, its coordinate net constructed as the asymmetric body of Leonardo's Vitruvian man, head up and feet down, eyes in front and arse in the back, left hand to the left, the right to the right. Thus, therefore, spake Zarathustra: "You say 'I' and you are proud of this word. But greater than this—although you will not believe in it—is your body which does not say 'I' but performs 'I'" (Nietzsche 1976, p. 146; my rendering, Olsson, 1991, p. 122). Body politics undressed, for most will agree that it is more honest to preach as you live than to live as you preach.

A circling tale of no beginning and no end, the taken-for-granted present everywhere, visible nowhere. Thus it would indeed be strange if not I too were a product of my own time and place, in this case the Swedish welfare state of the postwar decades. And even though by heritage, choice, and inclination I was never drawn to the Social Democratic Party per se, it is impossible not to be impressed by its vision of equality and social justice, including the idea that the bright new world should be erected on a foundation of causal theories and well-calibrated models. Such were the 1950s and early 1960s: the high noon of social engineering, the dream of a happy marriage between scientific knowledge and political action come true, the maximizing principles of utilitarian ethics institutionalized, Alva and Gunnar Myrdal the high priests in a congregation of politically anchored experts who took it as their mission to turn Sweden into a People's Home, a state of rationality in which the physical infrastructure (not least the architecture of the living quarters, especially the kitchens and the communal washing-rooms) was designed to ensure that the users would have no choice but to behave accordingly, at bottom a positivist belief that the road to mental hygiene and proper thinking goes via the body, an ideology well captured by Axel Hägerström's (1911) rejection of metaphysics and his advocacy of value nihilism—his well-known motto *praetera censeo metaphysicam esse delendam*, a paraphrase of Cato's "Carthage must be destroyed." But not everyone was born with genes deemed good enough for the future, an argument which was readily extended to the widespread practice of forced sterilization. *Zeitgeist* is the term, in the same breath an excuse and an accusation, for "when I obey a rule, I do not choose. I obey the rule *blindly*" (Wittgenstein, 1953, p. 219).

To the budding geographer the time-bound message could not be misunderstood: Capture the power of social relations in a net of scientific laws and then, like your friends in physics, chemistry, and medicine, you too will have acquired the means not merely for understanding the world but for changing it as well. If the natural scientists know how to construct rockets that take them to the moon, if they know how to generate energy by enriching uranium, if they know how to save lives by transplanting hearts, then your duty as a social scientist is to discover similar techniques for eradicating poverty! Before you accept that challenge, though, be sure to ask yourself first why no one now reads Plato and Aristotle for what they had to say about physics or medicine, then why so many continue to return to the plays of Sophocles and Shakespeare for their insights into the human condition of hopes and fears, love and hate. How does the circumstance that we have accumulated knowledge in some areas and not in others relate to Aristotle's remark that we should look for precision in each class of things just as far as the nature of the subject admits and that it would be equally foolish to accept probable reasoning from a mathematician as to demand scientific proofs from a rhetorician?

No small order given to a young man inexperienced in the actions that occur in life and therefore prone to pursue each object as passion directs. And yet, how could I possibly have ignored the challenge? GO ON, GO ON.

*

The list of required readings included the classics of location theory, cognitive science, decision theory, systems analysis, matrix algebra, probability theory, spatial statistics, and a sprinkle of historical geography, all of it somehow yoked together in Walter Isard's conception of Regional Science and its extension into Peace Science, the latter firmly anchored in the Quaker-thin interface of scientific knowledge and political action, John Dewey's pragmatism and the collections of the Barnes Foundation never far away. A formative experience it was, the handsome fellowship that in 1963–1964 took me to North Armorica and the intellectual hubs of the Wharton School, Berkeley, and Northwestern.

Great. Yet, in hindsight, the seeds might well have been planted 10 years earlier by the odd gymnasium teacher who did whatever he could to introduce his rowdy pupils to the concentric rings of von Thünen's isolated state and the cost curves of Alfred Weber's isodapanes. Perhaps I was the only one to pay attention, but the truth is that I can still feel in my body the boy's excitement when he literally *saw* why there were so many gauchos on the Pampas and so many steel mills along the Ruhr. The rhetorical power of geometric construction on the high wire, von Thünen's agricultural landscape depicted as an archer's target with the bull's eye as the central city on a homogeneous plain (more correctly the Junker's own estate), Weber's factory finding its place of least cost, the Archimedean point that is located at the center of a Euclidean triangle whose corners are the concepts of transportation, labor, and agglomeration. Deep roots it has, the subsequent definition of geography as a geometry with names, essentially an exercise in the drawing and baptizing of points, lines, and planes. Picture and story merged into one.

So there it is, the glue of socialization decomposed: Vico's *verum factum*—the true and the made are convertible—long before I knew the name; Wassily Kandinsky's abstract expressionism as a social scientific practice years ahead of my first visit to Dessau; Euclid's *Quod Erat Demonstrandum* overruled by his *Quod Erat Faciendum*—that which was to be demonstrated overruled by that which was to be shown—the beliefs of the former lodged in the socialized mind, the convictions of the latter in the individual body. These fix-points revealed, I can now better understand why once upon a time every Swedish school room was equipped with a blackboard, a ruler, a compass, and a square, these four implements serving as the teacher's pedagogical tools par excellence, to every generation after Plato the very key to understanding how we understand. In that context of knowledge creation, it should also be added that Immanuel Kant—*the* philosopher of limits—often referred to his own work as a form of architecture. In my mind the three Critiques may profitably be read as a report from the masterbuilder's experiments with different construction materials, one cement for the palace of pure reason, another for the house of practice, a third for the court of judgment.

And this interplay of reasoning modes is exactly why August Lösch's *Die räumliche Ordnung der Wirtschaft* (1943/1954) is such a groundbreaking book and why he himself was such an exceptionally interesting person, the conflict between Jahweh and Vico embodied. As the 33-year-old put it in the fateful autumn of 1939:

> The natural equilibrium of economics differs from the equilibrium of nature exactly as the moral differs from the mechanical. Nature works according to laws, but man acts according to his *idea* of laws. In other words, nature *must*, man *may*, act correctly. In order to do so he must have some conception of how he shall act. As to economic equilibrium this means that *in order to guide his activities he needs insight into the conditions of this equilibrium*. This is especially true for the lawmaker, since all others are bound by his precepts even though unable to perceive their rationality. (p. 93, emphasis in the original)

With that link between knowledge and action firmly established, Lösch then proceeded to the formulation of a general theory of location, a derivation based on the principle of profit maximization rather than cost minimization, the lattice of nested hexagons its most spectacular outcome. As he put it in the book's preface, the mathematical calculations are there "because it is reprehensible not to trust reason and rest content with vague words and hazy statements" (p. xv). Heaving a sigh of relief that the number of equations coincided with the number of unknowns, he nevertheless exclaimed: "If only we had a method that combined the generality of equations with the clarity of geometrical figures!" (p. 100)

The rhetorical point is well taken: If I want to be believed, it is not enough to tell a trustworthy story, I must also know how to paint the picture that goes with it. Rephrased, the credibility of a given argument is immensely increased if it is expressed not only in one but in both of the major modes of communication. Therefore,

> theory may be compared with reality for various ends, according to the sort of theory held. If it is to *explain* what actually is, the examination attempts to discover whether it started with a correct idea of its subject and arrived at an explanation that not only seemed possible but also corresponded with reality. On the other hand, if theory is to *construct* what is

rational, its assumptions may still be tested by facts, but not its results. Its author can discover from an examination of the facts whether he has built on adequately broad experience, whether he has taken all objective or subjective essentials into consideration. His procedure resembles the preliminary work of an architect, who cannot lightly neglect the characteristics of a site, the laws of nature, and the wishes of the owner. But a comparison with existing structures will not show whether his blueprints are accurate; in our case, that is, whether the theoretical structure has been properly erected. For the existing structure may be as faulty as the projected one. No! *Comparison now has to be drawn no longer to test the theory, but to test reality!* (Lösch, 1943/1954, pp. 363–364, emphasis added)

German idealism lodged in a thinker who has been described as

a combination of rare strength of character, intellect, and warmth of personality, [a man] who died shortly after the end of the hostilities on May 30, 1945, at least partially as the result of that very strength of character which forbade him to make any compromises with the National Socialist regime. (Hoover in Lösch, 1943/1954, p. vii)

His hands tied, it was the mind that carried him back to the place where his unconscious had been formed. In Lösch's own words:

It was not easy for me largely to forego the attractive task of applying what has thus been tested to our more complicated German conditions and analyzing the pertinent facts. But apart from all foreign studies [mainly based on U.S. data] and the wide applicability of the resulting ideas, my youthful experiences in a little Swabian town constitute the real background of this book. [To] have my original experiences there confirm my final theories gives me a real sense of security, and so I dedicate this book to the land of my birth, the land that I love. (Lösch, 1943/1954, pp. xv–xvi)

It is difficult not to cry, especially if one compares the fate of Lösch's life and work (1906–1945) with that of Walter Christaller (1898–1969), the first edition of Lösch's *Die räumliche Ordnung der Wirtschaft* appearing in 1940, the second edition in 1943, Christaller's *Die zentralen Orte in Süddeutschland* in 1933. In the present context of thought-in-action, it is simply impossible to ignore the fact that whereas Lösch paid a high price for his refusal to swear a personal oath of allegiance to the Führer, Christaller's political views (hence by extension his built-in attitudes to intentional action) were fluttering in the wind, like the LORD himself consistently inconsistent. The record is there for anyone to inspect. First, the trenches of World War I turned Christaller into a card-carrying Social Democrat. Second, in the summer of 1934, when that party had been banned, he fled on his bicycle to the liberty of France, from where he was promptly lured back to a job offered him by Konrad Meyer, an SS professor of agronomy, who already at that stage was working directly under Heinrich Himmler. Third, in the summer of 1940 Christaller joined the National Socialist Party (membership number 8 375 670). Fourth, immediately after the war that same(?) person enrolled as a member of the West German Communist Party and in 1953 was accused of collaborating with his comrades in the DDR. Fifth, after 14 years as a Communist he resurrected himself as a Social Democrat, just in time for his plenary lecture at the historic meeting of the International Geographical Union Symposium in Urban Geography in Lund, Sweden, in August 1960. To only partial avail, however, for even though the conversion might have paved the way to an honorary doctorate at Lund, it failed to get him the visa that would have taken him to the United States and the lecture tour of his life. Broken was the icon when the young man met him about 5 years before he passed away, the sadness of his eyes forever etched into my memory.

Water in water, a palimpsest hard to decipher, a mille-feuille bound to cause indigestion. But who am I to judge? What does a Swede born in 1935 know of blaring sirens, exploding bombs, ruins, terror, death camps, starving children without shoes? As so often before, I am once again drawn into Wittgenstein's struggle with solipsism:

> I am my world. There is no such thing as the subject that thinks or entertains ideas. If I wrote a book called *The World as I found* it, I should have to include a report on my body, and should have to say which parts were subordinate to my will, and which were not, etc.,…. The subject does not belong to the world: rather it is a limit of the world…. There is no *a priori* order of things. (Wittgenstein, 1921/1961, 5.63–5.632, 5.634)

✳✳✳

Drawing the limits of the world is exactly what the joint history of human geography and regional planning is about. And in that essentially political enterprise references to central place theory have often been used to legitimate some drastic intrusions into the daily lives of entire populations. All for their own good, of course.

For understanding these connections between text and context, it is important to know that Christaller's and Lösch's shared goal was to detail how a given area is colonized or settled, especially how a set of hierarchically nested and hexagonally distributed centers are (or, more accurately, *should* be) tied together into a functional whole. In that sense they were more immediately concerned with the geometry of the stage than with the actors' movements across it, more focused on scenography than on dialogue. The outcome was in both cases a script of power. And for that reason the critic should never forget that

> what distinguishes the worst architect from the best of bees is that the architect raises his structure in the imagination before he erects it in reality. At the end of every labor-process, we get a result that already existed in the imagination of the laborer at its commencement. He not only effects a change of form in the material on which he works, but he also realizes a purpose of his own that gives the law to his modus operandi, and to which he must subordinate his will. (Marx, 1867/1967, vol. I, p. 178)

An outstanding example comes from the Dutch polders, lands reclaimed from the sea and therefore at constant risk of being flooded. That likelihood must, of course, be carefully controlled and the condition of the dikes and pumps minutely monitored, a duty which since the eleventh century has been entrusted to an especially elected local authority appropriately called the *Hoogheemraadschap*. By law a modus operandi to which everyone must subordinate their will, the oldest democratic institution in the country.

These newly reclaimed lands are obviously both flat and nonpopulated, hence as close to the theoreticians' conception of a homogeneous plain as any social engineer could ever dream of. And exactly as the Marx quotation suggests, the planners actually *did* raise the structure of the new villages, towns, and cities in their imagination before they erected them in reality, a wonderful illustration of how the abstractness of Platonic forms is turned into the concreteness of visible objects. Seemingly a textbook application of practical reason, the intentionality of the plan preserved in the materiality of physical structures. Only seemingly, though, for in the case of the early Zuiderzee polders the impact of technological change was seriously underestimated. To make a long and complicated story short and simple, the constructed places proved to be too many, too small, and too closely packed, the location of the brick-built stores, schools, police stations, and hospitals obsolete before the mortar had dried. In addition, and because roads and houses are costly both to build and to tear down, the spatial nonoptimality tends to stick. *The* Achilles-heal of every optimizing location theory.

Lösch's remarks about the comparison between rational theory and faulty reality come readily to mind, Hegel's epistemology of self-conscious reevaluation as well. The reason is that the planning of the later polders, especially the Oostelijk and the Zuidelijks Flevolands, has become increasingly sophisticated. But that development rather heightens than lessens my surprise that Christaller's static, deterministic, and inelegant theory was used at all. The only excuse I can think of is that we are all children of our own time and place, the Dutchmen of 1930 as much as I at eighty. And what a happy circumstance that is. For what saved the subjects of the great polder project was not the machinations of social engineering but the circumstance that Holland is an open society, its citizens free to design their honeycombs as their fancy fancies.

In that respect the Third Reich was obviously different. But what richer pasture could the likes of Konrad Meyer and Walter Christaller have wished for than the newly conquered *Lebensraum* (living space) of Eastern Europe, a vast area showered down on them as a gift from the Führer's heaven. Like the Dutch polders, also the territory that the *Reichskommissariat für die Festigung deutschen Volkstums* (Reich Commission for German Resettlement and Population Policy) was commissioned to settle had the characteristics of a homogeneous plain, the techniques of ethnic cleansing as merciless in Poland, Lithuania, Belarus, and Ukraine as anywhere else. The clearing of sufficient living space in the East was de facto *the* cornerstone of Nazi foreign policy, the very precondition for the Germanization that was meant to follow, the *Entfernung* (removal) of foreign elements setting the stage as effectively as the digging of the dikes in Holland. As an amateur artist, Hitler surely knew that without a properly prepared canvas there will never be any painting. And as the Leader of a populist movement he was well aware that no political battle is more decisive than that about the boundary between identity and difference, one and many, us and them, me and you. Such was consequently also the purpose of the charts, tables, and maps that came out of Meyer's office: the utopia of a totalitarian *Herrschaft* (rule) projected into optimally located settlements, everything and everyone in its proper place. Seventy-five years later the whole affair strikes me as a Dadaesque blend of Kandinsky's Bauhaus, Malevich's suprematism, Picasso's cubism, Ernst's surrealism. The irony of the *entartete Kunst* (degenerate art) in its proper perspective.

The outline of this new world was drawn in *Generalplan Ost* (General Plan for the East), a strictly confidential document prepared in the period 1939–1942, deliberately destroyed in May 1945 lest it be used as incriminating evidence, by later historians eventually pieced together again. It consisted of two parts, the Small Plan which covered actions to be taken during the *Blitzkrieg*, and the *Big Plan* which outlined what was to follow in the 30-year period thereafter. The text of the latter is simply too much for sensible analysis (a total of 31 million undesirables to be moved to West Siberia, the remaining to be treated as slaves), but the figures of the former are even more staggering. (Between October 12 and December 31, 1939, about 1,700,000 Jews and Poles were actually deported to places with names now well known, another five million classified as unsuitable for assimilation.) The machinelike horrors of the *Entfernung* set the stage not merely for what was *meant* to come but for what actually *did* come.

It is now well established that Walter Christaller was directly involved in the German settling of Warthegau, the Polish territory occupied by the German forces in September 1939—a story forcefully told by Barnes (2015) and much elaborated in the works of Bauman (1989), Kamenetzky (1961), Madajcyk (1994), Rössler (1989), and many others. A moment of truth for any theoretician eager to see his abstract imaginations metamorphosed into concrete reality. Yet nothing compared to what was to come with Christaller's appointment to the staff of Konrad Meyer, the mentor who under Himmler's personal supervision was charged with the task of finalizing the plans for the still unconquered *Lebensraum*. Included in the directives was the megalomaniac idea of a fortified string of SS garrisons and "pearl settlements" that would run all the way from Arkhangelsk on the Northern Dvina River to Astrakan in the Volga delta, the *Übermenschen* (superior humans) in the west securely separated from the *Untermenschen* (subhumans) in the east. The surviving records occasionally refer to Christaller's theory, but there is no explicit mention of any detailed plans; who knows, perhaps they were not Aryan enough. Crucial indeed, for every judgment of guilt and punishment should be based on the here-and-now of particular circumstances, not on the there-and-then of general principals. On the surface a matter of alternative descriptions, deeper down an entangled skein of modal logics.

It is the struggle with the latter that now brings me to the intricacies of the word *can*, like all modal verbs of vital importance to any critique of power, by extension, to any worthwhile understanding of the relations between knowledge and action (Ofstad, 1961, pp. 328–337; see also Olsson, 1980, pp. 118b–115b). The reason is that the "all-in can" (forty-seven of them) is essentially a combination of two "sub-cans," one denoting ability, the other opportunity. For instance, there is no doubt that Walter Christaller already in 1933 knew how to deduce an optimal settlement pattern from a set of (un)realistic assumptions, but it was only after Hitler's *Drang nach Osten* (drive toward the east) that he got a chance to apply his knowledge and in that manner show the world who he really was. Hand in glove, a temptation hard to resist, a mixture of pleasures and nightmares, a situation he shared with many others, Martin Heidegger most prominent among them. The pivotal question is, of course, whether, given the circumstances, he could have acted otherwise. If not, he should not be held responsible, regardless of his political (in)stability. Purgatory has many chambers, and in some congregations you get to Paradise because of your beliefs, in others because of your deeds. "In this connection," wrote Albert Speer (1969/1970) in a passage of direct relevance for the assessment of spatial planning,

> I must mention [Hitler's] plan for founding German cities in the occupied areas of the Soviet Union. On November 24, 1941, in the very midst of the winter catastrophe, Gauleiter Meyer [Alfred, not Konrad], deputy of Alfred Rosenberg, the Reich Minister for the occupied eastern territories, asked me to take over the section on 'new cities' and plan and build the settlements for the German garrisons and civil administrations. I finally refused this offer at the end of 1942 on the grounds that a central authority for the city planning would inevitably lead to a uniform pattern. I insisted instead that the great German cities each stand as sponsor for the construction of the new ones. (p. 182)

For Oberführer Konrad Meyer-Hertling the situation was less clear. Like Speer, he too was convicted at Nuremberg, but unlike the genius of organizational dynamics, his crimes were deemed so small that immediately after the trial he was set free for time served, a whitewash paper written by Walter Christaller being part of the evidence. In the judges' opinion Meyer's contribution to *Generalplan Ost* was "a strictly independent scientific study" (Rössler, 1989, p. 427)—in Marx's dialectics something imagined that never made it into reality; in my own terminology, an ontological transformation aborted.

No serious wrong-doing proven and in 1956 the University of Hanover appointed Meyer Professor Ordinarius (full professor) of Land Planning, a post he occupied until his retirement. The pragmatism of expert knowledge and political action undressed, H. C. Andersen's emperor as he must have appeared to the lackeys, who continued to carry the fabulous train that did not exist. The boys in the gutter saw it differently. For even though they had never attended Meyer's and Christaller's alma maters, they still knew that ethics is the only ordered discourse that has thought-and-action as its defining subject matter. In addition, they were soon to learn the Foucauldian lesson that it is in the prison and madhouse that we discover what is normal, indeed what it means to be human. As Arendt (1977) put it, there are strong streaks of banality in evil; the institutions of modernity a precondition for the Holocaust. It is telling that Heidegger's postwar critique of technology paid much attention to the verb *can* and its tendency to turn into a *may*, the *may* into an *ought*, the *ought* into a *shall*, the *shall* into a *must*.

***

Mind-boggling are the German vignettes, the offered interpretations part and parcel of the same epistemology of extremity that for 50 years has served me so well. Come to think of it, it may well be that same attitude that has made me less responsive to the political calls for changing the world and more focused on the hidden in my own taken-for-granted, the latter the only critique that to my solipsist mind is honest enough. That remark is obviously not an excuse for the shallowness of what I have just written about Hitler, Himmler, Meyer, and Christaller, merely a way of saying that it is by detecting the beam in my neighbor's eye that I become aware of the mote in my own. And what a painful experience that is, learning to roll with the punches, a technique which Marlene Dietrich practiced to perfection:

It's not cause I wouldn't
It's not cause I shouldn't
And you know it's not cause I couldn't
It's simply because I'm the laziest gal in town.

In that mood I shall now proceed to the spatial set-up of the Swedish welfare state. As Shakespeare (1602/n.d.) put it in *The Merry Wives of Windsor*, "the world's mine oyster, Which I with sword will open" (Act II, Scene II, 2–3).

*

The story goes a long way back, not least to Gustav Eriksson Vasa, the guerilla leader who in 1523 threw the Danes out, united the Swedes into one country, and let himself be elected king to crown it off. Once that goal had been achieved, he faced the problem of paying back the money he had borrowed to finance his campaign, a problem he solved by confiscating the riches of the Church, converting to the Lutheran faith, and translating the Bible in the process. An expert in Machiavellian rhetoric and the logistics of tax collection, he penetrated so deeply into the minds of his subjects that a Swede of the twentieth century readily recognizes the similarities. *Allt förändras, allt förblir ändå det samma*, or, as the French have it, *Plus ça change, plus ça reste la même chose*, alternatively, the more things change, the more they stay the same. In the farewell speech Gustav gave to Parliament on June 16, 1560:

I know that in the minds of many I have been a harsh king. But the times shall come when the children of Sweden will want to tear me up from the ground, were that within their might. I also know that the Swedes are quick to agree and late to question. I predict that many pretenders and false prophets will be forthcoming. Therefore I beg and advise you: Stick firmly to God's words. Listen carefully to your superiors and stand united together. My days will soon be gone. For telling me that I need neither stars nor any other sorcery. I feel in my body the signs that I will soon be taken away. Follow me then with your sincere prayers and, when I have closed my eyes, let my body rest in peace. (Retrieved November 10, 2015, from http://sv.wikipedia.org/wiki/Vasakoret, my translation)

Quick to agree and late to question, well organized by their superiors.

Following in his grandfather's footsteps was Gustavus Adolphus, in 1632 killed in the mist-enveloped battle at Lützen, his military forays clearly proving that Sweden from then on was a power to reckon with. The road to success was forged by his genial chancellor, Axel Oxenstierna, the man who invented the administrative set-up that made it all possible, its basic outline still with us.

It is this historical stickiness that now prompts me back to the 1950s and some fundamental problems which Christaller's theory was then called upon to settle. To put it very simply, the old parishes and communes—often with boundaries unchanged since Oxenstierna's time—was a harness too small for the expanding welfare state. Something had to be done, and on January 1, 1952, the number of rural communes was cut from 2281 to 816. Not enough, however, and 10 years later a new and wider reform was set in motion, the number of communes (including the towns and cities) presently down to 290.

These administrative reforms have had a revolutionary impact on the daily life of every Swede, the redrawing of the political boundaries directly related to the where, when, and how you happen to be born; to the when, where, and how you will eventually die; to every whatever that may or may not lie in-between. The underlying ideology is, of course, that just as all citizens should have equal rights regardless of whether they are rich or poor, so the same should hold regardless of where they happen to live. No small deal but a tacit admission that the whereness of spatial form bears directly on the whatness of social relations. Whether form follows function or function follows form is in that perspective a moot point, the geographer's inference problem when it matters.

The blueprint of this brave new world was drawn by a politically appointed committee supported by a set of experts, the result submitted to the Minister of the Interior as number 1961:9 of *Statens Offentliga Utredningar*—The State's Official Investigations. The pivotal parts of this document were written by Sven Godlund and Torsten Hägerstrand, two up-to-date geographers who explicitly anchored their reasoning in Christaller's theory. Their basic argument was that whereas the drastic changes in transportation technology had led to novel forms of shopping behavior and thereby to the spontaneous establishment of larger market areas, the administrative units were legally sanctioned leftovers from a previous era—the commercial system was efficient, open, and modern; the legal was outdated, closed, and obsolete. The committee therefore recommended that the boundaries of the latter should be redrawn to coincide with the hinterlands of the former. And in that twist from the economist's *is* to the politician's *ought*, the play was changed in the middle of the act, the utopian dreams of justice disappearing in the wings, fatally stabbed by the reality it was supposed to replace. Exit man with his precious visions, hopes, and fears. Enter the Thiessen polygons with their crude distance minimizations and cost-benefit ratios. Ideology and methodology in profound and irresolvable conflict.

The root of the problem lies in the social gravity model, a formulation which in the heydays of the 1960s lay at the frontier of quantitative geography, the page-turner of my own conception of thought-in-action and action-in-thought. Although originally conceived as an analogue to Newton's law of gravitation—the interaction between two objects directly proportional to the size of their masses and inversely proportional to the square of the distance between them—its social science application a special case of Vilfredo Pareto's optimality principle, the latter a sociological generalization with deep roots in the mathematics of the negative exponential (see, e.g., Arrow, 1951; Sen, 1993). The irony is that even though Pareto, Hägerstrand, and Godlund knew perfectly well that they were describing the world as it was, Italian fascists and Swedish democrats read their texts as recipes for how a better world could be constructed. As Marx put it, the philosophers have hitherto only interpreted the world, the point is to change it. This (mis)reading was in no way inevitable, for Pareto argued very explicitly that observed behavior belongs to the same category of "logical action" as economic profit maximization, Machiavellian politics, and scientific work. But to sanctify observed behavior as logical action is nothing but a rhetorical technique for legitimating the status quo. The history of the social gravity model provides an excellent example, for although in the beginning it was treated as a formulation of great explanatory power, later generations have come to see it as an expression of autocorrelation. As Tobler's (1970) first law of geography has it, "everything is related to everything else, but near things are more related than distant things" (p. 236). A planning tool tailor-made for unintended side effects.

In that perspective Pareto's conception of logic appears just as narrow as the dogma of any other religion. Rather than perpetuating the belief that the reasoning rules represent objective and unassailable a priori principles, we must therefore constantly remind ourselves that they are neither ethically nor aesthetically neutral. If we are prepared for that volte-face, then we too, like Vico, Nietzsche, and Heidegger before us, will discover how it is grammar that tells us what kind of object anything is, not the other way around. As a consequence, we will then understand that the role of all languages, deductive logic included, is not to furnish labels for the objects we are talking *about* but to shape the categories we are thinking and talking *in*. And thus it is by no coincidence that the tautological **a = a** is the linchpin of conventional logic just as the evasive **I am who I am** is the self-proclaimed name of God the Father. And so it is that every concept is a tool of human making, intelligible only in the context of our personal and social lives.

If we dare not admit that our analytical languages have these characteristics, then we run the risk of imposing on reality a strictness that it neither has nor ought to have. And if in our many-facetted roles as experts, citizens, and social engineers we choose to ignore this hallmark of critical theory, then we will inevitably produce a society that both mirrors the techniques by which we measure it and echoes the languages in which we talk about it. By extension a dystopia of human puppets with no dreams to dream and nothing to be sorry for. And thus it is that Pareto's *ought* cohabits with the *is* of the elite, exactly as it was propagated in the ethical theory of Hägerström (1911; see also Marc-Wogau, 1968) and the legal principles of Lundstedt (1932–1936) and Olivecrona (1942), legitimating shapers of Swedish ideology. The outcome is that the law of large numbers rules supreme, the emerging relations between individual and collective a classic case of double bind. And in that sense the negative exponential serves the purposes of populists and elitists alike. The utilitarians should be more cautious, for it is the very kernel of their ethics that every act should be judged in terms of its consequences, not in terms of the intentions behind it.

*

The statistics are equivocal, especially when it comes to education and health care, by all accounts key ingredients of any welfare system. Thus, there is general agreement that the Swedish school system is in deep crisis, the results no longer at the top of the evaluations generated by the OECD's Programme for International Student Assessment (PISA) but regularly below average and steadily sliding; among the 40 countries listed in the 2013 evaluation, Sweden is ranked as number 36 in reading and 38 in mathematics. Little wonder that in a press release (May 4, 2015) the OECD concluded that

Sweden has failed to improve its school system despite a series of reforms in recent years. A more ambitious, national reform strategy is now urgently needed to improve quality and equity in education....No other country taking part in PISA has a steeper decline. (Retrieved November 10, 2015, from par. 1–2, http://www.oecd.org/Sweden/Sweden-should-urgently-reform-its-school-system-to-improve-quality-and-equity.htm)

Much to mourn but most alarming are the figures that Swedish eighth-graders' command of mathematics is now at the same level as that of seventh graders' a decade earlier and that one quarter of the boys fail to comprehend what they are reading. The social and economic inequalities are following suit, a new class of unemployables growing up, a development most pronounced in the ethnically seg-regated areas of Malmö and Stockholm. Counterfinality is the term for the mis-match between intentionality and consequence, the infected sore of utilitarian ethics and the source of an intense debate with immediate ties to the administrative reforms of the 1960s. The turning point came in 1991 when the political *cum* administrative responsibility for the schools was shifted from the state to the local municipalities, a reorganization that in one stroke—and very deliberately—lowered the status of the teachers. The result is that more than half of them are officially unqualified for their jobs! An ocean liner to turn around, the *Titanic* heading for the iceberg.

In the meantime the health-care system is struggling with an attitudinal problem of its own. To be precise, the 2011 Commonwealth Fund International Health Policy Survey of eleven comparable countries placed Sweden at the bottom of the list in terms of health-care availability. Similar figures hold for the sense of dignity, respect, and empathy that the patients thought they had the right to expect but did not receive, one third of the doctors demonstrating that they knew little or nothing about their clients' medical history. Since with growing age we tend to forget first what we learned last, many immigrants from the 1950s, now in nursing homes, have lost their Swedish and are therefore, unbeknownst to themselves, reverting back to their mother tongues, idioms typically unknown to their helpers. Sadder than sad, the art of dying a question of *chairos* rather than *chronos*, an issue of the right moment rather than the orderlies' work schedule. But just as eugenics is not eutha-nasia, so euthanasia is not suicide.

In the meantime all surveys agree that although everyone considers the level of expert medicine to be outstanding, the proportion of patients who doubt that they are receiving the best treatment available is higher in Sweden than in any of the comparable countries, the sense of shared trust no longer what it used to be. To put it bluntly, Swedish health care sees a diagnosis, not a human being. Political dyna-mite, not least because the degree of (dis)satisfaction varies between socioeconomic groups—the higher the education, the higher the trust, the professors of geography and anesthesia the best of friends. Human, all too human. Gustav Vasa echoes back: Listen carefully to your masters, be quick to agree and late to question. But there is an echo of *The Phenomenology of Mind* as well, for

just as lordship shows its essential nature to be the reverse of what it wants to be, so too, bondage will, when completed, pass into the opposite of what it immediately is: being a consciousness repressed within itself, it will enter itself, and change around into real and true independence. (Hegel, 1807/1967, p. 237)

Hegel's remarks notwithstanding, the empirical truth remains: The values of the strong today are metamorphosed into the facts for the weak of tomorrow. The point is not that the Swedish welfare state *is* a tragedy but that it is *structured* like a tragedy: everything beautifully right in the beginning, everything horribly wrong at the end, no one to blame in between. To understand human action is therefore not to blame but to see that actors are so entrenched in their roles that they take the shadow play for reality and reality for the play. It is indeed an integral part of all internal relations (logic and money being paradigmatic examples) that we obey their commands without hearing them and without knowing where they come from. And for that reason I am eternally grateful that I was born in Per Albin Hansson's Sweden and not in Adolf Hitler's Germany or Joseph Stalin's Soviet Union. But this fortunate circumstance must not keep me from realizing that everything comes with a price, the politics of the welfare state included. For instance: How do I insult a power which is so powerful that it is faceless? How do I learn about difference when difference is defined away? How do I topple a regime that has no statues erected in its honor? How do I find my way in a jungle of paragraphs? How do I live in a culture so proud of its penis that it is unaware of its Phallus? Why is it so hard to detect the relations between the *Nom-du-Père* and the *Non-du-Père*?

Servitude and (in)equality exposed, King Oedipus blood-soaked before us.

***

On my reading, Sophocles' *Oedipus Tyrannus* (ca. 440 BC) is a paradigmatic example of Bertrand Russell's theory of proper names and definite descriptions, his formula for how a given statement can at the same time be both true and informative. And in this sense the tragedian and the atheist are alike that both were driven to truth by their ignorance of truth, their engagements a relentless pursuit of knowledge no matter where it would lead them. From beginning to end a struggle with tautology, the latter by definition always true but never informative.

In the play's prologue, Oedipus, the king with the swollen foot, he who once had saved the city from the sphinx, is asked to become what he had once been before. In the petitioner's words:

> You are not one of the immortal gods, we know;
> Yet we have come to you to make our prayer
> As to the man surest in mortal ways.
> [Once], years ago, with happy augury,
> You brought us fortune; be the same again!
> (Sophocles, trans. 1949, pp. 4–5)

On this occasion the charge is to save the city from the plague. But whereas solving the riddle of the Sphinx had led him to the dignity of man, solving the problem of the plague will take him to himself. In his search he is pushed to truth by his blindness to truth, and, when he finally sees it, he blinds himself, thereby to see more clearly. At the end he saved the city but destroyed himself, neither result on purpose, even though everything started with a purpose. All is fate, except that each step along the way could have been avoided. Freedom and necessity are mixed, the forces of certainty and ambiguity embracing each other. In the beginning everything is right, in the end it shall all be wrong. Be the same again!

Once the stage has been set, the crucial question: "Who were my parents?" The chorus replies:

> Bewildered as a blown bird, my soul hovers and can not find
> Foothold in this debate, or any reason or rest of mind. (Sophocles, trans. 1949, p. 25)

After a row of excruciating interrogations, the bewildering ambiguities finally spring into unquestionable certainty. When that happens Jocasta can no longer contain herself, no longer equate the name "Oedipus" with any of the alternative descriptions, "my king," "my husband," "father of my children." First praying "May you never learn who you are!" she cries out:

> Ah, Miserable!
> That is the only word I have for you now.
> That is the only word I can ever have. (Sophocles, trans. 1949, p. 56)

In the new context any other word would be false. And she exits into her apartment, her hair clutched by the fingers of both hands, closing the doors behind her. A long scene later, when also Oedipus has convinced himself that logic had run its course and that all his premonitions had been right, he breaks the door open and rushes in. As a messenger reports,

> And there we saw her hanging, her body swaying
> From the cruel cord she had noosed about her neck.
> A great sob broke from him, heartbreaking to hear,
> As he loosed the rope and lowered her to the ground.
> I would blot out from my mind what happened next!
> For the King ripped from her gown the golden brooches
> That were her ornament, and raised them, and plunged them down
> Straight into his own eyeballs, crying, "No more,
> No more shall you look on the misery about me,
> The horrors of my own doing! Too long you have known
> The faces of those whom I should never have seen,
> Too long been blind to those for whom I have been searching!
> From this hour go in darkness!" And as he spoke,
> He struck at his eyes—not once, but many times;
> And the blood spattered his beard,
> Bursting from his ruined sockets like red hail. (p. 67)

Millennia later we keep returning. And as times go by, as they eventually did for Oedipus too, we come gradually to understand that in every already there is always a not yet, in every not yet always an already. Finding out who he was may or may not have rid the city of the plague; Sophocles never bothered to say. What he did tell us, though, is that at the crossroads, the place where Laïos was killed, nobody knew, in the palace, where the truth was revealed, nobody rejoiced. Honesty is in pursuit and pursuit in tragedy, life itself a game of dice played by men and watched by gods.

As the tragic hero eventually understood and accepted, whatever fate there is we bring onto ourselves. To do otherwise would be to be dishonest to oneself, to break the rules of one's own game, to be utterly lost. In the long run that is impossible. For everyone is one with his own map.

Fig. 4.1 Gunnael Jensson, *Mappa Mundi Universalis.* Glass tetrahedron on granite base, 25 × 25 × 19¼ in. Mixed media (Kalmar granite, Weissglass, gold, ruby). Museum Gustavianum, Uppsala. First exhibited in the Uppsala Cathedral, September, 2000 (Photo by the author)

***

And for that cartographic reason I must now briefly turn to the sculpture *Mappa Mundi Universalis* (Olsson, 2007, pp. 411–437; Jensson, 2015; see also Jensen, 2012), in the same expression a mapping of power-and-knowledge and a self-referential presentation of the fix-points, sight lines, and projection planes of understanding, in every respect the joint effort of myself and my friend and former student Ole Michael Jensen. So close was in fact our cooperation that in the end we reported our findings not under our individual names but under the amalgamated imprint of Gunnael Jensson. Seemingly not a map at all, just a tetrahedron of transparent glass grown out of a square slab of granite (Fig. 4.1). Not much, yet enough to last us for a lifetime.

To understand why, imagine how a long time ago a drama was set in motion. The stage-floor is a flat rock that gently slopes into the sea, the actors some strange creatures that emerge out of nowhere, aimlessly spreading across the homogeneous plain. A foot gets stuck in a crevice and for the first time ever there is a difference different enough to make a difference. The others notice, they point and they mutter, every gesture an attempt to force the bothering difference into graspable identity. An event of tremendous consequences, for what we are now about to witness is the very first sacrifice, *the* act through which the indefinable creatures are changed into human beings, a species whose individuals are held together and kept apart by their use of signs, every sign an ironic expression of Signifier and signified merged into one.

When the foot is pulled out of the rock, a well of blood springs up, a constant reminder of what happened when the original deviance was turned into a nonwilling scapegoat, the baring of the navel of what it means to be human. In the materialized version of Jensson's sculpture, the place of this remarkable event is shown by a red ruby, a godly symbol which in the accompanying text is called a. Not because it *is* a but because the semiotic animal must call it something.

In the definitional struggle that now follows the mute difference is transformed into a set of communicable identities, like every translation an act of violence. More precisely, the foot in the crevice splits into a trinity of reformulations, a set of provisional reincarnations that in due course, and after much swirling around, find their positions in the corners of an equilateral triangle. Subsequently, each of the cornered aliases adopts a name that reflects the pain with which it was born: the shadowy a; the tautological $a = a$, the informative $a = b$. Atoms of understanding captured in a mushroom cloud of perpetual fission.

When the tension reaches its limit, the rock bursts and out of the lava grows a glass tetrahedron, a crystal palace sometimes known as the crucible of man, sometimes as the prison house of language. The floor and the three walls of this enchanting structure are all built as equal-sized equilateral triangles, the walls transparent, the foundation sunk into the granite ground, the ruby-covered well at its center. In a twist of cultural survival, the three reformulations (a, $a = a$, $a = b$) now rise from the base, stretch upwards, and meet again at the tetrahedron's top, the multitudes of Greek polytheism converging in the singularity of Abrahamic monotheism. Like every mapping, also this one is a triangulation, the a and its three restatements coming together in the vanishing point of the pinnacle, the locus of a tautological entity that by definition is what it is—a = a = b—a contradictory condensation of difference and identity, God's name (if a name it is). And from its inception this Absolute speaks. *Let there be!* And there is. A universe flowing out of the creator's mouth, in James Joyce's conception a commodious vicus of (p) recirculation.

In the coolness of the evening, the utterer listens back to what he has heard his tongue say, claiming first that it is very good, then that he alone has the right to judge. Tolerating neither idols nor false prophets, he declares that all usurpers will be killed and that every critique will be censored. Hereafter, there shall be neither pictures nor stories, hence no maps either. Impressed by his own achievements, he proclaims a day of rest, a Sabbath without work, 24 h devoted to the glorification of himself and his faithful.

Such is the subjection of subjects. Such is the structure of power. Such are the techniques by which we are made so obedient and so predictable.

*

The crystal palace is a well-guarded castle, its ruling resident the tyrant of tyrants. Admittedly a rhetorical exaggeration, for no Absolute is absolutely absolute, no crook crooked enough to live on forever.

But the palace is also a marvelous movie theater, one projector in each of the basement corners, golden rays carrying the alternative translations from the machine rooms to the screens of the opposite walls: the glass of Marcel Duchamp's *La mariée mise à nu par ses célibataires, même* (1914) (The Bride Stripped Bare by Her Bachelors, Even); the limestone wall of Plato's cave; the wood panel of Fra Angelico's *Annunciation;* all found again in the *mappa* of cartographic reason. And when the projections of the imagined identities hit the sheets of glass, they miraculously change into a set of Peircean signs, no longer the private fantasies of their inventor but communicable bits in an evolving discourse. To be technical, the *a* becomes the symbol of a, the *a = a* the icon of $a = a$, the *a = b* the index of $a = b$. But just as the painter's canvas must be properly prepared for the paint not to crack or run off, so must our minds be indoctrinated to ensure that all that is solid does not melt into air. Three grand institutions have risen to the task: religion (with its belief in the *a* of shared conventions), art (with it's *a = a* striving for perfect resemblance), science (with it's *a = b*, the *as-if* knowledge of provisional truth). Each mode of understanding entrenched within its own self-supporting power structures, rituals, rules, and regulations.

If these rituals could be perfectly performed, then the projection lines would strike the screening planes at 90° angles, every message going straight back to the cornered restatement it came from, nothing learned in the process. But even though the Saussurean/Lacanian sign is steeped in mimetic desire, the diverse ontologies of Signifier and signified guarantee that this perpetual urge can never be satisfied. Hence the fortunate consequence that no translation can ever be perfect. It follows that in actuality the inclination of the (en)lightening rays is never *right on* and that the projections, instead of returning to the original identities unchanged, they begin to bounce between the walls. In turn, this slight deflection means that whatever I happen to think, say, and do is never pure and simple but always a nondissolvable blend of religion, art, and science. And suddenly I see where the trigger of tragedy lies: in the purifying spirit of the right angle, in the hatred of the other which is built into the desire of every identity formulation. Hitler's *Lebensraum,* Stalin's *Gulag,* the Rwanda genocide, the iconoclastic controversy, *Jyllands-Posten*'s Mohammed pictures—all of them variations on the same theme. Murderous is our history, murky the connection between knowledge and action.

In turn, this analysis explains why for 40 years tragedy has occupied such an important place in my own conception of what it means to be human, indeed why I take it to be the most insightful of all available conceptions of thought-in-action and action-in-thought. The original setting is crucial, for Sophocles—a Janus-like figure who with one eye was scanning the old, with another was imagining the future— lived his long life in the abyss between the *mythos* of Homer and the *logos* of Plato. What he then discovered was that the greatest tension of his time lay in the attitudes to predicament, for while the archaic poets had taken a person's social standing to reflect his or her ability to handle contradiction, the new philosophers defined paradox as the greatest threat to the cohesion of human reason, an enemy to be fought by all means. As Wittgenstein (1921/1961) later put it, "without philosophy thoughts are, as it were, cloudy and indistinct: its task to make them clear and to give them sharp boundaries" (4.112). But in Sophocles' eyes religion itself was nothing but a human invention designed to keep people in place, like other laws issued by the humans of the polis, not by the gods of Olympus.

In my mind this pre-Christian circumstance explains both why the tragedians assigned such a crucial role to the chorus and why the recurring convulsions of the late twentieth and early twenty-first centuries are essentially a political crisis, an orgy in promises that cannot be kept and therefore should never be given, the election results bought with junk bonds issued in the voters' own names. Whereas the problem for the tragedians was the exact drawing of the boundary between the humans and the gods, the problem for the postdemocrats is that although all animals are equal, some pigs are more equal than the others. In my readings it is exactly these relations between religion, arts, and science that permeate also the cascading reflections of writers like Giorgio Agamben, Alain Badiou, Peter Sloterdijk, and Slavoj Zizek. Getting crowded is the crystal palace, the prophets moving in.

***

In the history of the *longue durée*, the examples of Swedish welfare, central place theory, geography, and planning deserve little but a footnote. Yet they too spring from the tension of trust and verification that lies at the heart of European culture, perhaps of all cultures, the tales about Oedipus' foot and Odysseus' scar pulling in one direction, the paragraphs of Moses' first stone tablet in the other. In the cleft in-between hides everything inter-esting, including the scientist's testable theory and operationalized model, in the same breath a reified deification and a deified reification, the potentially informative $a = b$ turning into the tautological I am who I am. In that context the lawmakers' grasp of human action as a magic game of ontological transformations is truly remarkable: "Thou shalt not make unto thee any graven image, or any likeness of any thing that is in heaven above, or that is in the earth beneath, or that is in the water under the earth; Thou shalt not bow down thyself to them, nor serve them" (Exodus 20:4–5, Deuteronomy 5:8–9, King James Version).

Well decreed. For in the empirical now-here of the utopian No-where, nothing is more inhibiting than our inability to be abstract enough. As Abraham responded on his way to the *akedah* (Genesis 22:1, King James Version): "Here I am." And the two went on together, world literature's most pregnant silence.

The spiral is closing in, every thought emitting a throw of dice. Hazerdous is the hazard. In the Vico-inspired language of Norman O. Brown's (1974) *Closing Time*:

The true (*verum*) and the made (*factum*) are convertible
Verification is fabrication
Homo faber
Man the forger; at his forge
Forging the uncreated conscience of his race. (p. 18)

References

Abrahamsson, C., & Gren, M. (Eds.). (2012). *GO: On the geographies of Gunnar Olsson*. Farnham: Ashgate.

Arendt, H. (1977). *Eichmann in Jerusalem: A report on the banality of evil*. Harmondsworth: Penguin.

Aristotle. (1941). Nicomachean ethics. (W. D. Ross, Trans.). In R. McKeon (Ed.), *The basic works of Aristotle* (pp. 927–1112). New York: Random House. (Original work written ca. 330 BC)

Arrow, K. J. (1951). *Social choice and individual values*. New York: Wiley.

Barnes, T. J. (2015). "Desk killers": Walter Christaller, central place theory, and the Nazis. In P. Meusburger, D. Gregory, & L. Suarsana (Eds.), *Geographies of knowledge and power* (pp. 187–201). Knowledge and Space: Vol. 7. Dordrecht: Springer. doi:10.1007/978-94-017-9960-7

Bauman, Z. (1989). *Modernity and the holocaust*. Ithaca: Cornell University Press.

Brown, N. O. (1974). *Closing time*. New York: Vintage Books.

Christaller, W. (1933). *Die zentralen Orte in Süddeutschland. Eine ökonomisch-geographische Untersuchung über die Gesetzmäßigkeit der Verbreitung und Entwicklung der Siedlungen mit städtischer Funktion*. [Central places in southern Germany: An economic-geographical study of the inherent laws of the distribution and development of settlements with urban function]. Jena: Gustav Fischer.

Hägerström, A. (1911). *Om moraliska föreställningars sanning* [On the truth of moral conceptions]. Stockholm: Bonnier.

Hegel, G. W. F. (1967). *The phenomenology of mind*. (J. B. Baille, Trans.). New York: Harper Torchbooks. (Original work published 1807)

Jensen, O. M. (2012.). To be human (the secret of the pyramid). In C. Abrahamsson & M. Gren (Eds.), *GO: On the geographies of Gunnar Olsson* (pp. 349–363). Farnham: Ashgate.

Jensson, G. (2015). Mappa mundi universalis. In F. Sjöberg (Ed.), *Freikörperkultur* (pp. 67–86). Stockholm: Arvinius+Orfeus.

Kamenetzky, I. (1961). Lebensraum in Hitler's war plan: The theory and the Eastern European reality. *American Journal of Economics and Sociology, 20,* 313–326. doi:10.1111/j.1536-7150.1961.tb00589.x

Lösch, A. (1954). *The economics of location* (W. H. Woglom & W. F. Stolper, Trans.) (2nd rev. ed.). New Haven: Yale University Press. (Original work published 1940, 2nd ed. 1943)

Lundstedt, A. V. (1932–1936). *Die Unwissenschaftlichkeit der Rechtswissenschaft* [The unscientific nature of jurisprudence]. 2 Vols. Berlin: W. Rothschild.

Madajcyk, C. (Ed.). (1994). *Vom Generalplan Ost zum Generalsiedlungsplan* [From the master plan East to the master settlement plan]. Munich: K. G. Sauer.

Marc-Wogau, K. (1968). *Studier till Axel Hägerströms filosofi* [Studies on Axel Hägerströms philosophy]. Stockholm: Prisma.

Marx, K. (1967). *Capital: Critique of political economy: Vol. 1. The process of capitalist production* (S. Moore & E. Aveling, Trans.). New York: International Publishers. (Original work published 1867)

Nietzsche, F. (1976). On truth and lie in an extra-moral sense. In W. Kaufmann (Ed. & Trans.), *The portable Nietzsche* (pp. 42–50). London: Penguin Books. (Original work written 1870–1873; additional copyrights New York: Viking Press 1954 & 1968)

Ofstad, H. (1961). *An inquiry into the freedom of decision*. Oslo: Norwegian Universities Press.

Olivecrona, K. (1942). *Om lagen och rätten* [On the law and the right]. Lund: Gleerup.

Olsson, G. (1980). *Birds in egg/Eggs in bird*. London: Pion.

Olsson, G. (1991). *Lines of power/Limits of language*. Minneapolis: University of Minnesota Press.

Olsson, G. (2007). *Abysmal: A critique of cartographic reason*. Chicago: University of Chicago Press.

Rössler, M. (1989). Applied geography and area research in Nazi society: Central place theory and planning, 1933–1945. *Environment and Planning D: Society and Space, 7,* 419–431. doi:10.1068/d070419

Sen, A. (1993). Markets and freedom: Achievements and limitations for the market mechanism in promoting individual freedom. *Oxford Economic Papers, 45,* 519–541.

Shakespeare, W. (n.d.). The merry wives of Windsor. In *The complete works of William Shakespeare* (with an introduction and glossary by B. Hodek) (pp. 41–65). London: Spring Books. (Play originally published 1602)

Sophocles (1949). *The Oedipus cycle* (D. Fitts & R. Fitzgerald, Trans.). New York: Harcourt, Brace and World, Harvest edition. (Original work written ca. 430 BC)

Speer, A. (1970). *Inside the Third Reich* (R. Winston & C. Winston, Trans.). New York: Macmillan. (Original work published 1969)

Tobler, W. (1970). A computer movie simulating urban growth in the Detroit region. *Economic Geography, 46,* 234–240.

Wittgenstein, L. (1953). *Philosophical investigations* (G. E. M. Anscombe, Trans.). Oxford: Basil Blackwell.

Wittgenstein, L. (1961). *Tractatus Logico-Philosophicus* (D. F. Pears & B. F. McGuiness, Trans.). London: Routledge and Kegan Paul. (Original work published 1921)

Chapter 5
Perverse Expertise and the Social Unconscious in the Making of Crisis

Richard Peet

This chapter stresses the social construction of the knowledge guiding social action. I focus on social construction as opposed to the individual's psychology of knowledge. The individual always has his or her own mentality, but what matters in the making of history are the broad social and cultural trends in thought, imagination, and comprehension. Further, I discuss social construction as it is meant in the critical tradition—Marx's ideology, Gramsci's hegemony—whereby class forces lead, direct, and control the production of knowledge. Knowledge production serves a class interest. As Marx and Engels (1845/2004) put it,

> The ideas of the ruling class are in every epoch the ruling ideas, i.e. the class which is the ruling material force of society, is at the same time its ruling intellectual force. The class which has the means of material production at its disposal, has control at the same time over the means of mental production, so that thereby, generally speaking, the ideas of those who lack the means of mental production are subject to it. The ruling ideas are nothing more than the ideal expression of the dominant material relationships, the dominant material relationships grasped as ideas; hence of the relationships which make the one class the ruling one, therefore, the ideas of its dominance. (p. 64)

If the problems that beset capitalism result from the actions of capitalists—if the financial crisis that began in 2007 was caused by speculation by finance capitalists—then, the dominant interpretations will be those of the causal agents.

The rush of contemporary events is thus testing the ideas available for understanding them. This testing holds for the ideas developed to think through the immediate onslaught of rebellions, crises, and catastrophes. It also holds for the concepts needed to guide a more long-term movement into a different kind of society. Narrowly economic categories are insufficient for thinking about society as a whole. At the least, political-economic-cultural ideas are needed. Clearly, one cannot just regard a single country to be a *society* and must therefore consider geoeconomic or

R. Peet (✉)
Graduate School of Geography, Clark University, Worcester, MA, USA
e-mail: rpeet@clarku.edu

© The Author(s) 2017
P. Meusburger et al. (eds.), *Knowledge and Action*, Knowledge and Space 9,
DOI 10.1007/978-3-319-44588-5_5

geopolitical notions—or rather, geopolitical-economic concepts—adequate for a globalized existence. A new, critical conceptual apparatus is needed. But this critical conception is prevented by hegemonic control that a combination of perverse expertise and mass social unconsciousness exerts over imaginaries. At the juncture between modern knowledge and practical action lies expertise. When the mass mind loses its capacity to think rationally, the outcome is social unconsciousness. The elite practice perverse expertise, and the masses respond unconsciously. This mindset moves capitalist society into an era of perpetual crisis.

Neoliberalism, Finance Capitalism, and Crisis

I offer a proposition worthy, perhaps, of consideration. Several major, powerful blocs of countries have changed from societies with economies characterized by industrial capitalism to a new kind of society one might call *finance capitalism*. In the United States, the timing of this transformation is clear. Profits from manufacturing were far larger than profits from other corporate sectors until the 1980s, when profits in FIRE corporations (finance, insurance, and real estate) all of a sudden grew rapidly. They overtook those in manufacturing in the 1990s and have remained greater ever since. Financial corporations are now the dominant economic institutions in capitalist societies that have transitioned from production to the provision of services, especially financial services (Peet, 2011).

This transition results from secular change in the distribution of income. Figure 5.1, derived from U.S. income-tax statistics computed by Emmanuel Saez from the University of California, shows that the 1% of the U.S. population at the highest end of the income scale received 15–25% of total income in the Liberal period of U.S. capitalism (1917–1941). For the subsequent 40 years under Keynesian capitalism, that group received a fairly steady 10%, a figure that began to rise suddenly in the early 1980s, under Neoliberalism, reaching 20–24% in the 2000s. Economic growth since 1980 has almost exclusively produced higher incomes for the already rich (Piketty & Saez, 2003). At the other end of the class spectrum, real incomes have fallen for the poor and have remained steady for just about everyone else. Increasing inequality is the central socioeconomic characteristic of finance capitalism.

Finance capitalism exercises power by controlling access to the markets through which capital accumulations become investments, directing flows of capital (e.g., equity purchases, bond sales, and direct investment) to places and users approved by the financial analytic structure of the banks, investment firms, and bond sellers on Wall Street and in the City of London. In terms of expertise, it is the investment analyst's global gaze, representing the confidence of the market, by which societies and economies are ordered, ranked, and adjudicated. Although investor confidence is presented by the business media as a neutral, technical, and necessary factor—in everyone's best long-term interest—it is actually a committed, financial capitalist interest based on utterly biased knowledge. An instructive example is the global bond market. The interest paid on sovereign bonds is determined by the risk of

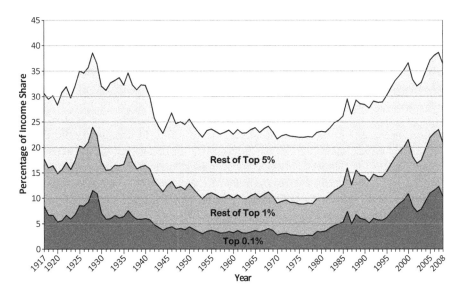

Fig. 5.1 Percentage income (including capital gains) going to the three highest income groups, United States, 1917–2008. (Source: Designed and drawn by the author. Statistical data from Alveredo, Atkinson, Piketty, & Saez (2011))

default, with experts employing formulae stemming from long experience measured statistically—apparently scientific and necessary. Yet it is actually a few thousand experts representing the interests of accumulated capital who tell governments how to run their economies. At the very least, they represent undemocratic expertise.

At the confluence of knowledge and action lies expertise, by which is meant high-quality, specialized, theoretical, and practical knowledge. The process that produces sophisticated, but inimical, knowledge is what I call *perverse expertise*. It is expertise in that some of the world's finest minds, such as professional economists, do the intellectual and practical modeling and are well paid and respected for doing so. The process is perverse because knowledge is accumulated in order to continue augmenting the incomes of already wealthy people, the capitalist class. The only valid economic reason for gross distortions in income distribution of the kind that characterizes neoliberal, finance capitalism is that wealthy people are so rich that they cannot possibly spend all the money they receive and are therefore forced to save. The resulting vast accumulation of saved incomes becomes the main source of investment capital. Properly invested, capital can be used for research and innovation that results in more productive or sustainable economies. Badly invested, capital can be used for speculation that results in unstable economies. Knowledge and expertise make the difference.

Accordingly, Neoliberalism is a way of running the economy that produces dramatic price rises on the stock exchange, where the rich put their money to make ever more of it. But stocks and shares are a relatively safe bet compared to Neoliberalism's irrational exuberances, such as the sprawling financial apparatus surrounding the swollen credit market. Disaster strikes when, as in 1929 and 2007, the amount of money going to the 1 % superrich approaches 25 % of total income generated in the country, far exceeding requirements for productive investment and *necessitating* speculation to enhance returns. For the price of high returns is eternal risk. Any investment fund that does not generate quick and large returns and that thereby avoids extreme gambles suffers disinvestment in highly competitive markets, where money changes hands in a computer-aided flash. There is thus a competitive compulsion for experts to be ever more daring as they seek to maximize returns that temporarily attract investment. Financial managers, who oversee capital accumulations, compete for control over assets by promising these high returns. Those who fail to deliver high profit rates disappear to be replaced by even more aggressive investment analysts. Debt, speculation, hazard, and fear are thereby structurally endemic to finance capitalism in what Walks (2010) calls "Ponzi Neoliberalism." Fear itself becomes the source of further speculation, as with buying gold or futures. Debt and gambling spread from Wall Street into all sectors of society—house prices, state lotteries, casinos, numbers games, bingo at the church hall, sweepstakes, and Pokemon cards. Everyone gambles, even children. Production, consumption, economy, culture, and the use of environments are subject to an ever more removed, abstract calculus of power in which ability to contribute to short-term financial profit becomes the main concern. The structure of the system compels expertise into perversity. The particular thinker, with his or her own psychological structure and thinking processes, has little to do with structural compulsions in the relations between knowledge and action.

The interlocking of these speculations is the source of their intractability. The financial crisis that began in 2007 was thus marked by vastly overpriced housing, particularly near booming financial centers; competition among financial institutions to offer easy credit that made many people hopelessly indebted; the bundling of home mortgages and other debts into tradable paper; exorbitant levels of leveraging; and the use of assets whose value can disappear in an instant to securitize other, even chancier investments. It was not just that crisis spread from one area to another. It was that crisis in one area (such as the inevitable end to the housing price bubble) had exponential effects on the others (investment banks that were overextended into high-risk speculation) to the degree that accumulated losses tested the capacity of even client states and governance institutions to rescue the situation. In a nutshell, inequality is not merely unethical, it is dangerous. The combination of debt and speculation, deriving from inequality, produces an inevitable tendency toward repeated financial crises.

Buying the State

Why are the colossal incomes of the already rich not taxed out of existence? How can extreme inequality survive in democracies where people are, at least apparently, free to vote for anyone they choose? The main thing about so-called free elections is that they are not free. Elections are expensive. Public opinion is made by media persuasion. Political images are costly to produce, in part because sharp minds ponder every persuasive aspect, ransack each emotion, and raid the collective memory to sell candidates for office. Such images are expensive to distribute, especially because the image of the politician has to compete with images of other commodities that taste nice and look even better than the politician. Politicians therefore have to raise a great deal of money to run for office when elections are decided almost exclusively by image projection in Fordist societies.

In 1976 and 1980, the last U.S. elections under Keynesian capitalism, presidential candidates collectively raised and spent about $1.75 billion per election. As Neoliberalism took hold, the cost of elections soared. In the 2008 U.S. presidential election, candidates collectively raised ten times more—just under $17.49 billion, with the total cost of the election amounting to just over $5.28 billion. In the 2010 midterm elections, congressional candidates raised $ 1.08 billion—and senatorial candidates, $ 742 million—in an election fought almost entirely on the basis of attack ads (data from Center for Responsive Politics, n.d.). The 2012 presidential elections made even these enormous amounts seem like pocket money. In the few months of the early presidential campaign up to the end of June 2012, and before things really intensified, President Obama spent $400 million, and eventually $1 billion. In addition, the U.S. Supreme Court, in Citizens United vs. FEC (2010), ruled that under the First Amendment of the U.S. Constitution (which deals with the freedom of speech) the government could not restrict the size of corporate donations to Super Pacs (Political Action Committees) that indirectly support candidates for public office by supporting causes that they stand for. A billion dollars is needed to run a high-level campaign.

Where does one acquire a billion dollars to run a campaign or support a cause? Answer: from people who have a billion dollars. About one tenth of 1 % of the U.S. adult population (231,000 people) donate over $2000 each to political campaigns, and these donations make up 75 % of the total contributions; a mere 26,000 people donate 36 % of total contributions (Center for Responsive Politics n.d.). In other words, a candidate must raise hundreds of millions of dollars from 200,000 rich people to be able to run a campaign. Candidates who do not appeal to the rich or who are not wealthy themselves never have a chance. They raise a few million dollars at most (independent candidate Ralph Nader raised $4 million in 2008), they cannot run television ads, they are not present at media debates, and most of the electorate never hears of them. Rich people choose the political candidates who run for office. Under finance capitalist democracy, the electorate decides which rich people's candidates are elected to office. And the information spread by costly advertising? Most messages are attack ads presenting unfavorable information about the candidate or cause they oppose. Most of the rest are image ads presenting favorable pictures of the candidate they support. The real content, by which I mean substantiated and sustained information about a candidate's positions and policies, hardly appears. Images, attack ads, and the like constitute perverse political knowledge produced by perverse expertise. It produces perverse democracy.

Once in office, politicians are kept in line by lobbying. Companies, labor unions, and other organizations, in addition to making campaign contributions, spend $3.5 billion each year on efforts to influence the U.S. Congress and federal agencies. In the period between 1998 and 2010, the insurance, business association, and securities sectors spent $33.6 billion on lobbying, whereas labor spent about $30 million a year. Some 130 former members of congress are lobbyists, and lobbies employ nearly half the politicians and congressional aides who return to the private sector. Such money and connections do not spread scientific or factual knowledge. They project information based on superficial, biased knowledge thought up to support powerful interests. Lobbyists are yet another example of perverse political expertise.

Finance Capitalism and Environmental Crisis

During the unusually hot summers of 2010, 2011, and 2012, capitalist society fell prey to two crises: an economic depression that states or markets could not end and a sequence of environmental tragedies brought on by global warming. Did the two crises coincide by mere chance? Or did they stem systematically from the same structural causes? The answer might seem obvious were it not for media that must confuse on causation as they inform on details. Both economic depression and environmental catastrophe result from the extreme risks that must be taken by prominent actors under finance capitalism—meaning that anyone who does not stake everything is eliminated from power. Crises that threaten humanity are structurally endemic to finance capitalism.

Financial and economic crisis lead to periodic recessions, depressions, and downturns punctuated by hopelessly optimistic upturns in the *markets*, bringing on the terrible social outcome of millions of people losing their jobs, homes, and dignity. But the worst is yet to come as the environment strikes back. The hazards endemic to finance capitalism extend to precarious environmental relations. The bearers of capitalist culture become risk-ridden, short-term in memory and anticipation, and careless about consequences. They live for the moment, without regard for the environmental future. Production, consumption, the economy in general, and the use of environments are subject to a remote, abstract calculus of power wherein the ability to promote short-term financial profit becomes primary and long-term impacts are not so much ignored as glossed over through sophisticated corporate advertising, think-tank excuses, and pseudogreen propaganda ("We, too, care about the environment"). By generating above-average profits, corporate leaders who make environmentally perilous decisions—to drill in deep water, for instance—win the investor confidence that enables them to borrow, invest, and expand and allows them to pay their upper management well. CEOs who demonstrate an environmental conscience do not win the market's confidence. Environmental risk (mitigated by quality public relations to excuse the occasional mistakes) represents the frontier in profit-making and business success. Every time a disaster such as British Petroleum's

2010 oil spill in the Gulf of Mexico is cleaned up, excused, and forgotten, the agents of the risk business just become more knowledgeable and slicker at its politicocultural operations. As BP was restoring investor confidence in the summer of 2010, the company announced that it was selling its onshore drilling operations to concentrate even more on deep-sea drilling. The danger that produces economic catastrophe also creates environmental crises.

The neoliberal globalization that has deindustrialized the First World and industrialized parts of the Third World—Brazil, South Korea, China, and India—has resulted in a spectacular globalization of environmental destruction. Globalization of this neoliberal, financial kind means that economic growth rates slow in the deindustrialized center but accelerate rapidly (rates of 8–10% a year) in some peripheral industrializing countries. China's economy grew 14-fold between 1980 and 2006 to the equivalent of a GDP of $4.4 trillion, and India's economy grew sixfold, to $1.2 trillion, with carbon dioxide emissions increasing proportionately. China's carbon dioxide emissions from burning fossil fuels amounted to 407 million metric tons in 1980 and nearly 2.25 billion in 2010; India's went from 95 million metric tons in 1980 to 564 million in 2010 (Boden & Blasing, 2012).

Much of this production and pollution is connected to consumption in the First World. Some 40% of China's product is exported, as is 20% of India's, and both economies have become dramatically more export oriented. These statistics show the globalization of an economy still centered on consumption in the high-income countries. This fixation has led to an intensification of pollution's globalization, as evidenced by carbon dioxide emissions. In 2010 global fossil-fuel carbon emissions amounted to 9.13 billion metric tons of carbon. In global terms, more than 500 billion metric tons of carbon have been released into the atmosphere from the burning of fossil fuels and cement production since 1750, and half of these emissions have happened since the mid-1970s, when it was already known that greenhouse gasses caused global warming—perverse environmental knowledge.

The point is that environmental pollution is driven by economic necessity under capitalism. It is necessary to pollute so that money can be made. Within the existing politicoeconomic context, only economic recession can bring about a drastic decrease in pollution. Indeed, global carbon dioxide emissions from burning fossil fuels temporarily declined by 5.9% from 2008 through 2009. This reduction came about because of a 2.5% fall in global GDP, a decrease of 11.5% in the manufacturing production index, and a reduction of 40% in raw steel production. Yet it is politically impossible for parties or governments to suggest, in effect, that the necessary price of ending environmental destruction is a declining economy. The solution is to elevate discussion from the national to the international scale. Upward displacement in the environmental discourse necessarily takes the form of UN conferences, Earth summits, and unenforceable protocols. Economic necessity produces endless political evasion of the environmental issue. Yet under Neoliberalism the significance of government regulation of development—and development's relations with the environment—is diminishing because of the intensification of neoliberal and mass beliefs, including mass beliefs, about government, markets, and policies. Hence, the Tea Party movement in the United States is founded on the idea of reducing the size and interventional zeal of government at a time when state intervention through environmental regulation is all that exists in the way of collective response to the destruction of nature.

In brief, environmental knowledge has escalated as environmental destruction has intensified. It is a case of perverse knowledge.

Social Unconsciousness

Were these issues the only ones, the world's people might still survive to criticize the system yet again. The business–state–media power complex, led by finance capital and driven by the quest for superprofits and fantastic incomes, cannot be opposed with any degree of success except by social movements arising from an informed, enraged, and rational populace. There has to be a critical, rational, activist We-for-Us-to-save-the-world. Yet the other, popular side of finance capitalism is consumptive excess enabled by the cheap commodities that flood in from globalized production. The priority of social reproduction shifts from socializing people to become workers to socializing people to become consumers. A new type of human being is emerging, the consumptive person. The culture of overconsumption produces mass, popular apathy (*I like*, rather than *I think*). Overconsumption is a social addiction, a radical, selfish individualism that I characterize as the social unconscious. It is *unconscious* in that conscious awareness is missing, has not been constructed, has not been allowed to develop even from the interpretation of everyday experience (common sense), and it is *social* in that many people share similar characteristics. The culture of overconsumption is not so much a case of deliberately producing mass stupidity, although mass advertising comes close to a corporate conspiracy. It is more that the trivialization of everyday life produces unconsciousness. Utter trivialization gives rise to a new kind of soft, shallow, compliant personality encased in the kind of fat body that results from total absence of self-control—35.7 % of American adults are obese, as are 17 % of American children (*Adult Obesity Facts,* 2013). Reality is a show. Entertainment is all that is. Because every commodity must have a body to bear its message and because every service is energy-intensive, overconsumption, overproduction, and the concomitant overuse of resources create environmental risk for society as a whole.

Essentially, the ability to respond in a radical, collective, socially rational way—to control an activist, interventionist state democratically, for instance—has been consumed away in vast segments of the population living in the global centers of power. And the leading ideas produced by experts in the service of power are ideological diversions rather than means of collective rational intervention.

My conclusion is that the intersecting economic and environmental crises will continue *ad infinitum* because the existing hegemonic knowledge cannot guide effective social action.

References

Adult Obesity Facts. (2013). Retrieved October 16, 2013, from Centers for Disease Control and Prevention, Division of Nutrition, Physical Activity, and Obesity Website at http://www.cdc.gov/obesity/data/adult.html

Alveredo, F., Atkinson, T., Piketty, T., & Saez, E. (2011). *The world top income database.* Retrieved from http://g-mond.parisschoolofeconomics.eu/topincomes/

Boden, T., & Blasing, T. J. (2012). *Record high 2010 global carbon dioxide emissions from fossil-fuel combustion and cement manufacture.* Retrieved from the U.S. Department of Energy, Office of Science, Dioxide Information Analysis Center Website at http://cdiac.ornl.gov/trends/emis/prelim_2009_2010_estimates.html

Center for Responsive Politics. (n.d.). https://www.opensecrets.org Accessed several times from 2010 to 2011.

Citizens United vs. Federal Election Commission, No. 08–205. U.S. 310. Argued March 24, 2009—Reargued September 9, 2009—Decided January 21, 2010.

Marx, K., & Engels, F. (2004). *The German ideology: Part one with selections from parts two and three and supplementary texts* (C. J. Arthur, Ed.). New York: International Publishers. (Original work published 1845)

Peet, R. (2011). Contradictions of finance capitalism. *Monthly Review, 63*(7), 18–32. Retrieved from http://monthlyreview.org/2011/12/01/contradictions-of-finance-capitalism

Piketty, T., & Saez, E. (2003). Income inequality in the United States, 1913–1998. *Quarterly Journal of Economics, 118,* 1–39. doi:10.1162/00335530360535135

Walks, A. (2010). Bailing out the wealthy: Responses to the financial crisis, Ponzi Neoliberalism, and the city. *Human Geography, 3*(3), 54–84.

Chapter 6
How Much Knowledge Is Necessary for Action?

Joachim Funke

How much knowledge is necessary for action? This question is fundamental because it suggests that the link between knowledge and action is debatable, that there is no given, fixed causal relationship between knowledge and action. In addition, there seems to be no fixed causal direction. Knowledge can be a prerequisite for action but also a consequence of an action. My opening question relates two key words in psychology. One of them is *knowledge*, about which a large body of knowledge exists (e.g., Halford, Wilson, & Phillips, 2010)—about its different types (e.g., procedural, declarative), styles of acquisition (implicit, explicit), and degrees of accessibility (conscious, subconscious, unconscious). The other word is *action*, about which there are various theories describing human behavior with respect to intention (e.g., Fishbein & Ajzen, 2010). In this introductory section I try to give an overview of these conceptions and of the relation between knowledge and action.

The issues around the keywords *knowledge* and *action*—which constitute the title of a book by Frey, Mandl, and von Rosenstiel (2006)—are captured by the following four main aspects, which generate corresponding questions.

1. The relation between knowledge and action. From the perspective of the psychology of knowledge (e.g., Strube & Wender, 1993), knowledge is a competence for action, a precondition. What is known about the relation between knowledge and action and what is not known? How much of human action is governed by routines, experience, intuition, and knowledge? What is the trade-off between taking action and improving knowledge?
2. Types of knowledge and different phases. To what extent do various types of knowledge (e.g., implicit or explicit) influence the steps from cognition to action (e.g., aspirations, attention, decision-making, problem-solving, the evaluation of situations, the search for alternatives, and the implementation of intentions)?

J. Funke (✉)
Department of Psychology, Heidelberg University, Heidelberg, Germany
e-mail: joachim.funke@psychologie.uni-heidelberg.de

© The Author(s) 2017
P. Meusburger et al. (eds.), *Knowledge and Action*, Knowledge and Space 9,
DOI 10.1007/978-3-319-44588-5_6

3. Rationality and knowledge. What categories of rationality should be identified? Concepts of rationality are common ground in social and economic theories, but rationality in everyday life seems to be something else. To what degree does the concept of bounded rationality (Simon, 1947, p. 61–65) weaken the link between knowledge and action? Is there a threshold of minimal knowledge that is necessary for action?

4. Action theory and language. How constitutive is language use for action? Searle (1969), with his concept of speech acts, points out that speaking can be acting. To speak about X requires knowing something about X. If someone is not able to speak about Z, can that person act upon Z or does the inability to speak about Z imply the inability to act upon Z? What about the idea that "actions speak louder than words" (Tanner, Brügger, van Schie, & Lebherz, 2010)?

The contribution from my own empirical work addresses mainly the first and at least in part the second of these four main aspects, leaving many of the other questions to the reader.

After a short section on definitions, I ask whether action is possible without knowledge and afterward venture the question of whether it is possible for people to act against their own knowledge. Thereafter, I review some of the standard views on the relation between knowledge and action, interpretations that may help this chapter's exploration of that connection through three theories: planned behavior, unconscious thought, and the option-generation framework. The chapter then continues with empirical evidence from my own research area, problem-solving, and shows that the relation between knowledge and action is strong within that area.

Definitions of Knowledge and Action

Knowledge and Belief

Knowledge is not always knowledge; it is necessary to distinguish between knowledge and true belief. A person who believes that leaves of a red tree are green definitely knows about his or her belief. Hence, there is knowledge that depends on states in the outer world (it being a purely empirical question whether the leaves are green or red) and on other knowledge that is a priori true (i.e., my knowledge about my beliefs). In the philosophy of language, this position is called *externalism*. For the issues considered in this chapter, it suffices to state that I am talking about the person's internal knowledge not at a metalevel but rather at the level of assertions that are believed to be true.

Types of Knowledge

The distinction between explicit (verbalizable, declarative) and implicit (nonverbalizable, tacit) knowledge is well known and relates to the distinction between conscious and nonconscious knowledge. Cognitive processes in general are often seen as working in two modes, a deliberate, conscious one and an automatic nonconscious type of processing (e.g., Evans, 2008; Kahneman, 2011).

Action

The definition of action as goal-directed human activity helps set it apart from pure behavior (e.g., sneezing, which is not directed to any particular goal). Action is that part of behavior which occurs intentionally. Keep in mind that even trial-and-error behavior could be classified as action if it happens intentionally.

Is Action Possible Without Knowledge?

Is action possible without knowledge? Can one really posit that idea as a serious option? If one takes the term *action* to mean goal-directed human activity, the answer must be no. Action implies goals, and in order to realize goals a person needs appropriate means. The means–end connection is knowledge—to know that one can use bamboo sticks to fetch a banana lying just beyond arm's reach outside the bars of a cage was an important insight to Sultan, the most intelligent chimpanzee analyzed by Köhler (1925).

But what is the relation between goals and knowledge? Are goals part of what people call knowledge or are they a separate entity only derivative of knowledge? In my understanding, knowledge is a piece of subjectively acquired information about the world. In German one would say that knowledge about the world is *angeeignet* (appropriated, assimilated, internalized). In a certain sense it could be construed as embodied information.

But how is embodied information linked to goals? Goals are representations of future states and derive their power from the possibility of finding a way from the given present state to an envisioned future state. When talking about goals, people always talk about degrees of distance between the given and the goal state. Because the path from the given state to the goal state is sometimes not easy to discover, problem-solving comes into play. Indeed, the epistemologist Karl Popper (1999) argued that "all life is problem solving."

To answer the question of whether action is possible without knowledge, I must thus conclude that the use of the word action logically implies the connection to some background representation, which is normally called knowledge.

Is Action Possible Against One's Better Knowledge?

It may be more interesting to ask whether action is possible *against* knowledge. The question is related to the understanding of human rationality. Newell (1981) stated the principle of rationality simply by saying, "if an agent has knowledge that one of its actions will lead to one of its goals, then the agent will select that action" (p. 8). This principle would not allow a person to act against her or his goals.

Yet everyday experience brims with examples to the contrary. People love animals—but at the same time do not hesitate to slaughter them professionally in the slaughterhouse. Concern about climate change is widespread, though people continue to pollute the environment by driving big cars. The gaps between attitude and behavior are large, but are attitude and behavior the same as knowledge and action? Take smoking for example. Evidence indisputably shows that smoking is detrimental to human health, but people continue to smoke despite their knowledge of this fact. Are they acting against their knowledge? I would say, no! Given even such blatant violations of their own attitudes, people follow principles of bounded rationality. When smoking despite knowledge about the negative consequences of that behavior, a person might argue, "Yes, I know about the negative effects, but my family has a very good gene pool, so I do not assume I'll get cancer as easily as normal people will." This argumentation conveys a kind of justification for behavior that, from the viewpoint of the individual, is no longer irrational but instead has its own limited rationality.

Can Knowledge Impede Action?

Planning before taking action is usually thought to be wise, but it can have disadvantages. Although having plans generally makes people more likely to act on a goal than they would without them, an experiment reported by Masicampo and Baumeister (2012) showed that subjects who had devised plans to achieve a goal failed at that task, particularly when it was essential to recognize and seize an alternative opportunity in order to succeed. The authors concluded that with sufficient (unlimited) time a previously learned specific plan increased attainment of the goal, replicating the usual benefit of planning. With insufficient time, however, the specific plan impaired performance because participants failed to capitalize on an alternative opportunity for accomplishing the goal. The final conclusion by Masicampo and Baumeister was that plans can drastically decrease overall rates of attainment when openness to alternatives is crucial to success.

The Relation Between Knowledge and Action

What are the standard views on the relation between knowledge and action? I concentrate on three approaches that posit assumptions about this relationship: (a) the theory of planned behavior (Ajzen, 1991), (b) the theory of unconscious thought (Dijksterhuis & Nordgren, 2006), and (c) the option-generation framework (Kalis, Mojzisch, Schweizer, & Kaiser, 2008).

The Theory of Planned Behavior

The theory of planned behavior formulated by Ajzen (1991) has become one of the best-known theories in psychology. Roughly, it states that behavior depends on the intention or resolve of the individual to behave in a certain way, say, to exercise at least five times a week. Intention itself depends on a behavioral attitude (e.g., exercising at least five times a week would be good/bad), subjective norms (e.g., most people important to the person think that she or he should exercise at least five times a week), and perceived behavioral control (e.g., exercising at least five times a week would be easy/difficult). This theory, in its new versions, is referred to as the "reasoned action approach" (Fishbein & Ajzen, 2010).

As depicted in Fig. 6.1, action depends on previous knowledge in the form of intention. The empirical evidence bearing out this theory is impressive, with meta-analyses of empirical studies (Armitage & Conner, 2001; Manning, 2009) overwhelmingly showing a strong connection between intention and subsequent

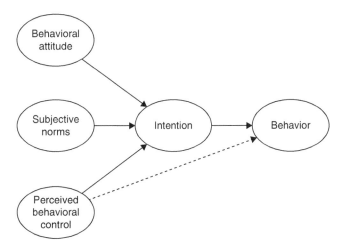

Fig. 6.1 The main elements that constitute the theory of reasoned action. Behavioral attitude, subjective norms, and perceived behavioral control causes intention that brings about behavior (with additional influence from perceived behavioral control)

behavior. But is this finding really a surprise? Werner Greve, a psychologist from Hildesheim University, has argued that the empirical success of the theory of planned behavior is not astonishing. According to him, the connection between intention and action is logical, not causal. In his article "Traps and Gaps in Action Explanation" (2001), he stated that intention is an inherent part of what is called action. Speaking about action therefore implies the assumption that an intention must exist to carry out a certain action.

The consequence of Greve's (2001) argument is clear. In his view most of the empirical studies on the theory of planned action are pseudoempirical research in that things that are true *a priori* are proven empirically. If a person intends to diet and sometime later starts to undergo dietary treatment, that action comes as no surprise. It is a logical consequence of the fact that at some time *t* a person decides to begin dietary treatment and then at time *t + 1* the diet really commences. But what about the cases in which persons do *not* start their dietary treatment? Would their lapse falsify the logical connection between intention and action? No, it would only mean that the intention was not strong enough to reach a threshold needed to turn intention into behavior.

The Theory of Unconscious Thought

A second approach is the theory of unconscious thought (Dijksterhuis & Nordgren, 2006). The basic idea is that the quality of decision-making depends on conscious and unconscious thought simultaneously. The term *conscious thought* is understood to mean a mental state that encompasses a person's rational awareness, whereas the term *unconscious thought* refers to the underlying influence, of which one is typically unaware and which has an impact on one's behavior. Unconscious thought takes place when conscious attention is directed elsewhere. Unconscious thought tends to outmatch conscious thought, especially in complex and untransparent situations.

The relative impacts that conscious and unconscious thought can have on decision-making become evident in the data from experiments by Dijksterhuis, Bos, Nordgren, and van Baaren (2006). The task for participants was to choose the most favorable car from a selection of cars that were described by only four aspects (the simple situation) or as many as twelve aspects (complex situation). Part (a) of Fig. 6.2 shows the percentage of persons who chose the best option; part (b), as a secondary measure, shows the difference in attitude toward the best option. The left-hand set of two bars in part (a) shows that most of the subjects made the correct decision in the simple situation if they were in a conscious-thought mode (represented by the white bar). But when the complexity of the task increased to twelve aspects, as is shown in the right-hand set of bars in part (b), the mode of unconscious thought has a great advantage over that of conscious thought, a finding that supports the theory by Dijksterhuis and Nordgren (2006). As part (b) of Fig. 6.2

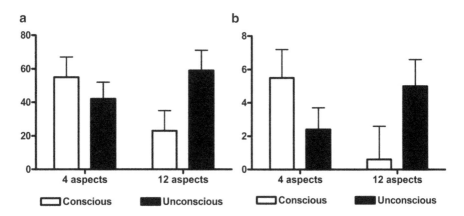

Fig. 6.2 Decision-making criteria for choosing a car: (**a**) Percentage of participants who chose the most desirable car as a function of complexity of decision and of mode of thought ($n = 18$ to 22 in each condition). Error bars represent the standard error. (**b**) Difference in attitude (on a scale of -25 to $+25$) toward the desirable and undesirable car as a function of complexity of decision and of mode of thought ($n = 12$ to 14 in each condition). Error bars [the *vertical lines* above the bars] represent the standard error (Reprinted from Dijksterhuis et al. (2006, p. 1005) with permission from the American Association for the Advancement of Science)

illustrates, not only are the decisions improved by unconscious thought but the attitude toward the desirable and undesirable car depends on the mode of thought.

The Option-Generation Framework

A third theory that deals with the relation between knowledge and action is the option-generation framework by Kalis et al. (2008). Studying the weakness of will (a phenomenon known as acrasia), these researchers concentrated on option generation, a little-understood process that precedes option selection and action initiation.

Figure 6.3 illustrates the idealized process of option generation, option selection, and action initiation and gives the background of the ideas that Kalis et al. (2008) have about degenerative processes in this area. Table 6.1 affords an overview of the ways in which dysfunctions in option generation can result in irrational behavior. The table presents two dimensions—dysfunction in the quantity of options (*hypo*generation and *hyper*generation) and dysfunction in the quality of options. The two rows separate instrumental irrationality from noninstrumental irrationality, meaning that options can be seen either as a means to realize certain goals (i.e., the instrumental understanding) or as irrationality in the goals themselves (i.e., noninstrumental irrationality). This concept links knowledge and action in a special way: It makes a connection between options and actions.

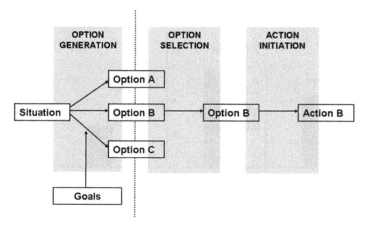

Fig. 6.3 Stages of decision making in our model. (Kalis et al., 2008, p. 403) (Copyright 2008 by Springer Science + Business Media. With permission of Springer)

Table 6.1 Six types of irrational behavior

	Dysfunction in quantity of options		Dysfunction in quality of options
Irrationality	Hypogeneration	Hypergeneration	
Instrumental	(1) Absence of options leads to leads to reduced effectiveness in attaining one's goals.	(2) An increase in the number of options leads to problems in selection and initiation.	(3) Options are inadequate means to one's goals.
Noninstrumental	(4) Absence of goals leads to a reduction in one's options.	(5) An increase in the number of goals leads to defocused option generation.	(6) Options are means to goals that are themselves irrational.

Based on Kalis et al. (2008, pp. 407–411)

This walk through the three theories on the connection between knowledge and action gives an understanding of current approaches to that area of inquiry. In this chapter's final section I bring to this subject empirical evidence from my own research area, problem-solving.

Evidence From Problem-Solving Research

What is meant by problem-solving? In my understanding, problem-solving is the intentional generation of knowledge for action instead of simple trial-and-error behavior. From the perspective of a problem-solving approach, the connection between knowledge and action is a classical means–end relation. The question remains how one can demonstrate that subjects generate knowledge intentionally for action? My tentative answer comes from experiments in which researchers present subjects with problems by using multistep tasks of reasonable complexity (Funke, 2010).

Figure 6.4 illustrates the MicroDyn approach, which was implemented for the 2012 cycle of the OECD's worldwide Programme for International Student Assessment (PISA) (Wüstenberg, Greiff, & Funke, 2012). In the upper part is a screenshot of a small scenario, called "Handball Training." It involves three types of training—A, B, and C (input variables). The task of the problem-solver is to find out how the types of training influence the three output variables (motivation, power of throw, and exhaustion). The problem-solver can change the amount of training and will see the response on the side displaying the output variables. Giving certain amounts of input, as in this example, seems to increase the motivation level and decrease exhaustion.

The experiments that my colleagues and I have designed and conducted typically have three stages (see Fig. 6.5). First, subjects have to explore the system for about 3 min. This stage is "information retrieval" because in unguided explorations subjects generate information for the second stage, "model-building." This second stage requires reflection about the causal model behind the different entities. There are assumed connections between input and output; training A, for example, increases motivation only. The third stage is "forecasting" and requires the subjects to achieve given values on the various endogenous variables—the output variables in this example—by entering the correct values into the system. In such experiments subjects have to work on many similar tasks. This requirement allows for psychometrically sound measurement of the three abilities—information retrieval, model-building, and forecasting (for more details, see Greiff & Funke, 2009; Wüstenberg et al., 2012).

As demonstrated by the results of the studies reported in this section, a clear connection exists between the generation of knowledge and the application of that knowledge (action). This structural equation model with three latent variables shows that model-building is a major prerequisite for the two other postulated abilities, forecasting and information retrieval. The fit between this model and the data is fine and allows acceptance of the model. My colleagues and I have also constructed a measurement model that sequences the three abilities—*information retrieval, model-building,* and *forecasting.* It is simple, another characteristic that fits the data well. Our empirical results thus reveal strong connections between knowledge and action. Acting on a system requires knowledge about the system's structure if goals are to be attained successfully.

Berry and Broadbent (1984) argued that this system knowledge need not be verbalizable and explicit and that, instead, implicit knowledge might guide the action of subjects controlling a system. They even postulated a negative correlation between control performance and verbalizable knowledge. But Buchner, Funke, and Berry (1995) showed that this explanation is not fully convincing, for the only subjects who acquired knowledge about the system were those who were *not* able to accomplish the given goal immediately.

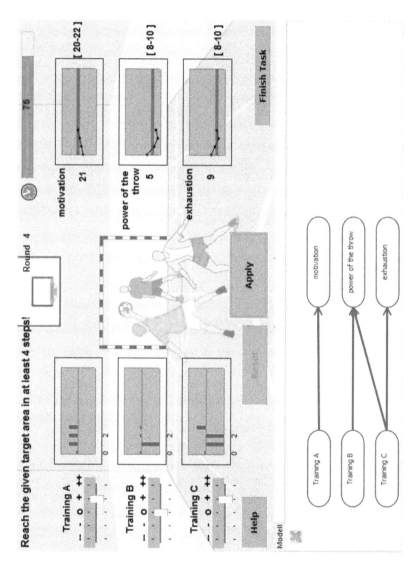

Fig. 6.4 Screenshot of the MicroDYN item "handball-training" control phase. The controllers of the input variables range from "−" (value = −2) to "++" (value = +2). The current value is displayed numerically and the target values of the output variables are displayed graphically and numerically (Reprinted from Wüstenberg et al. (2012, p. 202) with permission of Elsevier)

Fig. 6.5 Internal structure of MicroDYN processes including intercorrelations and communalities (*n* = 114). Note: Standard error in parentheses. Variances of the latent variables were set to 1.0. Residuals of the items within a task (not depicted) were not allowed to correlate. *p < .05; **p < .01 (Reprinted from Greiff, Wüstenberg, & Funke, 2012, p. 202) with permission of Sage Publications)

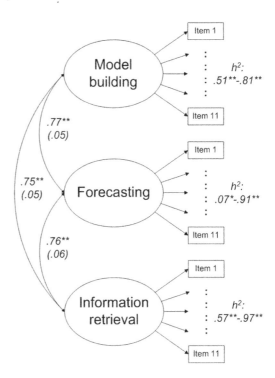

Conclusion

Knowledge and action is an interesting relationship! As I have shown, there are conscious and unconscious influences, and they are primarily logical, not causal. Kaiser, Wölfing, and Fuhrer (1999), who analyzed the relation between environmental knowledge, environmental values, and ecological behavior (intention as well as observed behavior), concluded on the basis of structural equation modeling that only 40 % of the variance in the intention that it entails was attributable to knowledge and values but that this intention explained 75 % of the variance in observed behavior. From the viewpoint of action, I have concluded that it is not possible to act *without* knowledge but that we humans can act—at least at a surface level—*against* our knowledge! For God's sake, may all persons in our small world act in concordance with their knowledge.

References

Ajzen, I. (1991). The theory of planned behavior. *Organizational Behavior and Human Decision Processes, 50*, 179–211. doi:10.1016/0749-5978(91)90020-T

Armitage, C. J., & Conner, M. (2001). Efficacy of the theory of planned behaviour: A meta-analytic review. *British Journal of Social Psychology, 40*, 471–499. doi:10.1348/014466601164939

Berry, D. C., & Broadbent, D. E. (1984). On the relationship between task performance and associated verbalizable knowledge. *Quarterly Journal of Experimental Psychology, 36A,* 209–231. doi:10.1080/14640748408402156

Buchner, A., Funke, J., & Berry, D. C. (1995). Negative correlations between control performance and verbalizable knowledge: Indicators for implicit learning in process control tasks? *Quarterly Journal of Experimental Psychology, 48A,* 166–187. doi:10.1080/14640749508401383

Dijksterhuis, A., Bos, M. W., Nordgren, L. F., & van Baaren, R. B. (2006). On making the right choice: The deliberation-without-attention effect. *Science, 311,* 1005–1007. doi:10.1126/science.1121629

Dijksterhuis, A., & Nordgren, L. F. (2006). A theory of unconscious thought. *Perspectives on Psychological Science, 1,* 95–109. doi:10.1111/j.1745-6916.2006.00007.x

Evans, J. S. B. T. (2008). Dual-processing accounts of reasoning, judgment, and social cognition. *Annual Review of Psychology, 59,* 255–278. doi:10.1146/annurev.psych.59.103006.093629

Fishbein, M., & Ajzen, I. (2010). *Predicting and changing behavior: The reasoned action approach.* New York: Psychology Press.

Frey, D., Mandl, H., & von Rosenstiel, L. (Eds.). (2006). *Knowledge and action.* Göttingen: Hogrefe & Huber.

Funke, J. (2010). Complex problem solving: A case for complex cognition? *Cognitive Processing, 11,* 133–142. doi:10.1007/s10339-009-0345-0

Greiff, S., & Funke, J. (2009). Measuring complex problem solving: The microDYN approach. In F. Scheuermann (Ed.), *The transition to computer-based assessment—Lessons learned from large-scale surveys and implications for testing* (pp. 157–163). Luxembourg: Office for Official Publications of the European Communities.

Greiff, S., Wüstenberg, S., & Funke, J. (2012). Dynamic Problem Solving: A new measurement perspective. *Applied Psychological Measurement, 36,* 189–213. doi:10.1177/01466 21612439620

Greve, W. (2001). Traps and gaps in action explanation: Theoretical problems of a psychology of human action. *Psychological Review, 108,* 435–451. doi:10.1037/0033-295X.108.2.435

Halford, G. S., Wilson, W. H., & Phillips, S. (2010). Relational knowledge: The foundation of higher cognition. *Trends in Cognitive Sciences, 14,* 497–505. doi:10.1016/j.tics.2010.08.005

Kahneman, D. (2011). *Thinking, fast and slow.* New York: Farrar, Straus and Giroux.

Kaiser, F. G., Wölfing, S., & Fuhrer, U. (1999). Environmental attitude and ecological behaviour. *Journal of Environmental Psychology, 19,* 1–19. doi:10.1006/jevp.1998.0107

Kalis, A., Mojzisch, A., Schweizer, T. S., & Kaiser, S. (2008). Weakness of will, akrasia, and the neuropsychiatry of decision-making: An interdisciplinary perspective. *Cognitive, Affective, & Behavioral Neuroscience, 8,* 402–417. doi:10.3758/CABN.8.4.402

Köhler, W. (1925). *The mentality of apes* (E. Winter, Trans.). New York: Harcourt, Brace & World.

Manning, M. (2009). The effects of subjective norms on behaviour in the theory of planned behaviour: A meta-analysis. *British Journal of Social Psychology, 48,* 649–705. doi:10.1348/014466 608X393136

Masicampo, E. J., & Baumeister, R. F. (2012). Committed but closed-minded: When making a specific plan for a goal hinders success. *Social Cognition, 30,* 37–55. doi:10.1521/soco.2012.30.1.37

Newell, A. (1981). The knowledge level. *AI Magazine, 2*(2), 1–33.

Popper, K. (1999). *All life is problem solving.* Hove: Psychology Press.

Searle, J. R. (1969). *Speech acts: An essay in the philosophy of language.* Cambridge: Cambridge University Press.

Simon, H. A. (1947). *Administrative behavior: A study of decision-making processes in administrative organizations.* New York: Macmillan.

Strube, G., & Wender, K. F. (Eds.). (1993). *The cognitive psychology of knowledge*. Amsterdam: North-Holland, Elsevier Science Publishers.

Tanner, C., Brügger, A., van Schie, S., & Lebherz, C. (2010). Actions speak louder than words: The benefits of ethical behaviors of leaders. *Zeitschrift für Psychologie, 218*, 225–233. doi:10.1027/0044-3409/a000032

Wüstenberg, S., Greiff, S., & Funke, J. (2012). Complex problem solving—More than reasoning? *Intelligence, 40*, 1–14. doi:10.1016/j.intell.2011.11.003

Chapter 7
Knowing and Not Knowing

Nico Stehr

> *The outstanding feature of a man's life in the modern world is his conviction that his life-world as a whole is neither fully understood by himself nor fully understandable to any of his fellow-men. Alfred Schütz (1946, p. 463)*
>
> *In the presence of the total reality upon which our conduct is founded, our knowledge is characterized by peculiar limitations and aberrations. Georg Simmel (1906, p. 444)*

As aptly as these introductory words by Schütz and Simmel summarize my own hypothesis on the presumed phenomenon of non-knowledge,[1] I note that it is captured still more precisely by economist Joseph Stiglitz's (2005) formulation about the "invisible hand" (p. 133) ostensibly operating in the market place. Asked why the invisible hand is invisible, Stiglitz gave a straightforward answer: because it does not exist. Similarly, I ask in this chapter why non-knowledge is difficult to grasp. And my equally analogous response is: because there is no such thing as non-knowledge.

Not wishing to capitulate already at this early point, I concentrate in this chapter on scientific discourses in which participants maintain that something like non-knowledge does exist. The knowledge/non-knowledge dichotomy appears in many discussions on the subject as a kind of performative speech act (Sartori, 1968). However, it recommends only one side of that which it designates, namely, knowledge. I cannot quite sustain my doubt about the existence of not-knowing; from time to time I have to deviate from it and maintain that non-knowledge does exist. At the same time, I draw attention to other terms that are empirically and theoretically more productive than the naked assertion that non-knowledge exists. Finally, I will point to a number of intriguing, but rarely studied topics relating to the question of the societal function or societal treatment of apparently insufficient knowledge.

---

[1] My usage of the term *non-knowledge* follows the convention in the literature that discusses the absence of knowledge. The term is synonymous with *not knowing* and has a close affinity but not identity with *ignorance*. In German the term is *Nichtwissen*.

N. Stehr (✉)
Karl Mannheim Professor for Cultural Studies, Zeppelin University,
D-88045 Friedrichshafen, Germany
e-mail: nico.stehr@t-online.de

© The Author(s) 2017
P. Meusburger et al. (eds.), *Knowledge and Action*, Knowledge and Space 9,
DOI 10.1007/978-3-319-44588-5_7

Freud and Hayek: Why Quit?

The treatment of non-knowledge by Sigmund Freud and Friedrich von Hayek is of particular interest in this context because their approach is, if I am not mistaken, quite representative for much of scientific discourse. Both Freud and Hayek recognized that there can be no such thing as a researchable subject called non-knowledge, but, unimpressed by their own conclusion, they continued to examine something that does not exist. Their grappling with this issue gives me the opportunity to ask why concerning oneself with the subject of non-knowledge is typical especially for the German-speaking scientific community. Is it a sort of eccentricity?

Freud's (1924/1963) theory of the dream as a psychic phenomenon is based on the primary conviction that the dreamer himself should "say what his dream means" (p. 100). But an evident fundamental obstacle to doing so is that the dreamer is, as a rule, firmly convinced that he does not know what his dream means. As Freud notes, "the dreamer always says he knows nothing" (p. 101). The lack of information from the dreamer confronts Freud with an apparent scientific and methodological conundrum defying sound interpretation of dreams. "Since he [the dreamer] knows nothing and we [the psychoanalyst] know nothing and a third person could know even less, there seems to be no prospect of finding out [the dream's meaning]" (p. 101).

Instead of accepting these findings as a sound conclusion and therefore forsaking any further search for the meaning of dreams, Freud (1924/1963) considered another possibility: "For I can assure you that it is quite possible, and highly probable indeed, that the dreamer *does* know what his dream means: *only he does not know that he knows it and for that reason thinks he does not know it*" (p. 101). This interpretation seems to be confusing and self-contradictory. Freud even asked himself whether a contradiction in terms might exist in his hypothesis that there are "mental things in a man which he knows without knowing that he knows them" (p. 101):

> Where, then, in what field, can it be that proof has been found that there is a knowledge of which the person concerned nevertheless knows nothing, as we are proposing to assume of dreamers? After all, this would be a strange, surprising fact and one which would alter our view of mental life and which would have no need to hide itself: a fact, incidentally, which cancels itself in its very naming and which nevertheless claims to be something real—a contradiction in terms. (pp. 102–103)

For Freud what followed from these observations was the conclusion that one ought to abandon this method of dream interpretation as lacking any substance. But Freud did not. After all, the knowledge does not really hide from the observer. One has only to search for it persistently. "It is very probable, then, that the dreamer knows about his dream; the only question is how to make it possible for him to discover his knowledge and communicate it to us" (p. 104).

Hayek, confronted with a similar dilemma, decided, just like Freud, to ignore it. In his essay entitled "The Creative Powers of a Free Civilization" (1960/1978), in which the lack of knowledge is a question of the distribution of knowledge in markets, Hayek first noted that any progress in civilization is the result of an increase of knowledge. In the real world, according to Hayek (1960/1978), it simultaneously holds true that "the individual benefits from more knowledge than he is aware of"

(p. 22), and he added that "this fundamental fact of man's unavoidable ignorance of much on which the working of civilization rests has received little attention" (p. 22) in science.[2] Human knowledge is far from being complete.

The key passage in Hayek's (1960/1978) analysis of the difference between what he called the "boundaries of ignorance" (p. 22) or man's "unavoidable ignorance" (p. 22) and "conscious knowledge" (p. 24) is: "It must be admitted, however, that our ignorance is a peculiarly difficult subject to discuss....We certainly cannot discuss something intelligently about which we know nothing" (p. 23). Hayek takes recourse to a kind of Münchhausen maneuver: "We must at least be able to state the questions even if we do not know the answers....Though we cannot see in the dark, we must be able to trace the limits of the dark areas" (p. 23). Nevertheless, as Hayek emphasizes, "If we are to understand how society works, we must attempt to define the general nature and range of our ignorance concerning it" (p. 23).

The Excess Boom in Non-knowledge

Despite of the problems that Freud and Hayek quite obviously had with the concept of non-knowledge, why has the term resonated so much in the contemporary cultural and social sciences, particularly in German-speaking countries? In the media and public discourse alike, the category of non-knowledge is increasingly becoming a prominent and trenchant monetary unit as the shady side of knowledge, but why is it gaining currency?

The boom in reflection on non-knowledge certainly has to do with the essentially controversial concept of knowledge as well as with the common understanding of the modern conditions for the production of knowledge, with the societal role often attributed to knowledge, and with the theory of modern society as a knowledge society. Is the difference between knowledge and non-knowledge an example of the typically static conceptual polarity of Old European philosophy? Or is that difference basically only the widespread cultural criticism that the individual—given the extensive and growing volume of objectified knowledge in modern societies and given the sophisticated new technical and complicated methods of accessing it— disposes over only a minute (and probably diminishing) share of all knowledge? Are the widely discussed findings on the average voter's alleged political ignorance, stupidity, and disenfranchisement and on the danger it poses to democracy a cause of the topicality of the subject of non-knowledge?

Is it, on the other hand, unrealistic to assume that the average citizen, including the well-educated contemporary citizen, has (or should have) sufficient *technical* expertise to intervene, for example, in the complex decision-making on economic questions of the goal conflict between inflation and unemployment? At root, does the concept of non-knowledge merely mean the societally necessary *distribution* of

---

[2] The German wording that Hayek chose as translations of two central concepts in his English original is of interest, and is, in my opinion, fully adequate. "The boundaries of his ignorance" and "man's unavoidable ignorance" are rendered as *Grenzen seines Unwissen* and *unvermeidlichen Unkenntnis des Menschen* (Hayek, 1960/2005, p. 31). In other words, there is no reference to non-knowledge (*Nichtwissen*).

knowledge? Does the concept of non-knowledge perhaps refer primarily to the future present, about which one is really little informed? Does the origin of the boom in observations about non-knowledge lie, under certain circumstances, in an overestimation of the societal role of allegedly unquestioned scientific knowledge and in an underestimation of the societal roles of knowledge?

In my view the societal phenomena perceived as non-knowledge can be better captured by other terms, such as "systemic ignorance" (Moore & Tumin, 1949, p. 789), that express how a lack of knowledge or information is manifested in modern societies and how people can deal with knowledge gaps. In any case, two keys to recognizing the myth of non-knowledge are the concept of knowledge itself and the complicated question of distinguishing between information and knowledge.

Knowledge as a Societal Construct

The discussion on the concept of non-knowledge often reflects a liberal intermingling of the terms *knowledge* and *information*. I assume that one should distinguish between the two, even if this differentiation is difficult to maintain in practice. A lack of information is not non-knowledge.[3] Just exactly what knowledge is and how knowledge differs from information, human capital, or other intellectual or cognitive characteristics is an essentially controversial question. Neither the concept of knowledge nor the manner of knowledge's production, distribution, use, or consequences can be taken for granted. They constitute foregone conclusions, at least for the scientific observer.

I would like to define knowledge as the capacity for societal action (the capacity to act), as the possibility to get something going. Knowledge therefore refers to process knowledge. Knowledge is a model for reality. Shannon (1948/1949), for example, explained how words and images can be converted into characters and transmitted electronically. He thus contributed to realizing the Digital Revolution.[4] According to Shannon, the expansion of knowledge represents a broadening of the horizon of possibilities. Whether the broadening of the possibilities for action also automatically represents an increase in the possibilities for disappointment (often also understood to be an increase in non-knowledge) has to be regarded as controversial. Insufficient knowledge on the part of an individual or a group accordingly means the inability of those actors to mobilize knowledge in order to put something in motion.

---

[3] For instance, Wehling (2009, p. 99) characterizes the insufficient information "Does the guest arrive at 5 or 6 p.m.?" as a case of non-knowledge. This example is at best vague information, as I show more precisely in this chapter.

[4] Dyson (2011) described Shannon's case: "In 1945 Shannon wrote a paper, A Mathematical Theory of Cryptography, which was stamped SECRET and never saw the light of day. He published in 1948 an expurgated version of the 1945 paper with the title 'A Mathematical Theory of Communication'. The 1948 version appeared in the *Bell System Technical Journal*, the house journal of the Bell Telephone Laboratories, and became an instant classic. It is the founding document for the modern science of information. After Shannon, the technology of information raced ahead, with electronic computers, digital cameras, the Internet, and the World Wide Web" (par. 13).

Knowledge exercises an active function in the societal sequence of actions only when action is not carried out in essentially stereotyped habitual (effortless) patterns or is otherwise largely regulated, that is, where there is leeway and the need for decisions and where this situation necessitates mental exertion.[5],[6] The societal practices in which decisions are possible and necessary represent the ecology of knowledge or, more exactly, of its application.

Every implementation of knowledge, not only of great scientific experiments, requires control of the circumstances of action (the initial conditions) through active agents, who, for example, want to translate laboratory successes (or a thought experiment) into practice. In other words, when "scientific knowledge is to be 'applied' in society, adaptation to the initial conditions prevailing there has to be made, or societal practice has to be remodeled according to the standards set by science" (Krohn & Weyer, 1989, p. 354).[7]

Information and Knowledge

I define information in distinction to the concept of knowledge as follows: The content of information concerns the characteristics of products or results (output, condition, supply), whereas the stuff that science consists of refers primarily to the qualities of processes or resources (input, procedures, business enterprises), which are used in processes. Knowledge is the capacity to act, whereas information does not enable one to set anything in motion.

It is just as important to emphasize from the outset that information and knowledge have, to a limited extent, common attributes. The most important basic common denominator is that neither information nor knowledge can be understood independent of societal contexts. In daily life, as in the scientific discourse, the conceptual interchangeability of information and knowledge is extensive. It is nonetheless notable that public places such as airports, shopping centers, railroad stations, and highway roadhouses commonly do not have a knowledge stand but rather

---

[5] A variant of these thoughts worth considering—one quoted by Hayek (1960/1978, p. 22)—can be found in Whitehead's (1911) *Introduction to Mathematics*: "Civilization advances by increasing the number of important operations which we can perform without thinking about them. Operations of thought are like cavalry charges in a battle—they are strictly limited in number, they require fresh horses, and must only be made at decisive moments" (p. 61).

[6] Luhmann's (1992) observations about the preconditions for the possibility of making a decision may permit a still broader application of knowledge. "One can only decide," as he very plausibly underlines, "when and to which extent it is not certain what will happen" (p. 136). On the premise that the future is highly uncertain, the lack of knowledge in decision-making processes can extend over many other societal contexts, too, and thereby also to those that are normally characterized by routines and habitual behavior.

[7] Hans Radder (1986) arrived at a similar conclusion when he pointed out that material as well as social prerequisites ultimately have to be met for long-term practical success in technical production: "The creation and maintenance of particular social conditions (for example, a bureaucratic and centralist administration in the case of nuclear energy) is necessary in order to be able to guarantee the permanent technological success of a project" (p. 675).

an information stand. The blending of these terms will probably continue to prevail in practice, in science and everyday life alike, because who can distinguish between the information society and the knowledge society?

Observing Non-knowledge, and Some of the Questions I Ask Myself in the Process

With these observations in mind, I try to ascertain what could or could not be meant when one speaks of non-knowledge. People's actions are guided by knowledge. Knowledge of others and self-knowledge are prerequisites for socialization. Hence, as Simmel (1906) noted, knowledge is an anthropological constant: "All relationships of people to each other rest, as a matter of course, upon the precondition that they know something about each other" (p. 441). There can be no societal actors without knowledge. One is just as far from being unknowing *without* knowledge as one is naked without a headscarf. A society without secrets is inconceivable. Ignoring knowledge and information is sensible, even rational. A society in which there is total transparency is impossible. Knowledge is never created out of nothing. Knowledge, or the revision of knowledge, arises out of already existing knowledge (not out of forms of non-knowledge). The existence of a *non*-knowledge society is just as questionable as that of a human society without language. Humans live in a complex society marked by a high degree of functional differentiation in which almost all of its members are non-knowledgeable about almost all knowledge. Knowledge in the broad sense meant in this chapter is not restricted to any particular social system in modern societies. Thus, knowledge is everywhere (Luhmann, 1990, p. 147).

It is useful to ignore information and knowledge. Each individual knows that his or her knowledge is limited. Yet people profit a great deal from knowledge they are not acquainted with. What indicators could be used to characterize a non-knowledge society empirically? Almost half of the American population is convinced that the Earth is younger than 10,000 years old. Is the American society for that reason a non-knowledge society?

Who or what is the standard of comparison when one speaks of the duality of non-knowledge and knowledge or of the relationship of knowledge to non-knowledge (as *known unknowns*)? Is it the individual or rather a collective? Privileging the individual is common. To put it more stringently, does the concept of non-knowledge mean a single process, a single quality (information), or the prognosis of an occurrence? How long must (or can) non-knowledge be perceptibly recognizable in order to be non-knowledge? Can cluelessness, for example, last only for seconds? Does one refer to individual forms of knowledge (or information) that the isolated individual (e.g., a scientist) or a non-knowledgeable collective does not— and cannot—have because one always proceeds selectively or is forced to filter?

Knowledge, by contrast, is a variable societal phenomenon that lies on an indivisible continuum and points to the existence of the elementary distribution of knowledge in complex societies. No clear-cut difference between knowledge and non-knowledge exists. Knowledge is a total societal phenomenon.

There is no comprehensive knowledge; nobody can know everything. Acting under conditions of uncertainty is commonplace. Knowledge of these gaps is knowledge. But knowledge of gaps does not belong in the category of non-knowledge if it is a case of negative knowledge (to the extent that one finds this designation helpful). Actually, one can often close this gap quickly because it is possible to know or find out who might know it (a task fulfilled by the role of experts, for instance). On the other hand, there are things that everyone, or almost everyone, knows or about which almost everyone is informed (e.g., the fact that almost every human has two eyes or that there is such a thing as weather or climate). There are a number of expressions that are both empirically and practically more productive than *non-knowledge* and nonetheless illuminate the horizon of problems that non-knowledge allegedly comprises. In the following section I limit myself to just one of these possibilities.

Asymmetric Information/Knowledge

In an influential article entitled "The Market for Lemons," the economist and later Nobel Laureate George Akerlof (1970) paved the way to a systematic analysis of asymmetric information by conducting an exemplary analysis of the respective information that buyers and sellers of used cars had. An asymmetric state of information is one of the fundamental characteristics of various classes of participants in the used-car market. As a rule, the owner and the driver of the used car on sale have much more detailed knowledge about the dependability and history of the vehicle's mechanical problems than the potential purchaser does. In a credit agreement the debtor is guided by certain intentions to repay the credit or not. The lender usually has no access to that information. Nor can the lender be certain that the debtor's intended investment will actually be profitable. Generally speaking, asymmetric information on the part of market participants should lead to market failure.

Buyers and sellers, lenders and debtors are often conscious of the fact that there is or can be a state of asymmetric information. It follows that the buyer or lender seek indicators that diminish the mistrust in the available information or allow that information to be considered more or less reliable. Because the transaction costs of the acquisition of relevant information might be high, the very accessibility of the information on the seller's or debtor's social reputation will likely be an important indicator for the lender or buyer.

From Akerlof's deliberations and those of other economists (e.g., Chappori & Salanie, 2000; Sharpe, 1990; Wang, 2012), I derive the following general lesson for my analysis of the antithesis of information and knowledge: Because societal knowledge is scattered asymmetrically rather than evenly distributed, one has to assume a cognitive-societal functional differentiation in all societal institutions.[8]

---

[8] In memory research an extreme example of asymmetric information has recently come under study—the few people who have "superior autobiographical memory" (Parker, Cahill, & McGaugh, 2006, p. 36), that is, the ability to recall every single day of their lives or to remember the occurrences of every single day.

In science such a cognitive division is not only perceived as a matter of course but is also generally understood to be a functional characteristic of science as an institution. Not every scientist can work on just any question. And the role of every scientist cannot be classified in relation to itself, but only in relation to that of other scientists. It is therefore natural to speak of a cognitive functional differentiation in all societal institutions. In other words, it can make sense only to speak of a range of knowledge in groups of actors in comparison to symmetrically limited knowledge in other groups of actors, and not of knowledge and non-knowledge.

On the Virtues (Advantages?) of Non-knowledge

The functional meaning of non-knowledge differs from one societal institution to the next. In an institution such as science it is a state of development of knowledge that must be overcome, a condition that acts as an incentive. In a highly stratified societal institution (e.g., a total institution) differing states of knowledge are a constitutive characteristic feature (a functional necessity) that is defended by all means. A society in which complete transparency prevails would be, as Merton (1949/1968) emphasized, "diabolical" (p. 345). In practice, a mutually transparent, complex society is unrealistic.

Moore and Tulmin (1949, p. 787), in their classical functionalist analysis of the societal functions of ignorance, therefore pointed to what in their opinion is the widespread opinion that ignorance is the natural enemy of societal stability and of the possibility for orderly societal progress and that every increase in knowledge automatically increases human welfare. A generally positive public attitude toward new knowledge, which was widespread in the years immediately following World War II, is at present losing ground to growing skepticism about new scientific and technical knowledge. It is not unusual anymore to encounter the opinion that people know too much. Explicit knowledge politics, that is, efforts to police novel knowledge, commences once new capacities for action have been discovered (Stehr, 2003).

There is a multitude of convincing references to the virtues and advantages of ignorance, a lack of knowledge, and invisibility. The discussion and formulation of the novel moral principle for an individual's "right to ignorance" by Jonas (1974, pp. 161–163) is clearly germane to a discussion of the political and ethical dilemmas generated by the dynamics with which knowledge grows. Jonas's moral principle is opposed by equally formidable ethical demands that insist on a right to know, especially at the collective level or from a macroperspective (Sen, 1981; Stiglitz, 1999). In everyday life, sentiments that support the virtue of not knowing find expression in such sayings as "What I don't know can't hurt me" and "Where ignorance is bliss, it is folly to be wise."

Opposition to excessive transparency of one's own behavior and that of other actors, as Merton (1949/1968, p. 343) also emphasized, stems from certain structural characteristics of societal groups. To these features belong, for instance, the institutionally sanctioned, but in reality also limited, negligence in complying with or enforcing existing social norms. The characteristics also include psychologically determined, variable opposition to maximum behavioral transparency (Popitz, 1968, p. 8).[9] In modern society technical and legal barriers and these conditions for opposition preclude an unlimited investigation of the behavior and convictions of individual actors—about whom one would like to know everything. The alleged goodwill or maliciousness of the thought police is irrelevant. For instance, new possibilities for avoiding technically mobilized monitoring keep turning up.

Popitz (1968), on the other hand, pointed to the *disencumbering* function that limited behavioral information has for the system of sanctions.[10] Limiting the available or requested behavioral information—a decision that is tantamount to relinquishing sanctions—is also a sort of "indeterminacy principle of social life" (p. 12). It "opens a sphere in which the system of norms and sanctions need not be taken literally without obviously giving up its claim to validity" (p. 12).

Lastly, there is a further (primarily cognitive) function of insufficient knowledge. It has repeatedly been claimed that knowledge arises from non-knowledge, or that non-knowledge can be transformed into knowledge. Just how this transformation is supposed to happen is scarcely addressed, however. The hypothesis that knowledge originates in non-knowledge as it were, in nothing (*ex nihilo*), completely overlooks the societal genealogy of knowledge, such as the close, even intimate relationship between scientific and practical knowledge. The birth of a scientific discipline is no parthenogenesis. The hypothesis of the transformation of non-knowledge into knowledge favors certain knowledge in that the origin of new knowledge is simply suppressed.

The Societal-Cognitive Functional Differentiation Between Non-knowledge and Societally Determined Knowledge Gaps

One of the self-evident realities in a modern society, with its functionally differentiated cognitive structure, is that individuals, societal groups, and societal institutions have long since given up as an illusion the wish, or the hope, for their knowledge to be self-sufficient. Limited knowledge alleviates. Knowledge is unequally

---

[9] Inasmuch as the disregard and sanctioning of existing social norms by certain incumbents of societal positions of a group is known, it must be decided whether "the basic formal structure of a group is being undermined by the observed deviations of behavior. It is in this sense that authorities can have *excessive knowledge* of what is actually going on, so that this becomes dysfunctional for the system of social control" (Merton, 1949/1968, p. 343; emphasis added).

[10] In this respect I note that the expression *non-knowledge* (*Nichtwissen*) in the title of Popitz's treatise does not appear a single time in the text. The work's title may be the work of the publishing house. The exposition shows that Popitz rightly avoided the term *non-knowledge* and more guardedly wrote of limited behavioral information and limited behavioral transparency.

distributed. As a rule, managers do not themselves have the technical knowledge of their employed laborers, engineers, or assembly-line workers.[11] Despite this lack of knowledge, managers still become managers.

Knowledge gaps or incomprehensive forms of knowledge distribution, *not* non-knowledge, are a constitutive element of functionally differentiated societies. Asymmetrical stocks of knowledge do not lead to society's collapse. A society's ability to act competently is not a function of the knowledge and information of isolated individual actors. A competent actor, for instance, as a politically active citizen, need not be comprehensively informed as an individual.

A society without this fundamental limitation, without this cognitive functional differentiation, is inconceivable. No one has to know everything. But this elementary fact, which determines the way society is, does not justify the conclusion that that non-knowledge is the opposite of knowledge. A being constantly caught up in non-knowledge cannot exist. The more collective knowledge increases,

> the smaller the share of all that knowledge becomes that any *one* mind can absorb. The more civilized we become, the more relatively ignorant must each individual be of the facts on which the working of his civilization depends. The very division of knowledge increases the necessary ignorance of the individual and most of this knowledge. (Hayek, 1960/1978, p. 26, emphasis added)

Abandoning the hope for autarkic knowledge, especially the *individual* self-sufficiency of knowledge, and giving up the conviction that knowledge is fundamentally limited (bounded) entails both costs and benefits. But the loss of autarky—inasmuch as autarky had ever existed, even in traditional societies—is never to be understood as a form of non-knowledge. Societal innovations such as the market and the scientific or political system help manage knowledge gaps (Pérez, Florin, & Whitelock, 2012).

Relevant functionally differentiated scales of knowledge differ according to facets such as their respective epoch, the type of society, the pattern of societal inequality, and the interests of the dominant worldview.[12] In modern complex societies the scale of knowledge is longer than in traditional societies. The distance to the sources of knowledge is often great. Personal acquaintance with the knowledge producer is not necessary. Only in exceptional cases does the knowledge that one does not have, but can obtain, include the knowledge that was necessary for the production, legitimation, and distribution of the knowledge acquired.

---

[11] Collinson's (1994) examination of labor resistance—based on two case studies—drew on the emphasis that Clegg (1989) placed on knowledge and information of subordinates and outlines generally "the importance of different forms of knowledge in the articulation of resistance" (p. 25). Collinson summarized his findings and pointed out that "specific forms of knowledge are a crucial resource and means through which resistance can be mobilized. Knowledge in organizations is multiple, contested and shifting. Employees may not possess detailed underpinnings of certain bureaucratic/political processes, but they often do monopolize other technical, production-related knowledges that facilitate their oppositional practices" (p. 28).

[12] The concept of the scales of knowledge has a parallel in the concept of the degrees of property rights, which are calibrated according to the labor, need, or performance, that is, the merits, of the owner (Neumann, 2009).

Outlook

The current intense debate among social scientists, with its radical polarization of knowledge and non-knowledge, is like an echo from a lost world or the wish to be able to live in this lost, but secure, world. It was a world in which knowledge was reliable, objective, ontologically well-founded, truthful, realistic, uniform, and undisputed. It was a world in which scientific knowledge was unique and the profane world of nonscientific knowledge was largely disqualified. It was a world in which more knowledge alone—such as that which enables one to act successfully in practice—was always superior to having no additional knowledge (knowledge bias). The world of unquestioned knowledge has vanished. Unclear is whether the disappearance of such knowledge is a real loss, as one is evidently supposed to believe from talk of the divide between non-knowledge and knowledge, or whether it is a form of intellectual emancipation.

The difference between knowledge and non-knowledge is an old European antithesis with an ancestry harking back to premodern cultures. The old European tradition of a dichotomy of non-knowledge and knowledge becomes apparent especially in the attribution of persons or groups to one of these two categories. Such ascription holds that the unknowing person or, more generally, the unknowing social class is not only helplessly exposed to the power of knowledge but also pitiable and backward. And inasmuch as the occurrence of non-knowledge applies to other societies and cultures, it is foreign knowledge—not one's own—that is non-knowledge. As described by Fleck (1935/1979): "Whatever is known has always seemed systematic, proven, applicable, and evident to the knower. Every alien system of knowledge has likewise seemed contradictory, unproven, inapplicable, fanciful, or mystical" (p. 22).

For that reason these traditional deliberations on the great divide between knowledge and non-knowledge come nowhere close to resolving the dilemma described by Luhmann (1991): "Is the generally held assumption that more communication, more reflection, more knowledge, more learning, more participation—that more of all of this would bring about something good or, in any sense, nothing bad—at all justified?" (p. 90, my translation). The emerging political field of knowledge politics is dedicated to this societal dilemma posed by the risks of knowledge (Stehr, 2003).

One should not insist on an absolute antithesis of knowledge and non-knowledge—there is only less or more knowledge and those who know something and those who know something else. The practical problem is always to know how much or how little one knows in a given situation. A person is not either knowledgeable or unknowing. A person has more knowledge in one context than in another: A person may know a great deal about tax regulations but hardly anything about playing golf.

Actors (including scientists) react to complex societal forms by simplifying mental constructs of these relationships. The mental constructs are, in fact, incomplete inasmuch as they do not depict reality in its full complexity. These simple models change, react to the unexpected, but are hardly non-knowledge. One of the advantages of liberal democracies is the consciousness that omniscience can be dangerous and that safeguarding privacy must remain a form of sanctioned ignorance.

Acknowledgements Robert Avila translated an early draft of this chapter from German. I am grateful to Jason Mast for his critical reading of the text. Volker Meja offered useful editorial advice. An initial version of the chapter was published as an article entitled "Knowledge and non-knowledge," in *Science, Technology and Innovation Studies, 8*, 3–13, 2012. For the purpose of this edited volume, the argument of that text has been considerably extended and enlarged.

References

Akerlof, G. A. (1970). The market for "lemons": Quality uncertainty and the market mechanism. *Quarterly Journal of Economics, 84,* 488–500. doi:10.2307/1879431

Chappori, P.-A., & Salanie, B. (2000). Testing for asymmetric information in insurance markets. *Journal of Political Economy, 108,* 56–78. doi:10.1086/262111

Clegg, S. R. (1989). *Frameworks of power.* London: Sage.

Collison, D. (1994). Strategies of resistance: Power, knowledge and subjectivity in the workplace. In J. M. Jermier, D. Knights, & W. R. Nord (Eds.), *Resistance and power in organizations* (pp. 25–68). London: Routledge.

Dyson, F. (2011). How we know. *The New York Review of Books, 58*(4). Retrieved from http://www.nybooks.com/articles/archives/2011/mar/10/how-we-know/

Fleck, L. (1979). *Genesis and development of a scientific fact* (F. Bradley & T. J. Trenn, Trans.; T. J. Trenn & R. K. Merton, Eds.; with a Foreword by T. S. Kuhn). Chicago: Chicago University Press. (Original work published 1935). Retrieved from http://www.evolocus.com/Textbooks/Fleck1979.pdf

Freud, S. (1963). *Introductory lectures on psycho-analysis* (Vol. 15, Parts I and II, 1915–1916). Translated from the German under the General Editorship of James Strachey in collaboration with Anna Freud. Assisted by Alix Strachey and Alan Tyson. London: Hogarth Press. (Original work published 1924).

Hayek, F. A. von. (1978). *The constitution of liberty* (reprint ed.). Chicago: University of Chicago Press. (Original work published 1960) http://www.libertarianismo.org/livros/tcolfh.pdf

Hayek, F. A. von. (2005). Die schöpferischen Kräfte einer freien Zivilisation [The creative powers of a free civilisation]. In F. A. von Hayek, *Gesammelte Schriften in deutscher Sprache, Abteilung B: Vol. 3. Die Verfassung der Freiheit* (4th ed., pp. 31–50). Tübingen: Mohr Siebeck. (Original work published 1960)

Jonas, H. (1974). *Philosophical essays: From ancient creed to technological man.* Englewood Cliffs: Prentice Hall.

Krohn, W., & Weyer, J. (1989). Gesellschaft als Labor: Die Erzeugung sozialer Risiken durch experimentelle Forschung [Society as a laboratory: The creation of social risks through experimental research]. *Soziale Welt, 40,* 349–373. Retrieved from http://www.jstor.org/stable/40877604

Luhmann, N. (1990). *Die Wissenschaft der Gesellschaft* [The science of society]. Frankfurt am Main: Suhrkamp.

Luhmann, N. (1991). Verständigung über Risiken und Gefahren [Understanding on risks and hazards]. *Die politische Meinung, 36,* 86–95.

Luhmann, N. (1992). *Beobachtungen der Moderne* [Observations on modernity]. Opladen: Westdeutscher Verlag.

Merton, R. K. (1968). *Social theory and social structure* (revised and enlarged edition). New York: The Free Press. (Original work published 1949)

Moore, W., & Tumin, M. M. (1949). Social functions of ignorance. *American Sociological Review, 14,* 787–796. Retrieved from http://www.jstor.org/stable/2086681

Neumann, M. (2009). Degrees of property. *Think, 8*(22), 75–91. doi:10.1017/S1477175609000104

Parker, E. S., Cahill, L., & McGaugh, J. L. (2006). A case of unusual autobiographical remembering. *Neurocase: The Neural Basis of Cognition, 12,* 35–49. doi:10.1080/13554790500473680

Pérez, L., Florin, J., & Whitelock, J. (2012). Dancing with elephants: The challenge of managing asymmetric technology alliances. *Journal of High Technology Management, 23,* 142–154. doi:10.1016/j.hitech.2012.06.007

Popitz, H. (1968). *Über die Präventivwirkung des Nichtwissens: Dunkelziffer, Norm und Strafe* [On the preventive effect of not knowing: Number of unreported cases, norm, and punishment]. Tübingen: J. C. B. Mohr (Paul Siebeck)

Radder, H. (1986). Experiment, technology and the intrinsic connection between knowledge and power. *Social Studies of Science, 16,* 663–683. doi:10.1177/030631286016004005

Sartori, G. (1968). Democracy. In D. L. Sills (Ed.), *International encyclopedia of the social sciences: Vol. 4.* (pp. 112–121). New York: Macmillan and Free Press.

Schütz, A. (1946). The well-informed citizen: An essay on the social distribution of knowledge. *Social Research, 13,* 463–478. Retrieved from http://www.jstor.org/stable/40958880

Sen, A. (1981). Ingredients of famine analysis: Availability and entitlements. *Quarterly Journal of Economics, 96,* 433–464. doi:10.2307/1882681

Shannon, C. (1949). Communication theory of secrecy systems. *Bell System Technical Journal, 28,* 656–715. Retrieved from http://www3.alcatel-lucent.com/bstj/vol28-1949/articles/bstj28-4-656.pdf (Original work published 1948)

Sharpe, S. A. (1990). Asymmetric information, bank lending and implicit contracts: A stylized model of customer relations. *The Journal of Finance, 45,* 1069–1087. doi:10.1111/j.1540-6261.1990.tb02427.x

Simmel, G. (1906). The sociology of secrecy and of secret societies (A. W. Small, Trans). *American Journal of Sociology, 11,* 441–498. Retrieved from http://www.jstor.org/stable/2762562

Stehr, N. (2003). *Wissenspolitik* [Knowledge politics]. Frankfurt am Main: Suhrkamp.

Stiglitz, J. E. (1999). On liberty, the right to know, and public discourse: The role of transparency in public life. *Oxford Amnesty Lecture,* Oxford, January 27, 1999. Retrieved October 27, 2013, from http://www1.gsb.columbia.edu/mygsb/faculty/research/pubfiles/1475/Stiglitz_OnLiberty.pdf

Stiglitz, J. E. (2005). The ethical economist. *Foreign Affairs, 84,* 128–134. Retrieved from http://www.foreignaffairs.com/articles/61208/joseph-e-stiglitz/the-ethical-economist

Wang, X. (2012). When workers do not know: The behavioral effects of minimum wage laws revisited. *Journal of Economic Psychology, 33,* 951–962. doi:10.1016/j.joep.2012.05.004

Wehling, P. (2009). Nichtwissen: Bestimmungen, Abgrenzungen, Bewertungen [Not knowing: Regulations, delimitations, evaluations]. *EWE, 20,* 95–106.

Whitehead, A. N. (1911). *Introduction to mathematics.* London: Williams & Norgate. http://www.gutenberg.org/files/41568/41568-pdf.pdf

Chapter 8
How Representations of Knowledge Shape Actions

Ralph Hertwig and Renato Frey

In 2009 the world found itself in the midst of the worst recession since the Great Depression. Events thought of as extremely unlikely, such as the burst of the U.S. housing boom, the meltdown of the financial system, and the bankruptcy of colossal companies, happened in breathtakingly fast succession. Why was the world so badly prepared for these improbabilities? One explanation is that the crisis of the financial industry preceding the economic recession occurred because the industry's supposedly optimal risk-management models failed to reckon with "black swans" (Taleb, 2007)—unexpected and unpredictable rare events that carry an enormous impact. Of course, modern risk-management paradigms were not alone in failing to take the black-swan event into account—so did individual players, such as many homeowners who could no longer afford their mortgages. Can psychological theories and findings account for such blind spots?

At first glance, the answer is no. Influential studies in behavioral decision research consistently suggest the opposite propensity: People are oversensitive to rare events. For example, they overestimate the chance of getting food poisoning or of contracting lung cancer from smoking (Lichtenstein, Slovic, Fischhoff, Layman, & Combs, 1978; Viscusi, 2002). Moreover, people are depicted as remembering past experiences by how they felt at their peak (rare moment) and end (Redelmeier & Kahneman, 1996). Such oversensitivity is not only empirically observed but also theoretically suggested. According to the most influential descriptive theory of risky choice, people overweight low-probability events (Tversky & Kahneman, 1992). In fact, cumulative prospect theory explains the puzzling co-occurrence of two

R. Hertwig (✉)
Center of Adaptive Rationality (ARC), Max Planck Institute for Human
Development, Berlin, Germany
e-mail: Hertwig@mpib-berlin.mpg.de

R. Frey
Center for Cognitive and Decision Sciences (CDS), Department of Psychology,
University of Basel, Basel, Switzerland

© The Author(s) 2017   127
P. Meusburger et al. (eds.), *Knowledge and Action*, Knowledge and Space 9,
DOI 10.1007/978-3-319-44588-5_8

behaviors—that the same people who purchase lottery tickets promising tiny chances of winning (thus being risk-seeking) also take out insurance against tiny chances of damage (thus being risk averse; Friedman & Savage, 1948)—on the assumption that small probabilities receive too much weight.

In light of people's ostensible oversensitivity to rare events, why did so many people, financial experts and laypeople alike, behave as though they were not cognizant of the rare events that triggered what some observers called a bona-fide depression (Posner, 2009)? Analyses have highlighted a variety of enabling factors, ranging from purportedly rational bankers who acted on strong incentives to take maximum risks in their lending (Posner, 2009) to humans' "animal spirits" (Akerlof & Shiller, 2009). However, there is another possibly enabling condition. The customary portrayal of humans as being oversensitive to rare events obscures the evidence that people, when recruiting their experience sampled across time to make risky decisions, tend to accord rare events (such as the burst of housing bubbles) less weight than they deserve according to their objective probabilities.

The Description–Experience Gap

Just as biologists use the *Drosophila* as one model organism, behavioral-decision researchers have used choice between monetary gambles as a model for risky choice, assuming that many real-world options have the same properties as gambles, namely, *n* outcomes and associated probabilities (Lopes, 1983). Moreover, many researchers have grown accustomed to presenting their respondents with one particular genus of the fruit fly: gambles in which all outcomes and their probabilities are stated and respondents make a single choice. Figure 8.1 illustrates typical description-based decision-making problems.

In everyday life, however, people can rarely peruse such descriptions of probability distributions—although there are a few exceptions, such as media weather forecasts stating probabilities of precipitation (Gigerenzer, Hertwig, Van Den Broek, Fasolo, & Katsikopoulos, 2005). When people decide whether to take out a loan or contemplate the success of a first date, there are no risk tables to consult. Instead, people need to rely on whatever experience they have had with these options, making decisions based on experience rather than on description (Hertwig, Barron, Weber, & Erev, 2004). Both kinds of decision can be understood as opposite poles on a continuum of uncertainty about what one is choosing between. In Knight's (1921) terminology, decisions from descriptions involve *a priori probabilities*, whereas decisions from experience involve *statistical probabilities*, which one must assess "if at all, by tabulating the results of experience" (p. 215), so they invariably fall short of the standards of accuracy set by a priori probabilities (Hau, Pleskac, & Hertwig, 2010).

In the 1950s and early 1960s, before modern behavioral-decision research, scientists who studied decision-making investigated decisions from experience. They examined, for example, whether and how people learn the probability structure of an outcome distribution through trial-by-trial feedback (for a review see Luce &

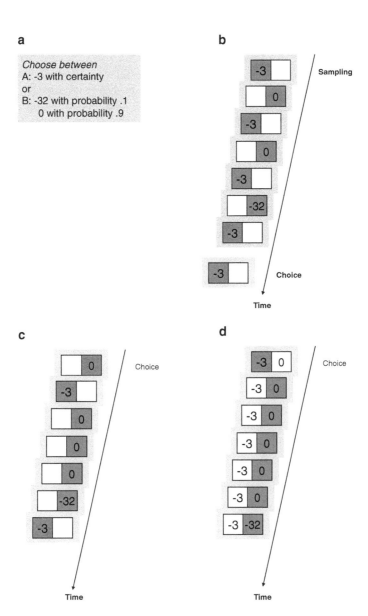

Fig. 8.1 How to study decisions from descriptions and experience. The choice task in decisions from description typically consists of two monetary gambles with explicitly stated outcomes and their probabilities (**a**). In decisions from experience, three paradigms have been employed. The *sampling paradigm* (**b**) consists of an initial sampling stage (here represented by seven fictitious draws) in which a person explores two payoff distributions without costs by clicking on one of the two buttons on the computer screen, followed by an outcome drawn from the respective distribution. The buttons chosen by a participant are marked in *red*. After terminating sampling, the person sees a choice screen (*green screen*) and is asked to select the button to draw once for real. The *partial-feedback paradigm* (**c**) combines sampling and choice, thus each draw represents both an act of exploration and an act of exploitation. The respondent receives feedback regarding the obtained payoff after each draw from the chosen button (*red box*). The *full-feedback paradigm* (**d**) is identical to the partial-feedback paradigm, except that it also provides feedback concerning the forgone payoff (i.e., the payoff that the person would have received had she chosen the other option; *white box*) (Reprinted from Hertwig and Erev (2009, p. 518) with permission from Elsevier)

Suppes, 1965). The impracticality of the research designs—purportedly hundreds of trials are needed before behavior stabilizes—may have been the reason that modern behavioral-decision research turned away from the transients of learning (for an exception see, for example, Busemeyer, 1985). Moreover, with the increasing importance of expected utility theory, the study of anomalies became pertinent, which required the conveying of perfect information about the probabilities of relevant events (Fig. 8.1a). Interest in issues of learning and experience-based decisions, however, remained alive in other fields, such as operation research (see literature on multiarmed bandit problems; Sutton & Barto, 1998).

Modern decision-making researchers' interest in decisions from experience has been rekindled by the recent observation of systematic and robust differences between them and decisions from description. Research on decisions from experience has come with a simple experimental tool, a "computerized money machine." Respondents see two buttons on a computer screen, each one representing an initially unknown payoff distribution. Clicking a button results in a random draw from the respective distribution. Three variations of this experimental tool have been employed. In the *sampling paradigm* (Fig. 8.1b), people first sample as many outcomes as they wish and only then decide from which distribution to make a single draw for real (Hertwig et al., 2004; Weber, Shafir, & Blais, 2004). In the *full-feedback paradigm* (Fig. 8.1d), there is a limited number of draws (typically 100), each of which contributes to people's earnings, and they receive draw-by-draw feedback on the obtained and the forgone payoffs (i.e., payoff received had the other option been selected; Yechiam & Busemeyer, 2006). The *partial-feedback paradigm* (Fig. 8.1c) is identical to the full-feedback paradigm, except that people learn about the obtained payoffs only (Barron & Erev, 2003; Erev & Barron, 2005). Unlike the first two paradigms, the partial-feedback paradigm presents respondents with an exploitation–exploration trade-off. Exploitation and exploration represent two alternative goals associated with every choice, namely, to obtain a desired outcome (exploitation) or to gather new information about other, perhaps better, actions (exploration; Cohen, McClure, & Yu, 2007).

Across all three experiential paradigms, a robust and systematic description–experience gap has emerged in numerous studies. Figure 8.2 illustrates this gap in six decision-making problems (Erev et al., 2010). Each one offers a choice between a risky option with two outcomes and a safe option. In the risky options, either the desirable outcome or the less desirable outcome occurs with low probability (.1 or less). In all three experiential paradigms, respondents tend to select the risky option when the desirable outcome occurs with high probability, and they select the safe option when the desirable outcome occurs with low probability. This tendency is reversed in decisions from description. The general pattern can be summarized as follows: In decisions from experience, people behave as if the rare events have less impact than they deserve according to their objective probabilities, whereas in decisions from description people behave as if the rare events have more impact than they deserve (consistent with cumulative prospect theory).

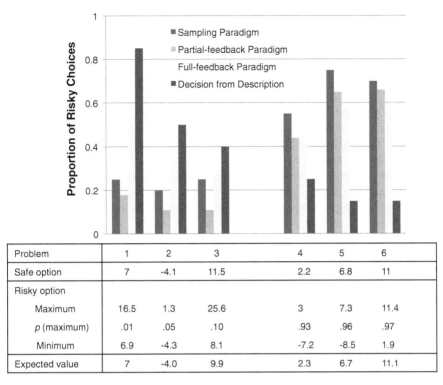

Problem	1	2	3	4	5	6
Safe option	7	-4.1	11.5	2.2	6.8	11
Risky option						
Maximum	16.5	1.3	25.6	3	7.3	11.4
p (maximum)	.01	.05	.10	.93	.96	.97
Minimum	6.9	-4.3	8.1	-7.2	-8.5	1.9
Expected value	7	-4.0	9.9	2.3	6.7	11.1

Fig. 8.2 Proportion of choices of the risky option as a function of the probability of the more desirable outcome in 6 of 120 problems studied in Erev et al. (2010). Each problem presents a choice between a risky option and a safe option. The decision-making problems and the expected values (EV) of the risky options are displayed below the plot. Each problem was studied using the four paradigms listed in Fig. 8.1 (Erev et al., 2010; the data from the full-feedback paradigm are unpublished). Participants (20 per paradigm) were paid (in shekels) for one of their choices, randomly selected. The partial- and full-feedback paradigms involved 100 choices per problem, and the reported proportions are the means over these choices and participants (Reprinted from Hertwig and Erev (2009, p. 519) with permission from Elsevier)

What Causes the Description–Experience Gap?

Several causes may be contributing to the description–experience gap.

Small Samples

Two classes of factors have been identified as shaping the search process in the sampling paradigm: properties of the decision-making problems (e.g., the magnitude of the incentives, see Hau, Pleskac, Kiefer, & Hertwig, 2008; and whether the outcomes are gains or losses, see Lejarraga, Hertwig, & Gonzalez, 2012) and individual characteristics, such as people's emotional state (Frey, Hertwig, & Rieskamp, 2014) or age (Frey et al. 2015). However, across numerous studies (reviewed in Hau et al., 2010), respondents typically proved restrained in their information search, with a median number of samples per choice problem typically ranging between 11 and 19. These results suggest that reliance on small samples is one factor that contributes to the attenuated impact of rare events (Hertwig et al., 2004). For small samples the chances are that a person does not even experience the rare events. More generally, one is more likely to undersample than oversample the rare event, for the binomial distribution of the number of times a particular outcome will be observed in n independent trials is markedly skewed when p is small (i.e., the event is rare) and n is small (i.e., few outcomes are sampled). Interestingly, reliance on small samples has also been discussed as a potential explanation for bumblebees' underweighting of rare events: Studying foraging decisions by bees in a spatial arrangement of flowers that promise with varying probabilities different amounts of nectar, Real (1991) concluded that "bumblebees underperceive rare events and overperceive common events" (p. 985). He explained this distortion in bees' probability perception as a consequence of their sampling behavior—"bees frame their decisions on the basis of only a few visits" (Real, 1992, p. 133)—and suggested that such reliance on small samples can be adaptive.

> Short-term optimization may be adaptive when there is a high degree of spatial autocorrelation in the distribution of floral rewards. In most field situations, there is intense local competition among pollinators for floral resources. When "hot" and "cold" spots in fields of flowers are created through pollinator activity, then such activity will generate a high degree of spatial autocorrelation in nectar rewards. If information about individual flowers is pooled, then the spatial structure of reward distributions will be lost, and foraging over the entire field will be less efficient. In spatially autocorrelated environments ("rugged landscapes"), averaging obscures the true nature of the environment. (p. 135)

Could there be any advantage to frugal sampling in experience-based decisions by humans? Hertwig and Pleskac (2008, 2010) proposed one possible advantage that rests on the notion of amplification. Unlike Real (1992), however, they argued that amplification proffers a cognitive rather than an evolutionary benefit. Through mathematical analysis and computer simulation, Hertwig and Pleskac (2010) showed that small samples amplify the difference between the options' average rewards. That is, drawing small samples from payoff distributions results in experienced differences of sample means that are larger than the objective difference. Such amplified absolute differences simplify the choice between gambles and thereby explain the frugal sampling behavior observed in investigations of decisions from experience—a conjecture for which Hertwig and Pleskac (2010) found empirical evidence.

The explanation of the description–experience gap in terms of small samples has prompted a critical response (Fox & Hadar, 2006) and has led to an ongoing debate. What appears to be underweighting of rare events in decisions from experience could be consistent with overweighting of low probabilities as assumed in cumulative prospect theory. When the probability experienced in a sample is smaller than the event's objective probability, people may still overweight this sample probability.

Despite this overweighting, the erroneous impression of underweighting would emerge if the *overweighting* did not fully compensate for the *underestimation* that results from the skew in small samples. In this view the description–experience gap is statistical (sampling error) rather than psychological in nature.

Several approaches have been taken to examine whether the gap observed in the sampling paradigm can indeed be reduced to sampling error. If sampling error was the sole culprit, then reducing the error by extending the sample should attenuate and eventually eliminate the gap. Increasing sample sizes substantially (up to 50 and 100 draws per choice problem) reduced but did not eliminate the gap (Hau et al., 2008, 2010). If sampling error caused the gap, then removing the error by aligning the sample's experienced probabilities to the objective probabilities should eliminate it. It did not (Ungemach, Chater, & Stewart, 2009). If sampling error was the sole root of the gap, then presenting respondents in the description condition the same information that others experienced (*yoking*) should eliminate the gap. In one study it did (Rakow, Demes, & Newell, 2008); in another it did for small samples but not for large ones (Hau et al., 2010; see these authors' discussion of trivial choices as one possible explanation for the mixed results obtained). The gap persisted even when people were presented both descriptions and experience rather than descriptions only (Jessup, Bishara, & Busemeyer, 2008).

In summary, the reality of the description–experience gap across the three experiential paradigms is unchallenged—its cause, however, is disputed. Some researchers have argued that the gap in the sampling paradigm is statistical in nature (Fox & Hadar, 2006; Hadar & Fox, 2009; Rakow et al., 2008); others have proposed that the sampling error is not the sole cause (Hau et al., 2008, 2010; Hertwig et al., 2004; Ungemach et al., 2009). Regardless of how this debate will advance, it is informative to go beyond the sampling paradigm. Reliance on small samples, for example, cannot be the reason behind the description–experience gap in the full-feedback paradigm (Fig. 8.1d) paradigm, in which the impact of rare events is attenuated even after a hundred trials with perfect feedback. Beyond sampling error, what psychological factors may be in play?

Recency

A psychological factor that may contribute to the description–experience gap is *recency* (Hertwig et al., 2004). Ubiquitously observed in memory, belief updating, and judgments (Hogarth & Einhorn, 1992), recency refers to the phenomenon that observations made late in a sequence receive more weight than they deserve (i.e., more than $1/n$). Recency is closely related to reliance on small samples: The small sample of recent events can reintroduce the aforementioned skew into large samples of experience. Although the original finding was that people give more weight to recent than to previous outcomes in the flow of their experience (Hertwig et al., 2004), little or no impact of recency was observed in later studies (Hau et al., 2010; Rakow et al., 2008; Ungemach et al., 2009).

Estimation Error

In theory, the description–experience gap could also be the result of a systematic estimation error (Fox & Hadar, 2006), with people systematically underestimating the frequencies of the rare event experienced in the sample. Studies of frequency and probability assessments, however, commonly report overestimation of rare events (Hertwig, Pachur, & Kurzenhäuser, 2005; Lichtenstein et al., 1978). Moreover, studies recording people's estimates of rare events in the sampling paradigm found them to be well calibrated or a little too high relative to the experienced frequency (Hau et al., 2008; Ungemach et al., 2009). That is, people do not systematically estimate rare things to be even rarer than they statistically are.

Contingent Sampling

Still another factor that could underlie the description–experience gap, especially in the feedback paradigm, is the notion that people inform their decisions by recruiting recent and past experiences garnered in similar situations (for related notions see Gilboa & Schmeidler, 1995; Gonzalez, Lerch, & Lebiere, 2003). Such contingent sampling is likely to be ubiquitous in the wild (Klein, 1999). For example, when firefighters need to predict the behavior of a fire, they appear to retrieve from memory similar instances from the past. Contingent sampling implies recency and reliance on small sampling to the extent that similarity decreases with time. Furthermore, in dynamic environments (e.g., the restless bandit problem; Whittle, 1988), reliance on similar experiences is an efficient heuristic (Biele, Erev, & Ert, 2009). Below, we turn to the manner in which the process of contingent sampling can be modeled.

Spatial Search Policies

Like any organism, humans can sample information in at least two very different ways from payoff distributions (e.g., flowers, ponds, other people, and gambles). Figure 8.3 depicts two paradigmatic sequential-sampling strategies based on two assumed options. In piecewise sampling, the searcher oscillates between options, each time drawing, in the most extreme case, the smallest possible sample. In comprehensive sampling, by contrast, the searcher samples extensively from one option and then turns to the other option to explore it thoroughly.

Taking these two sampling strategies as a starting point, Hills and Hertwig (2010) suggested that this spatial way of sampling foreshadows how people make their final decision. Specifically, they proposed that a person who samples piecewise will tend to make decisions as would a judge who scores each round of a boxing match: She determines which option yields the better reward in each round of sampling and ultimately picks the one that wins the most rounds. By contrast, a person using a comprehensive-sampling strategy will tend to gauge the average reward for each

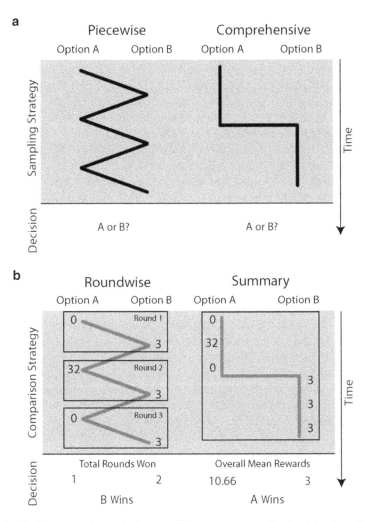

Fig. 8.3 (**a**) Representations of the sampling patterns associated with piecewise- and comprehensive-sampling strategies. Piecewise strategies repeatedly alternate back and forth between options. Comprehensive-sampling strategies take one large sample from each option. Following the sample phase, the participants make a decision about which option they prefer. (**b**) Representations of the comparison strategies associated with roundwise and summary strategies for a set of hypothetical outcomes. Roundwise strategies compare outcomes over repeated rounds and choose options that win the most rounds. Summary strategies compare final values (here, the overall expected value) and choose options with the better final value (Reprinted from Hills and Hertwig (2010, p. 1788) with permission from Associations for Psychological Science)

option and then choose the one promising the larger reward harvest. The reason for this dependency of the decision strategies on search is that the piecewise- and comprehensive-sampling strategy foster comparisons across different scales of information: rounds vs. summaries, respectively. Determining a winner who is ahead in most rounds and determining the one yielding the largest expected reward can lead to different choices even when both decisions-makers experience the same information. The reason is that the person using the former decision strategy weighs each round equally, ignores the magnitude of wins and losses, and thus acts as if it underweights rare, but consequential, outcomes. That link between sampling strategy and decision strategy is exactly what Hills and Hertwig (2010) found. Individuals who frequently oscillated between options were more likely to choose the round-wise winning options and to make choices as if they underweighted rare events than were individuals who switched options rarely.

In summary, modern behavioral decision research has been strongly focused on people's responses to descriptions of events. In recent years three experiential paradigms have been used to study how experience affects risky choice. A consistent picture has emerged. When rare events are involved, description-based and experience-based decisions can drastically diverge. We now turn to different ways of modeling decisions from experience.

Cognitive Strategies in Decisions from Experience

In attempting to capture the information search (learning) and decision-making processes in decisions from experience, researchers have proposed models that can be grouped into three classes. The first class—neo-Bernoullian models—rests on the premise that respondents form a mental representation of the relative frequency (probability) with which events occur in the process of sampling outcomes. Combined with outcome information, these probabilities then enter the evaluation of the two gambles' desirability. But do decisions from experience inevitably give rise to an explicit representation of probabilities? The second and the third class of models—associative learning models and heuristics—reflect the assumption that decision-makers can and will do without probabilities. In this section we discuss the three classes of models.

Neo-Bernoullian Models

Expected utility theory postulates that one can, or should, model human choice by assuming that people behave as if they have multiplied some function of probability and value and then have maximized it. Applied to decisions from experience, expected utility theory and related models require explicit representation of probabilities. An example is the "two-stage model" (Tversky & Fox, 1995, p. 279) of decision under uncertainty, in which it is assumed that decision-makers first estimate the probability p of an uncertain event A and then make a choice. The psychological impact of the event A with its associated (estimated) probability p is then measured in terms of cumulative prospect theory's probability weighting function π (Fox & Tversky, 1998).

Associative Learning Models

In this class of theories, human choice is conceptualized as a learning process (Busemeyer & Myung, 1992; Bush & Mosteller, 1955). Learning consists in changing the propensity to select a gamble according to the experienced outcomes. Good experiences boost the propensity of choosing the gamble associated with them, and bad experiences diminish it (e.g., Barron & Erev, 2003; Denrell, 2007; Erev & Barron, 2005; March, 1996). Two associative-learning models that have been proposed to capture decisions from experience are the value-updating model (Hertwig, Barron, Weber, & Erev,2006) and the instance-based learning (IBL) model (Gonzalez & Dutt, 2011).

The value-updating model stipulates that learners update their estimates of the value of the gamble after each new draw from it. Specifically, the model computes the weighted average of the previously estimated value and the value of the most recently experienced outcome. The model includes two parameters, namely, the number of draws and a recency parameter. The former parameter is determined empirically; the second is adjustable (i.e., fitted to the data). Importantly, the model does not necessitate representation of probabilities. Furthermore, the best fitting parameter in a model competition indeed suggested a substantial recency effect (Hau et al., 2008).

The IBL model also stipulates a learning process but goes beyond the relatively simple assumptions of the value-updating model: It is assumed that a choice (given that it is not automatically reproduced) represents the selection of the option with the higher utility (blended value). An option's blended value is a function of its associated outcomes and the probability of retrieving corresponding instances from memory (contingent sampling). Memory retrieval depends on memory activation, which, in turn, is a function of the recency and frequency of the experience. Activation is specified by the mechanism originally proposed in Adaptive Control of Thought—Rational (ACT-R; Anderson & Lebiere, 1998), a cognitive architecture used by cognitive psychologists to model problem-solving, learning, and memory. The IBL model is particularly attractive because it "predicts not only the final consequential choice but also the sequence of sampling selection" (Gonzalez & Dutt, 2011, p. 529; but see Hills & Hertwig, 2012) and because it offers a single learning mechanism (leading up to an instance's activation) across all experiential designs (Fig. 8.1b–d). Indeed, in a quantitative comparison of models, Gonzalez and Dutt (2011) were able to show that the IBL model predicts final experience-based decisions as well as or better than any other proposed model (including, for instance, the value-updating model and cumulative prospect theory).

Heuristics

Another class of models designed to describe both the process and outcome of choice are cognitive choice heuristics (see Brandstätter, Gigerenzer, & Hertwig,2006). Heuristics can be separated into two classes: those that use solely outcome information and exclude probabilities (outcome heuristics), and those that use at least rudimentary probability information (dual heuristics). Outcome heuristics such as maximax and minimax (Luce & Raïffa, 1957; Savage, 1954) were originally proposed as models for decision-making under ignorance in which people have no information whatsoever about probabilities.

Another cognitive heuristic that focuses on outcomes is the natural-mean heuristic (Hertwig & Pleskac, 2008). It works in two steps:

Step 1. Calculate the natural mean of outcomes for both gambles by summing, separately for each gamble, all n-experienced outcomes and then dividing by n.

Step 2. Choose the gamble with the larger natural mean (i.e., the gamble that had the best average outcome in the sampling phase).

The natural-mean heuristic was originally proposed in the context of n-armed bandit problems (Sutton & Barto, 1998) as a simple method for estimating the values of actions (e.g., the play of one of a slot machine's levers) and for using the estimates to select between actions: "The true value of an action is the mean reward received when the action is selected. One natural way to estimate this is by averaging the rewards actually received when the action was selected" (p. 27). The natural-mean heuristic totes up all experienced rewards (or losses) per gamble and then divides this sum by the sample size per gamble to arrive at the *natural mean*. One interpretation of the natural-mean heuristic is that in decisions from experience it is a simple and psychologically plausible instantiation of the expected-value calculus—particularly in continuous outcome distributions. Indeed, the natural-mean heuristic was not inferior to the more complex models described above and predicted a comparable number of correct predictions in decisions from experience (Hau et al., 2008).

In light of these models that do not require explicit representations of probabilities, we return to the question of what the possible codeterminants of the gap between description and experience are. The two associative-learning models and the natural-mean heuristic are format dependent. That is, they cannot capture decisions from description, for the input into these models consists of a sequence of outcomes that get integrated into one summary measure. They have no conceptual parameters with which to take probability information into account, and, in fact, probabilities are not directly apparent in decisions from experience. In decisions based on description, however, probabilities are made explicit to decisions-makers. Differences in description- and experience-based choices could therefore arise partly because different formats of mathematically equivalent information trigger different cognitive strategies (see Gigerenzer & Hoffrage, 1995, for a related argument in Bayesian reasoning).

Decisions from Experience: A Key to Otherwise Puzzling Human Behavior

The most famous eruption of Mount Vesuvius occurred in 79 AD, destroying many neighboring towns, among them Pompeii, the luxurious resort of wealthy Romans and now the most renowned still life of volcanic doom. This eruption, however, was not the most devastating one. As recent volcanological and archaeoanthropological studies have revealed, an earlier, Bronze Age eruption (around 3780 BC) covered the surrounding area as far as 25 km away, burying land and villages, causing a global climatic disturbance and the abandonment of the entire area for centuries. The loss of life and property was less extensive in the Bronze Age cataclysm than in the eruption of AD 79, but researchers recently discovered evidence of a mass exodus: a huge number of human and animal footprints pressed into the ash bed and all leading away from the volcano (Mastrolorenzo, Petrone, Pappalardo, & Sheridan,2006).

At present, at least three million people live within the area that was destroyed by the Bronze Age eruption. In fact, the periphery of Mount Vesuvius, which includes a significant chunk of the Naples metropolitan area, is among the most populated of any active volcano (Bruni, 2003). According to simulations by Mastrolorenzo et al. (2006), an eruption comparable in magnitude to the Bronze Age eruption would cause total devastation and mortality within a radius of at least 12 km (7½ miles). In addition, great quantities of fine ash in more distant zones might cause severe respiratory-tract injuries and fatalities due to acute asphyxia. Although it is impossible to predict the exact probability of such a catastrophe happening, volcanologists such as Michael Sheridan have argued that roughly 2000 years have passed since Pompeii's destruction and that "with each year, the statistical probability increases that there will be another violent eruption" of Vesuvius (Wilford, 2006). In light of these dire forecasts, one might expect that local residents would be keen to move away from the danger zone. On the contrary, relocating residents has proven extremely difficult, despite considerable incentives offered by the regional authorities. "In the shadow of Vesuvius, those residents have cultivated a remarkable optimism, a transcendent fatalism and a form of denial as deep as the earth's molten core" (Bruni, 2003, par. 12).

How can one explain the willingness of residents to defy fate? Perhaps it has become clear by now why the distinction between description-based and experience-based decisions may be key to understanding this and other puzzling risk-taking behavior. Personal experience tells residents in the vicinity of Mount Vesuvius that violent eruptions are extremely rare; in fact, in most people's lifetime, they have been nonexistent. Unless catastrophes have occurred recently, the relative indifference with which citizens and politicians often consider rare, but high-consequence, events like bursting levies, catastrophic earthquakes, and eruptions of volcanoes may be owed to the experience of their rarity (Weber, 2012). Just as residents in the vicinity of Mount Vesuvius have ignored incentives to relocate, people living in flood plains who make decisions about insurance based on their personal experience with floods—a rare event—have tended to turn down even federally subsidized flood insurance (Kunreuther, 1984).

At the same time, experiencing a rare, but highly consequential, event in reality can also have a lasting psychological impact. This possibility brings the discussion full circle. Generations growing up in a period of low stock returns appear to take an unusually cautious approach to investing, even decades later. In other words, young people who experienced the dramatic economic slump of 2008–2009 may enter the stock and housing market much more cautiously than their parents did.

Conclusion

Modern behavioral decision research has commonly focused on decisions from description. The observations stemming from this research suggest that humans overestimate and overweight rare events. Recent research on risky choice that takes into account the role of experience has found that people behave as if rare events are accorded less weight than they deserve relative to their objective probabilities. These observations are not contradictory; they describe how the mind functions in two different informational environments. In other words, research on description-based behavior and research on experience-based behavior should not be played against each other—their contrast is enlightening. However, to improve the understanding of how people make decisions with incomplete and uncertain information "in the wild" and how people respond to events that are rare but highly consequential, it is necessary to study the psychology and rationality of people's decisions from experience.

Acknowledgments This text is based largely on Hertwig and Erev (2009) and Hertwig (2012). We thank Elsevier, Sage, and Springer for granting the permission rights, and the Swiss National Science Foundation for a grant to the first author (100014–126558).

References

Akerlof, G. A., & Shiller, R. J. (2009). *Animal spirits: How human psychology drives the economy, and why it matters for global capitalism*. Princeton: Princeton University Press.

Anderson, J. R., & Lebiere, C. (1998). *The atomic components of thought*. Mahwah: Lawrence Erlbaum.

Barron, G., & Erev, I. (2003). Small feedback-based decisions and their limited correspondence to description-based decisions. *Journal of Behavioral Decision Making, 16,* 215–233. doi:10.1002/bdm.443

Biele, G., Erev, I., & Ert, E. (2009). Learning, risk attitude and hot stoves in restless bandit problems. *Journal of Mathematical Psychology, 53,* 155–167. doi:10.1016/j.jmp.2008.05.006

Brandstätter, E., Gigerenzer, G., & Hertwig, R. (2006). The priority heuristic: Making choices without trade-offs. *Psychological Review, 113,* 409–432. doi:10.1037/0033-295X.113.2.409

Bruni, F. (2003, August 26). San Giuseppe Vesuviano Journal: Who's afraid of Vesuvius? (Pompeii is history). *New York Times*. Retrieved from http://www.nytimes.com/2003/08/26/world/san-giuseppe-vesuviano-journal-who-s-afraid-of-vesuvius-pompeii-is-history.html

Busemeyer, J. R. (1985). Decision making under uncertainty: A comparison of simple scalability, fixed-sample, and sequential-sampling models. *Journal of Experimental Psychology: Learning, Memory, and Cognition, 11,* 538–564. doi:10.1037/0278-7393.11.3.538

Busemeyer, J. R., & Myung, I. J. (1992). An adaptive approach to human decision making: Learning theory, decision theory, and human performance. *Journal of Experimental Psychology: General, 121,* 177–194. doi:10.1037/0096-3445.121.2.177

Bush, R. R., & Mosteller, F. (1955). *Stochastic models for learning.* Oxford: John Wiley & Sons.

Cohen, J. D., McClure, S. M., & Yu, A. J. (2007). Should I stay or should I go? How the human brain manages the trade-off between exploitation and exploration. *Philosophical Transactions of the Royal Society B: Biological Sciences, 362,* 933–942. doi:10.1098/rstb.2007.2098

Denrell, J. (2007). Adaptive learning and risk taking. *Psychological Review, 114,* 177–187. doi:10.1037/0033-295X.114.1.177

Erev, I., & Barron, G. (2005). On adaptation, maximization, and reinforcement learning among cognitive strategies. *Psychological Review, 112,* 912–931. doi:10.1037/0033-295X.112.4.912

Erev, I., Ert, E., Roth, A. E., Haruvy, E., Herzog, S. M., Hau, R.,…Lebiere, C. (2010). A choice prediction competition: Choices from experience and from description. *Journal of Behavioral Decision Making, 23,* 15–47. doi:10.1002/bdm.683

Fox, C. R., & Hadar, L. (2006). "Decisions from experience" = sampling error + prospect theory: Reconsidering Hertwig, Barron, Weber & Erev (2004). *Judgment and Decision Making, 1,* 159–161.

Fox, C. R., & Tversky, A. (1998). A belief-based account of decision under uncertainty. *Management Science, 44,* 879–895. doi:10.1287/mnsc.44.7.879

Frey, R., Hertwig, R., & Rieskamp, J. (2014). Fear shapes information acquisition in decisions from experience. *Cognition, 132,* 90–99. doi:10.1016/j.cognition.2014.03.009

Frey, R., Mata, R., & Hertwig, R. (2015). The role of cognitive abilities in decisions from experience: Age differences emerge as a function of choice set size. *Cognition, 142,* 60–80. doi:10.1016/j.cognition.2015.05.004

Friedman, M., & Savage, L. J. (1948). The utility analysis of choices involving risk. *Journal of Political Economy, 56,* 279–304. doi:10.1086/256692

Gigerenzer, G., Hertwig, R., Van Den Broek, E., Fasolo, B., & Katsikopoulos, K. V. (2005). "A 30% chance of rain tomorrow": How does the public understand probabilistic weather forecasts? *Risk Analysis, 25,* 623–629. doi:10.1111/j.1539-6924.2005.00608.x

Gigerenzer, G., & Hoffrage, U. (1995). How to improve Bayesian reasoning without instruction: Frequency formats. *Psychological Review, 102,* 684–704. doi:10.1037/0033-295X.102.4.684

Gilboa, I., & Schmeidler, D. (1995). Case-based decision theory. *Quarterly Journal of Economics, 110,* 605–639. doi:10.2307/2946694

Gonzalez, C., & Dutt, V. (2011). Instance-based learning: Integrating sampling and repeated decisions from experience. *Psychological Review, 118,* 523–551. doi:10.1037/a0024558

Gonzalez, C., Lerch, J. F., & Lebiere, C. (2003). Instance-based learning in dynamic decision making. *Cognitive Science, 27,* 591–635. doi:10.1016/S0364-0213(03)00031-4

Hadar, L., & Fox, C. R. (2009). Information asymmetry in decision from description versus decision from experience. *Judgment and Decision Making, 4,* 317–325.

Hau, R., Pleskac, T. J., & Hertwig, R. (2010). Decisions from experience and statistical probabilities: Why they trigger different choices than a priori probabilities. *Journal of Behavioral Decision Making, 23,* 48–68. doi:10.1002/bdm.665

Hau, R., Pleskac, T. J., Kiefer, J., & Hertwig, R. (2008). The description–experience gap in risky choice: The role of sample size and experienced probabilities. *Journal of Behavioral Decision Making, 21,* 493–518. doi:10.1002/bdm.598

Hertwig, R. (2012). The psychology and rationality of decisions from experience. *Synthese, 187,* 269–292. doi:10.1007/s11229-011-0024-4

Hertwig, R., Barron, G., Weber, E. U., & Erev, I. (2004). Decisions from experience and the effect of rare events in risky choice. *Psychological Science, 15,* 534–539. doi:10.1111/j.0956-7976.2004.00715.x

Hertwig, R., Barron, G., Weber, E. U., & Erev, I. (2006). Decisions from experience: Sampling and updating of information. In K. Fiedler & P. Juslin (Eds.), *Information sampling and adaptive cognition* (pp. 71–91). New York: Cambridge University Press.

Hertwig, R., & Erev, I. (2009). The description–experience gap in risky choice. *Trends in Cognitive Sciences, 13,* 517–523. doi:10.1016/j.tics.2009.09.004

Hertwig, R., Pachur, T., & Kurzenhäuser, S. (2005). Judgments of risk frequencies: Tests of possible cognitive mechanisms. *Journal of Experimental Psychology: Learning, Memory, and Cognition, 35,* 621–642. doi:10.1037/0278-7393.31.4.621

Hertwig, R., & Pleskac, T. J. (2008). The game of life: How small samples render choice simpler. In N. Chater & M. Oaksford (Eds.), *The probabilistic mind: Prospects for Bayesian cognitive science* (pp. 209–235). Oxford: Oxford University Press.

Hertwig, R., & Pleskac, T. J. (2010). Decisions from experience: Why small samples? *Cognition, 115,* 225–237. doi:10.1016/j.cognition.2009.12.009

Hills, T. T., & Hertwig, R. (2010). Information search in decisions from experience: Do our patterns of sampling foreshadow our decisions? *Psychological Science, 21,* 1787–1792. doi:10.1177/0956797610387443

Hills, T. T., & Hertwig, R. (2012). Two distinct exploratory behaviors in decisions from experience: Comment on Gonzalez & Dutt, 2011. *Psychological Review, 119,* 888–892. doi:10.1037/a0028004

Hogarth, R. M., & Einhorn, H. J. (1992). Order effects in belief updating: The belief-adjustment model. *Cognitive Psychology, 24,* 1–55. doi:10.1016/0010-0285(92)90002-J

Jessup, R. K., Bishara, A. J., & Busemeyer, J. R. (2008). Feedback produces divergence from prospect theory in descriptive choice. *Psychological Science, 19,* 1015–1022. doi:10.1111/j.1467-9280.2008.02193.x

Klein, G. A. (1999). *Sources of power: How people make decisions.* Cambridge: MIT Press.

Knight, F. H. (1921). *Risk, uncertainty, and profit.* Boston: Houghton Mifflin.

Kunreuther, H. (1984). Causes of underinsurance against natural disasters. *The Geneva Papers on Risk and Insurance, 9,* 206–220.

Lejarraga, T., Hertwig, R., & Gonzalez, C. (2012). How choice ecology influences search in decisions from experience. *Cognition, 124,* 334–342. doi:10.1016/j.cognition.2012.06.002

Lichtenstein, S., Slovic, P., Fischhoff, B., Layman, M., & Combs, B. (1978). Judged frequency of lethal events. *Journal of Experimental Psychology: Human Learning and Memory, 4,* 551–578. doi:10.1037/0278-7393.4.6.551

Lopes, L. L. (1983). Some thoughts on the psychological concept of risk. *Journal of Experimental Psychology: Human Perception and Performance, 8,* 137–144. doi:10.1037/0096-1523.9.1.137

Luce, R. D., & Raïffa, H. (1957). *Games and decisions: Introduction and critical survey.* New York: Dover.

Luce, R. D., & Suppes, P. (1965). Preference, utility, and subjective probability. In R. Duncan, R. R. Bush, & E. Galanter (Eds.), *Handbook of mathematical psychology, Vol. III* (pp. 249–410). New York: John Wiley & Sons.

March, J. G. (1996). Learning to be risk averse. *Psychological Review, 103,* 309–319. doi:10.1037/0033-295X.103.2.309

Mastrolorenzo, G., Petrone, P., Pappalardo, L., & Sheridan, M. F. (2006). The Avellino 3780-yr-BP catastrophe as a worst-case scenario for a future eruption at Vesuvius. *Proceedings of the National Academy of Sciences of the United States of America, 103,* 4366–4370. doi:10.1073/pnas.0508697103

Posner, R. A. (2009). *A failure of capitalism: The crisis of '08 and the descent into depression.* Cambridge: Harvard University Press.

Rakow, T., Demes, K. A., & Newell, B. R. (2008). Biased samples not mode of presentation: Re-examining the apparent underweighting of rare events in experience-based choice. *Organizational Behavior and Human Decision Processes, 106,* 168–179. doi:10.1016/j.obhdp.2008.02.001

Real, L. A. (1991). Animal choice behavior and the evolution of cognitive architecture. *Science, 253,* 980–986. doi:10.1126/science.1887231

Real, L. A. (1992). Information processing and the evolutionary ecology of cognitive architecture. *American Naturalist, 140,* 108–145. doi:10.1086/285399

Redelmeier, D. A., & Kahneman, D. (1996). Patients' memories of painful medical treatments: Real-time and retrospective evaluations of two minimally invasive procedures. *Pain, 116,* 3–8. doi:10.1016/0304-3959(96)02994-6

Savage, L. J. (1954). *The foundations of statistics* (2nd ed.). New York: Dover Publications.

Sutton, R. S., & Barto, A. G. (1998). *Reinforcement learning: An introduction.* Cambridge: MIT Press.

Taleb, N. N. (2007). *The black swan: The impact of the highly improbable.* New York: Random House.

Tversky, A., & Fox, C. R. (1995). Weighing risk and uncertainty. *Psychological Review, 102,* 269–283. doi:10.1037/0033-295X.102.2.269

Tversky, A., & Kahneman, D. (1992). Advances in prospect theory: Cumulative representation of uncertainty. *Journal of Risk and Uncertainty, 5,* 297–323. doi:10.1007/BF00122574

Ungemach, C., Chater, N., & Stewart, N. (2009). Are probabilities overweighted or underweighted when rare outcomes are experienced (rarely)? *Psychological Science, 20,* 473–479. doi:10.1111/j.1467-9280.2009.02319.x

Viscusi, W. K. (2002). *Smoke-filled rooms: A postmortem on the tobacco deal.* Chicago: University of Chicago Press.

Weber, E. U. (2012). Doing the right thing willingly: Using the insights of behavioral decision research for better environmental decisions. In E. Shafir (Ed.), *The behavioral foundations of public policy* (pp. 380–397). Princeton: Princeton University Press.

Weber, E. U., Shafir, S., & Blais, A.-R. (2004). Predicting risk-sensitivity in humans and lower animals: Risk as variance or coefficient of variation. *Psychological Review, 111,* 430–445. doi:10.1037/0033-295X.111.2.430

Whittle, P. (1988). Restless bandits: Activity allocation in a changing world. *Journal of Applied Probability, 25,* 287–298. doi:10.2307/3214163

Wilford, J. N. (2006, March 7). Long before burying Pompeii, Vesuvius vented its wrath. *New York Times.* Retrieved from http://www.nytimes.com/2006/03/07/science/07volc.html

Yechiam, E., & Busemeyer, J. R. (2006). The effect of foregone payoffs on underweighting small probability events. *Journal of Behavioral Decision Making, 19,* 1–16. doi:10.1002/bdm.509

Chapter 9
Reflection and Impulse as Determinants of Human Behavior

Anand Krishna and Fritz Strack

The Missing Link Between Knowledge and Action

The experience of being and acting human is a universal theme of cultural expression. From movies to great literary works, great weight is placed on both of these aspects, being and acting. Literary figures that resonate in our minds do so both because of their heroic (or antiheroic) actions and their inner life—their motivations, feelings, and thoughts on their own existence and actions. Sometimes this inner life reflects a clever, reflective type of thinking, as with the Danaans in Homer's *Iliad* and their plan to defeat the Trojans by infiltrating the city in a wooden horse. But equally fascinating are the stories of protagonists who show an impetuous, impulsive side, such as Icarus, the Greek youth who flew too close to the sun and thereby melted his artificial wings despite his father's specific warning. Lastly, there are those figures who are faced with an inner conflict between reflection and impulse—Odysseus, for all his cleverness, cannot resist the temptation to hear the deadly song of the Sirens, yet his forethought in having himself tied to the mast of his ship defeats the impulse to drown himself trying to reach them.

These three Greek legends appear to show different ways of thinking that lead to different results. Coming up with complex plans such as the Trojan Horse requires reflection and active use of knowledge, whereas such deliberation would seem antithetical to Icarus' flight. However, these two different modes of thought do seem to come together in a fashion, as is in Odysseus' use of forward planning to defeat the consequences of his impulsive decision. In everyday life, as well, people often approach situations in these two ways—spending a while considering what to eat for lunch and making a deliberate selection but also automatically grabbing a sweet dessert without thinking about it at all. When considering how these mental

A. Krishna (✉) • F. Strack
Institute for Psychology, University of Würzburg, Würzburg, Germany
e-mail: krishna@psychologie.uni-wuerzburg.de

© The Author(s) 2017   145
P. Meusburger et al. (eds.), *Knowledge and Action*, Knowledge and Space 9,
DOI 10.1007/978-3-319-44588-5_9

processes work, it makes sense to look at the two styles of thinking separately to gain an understanding of their interaction and of their actual effect on behavior.

In this chapter we seek to illuminate the characteristics of these two processes, show their interactions with each another, and point out their common effect on behavior. To do so, it is first necessary to evaluate each system independently, examining historical and current perspectives on reflective and impulsive styles of thought. Thereafter, we present an integrative model of thinking and action in an endeavor to identify when which system of thought will be active and under what circumstances it will influence behavior.

A Short Overview of Reflective and Impulsive Styles of Thinking

Theories of Reflection

The idea that human behavior is based on active, reflective thought guided by the principle of attaining beneficial things is old and makes intuitive sense. It is difficult to argue why people would actively decide to act in a fashion that they know is bad for them without some belief that the action would ultimately be positive. In this conception of human thought, negative outcomes can be explained by a lack of information. The Greek philosopher Socrates, for example, proposed that people would otherwise act in ways that were good for them.

From a social psychological perspective, this kind of thinking is exemplified in expectancy-value theories and the concept of *homo oeconomicus* (e.g., Fishbein & Ajzen, 1975). The theory of planned behavior (Ajzen, 1985) is an established example of an expectancy-value model (Conner & Armitage, 1998). It depicts behavior as a function of several specific mental factors. In this conceptualization the three determinants of behavior are the attitude toward the behavior, the subjective norm relevant to the behavior, and the perceived behavioral control over the behavior. An attitude toward a specific behavior is generated by multiplying the evaluation of a possible perceived outcome of the behavior (a value) by the perceived likelihood of that outcome (an expectancy) and then summing the results of this multiplication for all possible outcomes. Similarly, the subjective norm is calculated by multiplying the actor's motivation to comply with another person's expectation by the perceived likelihood that that person holds that expectation over all persons. By contrast, perceived behavioral control is a function of the perceived power of behavior-inhibiting or behavior-facilitating factors multiplied by the likelihood that the actor has access to these factors.

The assumption in the theory of planned behavior is, therefore, that a human actor's calculation of these three determinants of behavior is optimally based on all available information. Once the determinants are established, the actor will integrate them for all possible behaviors and select the best option. This behavior is then initiated via a behavioral intention.

This idea is echoed in various domains, both historically and in more modern contexts, such as organizational psychology (Vroom, 1964), addiction research (Sutton, Marsh, & Matheson, 1987), and education (Wigfield & Eccles, 2000). There is solid empirical support for the ability of expectancy-value models to predict intentions and behavior (e.g., Armitage & Conner, 2001). However, even the strongest empirical studies do not conclude that this kind of thinking can completely predict behavior. In particular, it seems unlikely that behavior occurring without conscious thought could be dependent on this kind of deliberative, intentional processing (e.g., Langer, Blank, & Chanowitz, 1978). Therefore, one must consider alternative mental processes that are characterized by less deliberative processing.

Theories of Impulse

Expectancy-value models can describe the careful planning behind the Trojan horse well, but they seem less able to explain why Icarus would immolate his wings. The kind of action implied in the latter myth is apparently not influenced by the knowledge of the action's expected consequences. It may rather be seen as reckless, as based on an impulse that seems to instigate behavior automatically. This determinant of behavior differs from the rational assumptions of Socrates or the theory of planned behavior (Fishbein & Ajzen, 1975) and must be explained by other means. Historically, this point is recognized by Aristotle in the *Nicomanchean Ethics* (Crisp, 2000) when he argues that people may at times act against their judgment. In his view an overwhelming passion—physical feelings (e.g., hunger) and emotions (e.g., fear or pleasure)—directly implies a practical conclusion to act on it. This practical conclusion may at times overpower the conclusions reached by reason.

Psychology as a discipline has focused mostly on factors that affect the ability of reasoned conclusions to control passionate ones (Hofmann, Friese, & Strack, 2009). For example, children's ability to forgo a small, immediate reward in favor of a larger, delayed reward has been shown to depend on various factors, including opportunity to pay attention to the immediate reward and thinking happy or sad thoughts (Mischel, Ebbesen, & Raskoff, 1972). Muraven and Baumeister (2000) conceptualize the control of impulses as being achieved by a metaphorical "muscle" that is powered by limited resources and is subject to fatigue, a state called *ego depletion*. In this view, reasoned control of impulses will fail if remaining resources of self-control are insufficient to overcome impulse strength. Personality variables have been linked to the ability to control impulses (e.g., Block & Block, 1980; Carver, 2005), as have physiological variables such as blood glucose and alcohol levels (Bushman & Cooper, 1990; Gailliot et al., 2007) and situational factors such as the availability of tempting stimuli (Schachter, 1971).

Another approach to impulses and their effect on behavior is provided by research on implicit attitudes. Implicit attitudes are seen as spontaneous, automatic affective and behavioral responses to attitude objects (Greenwald & Banaji, 1995). The view that impulsive behavior comes from overwhelming passion caused by a situation maps well onto this idea that attitude objects may spontaneously cause affect and behavior via automatic processes. This view contrasts with the position that attitudes are evaluations of target objects (e.g., Eagly & Chaiken, 1993). The evaluative position implies a more deliberative assessment of object properties, which corresponds to processes similar to those described in the theory of reasoned action (Fishbein & Ajzen, 1975). Researchers studying implicit attitudes generally adopt indirect attitude measures such as the affective priming paradigm (Fazio, Sanbonmatsu, Powell, & Kardes, 1986) or the implicit association test (IAT) (Greenwald, McGhee, & Schwartz, 1998). These instruments typically use a combination of valent and categorical stimuli and measure their inhibition or facilitation of a target behavior. Affective priming studies show that people categorize evaluative adjectives such as *good* or *bad* faster when they are congruent in valence to an attitude object shown immediately beforehand (Fazio, 2001). The IAT measures the difference between reaction times when participants are asked to categorize an object by attitudinal categories via a key-press reaction also associated with a particular valence (Greenwald et al., 1998). These measures show that behavioral responses to specific stimuli are influenced by the valence of these stimuli. The difference between what these implicit measures capture and what traditional evaluative measures (e.g., self-report questions) assess is apparent from their only moderate correlations (Fazio & Olson, 2003) and by the relative robustness of implicit measures with regard to participants' conscious control (Banse, Seise, & Zerbes, 2001; Kim, 2003; but see Mierke & Klauer, 2001, and Fiedler & Bluemke, 2005, for critical discussions). One explains these results by stating that the spontaneous response to an attitudinal object is governed by associations that may differ in content from the results of a deliberative evaluation. These associations occur between perceived objects, behavior, and affect. The link between impulse and behavior has some theoretical basis—including the ideomotor principle (James, 1890) and the perception-behavior link (Bargh, 1997)—as does a direct link between perception and affective response (Zajonc, 1980). However, research on implicit attitudes has not succeeded in explaining what an implicit attitude actually is, beyond the tautological functional definition that an implicit attitude is what is measured by indirect measures (Strack & Deutsch, 2007). With evidence accruing that implicit attitudes may be strongly affected by the context (Wittenbrink, Judd, & Park, 2001) and type (Bosson, Swann, & Pennebaker, 2000) of the measurement, the question of what exactly an impulse might be is becoming ever more relevant.

Bridging the Gap: The Reflective-Impulsive Model

The research and models presented so far shed some light on the mysteries of human behavior. The careful plan behind the Trojan Horse seems rooted in deliberative, expectancy-value thinking, whereas Icarus' doomed flight into the sun might be seen as a lack of self-regulatory resources preventing him from automatically flying close to the bright sun. What has yet to be addressed is the question of the interaction of these systems—how does Odysseus defeat the Siren's call, or in more general terms, how do deliberative, rational thought and impulsive affect and action interact? In the past three decades many researchers have attempted to address this question. In the realm of social psychology, the challenge has been met with many different dual-process models (see Chaiken & Trope, 1999, for examples). These dual-process models stem from research on different topics, including persuasion (Chaiken, 1987; Petty & Cacioppo, 1986), stereotyping (Devine, 1989), causal attribution (Gilbert, Pelham, & Krull, 1988), and general cognition (Epstein, Lipson, Holstein, & Huh, 1992). Although these models deal with different aspects of human behavior and cognition, they share certain structural traits. In all cases, two modes of information processing are proposed, one of which is characterized by effortful, rule-based processing, the other by almost effortless, associative processing. This distinction is delineated clearly by Sloman (1996), who describes both of these modes in detail.

Many influential dual-process models conform to this structure, but not all models provide for interactions between the proposed processes (for an overview, see Smith & DeCoster, 2000). Even fewer models make statements about how both processes influence behavior and whether they are interdependent in doing so. Rather, they specify how information is processed at a cognitive level—they describe how people think about what to eat for lunch and how they process the information that sweet desserts are available, but these models do not go beyond the formation of a behavioral decision on what would be best to eat. They also cannot describe how behavior can be instigated independently from a decision (e.g., Strack & Neumann, 1996)—how it can be that one decides to eat a healthy lunch but still reach out for the sweet muffin. In order to address these issues and fill the gap between knowledge and action, an integrative model that incorporates both elements is needed. For this purpose, Strack and Deutsch (2004) propose the reflective-impulsive model (RIM), a dual-systems model conceived to clearly define and integrate the theoretical perspectives so far presented under the headings of impulsive and reflective.

The Reflective System

The RIM refers to the rational, rule-based system of thought as the reflective system. Slow and driven by resources of working memory, this system has limits on its capacity for information processing. It may be disengaged from processing under certain circumstances, but it is capable of generating knowledge via syllogistic inferences. It does so by activating concepts and possible relations between these concepts and then assigning a truth value to the proposition formed by the concepts and the relation. For example, the concepts *salad* and *health* may be activated, along with the relation of *is/is not*. In this case the reflective system would assign the value of *true* to the configuration, yielding the proposition *salad is healthy*. If the concept of *muffin* was activated instead of *salad*, the truth value might instead be *false*, yielding the proposition *muffin is not healthy*.

It is important to note that any other relation might be used beyond *is/is not*, such as *implies/does not imply*, *causes/does not cause*, or *is/is not a member of*, to name a few. If several related propositions are constructed, new knowledge may be generated by the combination of these propositions. In keeping with the example propositions given above—*salad is healthy* and *muffin is not healthy*—an additional proposition of *being healthy is good* might yield both the conclusion that salad is good and that muffins are not. Because the reflective system is able to assign truth values to statements, rule-based inferences can be drawn in order to maximize the consistency of the resulting representation (Gawronski & Strack, 2004). The ability of this mode of processing to help a person generate and infer conclusions makes it extremely flexible and useful for facilitating many operations typically associated with deliberative thought, including expectancy-value judgments and advanced social behavior (e.g., the discernment of people's states of belief; see Wimmer & Perner, 1983, for example) and the learning of new connections between concepts without much or any repetition.

The reflective system is limited by boundary conditions that constrain its ability to process information. Two of the most important of these conditions are working memory capacity and arousal. The activation of concepts and relations and the transformation of the resulting propositions are assumed to take place in the working memory (Baddeley, 1986). These dynamics provide a functional limit to the complexity and scope of reflective operations, in that the capacity of working memory may be insufficient to contain all the required propositions for a given operation concurrently. This statement is bolstered by studies showing that an impairment of working-memory capacity through a manipulation of cognitive load impairs logical reasoning (De Neys, 2006; DeWall, Baumeister, & Masicampo, 2008). Arousal, by contrast, affects reflective processing in a nonlinear fashion resembling the Yerkes-Dodson Law (Yerkes & Dodson, 1908)—intermediate levels of arousal facilitate the operation of the reflective system. Evidence exists that high levels of arousal reduce complexity in social judgments (Baron, 2000; Lambert et al., 2003; Paulhus & Lim, 1994), whereas low arousal, characteristic in a state of fatigue, for example, is also associated with lowered capacity to engage in reflective processing.

Important and ubiquitous cognitive phenomena rely upon the reflective system's ability to assign truth values to relations between concepts, an example of which is negation. The RIM predicts that negations of propositions can be processed only under circumstances in which the reflective system can be engaged, that is, under conditions endowed with resources sufficient for efforts to engage in processing. This statement differs from models based on the assumption that negations may be "tagged" onto propositions once and for all and henceforth no longer require reflective engagement (e.g., Gilbert, 1991), and it is supported by evidence that negations require cognitive resources to process (Wason, 1959).

Reflective processing is accompanied by a state of noetic awareness of whether something is the case or not. This awareness may sometimes be accompanied by a particular feeling that is processed consciously, a state of experiential awareness. It should be noted, however, that some operations in the reflective system may require so few resources that they can be processed without corresponding noetic awareness or a feeling of intentionality (Deutsch, Kordts-Freudinger, Gawronski, & Strack, 2009).

The Impulsive System

Aside from the reflective system, the RIM proposes the existence of an associative system of thought called the impulsive system. This system works continuously and effortlessly. Whereas the reflective system uses working memory capacity, the impulsive system can be seen as long-term memory and therefore has functionally unlimited capacity. The impulsive system forms associative links between individual elements that may be of varying strengths. When an element is activated, other elements linked to it are activated in accordance with the strength of the links to the original element, a form of spreading activation. Recent or frequent activation of an element also increases both the accessibility of that element and the likelihood of its continued processing if further activation occurs. Links between elements are based on the principles of contiguity and similarity, so that stimuli that occur a short time or distance from one another are more likely to become linked or to have existing links strengthened than is the case with temporally or spatially nonproximal stimuli. It is important to note that reflective processes activate corresponding patterns of impulsive elements, meaning that even elements that are never perceived together in the world may become associatively linked if they are often reflectively processed together. The activation of impulsive elements may be accompanied by an experiential state of awareness, with people experiencing a specific feeling without being able to say where it comes from. Such feelings are themselves elements in the impulsive system and may therefore be connected to other elements with varying link strengths.

This process of association is slow and enduring but also rigid. Although propositional processing in the reflective system may create associative links between concepts in the impulsive system, it is not necessarily the case that propositional processing can become completely automatic and effortless with enough practice (Deutsch et al., 2009). Instead, specific patterns of thought may become easier but lose or change their meaning under circumstances where reflective processing is hindered. As an example, African Americans who feel that whites perceive them negatively may often reflectively think "Blacks are not bad" as a response; in the impulsive system, however, the concepts of *black* and *bad* are being activated at the same time and thereby linked (Livingston, 2002). This simultaneity may counterintuitively lead African Americans to have additional negative feelings and associations with their in-group when they have no reflective resources with which to negate the associative relation. However, the rigidity of associative processing is somewhat alleviated by the effects of motivational orientation. When people are in an approach orientation, they are prepared to reduce the distance between themselves and some aspect of their environments, whereas an avoidance orientation is preparedness to increase this distance. These fundamental orientations can facilitate associative activation when this activation is compatible (e.g., approach orientation may facilitate the activation of positively valent elements). Therefore, the sight of a muffin might elicit the positive associations of *tasty*, *sweet*, and *good* more strongly when one is in an approach orientation, as when selecting what salad one would prefer for lunch, than when one is not. If one is currently in an avoidance orientation, having just read a brochure on calorie content and having selected the salad that would be least fattening, these associations might be weaker even before the activation of the reflective system. However, it is clear that the associative system alone, although it requires no resources and works very quickly, is generally far less flexible and adaptive than the reflective system.

Interaction of Systems

Now that we have described the basic operating principles of the RIM's two systems, it is necessary to show how they function together. The very structures of the two systems contain a first important point relevant to their interaction: the impulsive system is always effortlessly active, whereas the reflective system may also be inactive. The implication is that the reflective system, when it does operate, does so in parallel with the impulsive system, not in place of it. That is, reflective processing always occurs with parallel impulsive processing. It is also clear that the concepts that are transformed in working-memory space in the reflective system do not come from nowhere but from the long-term store of the impulsive system.

As the systems cannot interact when the reflective system is disengaged, it is adequate to examine how they interact from the beginning to the end of a reflective operation. When a reflective operation begins, perceptual input will already have activated several associative elements. For example, when thinking about what to have for lunch, a person may already have seen what is on offer in the cafeteria, a selection that will activate whatever associations that person has with the given meal options, but other perceptual data in the attentional focus (the presentation of the food, the attractiveness of the serving staff, and any number of other concepts) will also activate associations of their own. Some of these associations will achieve sufficient activation to attain awareness, so a particularly delicious-looking muffin might prompt an automatic expectation of a good taste. The reflective system then categorizes and relates the activated concepts, the result being that the muffin is recognized as tasting good, and activates additional relevant content in the impulsive system—such as health. This concept, in turn, changes the activation pattern in the impulsive system, so the associated concept of *salad* might become activated as well. This activation pattern is again categorized, and the process repeats until a decision or inference is reached. Such end results in the reflective system are driven by the principle of consistency of the propositions generated. For example *health is good*, *taste is good*, *health is more important than taste* might lead to the decision to select the healthy salad rather than the unhealthy one but also the tasty muffin, for this choice would be consistent with a greater number of propositions. However, the content of the propositions generated is necessarily limited by the activation pattern of the impulsive system—although tennis is also healthy, its activation potential in the environment of the cafeteria during lunch hour is very low, so the reflective system will not include it in processing without any prior link or further relevant perceptual stimuli.

Synergy between the systems occurs when the impulsive system's associations are valid and relevant to a consistent reflective solution. When the impulsive activation pattern is in synergy with reflective processing, concepts relevant to the focus of reflective processing become comparatively accessible, and cognitive effort is therefore reduced. The reflective system is not forced to perform extra categorizations and activations of concepts to achieve consistency, so subjective effort is lessened. This reduction may be accompanied by a feeling of flow (Winkielman, Huber, Kavanagh, & Schwarz, 2012), that is, ease of processing, which is then linked to positive affect. Therefore, when both systems are in accord, it feels easy and good to think and make decisions. As an example, if the only tasty option in the cafeteria were the healthy salad, people who ate there and cared deeply about their health (i.e., had a high accessibility of the concept health) would find it natural to choose the salad and, moreover, would feel good about how easy the choice was. A different picture emerges when the systems are at odds with each other, as when impulsive activation patterns present associations that are opposed to a consistent reflective conclusion and produce a feeling of conflict. It requires additional cognitive effort to activate new impulsive patterns and to form propositions that lead to a consistent end state. Once the muffin is added to the lunch options, the decision-maker must actively work against the temptation of the tasty dessert in order to generate the propositions about healthy eating that justify selecting the salad. This dependence of effortful processing on automatic activation has an interesting consequence: A fluently (synergistically) processed inference should have a higher truth value than a disfluently (antagonistically) processed inference does, unless the reflective system specifically corrects for the consequences of fluency (Allport & Lepkin, 1945; Begg, Anas, & Farinacci, 1992; Schwarz, Sanna, Skurnik, & Yoon, 2007). The

fluency of processing should affect both how sure a person is of a syllogistic inference and how securely she or he stands behind a given decision.

Common Pathway to Behavior

Having described how the reflective and impulsive systems are structured and how
they interact during the process of thought, we now turn to two issues that many
other dual-process models have not yet addressed: how these mental processes are
linked to behavior and especially how they interact when causing behavior. The
RIM seeks to provide an answer to this central question through the component of
behavioral schemata. In a general sense, behavioral schemata are clusters of elements in the impulsive system. They consist of specific motor representations of
behavior, the perceptual input of typical context factors for the behavior, and the
consequences of those factors. As elements of the impulsive system, specific behavioral schemata (e.g., how to grip a fork) will likely be associated with other behavioral schemata that are relevant to the context, the specific motor activation, or the
consequences of the behavior. This result leads to the conclusion that several specific, concrete behavioral schemata might form clusters that, in turn, can be seen as
behavioral schemata of greater abstractness. Gripping a fork and gripping a spoon,
for instance, are similar in terms of expected consequences (tasting food) and context (involving food, eating utensils, etc.). The more abstract behavioral schema in
this case might be termed *holding cutlery*, which might, in turn, connect to other
schemata to form a cluster of *eating politely*, and so on. This conceptual hierarchy
bears some relationship to other conceptualizations of schemata but is more specific
than its typical use (for a discussion see Fiske & Linville, 1980; Lodge, McGraw,
Conover, Feldman, & Miller, 1991).

If behavioral schemata are situated in the impulsive system, they are also subject
to spreading activation. In a way similar to that of nonbehavioral elements in the
impulsive system, behavioral schemata can be activated automatically if enough
other elements with sufficiently strong links to the schema are activated. In the case
of behavioral schemata, activation includes performance of the motor program
embedded within the schema. The reflective system, on the other hand, activates
behavioral schemata by propositionally connecting the self to the required behavioral schema by means of a behavioral decision. If the decision refers to a behavior
that is to take place in future, the reflective system additionally links the behavior's
expected relevant context with the cluster, creating an intention (Gollwitzer, 1999).
Although the systems encompass different precursors to behavior, they use the same
final gateway to enact behavior, namely, the activation of behavioral schemata, elements of the impulsive system. The implication is that the same principles of system
interaction that apply to purely mental operations in the RIM also apply to behavioral processes—fluent, synergistic processing of behavioral decisions leads to
behavior that is performed more smoothly and easily than disfluent, antagonistic
processing. In extreme cases of the latter, the impulsive activation of behavioral

schemata might be so strong that a reflective behavioral decision will not lead directly to behavior, as when one knows that eating the dessert is wrong and has decided not to, but the eyes and hands still seem to have their own volition to fixate on the forbidden. In this case the operating conditions of the systems will decide which behavior is performed. In states inimical to reflective processing, such as high arousal or reduced working memory capacity, the impulse to act will likely win out, whereas an unhindered reflective system might redirect the activation pattern in the impulsive system by, for example, diverting attention or actively linking negative consequences or attributes to the impulsive behavior. In this sense, there is little difference between mentally grappling with an unwanted impulsive idea, such as unwanted racist thoughts, and with an unwanted physical impulse, such as reaching for that tempting muffin.

Knowledge and Action: Bidirectional Connections

Having established that behavioral schemata are situated in the impulsive system, we note that an important additional implication of the RIM becomes clear. In the impulsive system, each element adheres to the mechanism of spreading activation, including behavioral schemata. Because behavioral schemata are linked to consequences and contextual stimuli, activating the behavior also activates related concepts. Therefore, behavior can directly influence cognition, both by creating and modifying associative links and by influencing what concepts are likely to become active in the reflective system. For example, the act of reaching for the muffin, if repeated often, may eventually become sufficiently associated with the sight of the muffin that the action is triggered by the sight. Similarly, this association makes the muffin more likely to come to mind when one is reaching for the salad, that is, when performing the very motor program associated with the muffin. This bidirectionality of influence—behavior to cognition as well as cognition to behavior—also holds for motivational orientation in that behaviors associated with approach will activate an approach orientation, whereas avoidance behavior has the opposite effect.

This link between behavior and cognition is not a new idea in principle. A similar effect is assumed in several influential theories, such as cognitive dissonance theory (Festinger, 1957) and self-perception theory (Bem, 1967). They also predict a change in attitudes as a specific form of cognition that is based on behavior, albeit via different mechanisms. The important difference lies in precisely these mechanisms. According to cognitive dissonance theory, a behavior that runs counter to an existing belief about the self causes an aversive motivational state that may be alleviated by changing existing beliefs or adding new ones, whereas the assumption in self-perception theory is that people infer their attitudes toward particular objects from their own behavior toward those objects. Both of these proposed mechanisms require propositional processing because they depend on a categorization of the behavior in question. The RIM, on the other hand, describes a direct link between behavior and cognition via the associative links between behavioral schemata and contiguously activated concepts in the impulsive system. It is not that cognitive dissonance and self-perception theory lack validity but rather that their path from behavior to cognitive change is not the only possible one.

When this perspective on the connection between behavior and implicit associative links is applied to the field of implicit attitudes, several interesting implications arise. From the perspective of the RIM, implicit attitudes measured by the IAT, affective priming, and other procedures based on reaction time reflect the strength of associative links between a target and a valence by means of a behavior associated with that valence.[1] In view of the attributes of the impulsive system, it follows that negated targets or valences should, under certain circumstances, have the same effect on reaction times as nonnegated ones do. Evidence supporting this logic comes from the Bona Fide Pipeline task (Fazio, Jackson, Dunton, & Williams, 1995), which was used in a study by Deutsch, Gawronski, and Strack (2006), who showed that positive prime words facilitated categorization of positive targets even when the prime was negated, whereas both negated and nonnegated negative prime words facilitated categorization of negative target. Although this effect is not universal (Deutsch et al., 2009), it provides evidence that impulsive associations are what implicit attitude procedures measure. Procedures used to change implicit attitudes, such as automatic stereotype reduction training (Kawakami, Dovidio, Moll, Hermsen, & Russin, 2000), can also benefit from the implications of the RIM's structure. In the original automatic stereotype reduction training, participants were induced to respond to stereotype-congruent pairings with a NO key and to stereotype-incongruent pairings with a YES key. Although this method was effective in reducing automatic stereotype activation, a study using only stereotype-incongruent pairings has shown the procedure to work (Gawronski, Deutsch, Mbirkou, Seibt, & Strack, 2008). The same studies also showed that negation of stereotype-congruent pairings alone actually increased implicit stereotyping, a prediction derived from the contrast between the propositional nature of negation and the associative nature of contiguous stimuli pairs.

The bidirectional link between behavior and cognition in the RIM also makes that model a valuable framework for studies that deal with embodied effects on cognition. The basic idea of embodiment research is that cognition is always founded in mechanisms of sensory processing and motor control (e.g., Wilson, 2002). The role of perceptual information and motor-processing in the impulsive system and the influence thereby exerted on the reflective system mirror this basic assumption. Precursor research to the current wave of embodiment movement, such as the pen study by Strack, Martin, and Stepper (1988) and the headphone study by Förster and Strack (1996), have already been discussed from the perspective of the RIM (Strack & Deutsch, 2004), but newer investigations into embodied processes might also be integrated into this model. For example, Zhong and Lijenquist (2006) show that washing hands reduced the effects of guilt on compensatory prosocial behavior. The authors explain the effect in terms of symbolic self-completion (Wicklund & Gollwitzer, 1981),

---

[1] The IAT is also capable of measuring associations other than valence, but because the argument is analogous to valence associations, it is omitted here.

but an alternative explanation offered by the RIM would be that the metaphorical association of purity with cleanliness might conflict with a negative activation of the self in the context of guilt and thereby alleviate the guilt's effects on behavior. Thus, an impetus is given for further inquiries into the precise mechanism behind embodiment effects.

Determinants of Systematic Behavioral Control

Having established the parameters and attributes of the two systems of the RIM and their parallel effects on behavior, we turn to explaining possible determinants of either system's dominance over the other in having these effects. If it is possible to identify variables that can affect which system determines behavior, one can vastly improve the predictive power of the RIM for behavior. Because the impulsive system is always active and processing, this question can be rephrased: Under what circumstances will the reflective system assert behavioral control when in conflict with the impulsive system?

Motivation and Opportunity

Fazio (1990) describes two modes of thinking—a spontaneous processing mode based on attitude accessibility, and a deliberative processing mode based on attitude behavior. These modes of thinking are remarkably similar in structure to the RIM's proposed systems, certain differences in mechanisms notwithstanding. Therefore, the MODE model (Fazio, 1990), which predicts when the deliberative mode will be engaged in processing the possible consequences of behavior, may be applicable to the RIM as well. In this conceptualization, engagement in deliberative processing depends on motivation and opportunity. Motivation in the MODE model is generated by the fear of invalidity (Kruglanski & Freund, 1983), a function of the perceived costliness of a judgmental mistake to the self, whereas opportunity is a function of the available time and resources for processing. Applying this framework to the RIM, one finds that the defined properties of the reflective system are in accord with these predictions. Reflective processing is accompanied by a feeling of subjective effort and so requires motivation, whereas both the reliance on the resources of working memory and the relatively slow speed of the reflective system make it clear that the reflective system can influence behavior only if the opportunity is given.

Evidence for this dependence on opportunity exists in many domains. Cognitive load, a manipulation often used to impair deliberative processing, has been applied in various different studies whose results can be explained with the RIM. Self-control (e.g., Lattimore & Maxwell, 2004; Wegner, Erber, & Zanakos, 1993), processing of negated stimuli (Deutsch et al. 2009), social judgments and attributions (Gilbert et al., 1988; Krull & Erickson, 1995; Trope & Alfieri, 1997), moral judgments (Greene, Morelli, Lowenberg, Nystrom, & Cohen, 2008), and general reasoning (De Neys, 2006) have all proven to be impaired by cognitive load in ways that are consistent with the RIM's predictions. The idea that working memory resources may also play a role in reflective processing has been tested in several studies, both by comparing individuals with dispositionally high or low working memory capacities (Hofmann, Gschwendner, Friese, Wiers, & Schmitt, 2008; Thush et al., 2008) and by specifically taxing resources of working memory (Deutsch et al., 2009). The conceptualization of working memory as "a domain-free limitation in ability to control attention" (Engle, 2002, p. 19) points to the conclusion that the effects of attentional cognitive load manipulations on reflective processing may be mediated by working memory capacity.

Self-Regulatory Resources

Vohs (2006) argues that the RIM's reflective system is, in fact, powered by self-regulatory resources (Baumeister, Bratslavsky, Muraven, & Tice, 1998). This account is based on the similarity between the idea of such resources and the cognitive resources discussed in relation to the RIM. Vohs & Faber, (2007) argue that impulsive spending, a phenomenon expected to occur under circumstances that inhibit reflective processing, does indeed occur more often when participants are depleted of self-regulatory resources. A structurally similar argument is made with respect to overeating among dieters (Vohs & Heatherton 2000). Further evidence for this integration of theories comes from research showing that effortful self-regulation has a detrimental effect on subsequent reasoning capabilities (Schmeichel, Vohs, & Baumeister, 2003). The bidirectionality of this effect, that is, a negative effect that prior reflective decision-making exerts on subsequent self-regulation, is shown in a laboratory paradigm encompassing many simple decisions followed by a self-regulatory exercise. The effect's bidirectionality also surfaces in a field study in which shoppers who reported having made effortful decisions previously solved fewer math problems than those who had engaged in fewer decisions during their shopping trip (Vohs et al., 2008). Although this evidence hints at a connection between self-regulatory and reflective cognitive resources, these studies do not show a direct link between the two. Other research shows that dietary standards and explicit target attitudes predict behavior only when self-regulatory resources are available; when it is not, implicit attitudes are better predictors (Friese, Hofmann, & Wänke, 2008; Hofmann, Rauch, & Gawronski, 2007). The fact that impulsive and reflective predictors diverge depending on the availability of self-regulatory resources underlines the conceptualization of self-regulation as a conflict between impulsive and reflective behavioral activation. Together with the evidence presented by Vohs (2006), these findings permit the conclusion that research on resource-based self-regulation can be integrated into the RIM. It remains to be seen whether self-regulatory resources are equivalent to working memory resources or whether they constitute their own construct.

Implications of the RIM

Thinking Is Tough!

Coming up with a complex plan of action is not a simple endeavor. The Trojan Horse required the cunning Odysseus to think hard for a long time, and this story is one of the main reasons he endures as a hero figure. In general terms, it is not easy to engage in reflective processing—beyond the subjective feeling of difficulty, there may be physical limits to the human ability to think (Gailliot et al., 2007). Although thinking may sometimes be facilitated when the reflective and impulsive systems are in accord, people must often use reflective processing against the pull of impulsive associations. Whether this struggle is due to temptation or to particularly complex challenges in the environment, the difficulty in staying the reflective course is clear.

However, cultivating moral or thoughtful habits may become easier with time. Specific propositional operations can become associated with the feeling of temptation if they are activated often enough, and even the experiential component of reflective operation (the feeling of effortful cognition) is itself represented in the impulsive system and may thus become associated with it. For careful planning habits, positive affect associated with successful plans may lead to the process of planning itself acquiring a positive valence, with these habits of thought perhaps eventually becoming inculcated through successful implementation. However, this effect is not sufficient to become truly automatic. Although reflective processing may become facilitated by such mechanisms, propositional reasoning itself cannot become automated. If resources are lacking, not even these habits of reflection will make for better control of impulses or careful planning. No matter how accessible the relevant propositional transformations may be in the impulsive system, reflective resources are required if a person is actually to bring those transformations to bear upon activated concepts.

The habit of critical metacognition is a particularly interesting case. Metacognition refers to thoughts about one's own thoughts, and critical metacognition is therefore those thoughts that evaluate the thinking process. In cognitive-behavioral therapy, thoughts are actively evaluated by the patient and classified as rational or irrational (Baer, 2003). The goal of such interventions is often to change dysfunctional behavior or thinking patterns, such as "catastrophizing" (Beck, 1976). Pursuing this kind of metacognitive thought alteration or suppression may be especially difficult because of the vast reflective resources required. A strong association between the metacognitive monitoring process and the undesired thoughts would eventually activate the latter rather than suppress them, requiring additional reflective resources to eliminate them. Evidence from studies on emotional disorders shows that metacognitive thought suppression does indeed increase the frequency of unwanted thoughts (Purdon, 1999). Although long-term use of metacognitive strategies may eventually divest undesired thoughts of their potency, it seems clear that the way there is a long and cognitively taxing one.

Sometimes No Means Yes If I Can't Process It

Given the research showing that negation is a reflective process that requires reflective resources (Deutsch et al., 2006, 2009; Grant, Malaviya, & Sternthal, 2004), one must wonder at the efficacy of negated persuasive messages. Evidence showing that older adults may be more likely to misremember explicitly negated information has been interpreted as a warning against negatively worded statements in healthcare materials (Wilson & Park, 2008). Wakefield et al.'s (2008) finding that antismoking campaigns funded by tobacco companies have few, if any, negative effects on teenagers' intentions to smoke may be partially due to the negated messages employed (e.g., "Think, Don't Smoke"; see Farrelly, Niederdeppe, & Yarsevich, 2003). These effects can be explained by a lack of processing resources in recalling the content of the messages. If advertisements or healthcare instructions convey associations that are negated in the message, then recall of the message may be confined to the association between the elements under circumstances of low reflective resources. This limitation can lead negated statements to be remembered as affirmed. Positively formulated messages (i.e., those whose association mirrors their propositional connection) are more effective, as with antismoking ads that depict smoking in combination with serious consequences for health (Biener, 2002).

This logic might also be generalized to ethical norms in everyday life. If presented as negated statements (such as *don't drink and drive*), strong ethical norms may have a behavioral effect opposite to what is expected. If people are continually reminded of what they should not do, the unwanted action will be continually activated in the impulsive system and thereby affect subsequent reflective and impulsive operations. If a sermon on the forbidden practice of adultery activates that concept and its influence on evaluations, the listener could see some other members of the congregation as attractive for possibly committing adultery with them. Of course, this possibility would be negated, but only if the listener had sufficient reflective resources available to perform the negation. It would be particularly problematic in cases where the forbidden behavior is hedonically attractive to start with; the activation of the concept would then also activate the expectation of the pleasant feeling associated with it and elicit an approach orientation. A better approach to ethics according to this logic might instead be to praise exemplars of morality or to prescribe morally positive acts as opposed to forbidding negative ones. Instead of saying no to vice, one should say yes to virtue.

Improving Implicit Self-Esteem

Implicit self-esteem is a much researched construct of recent years (e.g., Koole, Dijksterhuis, & van Knippenberg, 2001; Yamaguchi et al., 2007). In a general sense, implicit self-esteem is defined as an automatic evaluation of the self that occurs nonconsciously and affects spontaneous reactions to self-relevant stimuli (Bosson, et al. 2000). Implicit self-esteem has been shown to specifically predict diverse outcomes in a range of situations, including apparent anxiety in participants as they complete a self-relevant interview (Spalding & Hardin, 1999), levels of implicit gender bias in combination with implicit gender identity (Aidman & Carroll, 2003), and depressive symptomatology 6 months after measurement (Franck, De Readt, & De Houwer, 2007). Explicit self-esteem (i.e., explicit evaluations of self-worth), on the other hand, has specific predictive power for subjective well-being (Schimmack & Diener, 2003). It is the combination of the two constructs, however, that has excited most interest in recent years. In particular, the question of discrepant self-esteem has been examined (Zeigler-Hill, 2006). That is, what effects do high explicit but low implicit, or low explicit but high implicit, self-esteem have on behavior? One direct prediction based on psychodynamic theory concerns narcissism. The *mask model* of narcissism assumes that narcissistic individuals are characterized by deep self-doubt (corresponding to low implicit self-esteem), which they compensate for by projecting grandiose self-views (corresponding to extremely high explicit self-esteem) (Bosson et al., 2008). Empirical evidence supporting this model has remained mixed, however, perhaps partly because of the relative unreliability of measures of implicit self-esteem (Bosson et al., 2000).

By rather precisely spelling out the concepts involved, the RIM can contribute to the discussion of these and other phenomena of the implicit self. Implicit self-esteem might, for instance, be conceptualized as the total valence of the associative pattern linked with activation of the self in the impulsive system. This specification would imply recommendations for effective measures of implicit self-esteem—namely, measures that do not require any explicit judgment but rather depend solely on valence and behavior interference (e.g., the IAT, measures based on the logic of affective priming). In addition, the same logic that is applied to automatic stereotype reduction training (Gawronski et al., 2008) may be applied to the implicit self-esteem construct. Doing so yields a method through which to increase implicit self-esteem by consistently affirming positive pairings of valence and self (e.g., Dijksterhuis, 2004), suggesting a possible avenue for therapy of narcissism and other negative effects of low implicit self-esteem.

Conclusion

The RIM offers a multitude of predictions that can help improve the understanding of the link between knowledge and action, whether it be explaining the reasoning processes behind complex plans such as the Trojan Horse, the seemingly self-destructive flight of Icarus, or even the conflict between rationality and impulse as epitomized in Odysseus' suffering of the Siren's song. Although effortful, reflective processing may occur in fluent synergy with impulsive processing, there are often conflicts between the two systems. Their resolution is a question of available reflective resources and motivation to use them. But whether the systems work in concert or struggle against one another, the pathway to behavior is ultimately the same—behavioral schemata are activated depending on the results of both systems' processing. However, it is not just knowledge that may determine action in the context of the RIM. The bidirectional associative links between behavioral schemata and other elements of the impulsive system mean that action, in turn, influences knowledge. This bidirectionality in combination with the functioning of the two systems can tell much about what it means to think and act, when No might appear to mean Yes, and how to pinpoint and modify the elusive implicit self.

References

Aidman, E. V., & Carroll, S. M. (2003). Implicit individual differences: Relationships between implicit self-esteem, gender identity, and gender attitudes. *European Journal of Personality, 17,* 19–37. doi:10.1002/per.465

Ajzen, I. (1985). From intentions to actions: A theory of planned behavior. In P. D. J. Kuhl & D. J. Beckmann (Eds.), *Action control* (pp. 11–39). Berlin: Springer. doi:10.1007/978-3-642-69746-3_2

Allport, F. H., & Lepkin, M. (1945). Wartime rumors of waste and special privilege: Why some people believe them. *The Journal of Abnormal and Social Psychology, 40,* 3–36. doi:10.1037/h0058110

Armitage, C. J., & Conner, M. (2001). Efficacy of the theory of planned behaviour: A meta-analytic review. *British Journal of Social Psychology, 40,* 471–499. doi:10.1348/014466601164939

Baddeley, A. (1986). Working memory, reading and dyslexia. In E. Hjelmquist & L. G. Nilsson (Eds.), *Communication and handicap* (pp. 141–152). Advances in Psychology: Vol. 34. North-Holland: Elsevier Science. doi:10.1016/S0166-4115(08)61202-9

Baer, R. A. (2003). Mindfulness training as a clinical intervention: A conceptual and empirical review. *Clinical Psychology: Science and Practice, 10,* 125–143. doi:10.1093/clipsy.bpg015

Banse, R., Seise, J., & Zerbes, N. (2001). Implicit attitudes towards homosexuality: Reliability, validity, and controllability of the IAT. *Experimental Psychology, 48,* 145–160. doi:10.1026//0949-3946.48.2.145

Bargh, J. (1997). The automaticity of everyday life. In R. S. Wyer, Jr. (Ed.), *The automaticity of everyday life* (pp. 1–61). Advances in Social Cognition: Vol. 10. Mahwah: Lawrence Erlbaum.

Baron, R. S. (2000). Arousal, capacity, and intense indoctrination. *Personality and Social Psychology Review, 4,* 238–254. doi:10.1207/S15327957PSPR0403_3

Baumeister, R. F., Bratslavsky, E., Muraven, M., & Tice, D. M. (1998). Ego depletion: Is the active self a limited resource? *Journal of Personality and Social Psychology, 74,* 1252–1265. doi:10.1037/0022-3514.74.5.1252

Beck, A. T. (1976). *Cognitive therapy and the emotional disorders.* Madison: International Universities Press.

Begg, I. M., Anas, A., & Farinacci, S. (1992). Dissociation of processes in belief: Source recollection, statement familiarity, and the illusion of truth. *Journal of Experimental Psychology: General, 121,* 446–458. doi:10.1037/0096-3445.121.4.446

Bem, D. J. (1967). Self-perception: An alternative interpretation of cognitive dissonance phenomena. *Psychological Review, 74,* 183–200. doi:10.1037/h0024835

Biener, L. (2002). Anti-tobacco advertisements by Massachusetts and Philip Morris: What teenagers think. *Tobacco Control,* 11(S2), ii43–ii46. doi:10.1136/tc.11.suppl_2.ii43

Block, J. H., & Block, J. (1980). The role of ego-control and ego-resiliency in the organization of behavior. In W. A. Collins (Ed.), *Development of cognition, affect, and social relations* (pp. 39–101). The Minnesota Symposia on Child Psychology: Vol. 13. Hillsdale: Erlbaum.

Bosson, J. K., Lakey, C. E., Campbell, W. K., Zeigler-Hill, V., Jordan, C. H., & Kernis, M. H. (2008). Untangling the links between narcissism and self-esteem: A theoretical and empirical review. *Social and Personality Psychology Compass, 2,* 1415–1439. doi:10.1111/j.1751-9004.2008.00089.x

Bosson, J. K., Swann, W. B., & Pennebaker, J. W. (2000). Stalking the perfect measure of implicit self-esteem: The blind men and the elephant revisited? *Journal of Personality and Social Psychology, 79,* 631–643. doi:10.1037/0022-3514.79.4.631

Bushman, B. J., & Cooper, H. M. (1990). Effects of alcohol on human aggression: An integrative research review. *Psychological Bulletin, 107,* 341–354. doi:10.1037/0033-2909.107.3.341

Carver, C. S. (2005). Impulse and constraint: Perspectives from personality psychology, convergence with theory in other areas, and potential for integration. *Personality and Social Psychology Review, 9,* 312–333. doi:10.1207/s15327957pspr0904_2

Chaiken, S. (1987). The heuristic model of persuasion. In M. P. Zanna, J. M. Olson, & C. P. Herman (Eds.), *Social influence: The Ontario symposium* (pp. 3–39). The Ontario Symposium: Vol. 5. Hillsdale: Erlbaum.

Chaiken, S., & Trope, Y. (Eds.). (1999). *Dual-process theories in social psychology.* New York: Guilford Press.

Conner, M., & Armitage, C. J. (1998). Extending the theory of planned behavior: A review and avenues for further research. *Journal of Applied Social Psychology, 28,* 1429–1464. doi:10.1111/j.1559-1816.1998.tb01685.x

Crisp, R. (2000). *Aristotle: Nicomachean ethics.* Cambridge: Cambridge University Press. http://dx.doi.org/10.1017/CBO9780511802058

De Neys, W. (2006). Dual processing in reasoning: Two systems but one reasoner. *Psychological Science, 17,* 428–433. doi:10.1111/j.1467-9280.2006.01723.x

Deutsch, R., Gawronski, B., & Strack, F. (2006). At the boundaries of automaticity: Negation as reflective operation. *Journal of Personality and Social Psychology, 91,* 385–405. doi:10.1037/0022-3514.91.3.385

Deutsch, R., Kordts-Freudinger, R., Gawronski, B., & Strack, F. (2009). Fast and fragile: A new look at the automaticity of negation processing. *Experimental Psychology, 56,* 434–446. doi:10.1027/1618-3169.56.6.434

Devine, P. G. (1989). Stereotypes and prejudice: Their automatic and controlled components. *Journal of Personality and Social Psychology, 56,* 5–18. doi:10.1037/0022-3514.56.1.5

DeWall, C. N., Baumeister, R. F., & Masicampo, E. J. (2008). Evidence that logical reasoning depends on conscious processing. *Consciousness and Cognition, 17,* 628–645. doi:10.1016/j.concog.2007.12.004

Dijksterhuis, A. (2004). I like myself but I don't know why: Enhancing implicit self-esteem by subliminal evaluative conditioning. *Journal of Personality and Social Psychology, 86,* 345–355. doi:10.1037/0022-3514.86.2.345

Eagly, A. H., & Chaiken, S. (1993). *The psychology of attitudes.* Fort Worth: Harcourt Brace.

Engle, R. W. (2002). Working memory capacity as executive attention. *Current Directions in Psychological Science, 11,* 19–23. doi:10.1111/1467-8721.00160

Epstein, S., Lipson, A., Holstein, C., & Huh, E. (1992). Irrational reactions to negative outcomes: Evidence for two conceptual systems. *Journal of Personality and Social Psychology, 62,* 328–339. doi:10.1037/0022-3514.62.2.328

Farrelly, M. C., Niederdeppe, J., & Yarsevich, J. (2003). Youth tobacco prevention mass media campaigns: Past, present, and future directions. *Tobacco Control, 12*(S1), i35–i47. doi:10.1136/tc.12.suppl_1.i35

Fazio, R. H. (1990). Multiple processes by which attitudes guide behavior: The MODE model as an integrative framework. In M. P. Zanna (Ed.), *Advances in experimental social psychology* (Vol. 23, pp. 75–109). New York: Academic Press.

Fazio, R. H. (2001). On the automatic activation of associated evaluations: An overview. *Cognition & Emotion, 15,* 115–141. doi:10.1080/02699930125908

Fazio, R. H., Jackson, J. R., Dunton, B. C., & Williams, C. J. (1995). Variability in automatic activation as an unobtrusive measure of racial attitudes: A bona fide pipeline? *Journal of Personality and Social Psychology, 69,* 1013–1027. doi:10.1037/0022-3514.69.6.1013

Fazio, R. H., & Olson, M. A. (2003). Implicit measures in social cognition research: Their meaning and use. *Annual Review of Psychology, 54,* 297–327. doi:10.1146/annurev. psych.54.101601.145225

Fazio, R. H., Sanbonmatsu, D. M., Powell, M. C., & Kardes, F. R. (1986). On the automatic activation of attitudes. *Journal of Personality and Social Psychology, 50,* 229–238. doi:10.1037/0022-3514.50.2.229

Festinger, L. (1957). *A theory of cognitive dissonance.* Stanford: Stanford University Press.

Fiedler, K., & Bluemke, M. (2005). Faking the IAT: Aided and unaided response control on the implicit association tests. *Basic and Applied Social Psychology, 27,* 307–316. doi:10.1207/s15324834basp2704_3

Fishbein, M., & Ajzen, I. (1975). *Belief, attitude, intention, and behavior: An introduction to theory and research.* Reading: Addison-Wesley.

Fiske, S. T., & Linville, P. W. (1980). What does the schema concept buy us? *Personality and Social Psychology Bulletin, 6,* 543–557. doi:10.1177/014616728064006

Förster, J., & Strack, F. (1996). Influence of overt head movements on memory for valenced words: A case of conceptual-motor compatibility. *Journal of Personality and Social Psychology, 71,* 421–430. doi:10.1037/0022-3514.71.3.421

Franck, E., De Raedt, R., & De Houwer, J. (2007). Implicit but not explicit self-esteem predicts future depressive symptomatology. *Behaviour Research and Therapy, 45,* 2448–2455. doi:10.1016/j.brat.2007.01.008

Friese, M., Hofmann, W., & Wänke, M. (2008). When impulses take over: Moderated predictive validity of explicit and implicit attitude measures in predicting food choice and consumption behaviour. *British Journal of Social Psychology, 47,* 397–419. doi:10.1348/014466607X241540

Gailliot, M. T., Baumeister, R. F., DeWall, C. N., Maner, J. K., Plant, E. A., Tice, D. M., Brewer, L. E., & Schmeichel, B. J. (2007). Self-control relies on glucose as a limited energy source: Willpower is more than a metaphor. *Journal of Personality and Social Psychology, 92,* 325–336. doi:10.1037/0022-3514.92.2.325

Gawronski, B., Deutsch, R., Mbirkou, S., Seibt, B., & Strack, F. (2008). When "Just Say No" is not enough: Affirmation versus negation training and the reduction of automatic stereotype activation. *Journal of Experimental Social Psychology, 44,* 370–377. doi:10.1016/j.jesp.2006.12.004

Gawronski, B., & Strack, F. (2004). On the propositional nature of cognitive consistency: Dissonance changes explicit, but not implicit attitudes. *Journal of Experimental Social Psychology, 40,* 535–542. doi:10.1016/j.jesp.2003.10.005

Gilbert, D. T. (1991). How mental systems believe. *American Psychologist, 46,* 107–119. doi:10.1037/0003-066X.46.2.107

Gilbert, D. T., Pelham, B. W., & Krull, D. S. (1988). On cognitive busyness: When person perceivers meet persons perceived. *Journal of Personality and Social Psychology, 54,* 733–740. doi:10.1037/0022-3514.54.5.733

Gollwitzer, P. M. (1999). Implementation intentions: Strong effects of simple plans. *American Psychologist, 54,* 493–503. doi:10.1037/0003-066X.54.7.493

Grant, S. J., Malaviya, P., & Sternthal, B. (2004). The influence of negation on product evaluations. *Journal of Consumer Research, 31,* 583–591. doi:10.1086/425093

Greene, J. D., Morelli, S. A., Lowenberg, K., Nystrom, L. E., & Cohen, J. D. (2008). Cognitive load selectively interferes with utilitarian moral judgment. *Cognition, 107,* 1144–1154. doi:10.1016/j.cognition.2007.11.004

Greenwald, A. G., & Banaji, M. R. (1995). Implicit social cognition: Attitudes, self-esteem, and stereotypes. *Psychological Review, 102,* 4–27. doi:10.1037/0033-295X.102.1.4

Greenwald, A. G., McGhee, D. E., & Schwartz, J. L. K. (1998). Measuring individual differences in implicit cognition: The implicit association test. *Journal of Personality and Social Psychology, 74,* 1464–1480. doi:10.1037/0022-3514.74.6.1464

Hofmann, W., Friese, M., & Strack, F. (2009). Impulse and self-control from a dual-systems perspective. *Perspectives on Psychological Science, 4,* 162–176. doi:10.1111/j.1745-6924.2009.01116.x

Hofmann, W., Gschwendner, T., Friese, M., Wiers, R. W., & Schmitt, M. (2008). Working memory capacity and self-regulatory behavior: Toward an individual differences perspective on behavior determination by automatic versus controlled processes. *Journal of Personality and Social Psychology, 95,* 962–977. doi:10.1037/a0012705

Hofmann, W., Rauch, W., & Gawronski, B. (2007). And deplete us not into temptation: Automatic attitudes, dietary restraint, and self-regulatory resources as determinants of eating behavior. *Journal of Experimental Social Psychology, 43,* 497–504. doi:10.1016/j.jesp.2006.05.004

James, W. (1890). *Principles of psychology.* New York: Holt.

Kawakami, K., Dovidio, J. F., Moll, J., Hermsen, S., & Russin, A. (2000). Just say no (to stereotyping): Effects of training in the negation of stereotypic associations on stereotype activation. *Journal of Personality and Social Psychology, 78,* 871–888. doi:10.1037/0022-3514.78.5.871

Kim, D.-Y. (2003). Voluntary controllability of the Implicit Association Test (IAT). *Social Psychology Quarterly, 66,* 83–96. doi:10.2307/3090143

Koole, S. L., Dijksterhuis, A., & van Knippenberg, A. (2001). What's in a name: Implicit self-esteem and the automatic self. *Journal of Personality and Social Psychology, 80,* 669–685. doi:10.1037//0022-3514.80.4.669

Kruglanski, A. W., & Freund, T. (1983). The freezing and unfreezing of lay-inferences: Effects on impressional primacy, ethnic stereotyping, and numerical anchoring. *Journal of Experimental Social Psychology, 19,* 448–468. doi:10.1016/0022-1031(83)90022-7

Krull, D. S., & Erickson, D. J. (1995). Judging situations: On the effortful process of taking dispositional information into account. *Social Cognition, 13,* 417–438. doi:10.1521/soco.1995.13.4.417

Lambert, A. J., Payne, K. B., Jacoby, L. L., Shaffer, L. M., Chasteen, A. L., & Khan, S. R. (2003). Stereotypes as dominant responses: On the "social facilitation" of prejudice in anticipated public contexts. *Journal of Personality and Social Psychology, 84,* 277–295. doi:10.1037/0022-3514.84.2.277

Langer, E. J., Blank, A., & Chanowitz, B. (1978). The mindlessness of ostensibly thoughtful action: The role of "placebic" information in interpersonal interaction. *Journal of Personality and Social Psychology, 36,* 635–642. doi:10.1037/0022-3514.36.6.635

Lattimore, P., & Maxwell, L. (2004). Cognitive load, stress, and disinhibited eating. *Eating Behaviors, 5,* 315–324. doi:10.1016/j.eatbeh.2004.04.009

Livingston, R. W. (2002). The role of perceived negativity in the moderation of African Americans' implicit and explicit racial attitudes. *Journal of Experimental Social Psychology, 38,* 405–413. doi:10.1016/S0022-1031(02)00002-1

Lodge, M., McGraw, K. M., Conover, P. J., Feldman, S., & Miller, A. H. (1991). Where is the schema? Critiques. *The American Political Science Review, 85,* 1357–1380. doi:10.2307/1963950

Mierke, J., & Klauer, K. C. (2001). Implicit association measurement with the IAT: Evidence for effects of executive control processes. *Experimental Psychology, 48,* 107–122. doi:10.1026//0949-3946.48.2.107

Mischel, W., Ebbesen, E. B., & Raskoff, Z. A. (1972). Cognitive and attentional mechanisms in the delay of gratification. *Journal of Personality and Social Psychology, 21,* 204–218. doi:10.1037/h0032198

Muraven, M., & Baumeister, R. F. (2000). Self-regulation and depletion of limited resources: Does self-control resemble a muscle? *Psychological Bulletin, 126,* 247–259. http://dx.doi:10.1037//0033-2909.126.2.247

Paulhus, D. L., & Lim, D. T. K. (1994). Arousal and evaluative extremity in social judgments: A dynamic complexity model. *European Journal of Social Psychology, 24,* 89–99. doi:10.1002/ejsp.2420240107

Petty, R. E., & Cacioppo, J. T. (1986). *Communication and persuasion: Central and peripheral routes to attitude change.* New York: Springer.

Purdon, C. (1999). Thought suppression and psychopathology. *Behaviour Research and Therapy, 37,* 1029–1054. doi:10.1016/S0005-7967(98)00200-9

Schachter, S. (1971). Some extraordinary facts about obese humans and rats. *American Psychologist, 26,* 129–144. doi:10.1037/h0030817

Schimmack, U., & Diener, E. (2003). Predictive validity of explicit and implicit self-esteem for subjective well-being. *Journal of Research in Personality, 37,* 100–106. doi:10.1016/S0092-6566(02)00532-9

Schmeichel, B. J., Vohs, K. D., & Baumeister, R. F. (2003). Intellectual performance and ego depletion: Role of the self in logical reasoning and other information processing. *Journal of Personality and Social Psychology, 85,* 33–46. doi:10.1037/0022-3514.85.1.33

Schwarz, N., Sanna, L. J., Skurnik, I., & Yoon, C. (2007). Metacognitive experiences and the intricacies of setting people straight: Implications for debiasing and public information campaigns. In M. P. Zanna (Ed.), *Advances in experimental social psychology* (Vol. 39, pp. 127–161). New York: Academic Press. doi:10.1016/S0065-2601(06)39003-X

Sloman, S. A. (1996). The empirical case for two systems of reasoning. *Psychological Bulletin, 119,* 3–22. doi:10.1037/0033-2909.119.1.3

Smith, E. R., & DeCoster, J. (2000). Dual-process models in social and cognitive psychology: Conceptual integration and links to underlying memory systems. *Personality and Social Psychology Review, 4,* 108–131. doi:10.1207/S15327957PSPR0402_01

Spalding, L. R., & Hardin, C. D. (1999). Unconscious unease and self-handicapping: Behavioral consequences of individual differences in implicit and explicit self-esteem. *Psychological Science, 10,* 535–539. doi:10.1111/1467-9280.00202

Strack, F., & Deutsch, R. (2004). Reflective and impulsive determinants of social behavior. *Personality and Social Psychology Review, 8,* 220–247. doi:10.1207/s15327957pspr0803_1

Strack, F., & Deutsch, R. (2007). The role of impulse in social behavior. In A. W. Kruglanski & E. T. Higgins (Eds.), *Social psychology: Handbook of basic principles* (revised and expanded 2nd ed., pp. 408–431). New York: Guilford Press.

Strack, F., Martin, L. L., & Stepper, S. (1988). Inhibiting and facilitating conditions of the human smile: A nonobtrusive test of the facial feedback hypothesis. *Journal of Personality and Social Psychology, 54,* 768–777. doi:10.1037/0022-3514.54.5.768

Strack, F., & Neumann, R. (1996). "The spirit is willing, but the flesh is weak": Beyond mind-body interaction in human decision-making. *Organizational Behavior and Human Decision Processes, 65,* 300–304. doi:10.1006/obhd.1996.0031

Sutton, S., Marsh, A., & Matheson, J. (1987). Explaining smokers' decisions to stop: Test of an expectancy-value approach. *Social Behaviour, 2,* 35–49.

Thush, C., Wiers, R. W., Ames, S. L., Grenard, J. L., Sussman, S., & Stacy, A. W. (2008). Interactions between implicit and explicit cognition and working memory capacity in the prediction of alcohol use in at-risk adolescents. *Drug and Alcohol Dependence, 94,* 116–124. doi:10.1016/j.drugalcdep.2007.10.019

Trope, Y., & Alfieri, T. (1997). Effortfulness and flexibility of dispositional judgment processes. *Journal of Personality and Social Psychology, 73,* 662–674. doi:10.1037/0022-3514.73.4.662

Vohs, K. D. (2006). Self-regulatory resources power the reflective system: Evidence from five domains. *Journal of Consumer Psychology, 16,* 217–223. doi:10.1207/s15327663jcp1603_3

Vohs, K. D., Baumeister, R. F., Schmeichel, B. J., Twenge, J. M., Nelson, N. M., & Tice, D. M. (2008). Making choices impairs subsequent self-control: A limited-resource account of decision making, self-regulation, and active initiative. *Journal of Personality and Social Psychology, 94,* 883–898. doi:10.1037/0022-3514.94.5.883

Vohs, K. D., & Faber, R. J. (2007). Spent resources: Self-regulatory resource availability affects impulse buying. *Journal of Consumer Research, 33,* 537–547. doi:10.1086/510228

Vohs, K. D., & Heatherton, T. F. (2000). Self-regulatory failure: A resource-depletion approach. *Psychological Science, 11,* 249–254. doi:10.1111/1467-9280.00250

Vroom, H, V. (1964). *Work and motivation.* New York: Wiley.

Wakefield, M. A., Durkin, S., Spittal, M. J., Siahpush, M., Scollo, M., Simpson, J. A., Chapman, S., White, V., & Hill, D. (2008). Impact of tobacco control policies and mass media campaigns on monthly adult smoking prevalence. *American Journal of Public Health, 98,* 1443–1450. doi:10.2105/AJPH.2007.128991

Wason, P. C. (1959). The processing of positive and negative information. *Quarterly Journal of Experimental Psychology, 11,* 92–107. doi:10.1080/17470215908416296

Wegner, D. M., Erber, R., & Zanakos, S. (1993). Ironic processes in the mental control of mood and mood-related thought. *Journal of Personality and Social Psychology, 65,* 1093–1104. doi:10.1037/0022-3514.65.6.1093

Wicklund, R. A., & Gollwitzer, P. M. (1981). Symbolic self-completion, attempted influence, and self-deprecation. *Basic and Applied Social Psychology, 2,* 89–114. doi:10.1207/s15324834basp0202_2

Wigfield, A., & Eccles, J. S. (2000). Expectancy—Value theory of achievement motivation. *Contemporary Educational Psychology, 25,* 68–81. doi:10.1006/ceps.1999.1015

Wilson, E. A. H., & Park, D. C. (2008). A case for clarity in the writing of health statements. *Patient Education and Counseling, 72,* 330–335. doi:10.1016/j.pec.2008.02.008

Wilson, M. (2002). Six views of embodied cognition. *Psychonomic Bulletin & Review, 9,* 625–636. doi:10.3758/BF03196322

Wimmer, H., & Perner, J. (1983). Beliefs about beliefs: Representation and constraining function of wrong beliefs in young children's understanding of deception. *Cognition, 13,* 103–128. doi:10.1016/0010-0277(83)90004-5

Winkielman, P., Huber, D. E., Kavanagh, L., & Schwarz, N. (2012). Fluency of consistency: When thoughts fit nicely and flow smoothly. In B. Gawronski & F. Strack (Eds.), *Cognitive consistency: A fundamental principle in social cognition* (pp. 89–111). New York: Guilford Press.

Wittenbrink, B., Judd, C. M., & Park, B. (2001). Spontaneous prejudice in context: Variability in automatically activated attitudes. *Journal of Personality and Social Psychology, 81,* 815–827. doi:10.1037/0022-3514.81.5.815

Yamaguchi, S., Greenwald, A. G., Banaji, M. R., Murakami, F., Chen, D., Shiomura, K., Kobayashi, C., Cai, H., & Krendl, K. (2007). Apparent universality of positive implicit self-esteem. *Psychological Science, 18,* 498–500. doi:10.1111/j.1467-9280.2007.01928.x

Yerkes, R. M., & Dodson, J. D. (1908). The relation of strength of stimulus to rapidity of habit-formation. *Journal of Comparative Neurology and Psychology, 18,* 459–482. doi:10.1002/cne.920180503

Zajonc, R. B. (1980). Feeling and thinking: Preferences need no inferences. *American Psychologist, 35,* 151–175. doi:10.1037/0003-066X.35.2.151

Zeigler-Hill, V. (2006). Discrepancies between implicit and explicit self-esteem: Implications for narcissism and self-esteem instability. *Journal of Personality, 74,* 119–144. doi:10.1111/j.1467-6494.2005.00371.x

Zhong, C.-B., & Liljenquist, K. (2006). Washing away your sins: Threatened morality and physical cleansing. *Science, 313,* 1451–1452. doi:10.1126/science.1130726

Chapter 10
Planning and the Control of Action

Frank Wieber and Peter M. Gollwitzer

Planning has been found to have a powerful effect on human actions (e.g., Gollwitzer & Sheeran, 2006). But how do people plan? In this chapter we first introduce implementation intentions (e.g., Gollwitzer, 1999) as an efficient way of planning. Implementation intentions refer to specific plans in which individuals and groups can specify when, where, and how they intend to act using an if-then format (e.g., "If I come home from work on Fridays, then I will immediately put on my jogging shoes and go for a 30-minute run!"). After we examine how they support goal pursuit, we differentiate between spontaneous and strategic planning—two ways in which if–then plans can be made on the basis of goal-related knowledge.

With respect to spontaneous planning, we highlight the importance of the accessibility of goal-related knowledge. We introduce goal systems theory (Kruglanski, Shah, Fishbach, Friedman, Chun, & Sleeth-Keppler, 2002) as a conceptual framework because it addresses the question of how goals can increase the accessibility of knowledge about when, where, and how to pursue the goal. To illustrate how the accessibility of goal-related knowledge facilitates goal attainment, we discuss a set of recent studies. They show that individuals spontaneously grasp goal-relevant information in the form of implementation intentions (Marquardt, Tröger, Wieber, & Gollwitzer, 2016; see also Marquardt, 2011) even if it is incidentally provided in their environment and that they use this knowledge to improve their goal attainment without being prompted to do so.

F. Wieber (✉)
School of Health Professions, Institute for Health Sciences, ZHAW Zurich University of Applied Sciences, CH-8401 Winterthur, Switzerland

Department of Psychology, University of Konstanz, Konstanz, Germany
e-mail: frank.wieber@zhaw.ch

P.M. Gollwitzer
Department of Psychology, New York University, New York, NY, USA

Department of Psychology, University of Konstanz, Konstanz, Germany

© The Author(s) 2017
P. Meusburger et al. (eds.), *Knowledge and Action*, Knowledge and Space 9,
DOI 10.1007/978-3-319-44588-5_10

Regarding strategic planning, we argue that individuals' knowledge about their goals, potential obstacles during goal pursuit, and effective goal-directed actions is central to devising effective plans and to the successful control of action. We introduce Mental Contrasting with Implementation Intentions (MCII; Oettingen, Wittchen, & Gollwitzer, 2013; Oettingen, 2014) as an effective self-regulation strategy with which to systematize the selection of goal-relevant knowledge and the translation of that knowledge into if–then plans. In this chapter we discuss a recent experimental study suggesting that such strategic planning is very useful in unstructured situational contexts that require identification and selection of appropriate goal-relevant knowledge. We further suggest that strategic planning is less useful in structured situational contexts that prompt the goal-directed actions without requiring any knowledge about advantageous opportunities to act and about potential obstacles (Sailer et al., 2015). We conclude by emphasizing how useful spontaneous and strategic planning is for transforming individuals' goal-related knowledge into action.

Controlling Actions by Goals and Implementation Intentions

In the psychology of action (e.g., Lewin, Dembo, Festinger, & Sears, 1944; Gollwitzer & Bargh, 1996), two phenomena are thought to be relevant to goal pursuit: goal-setting and goal-striving. They are governed by different principles. Goal-setting is concerned with the choice of a desired end state for which to strive (What is being pursued?); goal-striving is associated with moving toward the desired end state (How is the goal being pursued?). Goals are thereby defined as desired end states that people intend to attain and to which they commit themselves (Gollwitzer & Oettingen, 2012). For individuals to commit themselves firmly to a goal, they must perceive it as highly desirable and feasible. These assessments are based on an individual's knowledge about a potential pursuit of the goal. Knowing that sunny weather has been forecast and having no commitments for the coming weekend, for example, one might judge a weekend trip to a nearby national park as both desirable and feasible and might consequently commit oneself to the goal of going on a weekend trip to that place.

Nonetheless, even when individuals have strongly pledged themselves to a goal, such commitment does not guarantee successful goal attainment. This fact is referred to as the intention–behavior gap (e.g., Sheeran, 2002). In a meta-analysis by Webb and Sheeran (2006), for instance, a moderate-to-large change ($d = 0.66$) in the strength of individuals' intentions resulted in only a small-to-moderate change in the individuals' behavior ($d = 0.36$). In considering why the transition of one's intention into goal-directed actions might fail, researchers (e.g., Gollwitzer & Sheeran, 2006) have identified several typical problems that have to be overcome during goal-striving. People must start acting on a goal, persist or even intensify their efforts in the face of difficulties or obstacles, shield their goal from interferences or distractions, abandon ineffective means or even the goal itself if it becomes obviously unattainable, and economize on their limited resources to self-regulate their actions. Knowledge about the when, where, and how of striving toward a goal is necessary, but not sufficient, for successfully attaining it. Even when individuals know how to pursue a goal, they might struggle to turn their knowledge into goal-directed actions. Strategies that allow effective regulation of one's thoughts, feelings, and actions during goal-striving are needed. One time- and cost-efficient strategy to promote individuals' goal-striving is to devise implementation intentions for planning when, where, and how one intends to act (Gollwitzer, 1993, 1999, 2014; overview by Wieber, Thürmer, & Gollwitzer, 2015b). In implementation intentions, people specify a well-suited or critical future situation and link an adaptive goal-directed response to it in an if–then format. For example, aa person intending to learn a new language might opt for one of the following implementation intentions: "If I am finished eating my Sunday morning breakfast, then I will work through one lecture of the language course on my computer," or "If 'New E-mail' notifications pop up while I am working on the language course on my computer, then I will ignore them."

What is so special about such simple if–then plans? Researchers studying the processes underlying the effects of implementation intentions have systematically tried to answer to this question. Essentially, implementation intentions are at the junction of controlled and automatic processes (e.g., Evans, 2008; Strack & Deutsch, 2004). The intentional formation of if–then plans typically emerges from deliberation on when, where, and how to act. By contrast, the implementation of goal-directed action in response to an existing, specified, critical situation entails features of automaticity (e.g., Bargh, 1994): Effects of implementation intentions have been observed to be immediate and efficient, and once the specified situation is encountered they come about without requiring extensive deliberation on how to respond (e.g., Aarts, Dijksterhuis, & Midden, 1999; Webb & Sheeran, 2007, 2008; Wieber & Sassenberg, 2006).

Indeed, empirical evidence suggests that forming implementation intentions in addition to mere goals leads to faster responses to critical situations (e.g., Parks-Stamm, Gollwitzer, & Oettingen, 2007) and improved performance in a secondary task without compromising the simultaneous performance in a primary task (i.e., speed-up effects are still evident under high cognitive load; e.g., Brandstätter, Lengfelder, & Gollwitzer, 2001). This research also suggests that there is no need for a further conscious intent to act in a critical moment. For instance, Bayer, Achtziger, Gollwitzer, and Moskowitz (2009) found that implementation intentions encouraged successful pursuit of a goal even when the critical cue was presented subliminally, that is, when it was not consciously recognized. Moreover, studies of the human brain have found evidence that implementation intentions change action control from slow top-down to fast bottom-up processes (e.g., Gilbert, Gollwitzer, Cohen, Oettingen, & Burgess, 2009; Schweiger Gallo, Keil, McCulloch, Rockstroh, & Gollwitzer, 2009; Hallam et al., 2015). In summary, implementation intentions strategically automate the control of goal-directed actions, instantly and efficiently activating the action response linked to a critical situation when the individual enters it.

The Role of Knowledge Accessibility in Planning and in the Control of Action

To assist the individual's pursuit of a goal effectively, implementation intentions need to specify relevant critical situations in the if-component and instrumental responses in the then-component (see also Gollwitzer, Wieber, Myers, & McCrea, 2009). Prior studies have generally observed that people can indeed identify and self-select suitable situations and responses (e.g., Adriaanse, de Ridder, & de Wit, 2009; Gollwitzer & Brandstätter, 1997). In fact, both experimenter-provided and self-generated implementation intentions have been shown to foster goal attainment effectively (Armitage, 2009). But how do people generate effective plans?

Individuals have to access goal-relevant knowledge before they can further process this information. Generally, psychological research shows wide agreement that knowledge accessibility is important for individuals' cognition and behavior (overview by Wyer, 2008). As for the accessibility of goal-related knowledge, goal systems theory (Kruglanski et al., 2002) affords a helpful conceptual framework for understanding how pursuing a goal affects the accessibility and application of knowledge that is relevant to planning. This theory rests on a cognitive approach to motivation. Its proponents apply a network conceptualization that allows for dynamic and malleable modeling of the activation and permits application of cognitive content to motivation content. Within this "motivation-as-cognition" approach, goal systems are defined as "the mental representations of motivational networks composed of interconnected goals and means" (Kruglanski et al., 2002, p. 333). Given this connectedness of goals and means, the activation of a mental representation of a goal should also activate the mental representation of suitable means to pursue this goal. When this idea is applied to planning, it follows that when one is pursuing a goal (e.g., to prepare a healthy dinner), knowledge of possible means that is relevant to planning the when, where, and how of goal-striving becomes easily accessible (e.g., thinking of the salad in one's fridge and of the tomatoes that one has to purchase on the way home).

Two properties of the interconnections are thus especially interesting for the activation of goal-relevant knowledge: structure and strength. As far as the structure of the interconnections are concerned, the number of means that are attached to a goal can vary. For one person, activating the physical fitness goal might activate only the means of going to the gym, but for another person it might activate a multitude of means (e.g., going to the gym, riding a bike to work, and taking the stairs). In addition to such interindividual differences, the number of means connected to a goal might also vary from one goal to the next. For instance, there might be numerous ways to pursue the goal of eating healthily (e.g., eating at least five portions of fruit and vegetables a day, drinking water rather than soft drinks) but only a few ways to pursue the goal of acquiring a driver's license (i.e., taking the official test). Concerning the strength of the interconnections, one may expect the strength of the cognitive association between the goal and the means for achieving it to be stronger when the number of those means is relatively low than when it is relatively high.

Going to the gym will probably be more likely to come to one's mind if it is the only means rather than one of several that are connected to one's physical fitness goal. In summary, the structure and strength of the goal–means interconnections relating to a given goal seem relevant to planning because the activation of knowledge about potential means is a starting point for individual planning. Thus, the activation of the goal should ease the access to the knowledge relevant to the when and where (the if-component) and to the how (the then-component) of implementing that goal.

Spontaneous Use of Incidentally Presented Goal-Relevant Information

Given the importance of accessibility, one might wonder whether incidental knowledge that is offered in an external context is also used by individuals to support their pursuit of a goal. In other words, are individuals capable of grasping goal-relevant knowledge about suitable opportunities, potential obstacles, and instrumental action strategies without much conscious effort?

Studies by Marquardt et al. (2016) addressed this question. They tested whether incidentally furnished goal-relevant information favors subsequent goal attainment. Moreover, they investigated whether the spontaneous use of incidentally provided implementation intentions depends on the activation of the particular goal. The authors expected that individuals would make spontaneous use of incidentally provided implementation intentions—but only when the goal had been previously activated.

Marquardt et al. (2016) first examined whether incidentally communicated plans can promote high school students' achievement in a school setting. Initially, the researchers implicitly activated the achievement goal of the participating students by having them work on a crossword puzzle containing either achievement-related words (achievement-goal condition) or neutral words (no achievement-goal-control condition). Priming the goal rather than asking individuals to set the goal themselves was intended to reduce the likelihood that they would try to plan consciously. To induce spontaneous implementation intention, all students in the study completed on paper a puzzle about sentence construction. It presented 34 sentence fragments in scrambled order. The task of the students was to (a) form six meaningful sentences by connecting the fragments and (b) write down these sentences. All six sentences had been composed as conditional phrases (if–then structure). The only difference between the intention conditions was that one of the six sentences in the implementation-intention condition was relevant to the subsequent creativity task ("If I have found a use, then I will instantly search for the next use."), whereas none of the six sentences in the no-achievement-goal condition and the mere-achievement-goal condition were relevant to the subsequent creativity task.

Students then worked on an ostensibly unrelated alternative- uses task (Guilford, 1967), in which they had to write down as many different ways of using a matchbox as possible. The number of different ways that students came up with was used to measure the effects of the manipulations of the goal and the plan. The results showed that participants in the achievement-goal-plus-implementation-intention condition found more uses for a matchbox than did the participants in the mere-achievement-goal and no-achievement-goal-control conditions. Thus, giving goal-relevant information (i.e., the implementation intention) improved goal attainment even when the information was delivered incidentally (i.e., before participants knew that it constituted an effective planning strategy for performing well on a later task). These findings tentatively bear out our argument that people can spontaneously use goal-related knowledge to bolster their goal attainment.

To corroborate these findings, Marquardt et al. (2016) ran a second study on the spontaneous use of goal-relevant knowledge. This time, the degree to which the individuals' healthy-diet goal benefited from incidentally shared plans to eat healthily was tested in a university cafeteria. The study was divided into two parts. The first part took place in the morning and served to manipulate participants' goal to eat healthily. Participants either read a short text of evidence-based arguments for a balanced diet with five portions of fruits and vegetables a day (healthy-diet goal condition) or a neutral text on nutrition science in Germany (no-goal-control condition), which was approximately the same length and had no words related to the healthy-diet goal.

Below the goal manipulation texts, a graphical display was positioned on the information sheet. This display was used to manipulate the incidentally offered plan. In all three conditions—no-healthy-diet-goal-control (A), mere-healthy-diet-goal (B), and mere-healthy-diet-goal-plus-implementation-intention (C)—participants received pictorial information on how to act on the healthy-diet goal. The graphical display consisted of three photographs showing the cafeteria's salad bar, the vegetable bar, and the fruit shelf (each seen from the perspective of an individual standing directly in front it). All participants therefore had identical information on the how of eating healthily at the cafeteria. However, only participants in condition C received two additional pieces of information. First, to the left of the three photographs, the participants saw one photograph of the cafeteria entrance. This image thus depicted a suitable opportunity for them to act on their healthy-diet goal and can be thought of as specifying the if-component of an implementation intention. Second, they saw an arrow pointing from the picture of the cafeteria entrance to the three photographs of the suitable responses (i.e., selecting salad, fruit, and/or vegetables). The arrow thereby connected the different pictures and was an equivalent to the link between the if-component and the then-component in verbal implementation intentions. In summary, participants in condition C received information on the how of goal pursuit (photographs of the salad bar, the vegetable bar, and the fruit shelf), the when and where (picture of the cafeteria entrance), and a graphical link between the pictures that implied the characteristic structure of the if–then condition.

The second part of the experiment took place during lunch time. Participants completed a questionnaire after they had finished their meal at the cafeteria. They indicated how many portions of salad, vegetables, and fruit they had consumed there on which day. The total sum was used to measure the effects that the goal and plan manipulation had on the diet of the participants. Participants in condition C consumed a greater quantity and variety of healthy foods than did participants in either condition A or B. Thus, passing on if–then information that was relevant to planning improved goal attainment even when this information came incidentally (in this case, through a graphical display).

Together, these findings further underline the importance of knowledge accessibility for individuals' goal pursuits. People readily used their newly acquired goal-related knowledge to conceive if–then plans for their goal attainment spontaneously. In our view, such spontaneous planning highlights the fact that automatic processes can be instrumental in the adaptive control of action. It is, however, important to note that the spontaneous planning occurred on the basis of an activated goal, further indicating that effects of implementation intention depend on the activation of a superordinate goal (Sheeran, Webb, & Gollwitzer, 2005).

Strategic Use of Goal-Relevant Knowledge with MCII

The use of goal intentions to guide action is aided by the coactivation of means associated with a goal. However, identifying and forming effective if–then plans might vary in difficulty, depending on the individual, the situation, and the specific goal. It may well be that neither the automatic activation of goal-related knowledge nor the spontaneous acquisition and use of incidentally presented goal-relevant information is enough to guide individuals' actions successfully when pursuing the goal is difficult (e.g., when that pursuit is cognitively or motivationally demanding). A goal can be difficult for reasons related to the individual, such as internal obstacles (e.g., ego control or procrastination; see Gollwitzer, Bayer, & McCulloch, 2005; Wieber & Gollwitzer, 2010, in press). Or it may be difficult because of the situation, that is, because of external obstacles (e.g., distractions; see Wieber, von Suchodoletz, Heikamp, Trommsdorff, & Gollwitzer, 2011). Whatever the case, individuals must carefully select the action they include in the if- and then-components of their implementation intentions. Depending on the goal at hand and on the existing ideas about goals and means, individuals might either narrow their focus to fewer situations and responses or extend the range of situations and responses they take into account when pursuing their goal. If people experience problems with sticking to a healthy diet when watching TV in the evening, they might want to address this situation specifically. Or when people experience problems with recognizing opportunities to exercise, they might want to expand the situations and means connected to their physical fitness goal.

A systematic guide to planning would be helpful for such challenging goal pursuit, and that guide exists—the preparation of if–then planning by means of mental contrasting (e.g., Oettingen et al., 2009; Oettingen, Pak, & Schnetter, 2001; for summaries see Oettingen, 2012, 2014). Mental contrasting brings individuals to actively search through their goal-relevant knowledge and select or even derive critical situations and suitable responses. In the application of the strategy, individuals are asked to formulate a personal wish, to imagine positive future outcomes of realizing that wish, and to mentally contrast these outcomes with current potential obstacles to their goal-striving. Mental contrasting thereby increases the accessibility of both a positive future vision and the current reality, instilling a sense that action is necessary. Moreover, mental contrasting is thought to activate relevant expectations that allow for an adjustment of personal goal commitment (a person's attachment to a goal or the decisiveness to reach it; Locke, Latham, & Erez, 1988). If the expectation of reaching the desired outcome is high, commitment is strengthened by mental contrasting; if it is low and effort might be in vain, commitment is weakened and individuals disengage.

In the next step, MCII guides individuals in using this knowledge of potential obstacles and in detecting instrumental responses to each of them. Corroborating the effectiveness of combining mental contrasting and implementation intentions, one study found that MCII participants reported greater success at reducing their unhealthy snacking consumption than did participants who used either only mental contrasting or only implementation intentions (Study 2 in Adriaanse et al., 2010). According to this line of thought, MCII is likeliest to contribute to one's goal attainment when the strategic search for one's goal-relevant knowledge and planning can make a difference. MCII is less likely to do so when one's environment prompts the when, where, and how of goal-directed actions to begin with.

One study by Sailer et al. (2015) addresses this argument. The authors ran an MCII intervention study on physical exercise in a clinical context. Previous research had indicated that regular exercise can have positive effects on both the physical and mental health of persons with schizophrenia. However, shortcomings in cognition, perception, affect, and volition make it especially difficult for people with schizophrenia to plan a behavior and follow through on it. As a result, studies that had incorporated exercise reported poor attendance and high drop-out rates, indicating that schizophrenic patients were not able to overcome the manifold barriers to physical activity. Sailer et al. therefore tested whether MCII helps convert schizophrenic individuals' exercise intentions into behavior while taking into account the supportiveness of the situational context.

The patients diagnosed with a schizophrenic spectrum disorder lived in either an autonomy-focused setting (a self-supply ward with daytime care by nurses, medical doctors, and psychologists) or a highly structured setting (a ward providing intense therapy to activate patients and affording continuous availability of psychiatric care). Whereas participants in the autonomy-focused setting had to manage attending the exercise groups on their own, those in the highly structured setting were actively reminded and invited to each exercise session. The authors predicted that engaging in MCII would help individuals attain their exercise goals in the autonomy-focused setting (in which each search and application of goal-relevant knowledge depended on the patients themselves) but not in the highly structured setting (in which the environment made the relevant information available in order to prompt the goal-directed actions). To test this prediction, participants who agreed to participate in the study were randomly assigned to an information-plus-goal-intention condition (control group) or an information-plus-MCII condition (MCII group). Patients in the control group read a nonfiction text on the benefits of physical activity and on potential obstacles for which one must prepare (e.g., motivational problems and tiredness). They then set the goal to attend jogging sessions and wrote it down. Patients in the MCII group read the same nonfiction text and then worked through the MCII strategy, listing three positive outcomes associated with attending the exercise session (e.g., losing weight) and three obstacles (e.g., feeling tired). Next, they identified their most important obstacle and, with their therapist, worked out a specific solution to this obstacle before translating it into an implementation intention in the if–then format: "If [obstacle], then I will [response]." In both groups participants were treated by a trained therapist during individual training sessions that involved an equal amount of contact between the therapist and each of the patients.

The attendance and persistence of the patients in the exercise program of the participating clinics during the 4 weeks after their treatment was measured as the dependent variable. In both the autonomy-focused and the highly structured setting, two jogging sessions were scheduled every week and did not conflict with therapies or other events. During jogging sessions, participants could run at their own pace and decide how long they wanted to run. Results in the highly structured setting showed that MCII and control participants alike attended about 70 % of the offered exercise sessions. In the autonomy-focused setting, however, control participants attended less than 40 % of the sessions, whereas the MCII participants continued attending about 70 % of them. When it comes to successful goal attainment, these findings demonstrate the importance of self-regulating one's goal pursuits and goal-striving in rather unstructured situations. When goal-directed actions were prompted contextually, MCII did not improve goal attainment, for it was already rather high. But when goal-related knowledge mattered because remembering and initiating the goal-directed actions was up to individuals, MCII did improve goal attainment. These findings imply that the MCII self-regulation strategy constitutes a time- and cost-efficient action-control tool that helps patients with severe mental illness (see also Toli, Webb, & Hardy, 2016) to achieve their health-related goals in an autonomous setting.

Strategic Planning of the Automatic Activation of Goal-Relevant Knowledge

In addition to the spontaneous and strategic planning described above, planning with implementation intentions can also be beneficial as a context-sensitive reminder of one's strategies or goals that supports reflective decision making and goal-directed actions. This strategic use of the automatic effects of planning with implementation intentions is related to the demands that have been postulated for human-centered computer systems in information management. The aim in the interaction between humans and computers in sociotechnical systems is to communicate the right information at the right time and the right place in the right way to the right person in order to empower that person to find and select the best goal-directed response (e.g., Fischer, 2012). Implementation intentions might also be used to achieve this end.

First, implementation intentions provide the relevant information about instrumental action responses in critical situations during goal pursuit. In a study on group decision-making (Thürmer, Wieber, & Gollwitzer, 2015a, 2015b), participants set themselves the goal of performing well. In keeping with this goal, they then either generated the specific goal of reviewing the advantages of the nonpreferred alternatives before making a group decision (control condition) or included this strategy in the implementation intention: "And when we finally take the decision sheet to note our preferred alternative, then we will go over the advantages of the non-preferred alternatives again" (Thürmer et al., 2015a, p. 104). As a result of this small difference in planning, implementation-intention groups succeeded more often than mere goal-intention groups at transforming their respective intentions into actions and thereby improving their goal attainment. Apparently, implementation intentions provided the strategy information to the group members just before the group decision was taken and thereby oriented them in their search for the best solution to the issue on which they were about to decide.

Second, implementation intentions have also been found to be capable of activating one's goal at a critical juncture and thereby increasing the impact of this goal on individuals' cognition and behavior (van Koningsbruggen, Stroebe, Papies, & Aarts, 2011). In a study on dieting, unsuccessful dieters either formed a think-of-dieting implementation intention ("The next time that I am tempted to eat chocolate [cookies, pizza, French fries, or chips], then I will think of dieting") or just indicated why it was important for them to resist the temptation to eat chocolate [cookies, pizza, French fries, or chips]. In a subsequent word-completion task, participants in the implementation-intention condition were instructed to fill in unfinished words (e.g., _ij_e_) that were preceded by one of the five food cues (e.g., chocolate). In completing the task, they used diet-related words (e.g., *lijnen*, Dutch for dieting) instead of neutral words (e.g., *tijger*, Dutch for tiger) more often than control participants did. Evidently, implementation intentions reminded individuals of their dieting goal when they encountered a tempting situation (Study 1) and thus empowered unsuccessful dieters to reduce their consumption of palatable foods (Study 2). Together, the findings of these studies (Thürmer et al., 2015a, 2015b; van Koningsbruggen et al., 2011; see also Wieber, Thürmer, & Gollwitzer, 2015a) demonstrate that strategic automation of action control by planning with implementation intentions can serve goal attainment even when a reflective decision needs to be made or when individuals are not aware of instrumental action strategies at the time of planning.

Conclusion and Outlook

In this chapter we have examined the role that knowledge has in planning and action control. We have stressed that knowing which goal one intends to pursue and committing oneself to that goal are often only the first step toward successful goal attainment. Planning when, where, and how to act with implementation intentions has proven to be an effective self-regulation strategy for reducing this intention–behavior gap. Regarding the acquisition and use of plan-relevant knowledge, we have argued that individuals have a variety of ways to form implementation intentions. They range from spontaneous planning of how to approach a goal on the basis of accessible goal-related knowledge to strategic planning that includes a systematic search of knowledge for critical situations and instrumental action responses.

With respect to spontaneous planning, we have argued that the activation of a goal coactivates goal-relevant knowledge and thus greatly facilitates the decision on when, where, and how to pursue the goal. Although this automatic coactivation is likely to be an adaptive mechanism that promotes successful control of action most of the time, it can also hinder behavioral change. For instance, having the goal of getting to work might automatically induce one to take the car rather than use public transport, even if one intends to adopt a sustainable lifestyle (e.g., Bamberg, 2000). In that sense, strategic planning is a powerful self-regulatory tool informing behavioral change. In fact, authors of meta-analyses of effects that implementation intention has on physical activity (Bélanger-Gravel, Godin, & Amireault, 2013) and eating behavior (Adriaanse, Vinkers, de Ridder, Hox, & de Wit, 2011) found that implementation intentions successfully aid the translation of individuals' intentions into action. The strategic automation of action control by implementation intentions has even been found to remind the individual of a useful reflective strategy (Thürmer et al., 2015a), to reinforce one's goal in a critical situation (van Koningsbruggen et al., 2011), or to foster the restructuring of automatic goal–means connections that are required to change habitual behavior (e.g., Adriaanse, Gollwitzer, de Ridder, de Wit, & Kroese, 2011). Combining mental contrasting and implementation intentions in order to extend planning has proven more effective than either mental contrasting or implementation intentions alone (Study 2 in Adriaanse et al., 2010). Hence, strategic planning with MCII appears to be an especially effective tool for encouraging individuals to make effective use of their goal-relevant knowledge and thus improve the attainment of their goals. In summary, the planning research we have presented in this chapter highlights the adaptive role of spontaneous and strategic planning in turning an individual's knowledge into action.

References

Aarts, H., Dijksterhuis, A., & Midden, C. (1999). To plan or not to plan? Goal achievement or interrupting the performance of mundane behaviors. *European Journal of Social Psychology, 29*, 971–979. doi:10.1002/(SICI)1099-0992(199912)29:8

Adriaanse, M. A., de Ridder, D. T. D., & de Wit, J. B. F. (2009). Finding the critical cue: Implementation intentions to change one's diet work best when tailored to personally relevant reasons for unhealthy eating. *Personality and Social Psychology Bulletin, 35*, 60–71. doi:10.1177/0146167208325612

Adriaanse, M. A., Gollwitzer, P. M., de Ridder, D. T. D., de Wit, J. B. F., & Kroese, F. M. (2011). Breaking habits with implementation intentions: A test of underlying processes. *Personality and Social Psychology Bulletin, 37*, 502–513. doi:10.1177/0146167211399102

Adriaanse, M. A., Oettingen, G., Gollwitzer, P. M., Hennes, E. P., de Ridder, D. T. D., & de Wit, J. B. F. (2010). When planning is not enough: Fighting unhealthy snacking habits by mental contrasting with implementation intentions (MCII). *European Journal of Social Psychology, 40*, 1277–1293. doi:10.1002/ejsp.730

Adriaanse, M. A., Vinkers, C. D. W., de Ridder, D. T. D., Hox, J. J., & de Wit, J. B. F. (2011). Do implementation intentions help to eat a healthy diet? A systematic review and meta-analysis of the empirical evidence. *Appetite, 56*, 183–193. doi:10.1016/j.appet.2010.10.012

Armitage, C. J. (2009). Effectiveness of experimenter-provided and self-generated implementation intentions to reduce alcohol consumption in a sample of the general population: A randomized exploratory trial. *Health Psychology, 28*, 545–553. doi:10.1037/a0015984

Bamberg, S. (2000). The promotion of new behavior by forming an implementation intention: Results of a field experiment in the domain of travel mode choice. *Journal of Applied Social Psychology, 30*, 1903–1922. doi:10.1111/j.1559-1816.2000.tb02474.x

Bargh, J. A. (1994). The four horsemen of automaticity: Awareness, intention, efficiency, and control in social cognition. In R. S. Wyer, Jr. & T. K. Srull (Eds.), *Handbook of social cognition, Vol. 1: Basic processes* (2nd ed., pp. 1–40). Hillsdale: Lawrence Erlbaum Associates.

Bayer, U. C., Achtziger, A., Gollwitzer, P. M., & Moskowitz, G. B. (2009). Responding to subliminal cues: Do if-then plans facilitate action preparation and initiation without conscious intent? *Social Cognition, 27*, 183–201. doi:10.1521/soco.2009.27.2.183

Bélanger-Gravel, A., Godin, G., & Amireault, S. (2013). A meta-analytic review of the effect of implementation intentions on physical activity. *Health Psychology Review, 7*, 23–54. doi:10.1080/17437199.2011.560095

Brandstätter, V., Lengfelder, A., & Gollwitzer, P. M. (2001). Implementation intentions and efficient action initiation. *Journal of Personality and Social Psychology, 81*, 946–960. doi:10.1037/0022-3514.81.5.946

Evans, J. S. B. T. (2008). Dual-processing accounts of reasoning, judgment, and social cognition. *Annual Review of Psychology, 59*, 255–278. doi:10.1146/annurev.psych.59.103006.093629

Fischer, G. (2012). Context-aware systems: The T "right" information, at the "right'" time, in the "right'" place, in the "right'''" way, to the "right" person. In G. Tortora, S. Levialdi, & M. Tucci (Eds.), *Proceedings of the international working conference on advanced visual interfaces* (pp. 287–294). New York: ACM. doi:10.1145/2254556.2254611

Gilbert, S. J., Gollwitzer, P. M., Cohen, A.-L., Oettingen, G., & Burgess, P. W. (2009). Separable brain systems supporting cued versus self-initiated realization of delayed intentions. *Journal of Experimental Psychology: Learning, Memory, and Cognition, 35*, 905–915. doi:10.1037/a0015535

Gollwitzer, P. M. (1993). Goal achievement: The role of intentions. *European Review of Social Psychology, 4*, 141–185. doi:10.1080/14792779343000059

Gollwitzer, P. M. (1999). Implementation intentions: Strong effects of simple plans. *American Psychologist, 54*, 493–503. doi:10.1037/0003-066X.54.7.493

Gollwitzer, P. M. (2014). Weakness of the will: Is a quick fix possible? *Motivation and Emotion, 38,* 305–322. doi:10.1007/s11031-014-9416-3

Gollwitzer, P. M., & Bargh, J. A. (1996). *The psychology of action: Linking cognition and motivation to behavior*. New York: Guilford Press.

Gollwitzer, P. M., Bayer, U. C., & McCulloch, K. C. (2005). The control of the unwanted. In R. R. Hassin, J. S. Uleman, & J. A. Bargh (Eds.), *The new unconscious* (pp. 485–515). New York: Oxford University Press. doi:10.1093/acprof:oso/9780195307696.003.0018

Gollwitzer, P. M., & Brandstätter, V. (1997). Implementation intentions and effective goal pursuit. *Journal of Personality and Social Psychology, 73,* 186–199. doi:10.1037/0022-3514.73.1.186

Gollwitzer, P. M., & Oettingen, G. (2012). Goal pursuit. In R. M. Ryan (Ed.), *The Oxford handbook of human motivation* (pp. 208–231). New York: Oxford University Press. doi:10.1093/oxfordhb/9780195399820.013.0013

Gollwitzer, P. M., & Sheeran, P. (2006). Implementation intentions and goal achievement: A meta-analysis of effects and processes. *Advances in Experimental Social Psychology, 38,* 69–119. doi:10.1016/S0065-2601(06)38002-1

Gollwitzer, P. M., Wieber, F., Myers, A. L., & McCrea, S. M. (2009). How to maximize implementation intention effects. In C. R. Agnew, D. E. Carlston, W. G. Graziano, & J. R. Kelly (Eds.), *Then a miracle occurs: Focusing on behavior in social psychological theory and research* (pp. 137–161). New York: Oxford University Press. doi:10.1093/acprof:oso/9780195377798.003.0008

Guilford, J. P. (1967). *The nature of human intelligence*. New York: McGraw-Hill.

Hallam, G. P., Webb, T. L., Sheeran, P., Miles, E., Wilkinson, I. D., Hunter, M. D.,...Farrow, T. F. D. (2015). The neural correlates of emotion regulation by implementation intentions. *PLoS ONE, 10,* 1–21. doi:10.1371/journal.pone.0119500

Kruglanski, A. W., Shah, J. Y., Fishbach, A., Friedman, R., Chun, W. Y., & Sleeth-Keppler, D. (2002). A theory of goal systems. *Advances in Experimental Social Psychology, 34,* 331–378. doi:10.1016/S0065-2601(02)80008-9

Lewin, K., Dembo, T., Festinger, L., & Sears, P. S. (1944). Level of aspiration. In J. M. Hunt (Ed.), *Personality and the behavior disorders: A handbook on experimental and clinical research* (pp. 333–378). New York: Ronald Press.

Locke, E. A., Latham, G. P., & Erez, M. (1988). The determinants of goal commitment. *Academy of Management Review, 13,* 23–39. doi:10.5465/amr.1988.4306771

Marquardt, M. K. (2011). When the mind forges its own plans: The phenomenon of the implicit emergence of implementation intentions (Doctoral dissertation, University of Konstanz, Germany). Retrieved from http://nbn-resolving.de/urn:nbn:de:bsz:352–175616

Marquardt, M. K., Tröger, J., Wieber, F., & Gollwitzer, P. M. (2016). *On the spontaneous use of goal-related information: Incidentially provided if-then plans support goal attainment*. Unpublished manuscript, University of Konstanz, Germany.

Oettingen, G. A. (2012). Future thought and behavior change. *European Review of Social Psychology, 23,* 1–63. doi:10.1080/10463283.2011.643698

Oettingen, G. A. (2014). *Rethinking positive thinking: Inside the new science of motivation*. New York: Penguin Random House.

Oettingen, G. A., Mayer, D., Sevincer, A. T., Stephens, E. J., Pak, H.-J., & Hagenah, M. (2009). Mental contrasting and goal commitment: The mediating role of energization. *Personality and Social Psychology Bulletin, 35,* 608–622. doi:10.1177/0146167208330856

Oettingen, G. A., Pak, H., & Schnetter, K. (2001). Self-regulation of goal-setting: Turning free fantasies about the future into binding goals. *Journal of Personality and Social Psychology, 80,* 736–753. doi:10.1037/0022-3514.80.5.736

Oettingen, G. A., Wittchen, M., & Gollwitzer, P. M. (2013). Regulating goal pursuit through mental contrasting with implementation intentions. In E. A. Locke & G. P. Latham (Eds.), *New developments in goal setting and task performance* (pp. 523–548). New York: Routledge.

Parks-Stamm, E. J., Gollwitzer, P. M., & Oettingen, G. (2007). Action control by implementation intentions: Effective cue detection and efficient response initiation. *Social Cognition, 25,* 248–266. doi:10.1521/soco.2007.25.2.248

Sailer, P., Wieber, F., Pröpster, K., Stoewer, S., Nischk, D., Volk, F., & Odenwald, M. (2015). A brief intervention to improve exercising in patients with schizophrenia: A controlled pilot study with mental contrasting and implementation intentions (MCII). *BMC Psychiatry, 15*(211). doi:10.1186/s12888-015-0513-y

Schweiger Gallo, I., Keil, A., McCulloch, K. C., Rockstroh, B., & Gollwitzer, P. M. (2009). Strategic automation of emotion regulation. *Journal of Personality and Social Psychology, 96,* 11–31. doi:10.1037/a0013460

Sheeran, P. (2002). Intention-behavior relations: A conceptual and empirical review. *European Review of Social Psychology, 12,* 1–36. doi:10.1080/14792772143000003

Sheeran, P., Webb, T. L., & Gollwitzer, P. M. (2005). The interplay between goal intentions and implementation intentions. *Personality and Social Psychology Bulletin, 31,* 87–98. doi:10.1177/0146167204271308

Strack, F., & Deutsch, R. (2004). Reflective and impulsive determinants of social behavior. *Personality and Social Psychology Review, 8,* 220–247. doi:10.1207/s15327957pspr0803_1

Thürmer, J. L., Wieber, F., & Gollwitzer, P. M. (2015a). A self-regulation perspective on hidden-profile problems: If–then planning to review information improves group decisions. *Journal of Behavioral Decision Making, 28,* 101–113. doi:10.1002/bdm.1832

Thürmer, J. L., Wieber, F., & Gollwitzer, P. M. (2015b). Planning high performance: Can groups and teams benefit from implementation intentions? In M. D. Mumford & M. Frese (Eds.), *The psychology of planning in organizations: Research and applications* (pp. 123–146). New York: Routledge.

Toli, A., Webb, T. L., & Hardy, G. (2016). Does forming implementation intentions help people with mental health problems to achieve goals? A meta-analysis of experimental studies with clinical and analogue samples [Special issue paper]. *British Journal of Clinical Psychology, 55,* 69–90. doi:10.1111/bjc.12086

van Koningsbruggen, G. M., Stroebe, W., Papies, E. K., & Aarts, H. (2011). Implementation intentions as goal primes: Boosting self-control in tempting environments. *European Journal of Social Psychology, 41,* 551–557. doi:10.1002/ejsp.799

Webb, T. L., & Sheeran, P. (2006). Does changing behavioral intentions engender behavior change? A meta-analysis of the experimental evidence. *Psychological Bulletin, 132,* 249–268. doi:10.1037/0033-2909.132.2.249

Webb, T. L., & Sheeran, P. (2007). How do implementation intentions promote goal attainment? A test of component processes. *Journal of Experimental Social Psychology, 43,* 295–302. doi:10.1016/j.jesp.2006.02.001

Webb, T. L., & Sheeran, P. (2008). Mechanisms of implementation intention effects: The role of goal intentions, self-efficacy, and accessibility of plan components. *British Journal of Social Psychology, 47,* 373–395. doi:10.1348/014466607X267010

Wieber, F., & Gollwitzer, P. M. (2010). Overcoming procrastination through planning. In C. Andreou & M. D. White (Eds.), *The thief of time: Philosophical essays on procrastination* (pp. 185–205). New York: Oxford University Press. doi:10.1093/acprof: oso/9780195376685.003.0011

Wieber, F., & Gollwitzer, P. M. (in press). Decoupling goal striving from resource depletion by forming implementation intentions. In E. R. Hirt, L. Jia, & J. J. Clarkson (Eds.), *Self-regulation and ego control.* San Diego: Elsevier.

Wieber, F., & Sassenberg, K. (2006). I can't take my eyes off of it: Attention attraction effects of implementation intentions. *Social Cognition, 24,* 723–752. doi:10.1521/soco.2006.24.6.723

Wieber, F., Thürmer, J. L., & Gollwitzer, P. M. (2015a). Attenuating the escalation of commitment to a faltering project in decision-making groups: An implementation intention approach. *Social Psychological and Personality Science, 6,* 587–595. doi:10.1177/1948550614568158

Wieber, F., Thürmer, J. L., & Gollwitzer, P. M. (2015b). Promoting the translation of intentions into action by implementation intentions: Behavioral effects and physiological correlates. *Frontiers in Human Neuroscience, 9.* doi:10.3389/fnhum.2015.00395

Wieber, F., von Suchodoletz, A., Heikamp, T., Trommsdorff, G., & Gollwitzer, P. M. (2011). If-then planning helps school-aged children to ignore attractive distractions. *Social Psychology, 42,* 39–47. doi:10.1027/1864-9335/a000041

Wyer, R. S., Jr. (2008). The role of knowledge accessibility in cognition and behavior: Implications for consumer information processing. In C. P. Haugtvedt, P. M. Herr & F. R. Kardes (Eds.), *Handbook of consumer psychology* (Vol. 4, pp. 31–76). New York: Taylor & Francis Group/Lawrence Erlbaum Associates. doi:10.4324/9780203809570.ch2

Chapter 11
Pragmatic Philosophy and the Social Function of Knowledge

Tilman Reitz

Even the members of the scientific community still do not know what it means to live in a "knowledge" society. Recent discussions of the issue are pervaded by a tension that is rarely noticed, for its aspects are situated within different academic disciplines. The social sciences mostly lack a well-considered definition of knowledge, whereas philosophical debates about such a definition usually fail to discuss the social constitution of knowledge. The following contribution presents an analysis of this problem, outlines a solution, and points out some of its implications.

Useful inspiration is found in pragmatic philosophy and in the efforts of social epistemology. Yet I argue that both of these approaches, too, overlook or repress a theoretical challenge: the spatial dispersion of social knowledge, which has been important since the invention of writing and storage media but which is pivotal in global networks of information. If knowledge is seated not only in the minds of individuals but also in the ways in which they collectively and collaboratively map their world, then it also matters where that knowledge is kept and how access to it is organized. The library thus serves as a paradigm of my account. The definition that will be developed permits inclusion of material resources and places in understandings of knowledge, and it can be noted at the outset that the very term *social epistemology* was coined in library studies (Shera, 1970).

I proceed in four steps. First, I illustrate the problematic tension of sociological characterizations and philosophical definitions of knowledge. The second step develops an alternative to dominant philosophical discussions of the issue. The intention is to arrive at a definition that allows one to conceive of knowledge as a complex of social practices and cultural artifacts. In the third step, I compare this approach to results of social epistemology and identify the problem of space. Lastly, I place my account in the context of reflections about the knowledge society.

T. Reitz (✉)
Institute of Sociology, Friedrich Schiller University Jena, Jena, Germany
e-mail: tilman.reitz@uni-jena.de

© The Author(s) 2017
P. Meusburger et al. (eds.), *Knowledge and Action*, Knowledge and Space 9,
DOI 10.1007/978-3-319-44588-5_11

How to Define and How to Obscure Knowledge

One may question whether sociological or economic accounts of the knowledge society need to define knowledge. As soon as they do, however, quite different views surface. The best examples (also in the sense of solid, not simply deficient considerations) are found in the classical theories on the topic. Drucker (1969), probably the first writer to offer a conception of the knowledge society, was brief in definitional matters. Using an approach that has since become widespread (outside philosophy), he also made a specific point: "Knowledge, that is, the systematic organization of information and concepts,... makes apprenticeship obsolete. Knowledge substitutes systematic learning for exposure to experience" (p. 268). In context, Drucker focused even more on issues of application: Knowledge is analyzed as crucial in increasing the productivity of labor.

Four years later, Bell (1973) highlighted the opposite side when he noted a "new centrality of *theoretical* knowledge, the primacy of theory over empiricism" (p. 343, his italics). Accordingly, basic science is the main reference when he defines knowledge as "a set of organized statements of facts or ideas, presenting a reasoned judgment or an experimental result, which is transmitted to others through some communication medium in some systematic form" (p. 175). This definition has remained popular in descriptions of the recent, computer-based take-off of the knowledge society (see Castells, 1996, p. 17, for example). But the focus on explicit statements cannot account for a central novelty that characterizes the work of contemporary knowledge workers or symbol analysts (Reich, 1991)—the importance of situated problem-solving, which demands capacities of embodied or organizational knowledge. Such a capacity is probably at stake when Willke (1998) tries to define knowledge in structures where it matters "not as truth but as a resource" (p. 161): "Whereas *information* designates systemically relevant differences, *knowledge* originates when such information is embedded in contexts of experience" (pp. 161–162, my translation).[1] Unlike the standardized situations Drucker had in mind, this experience presumably affords more than textbooks can convey.

Historical differences set aside, the given examples seem to offer three systematically distinguishable accounts of knowledge:

1. Knowledge as a systematic set of applicable recipes
2. Knowledge as an organized body of theoretical statements
3. Knowledge as a developed capacity of situated problem-solving

These accounts do not necessarily constitute or presuppose different concepts of knowledge. Maybe they are really only about different contexts in which knowledge matters and thus give different perspectives on the same thing. But if there should

---

[1] "Während *Informationen* systemspezifisch relevante Unterschiede bezeichnen, entsteht *Wissen*, wenn solche Informationen in bestimmte Erfahrungskontexte eingebunden sind." (Willke, 1998, pp. 161–162). An interesting question would be whether strict social systems theory is really compatible with the strong accent on experience, particularly that of the individual.

be an underlying concept of knowledge, it would be helpful to have a definition making it explicit.

The preceding quotations also hint at a strong option: They all identify knowledge as information that is relatively organized and that can thus orient perception and action. If one adds the concept of data to that approach, a clear structural picture emerges:

> Data is considered as a coded resource of operations, it is transformed into information when it is integrated into a relevant context where it makes a difference as a difference, it gains relevance and meaning relative to an integrating system. Information is transformed into knowledge when it is integrated into a context of experience. (Fuchs, 2004, par. 11).[2]

Such a model leaves open different possibilities of how information is organized and which kind of context is relevant. Following written instructions fits, as does employing individual mind maps in complex social constellations. Of course, both the definition of information and the notion of a context of experience call for further explication. As far as necessary, it is given below. But two more principal problems should be tackled first. On the one hand, the redundancy of organizing data into information and organizing information into knowledge gives pause. Is it really necessary to draw two distinctions of the same kind? If *knowledge* should not mean only very dense information (processed in human culture), one needs to spell out the specific ways in which it is organized and becomes operative. On the other hand, distinguishing knowledge from information may involve more than specifying a context. Semantically, knowledge is characterized by strong cognitive optimism—or by the kind of relation to truth that authors like Willke try to dismiss. Although information may be insufficient or misleading, knowledge is supposed to be about what is really the case. If someone says that you *know* and not only reasonably believe something (e.g., about natural laws, financial markets, the name of a country's president), she or he means you are right. I try to show how this peculiar trait matters in social analysis. But first and more basically, the question is what it means for the definition of knowledge.

At this juncture one naturally turns to philosophy. I leave aside some interesting knowledge philosophies of the past, namely, of knowledge as systematic self-reflection of a culture (Hegel) or as an elucidation of our being-in-the-world (Heidegger). I also refrain from concentrating on the special case of scientific knowledge and the philosophy of science. Instead, I consider contemporary debates about knowledge in general, discourses in which reduced ontological claims, precise definitions, and aims of wide conceptual extension are to be expected. Sadly, most of these debates turn out to be almost literally footnotes to Plato and not even based on a precise reading of the text. As a result of this discussion, the need for a fresh pragmatic account will become discernible.

---

[2] Fuchs (2004) does not quite agree with the structural outline (which he ascribes to authors such as Willke instead)—but only because his own project is a general theory for "all self-organizing physical, biological, and social systems" (par. 11). According to Fuchs, attention must thus be drawn to restrictions: "[T]he triad is not data-information-knowledge, but data-knowledge-practical knowledge as a manifestation of information in the human realm" (par. 11).

Where contemporary philosophers turn to defining knowledge, they almost inevitably start with the classic paradigm: justified true belief. The passages in Plato suggesting this definition of knowledge are found in the dialogues *Meno* (trans. 1990) and *Theatetus* (trans. 1996). In both dialogues, the term *epistéme* (knowledge or even science) is defined in similar ways:

- as *metà lógou alethés doxa*, true belief/opinion with reasoning/explanation (*Theatetus*, 201c) and
- as *orthé* or *alethés dóxa*, correct or true belief/opinion, together with *aitías logismós*, an account of the reason/origin (*Meno*, 97b–98a).

In one of the dialogues, the proposed definition fails; in the other it is accepted. What is of interest here is only what can be made of them (which actually involves one additional reference to the argument of *Meno*). Contemporary debates show that, for example, a narrow Cartesian interpretation is possible. Various authors accentuate that only individuals can believe and thus know something, and some commentators even take the degree of belief as decisive: Whoever is not certain is no candidate for knowing. I call this stance Cartesian because it makes individual consciousness central. Other scholars, such as the British philosopher Edward Craig (1990), have argued that belief does not matter at all (pp. 12–17) or have developed notions of group knowledge and belief (see below, section on Social Epistemology and Spatial Difference). The whole range of positions, however, leaves the structure of the Platonic definition remarkably untouched. This lack of conceptual innovation is even clearer from the fact that most discussions have focused on the meaning of *justified* or on the question in which sense reasons turn true belief into knowledge. A glimpse of these debates is useful to gain a sense of where the discussion got stuck.

The main idea of asking what *justified* means can serve as a starting point: What if I entertain a belief that is both justified and true, but only accidentally so? Examples and thought experiments relating to this question abound.[3] A simple one should be sufficient for my purposes in this chapter. Suppose, for instance, that I reasonably believe the refrigerator contains something to drink because I put orange juice in. And suppose that there actually is something to drink in there—but not the juice I am thinking about, for someone took it out and replaced it with milk without my realizing it. It would thereby not seem correct to say that I *know* the true state of affairs. Different solutions have been proposed, among them creative ones such as recurring to intellectual virtues (which, as virtues, imply success).[4] The general pattern may be derived from the initial question about the role of justification: *Justified true belief that is not just contingently true.*

Yet this extended definition is not the only possible solution. Goldman (1999), a main proponent of social epistemology, proposed distinguishing between different

---

[3] A major part of the debate refers to a short text by Gettier (1963), after whom the said thought experiments are named Gettier-style cases.

[4] A resulting definition reads: "Knowledge is a state of (true) belief arising out of acts of intellectual virtue" (Zagzebski, 1996, p. 271).

kinds or degrees of knowledge instead. In cases of "weak knowledge" (p. 23), true belief alone is sufficient. Reasons hardly matter when I ask, "Who in this room knows the capital of Cambodia?" But there are also cases where one insists on having "strong knowledge," which then has to be qualified by "some additional element or elements" (p. 23) "such as justification or warrant for the belief, and the exclusion of alternative possibilities" (p. 23). Goldman even develops a third model of quasi-infallible, "super-strong knowledge" (p. 23), but he does so mainly to show that there is little or no practical need for such a concept. This argument about context is also what I take to be the message of his account: It is necessary to ask which understanding of knowledge makes sense in what kind of everyday circumstances.

Following this line, a general critique of the debates in question can be mounted. It is certainly laudable that contemporary philosophers start with everyday language and intuitions when they discuss components and definitions of knowledge. But it is not sure that these sources are differentiated enough to pin down the true and exact meaning of a notion that signifies *diverse* and *complex* practices. Moreover, the usual approach focuses only on a very small segment of the various ways in which people actually talk about knowing and knowledge. An aspect that will turn out to be crucial is that analytic philosophers almost invariably explicate the verb *to know* when they want to find out something about the noun *knowledge*. In a classical study, for instance, Chisholm (1989) proposed the following "definition of knowledge" (p. 98): "h is known by S = Def (1) h is true; (2) S accepts h; (3) h is evident for S" (followed by an unnecessarily complicated fourth clause) (p. 98).

Unlike such definitions, everyday language seems to distinguish between verb and noun in important respects. Whereas *knowing* is exclusively attributed to persons (or, controversially, to quasi subjects like groups or clever animals), *knowledge* may also be situated in objective media or structures and transpersonal organizations. I do not really claim that my computer knows what I wrote during the last few years (even if it has it all stored), but no formal reason keeps me from saying that the knowledge of the National Security Agency (NSA) is frighteningly extensive, that the library of Alexandria housed most of the knowledge of classical antiquity, or that Wikipedia increasingly encompasses the basic common knowledge of the present world.

Such uses of language do not already imply an alternative definition of knowledge. They are as useful and potentially misleading as uses of *to know* are. But if there is no sensible way to decide where to start, it is appropriate to adopt an alternative strategy of using common language and practice to derive and test definitions. Instead of determining without ambiguity what is meant by *one specific* way to talk about knowledge and knowing—or, worse, intuitions about both—it would be instructive to ask which set of practices and capacities people *typically* refer to when applying these notions. Marginal cases such as group convictions and tacit or implicit knowledge may remain problematic then, but much is gained when they can at least be related to a core understanding.

Knowledge as Practice: Keeping Information Available

A new approach is thus not only desirable but apparent as soon as one specifies how a pragmatic philosophy of knowledge should proceed. It should not simply identify as true what proves useful (although a notion of use will indeed be important). It should ask how people act in contexts in which the concept of knowledge makes sense. The strategy just outlined has already been employed by Craig (1990), who introduced an additional reflection to make his point: What is called knowledge can be best constructed in contrast to a sociocognitive state of nature without or before it.

> If what I shall say is along the right lines, the core concept of knowledge is an outcome of certain very general facts about the human situation; so general, indeed, that one cannot imagine their changing whilst anything we can still recognise as social life persists. Given those facts, and a modicum of self-awareness, the concept will appear; and for the same reasons as caused it to appear, it will then stay (p. 10).

I do not try to be equally transhistorical. But I do subscribe to Craig's project to develop a "prototypical case" (p. 15) or a social core situation of knowledge use by spelling out what one could not do without it.

I am less satisfied with his answer. Craig (1990) constructs only a very basic original situation of knowledge, and he actively refuses to introduce necessary extensions. The basic problem he refers to is that reliable information is needed from someone else. It is this *other* person, not some presocial believer, to whom knowledge is typically (and prototypically) ascribed. This construction has two components. The first is unproblematic, but not sufficient: "To put it briefly and roughly, the concept of knowledge is used to flag approved sources of information" (p. 10). What is missing is, again, a specific way to distinguish knowledge from mere information, however approved its sources may be. Craig's way of solving the problem brings in the second component: Although there are many possible sources of information, only personal *informants* are said to have and convey knowledge. Once again, the verb *to know* is employed to make the distinction plausible, but Craig's text also includes a substantial pragmatic argument: Natural sources of information and even cultural artifacts cannot cooperate with the seeker of information; other members of her or his epistemic community can. The idea is most interestingly illustrated by books. Craig explains both why he does not want to attribute knowledge in this case and why some notion of knowledge still seems appropriate:

> Books and the like [are] excellent sources of information, but never, even in the spirit of metaphor, said to know anything…Not that specialist knowledge of any kind is required to unravel their secrets—a large part of their point is to provide a perspicuous source, accessible to anyone with a command of the language they use. But they have none of the psychology of the prototypical informant: they have no beliefs, they do not act, they are not felt to co-operate with us, and they cannot empathise with us so as to anticipate our purposes. Besides, they have a special place amongst the sources of information: they are the evidence laid down by creatures that *are* prototypical informants precisely as the most perspicuous vehicle of their information. (p. 38)

This description is fine, but Craig (1990) seems to overlook an obvious consequence—the human practice of knowledge may require both personal informants and storage media like books. The result is that Craig's prototype adds nothing substantial to the preconception of knowledge that has already emerged in social science accounts. He, too, could have defined knowledge as information (processed in human culture), and he may not even be able to give a satisfying account of culture. At root, an even vaguer summary seems adequate: "The human form of life demands good information, and the reliable flow of information. The concept of knowledge, along with related concepts, serves those needs" (Greco, 2009, p. 320).

This summary includes a minor mistake but it hints at a basic problem. Craig probably did not mix up the concept of knowledge with the practical structures it designates, but his account seems to lack important practical distinctions. In order to see what is lacking, one only has to ask whether the word *flow* applies equally well to both knowledge and information. As far as I see, both have different practical characteristics in this respect. Whereas information is typically transferred (and received as something new), knowledge is usually kept available over time. For example, one speaks of a flow of information when talking about communication technology but says that knowledge is kept in books and assembled in libraries. Even the information age could produce the sentence, "I store my knowledge in my friends." It goes without saying that these formulations may all only be manners of speaking and that society has also developed huge infrastructures for storing potential information or data. But the idea that it is an essential feature of knowledge to be kept available for future use is consistent with many other characteristics discussed so far in this chapter: its higher degree of organization, its versatile employability, even the semantic connection between knowledge and truth. Above all, I think this idea gives a specific answer to Craig's question of why there is occasion to apply the concept knowledge. It is because there are established practices of keeping correct beliefs or information available over time so that people can ask informants, use cultural sources of information, or just resort to their own mnemonic capacities when necessary.

Before I try and condense these initial reflections into a definition, I would like to offer my own footnote to Plato, who expressed similar intuitions about knowledge. When in *Meno* the question is asked what makes knowledge more valuable than mere true opinion, the answer is that it will not run away; reasons are ties that keep it fixed in the soul (*Meno*, 98a). One of Plato's own examples helps show how this image relates to the proposed account. If someone just happens to have a true opinion about the way to Larissa, she can give me the right information. But if that person really knows about it (or, even better, about the location of the city), she will be a steady, reliable informant in this respect. This interlocutor will, for instance, first check whether the place from which I set out is near Athens or near Thessaloniki, then think about roads going northwards or southwards from there, and so on. My informant may, in non-Platonic spirit, even use a map in order to refresh her knowledge or, as one might also say, have recourse to the cultural knowledge laid down in maps and the like.

Which definition can be drawn from this account? First, one needs basic elements such as the correct, useful opinions, beliefs, statements, or indications that figure in the given examples. As most examined contemporary theories suggest, information is an adequate term for grasping their common core. In other words, the material of knowledge consists of transferrable patterns that enable one to tell something about something in the world or that make a difference for operations of diverse systems in a changing environment. These patterns may be sentences explaining a travel route, a bee dance giving directions for collecting pollen, or even substances transmitting signals in an organism. The more exclusively human character of knowledge originates, second, when such information is assembled, integrated into a given framework, fixated, and stored for future use (practical or epistemic). None of these operations is redundant, but for the sake of brevity, integration into frameworks and fixation can be taken as implied in the exercise of assembly and structured storage. Most important, all operations are part of one process. They interact in the way information is organized, or reorganized, as a permanently available structure of orientation. Many versions of this interaction are conceivable. Assembling often includes generalizing and subsuming. Both operations usually occur within established logical or topical hierarchies. Fixation, too, involves ordering and aims at facilitating accessibility. Only where such organization takes place do books, experts, and universities, and not merely repositories or hard drives, have a role to play. Together, these considerations are sufficient for venturing a definition of knowledge:

Knowledge is information in the condition of being assembled and kept available for future use.

As a definition offered in pragmatic spirit, this formulation is open to empirical specification and maybe even substantial amendment. I immediately note the main variable aspects, indicating where I take them to be strengths and where I think additional reflection is needed.

1. The most obvious and voluntary openness of the proposed definition is that it does not specify media of knowledge. Information may be assembled and kept available in the minds of people, in cultural artifacts, and in social organizations. One can even argue that artifacts and social cooperation are a necessary part of the knowledge process, for people generally keep information available through symbols. (The person who knows that she put something in the fridge thus turns out to be a weak case, comparable to a squirrel that "knows" where it put the hazelnut.) This openness about media gives space for research on knowledge structures in the social sciences and humanities. The only restriction is that the practice of knowledge implies potential users of information.

2. What is also left open is the way in which information is actually organized, or how assembling, fixating, and keeping available work together. Maybe further reflection could carve out a clear functional scheme in this regard (e.g., a scheme oriented to the telos of availability), but I rather think that there are culturally and historically varying possibilities. One paradigmatic context where the concrete

organization of permanently available information can be studied is, obviously, the institution of science.

3. A less visible openness is implied in the perspective from which the definitional terms are chosen. As the notion of information exemplifies, they should work from the inside perspective of cultural participants as well as from an external focus on observable operations and causal relationships. The terms *assemble*, *keep available*, and *use* certainly have a participant bias—but they are nearly neutral, allowing for phenomenological, hermeneutic, semantic, and objectivist specification.

4. Finally, the definition does not systematically include the idea that a language community takes knowledge per se to be true. It only suggests why people do so: Information that is kept available for future use is deemed worthy of being kept. What counts as knowledge, not just as guess, opinion, belief, or conviction in intersubjective settings is understandably a stock of preserved, cultivated, proven, and tested insights and orientations.[5] Whether we—individuals, groups, cultures—are right to rely on it is a different question. In some cases we have very reliable clues, sometimes whole cultures turn out to be wrong. Any further inquiry would also have to see whether it is really the same kind of reliance in which they may be wrong. Perhaps the key words *episteme*, *scientia*, and *knowledge*, or even *knowledge*, *savoir*, and *Wissen*, do not designate the same thing.

The last reflection deserves further comment; it brings up problems of relativism. To avoid them, one could add that the information kept available for future use has to be correct, or reliable, or even organized as a true account of reality. Yet this criterion would force strong presuppositions into a mere definition. I prefer to leave even this consideration open by referring to the different possible views indicated in point 2, above. A deeper analysis from the *participant* perspective would have to make sense of several conflicting facts: that people cease to treat beliefs and statements as knowledge when they prove to be untrue, whereas people also know they risk error when they state or believe anything at all; that they disagree with the truth procedures of other cultures and times and yet would not deny that those cultures had knowledge; and so forth. Solutions may be either relativistic or objectivistic. For research in which the *observer* perspective predominates, however, it is sufficient to know what counts and functions as knowledge (or something very similar) in different sociocultural contexts. Researchers in social science (and epistemology) cannot avoid coming back to their own life world, but they do not need to become mired in efforts to make it transparent. Moreover, only reaching beyond the horizon of one's inherited language and practices may show just how much relativism is possible.

The proposed conceptual philosophical reflection thus allows me to come back to issues of sociocultural enquiry. This is precisely the desired effect. Yet the

---

[5] A stronger formulation would be that information is filtered before it is kept: "Knowledge…is the consequence of a filtering process; the process of filtering…facts through the ethical system or the intellectual system, or the system of scholarship…of the individual who receives it" (Shera, 1970, p. 96).

question remains whether a modestly innovative, pragmatic, philosophical definition of knowledge changes anything for the empirical disciplines.

Social Epistemology and Spatial Difference

Another theoretical detour will help find answers. Proponents of social epistemology have worked out an account that fits well with the purpose of the proposed definition. They, too, wish to avoid restricting the attribution of knowledge to individuals.
Instead, they situate knowledge in collectives and organizations. In doing so, they
offer instruments that may help analyze the changing social composition of knowledge and to advance from definitions of the concept to a discussion of concrete
conceptions. I introduce three innovations of this sort and discuss their perspectives
and limits. As already indicated, the main problem that will show up is a lack of
attention to the cultural media of knowledge and an ensuing space blindness—
against which more extensive sociodiagnostic opportunities will become apparent.

A difficult, but interesting, point of departure can be found in Gilbert (1994),
who is generally concerned with shared intentionality. Specifically, she also assumes
collective or group beliefs. According to her, such beliefs surface when a group
member expresses a view to which the others presumably (and legitimately) show
reactions of shocked surprise. All had agreed for a long while that John is an
unpleasant type, and suddenly Maggie comes up with the remark, "How nice John
was again yesterday!" A group of string-theory researchers sits down for lunch,
when a member sighs, "What nonsense this whole string theory is!" Gilbert argues
that appalled reactions such as "*What* did you just say?" are quite in order here.
Long-standing agreement (in the first example) and shared practice (in the second
example) have produced a kind of obligation not to utter the statements in question.
Such obligations may be unpleasant themselves, but they are to some extent
unavoidable and fulfill basic social functions:

> Apart from the general function of providing individuals with a sense of unity or commu-
> nity with others…, the collective beliefs evidently provide points from which people can go
> forward, not forever locked in the back and forth of argumentative conflict. (p. 253)

I momentarily refrain from evaluating this argument and step right ahead to a
second, more refined account of collective intellectual organization. Whereas
Gilbert's (1994) model refers only to the most basic practice of knowledge, the
preservation of belief, this second account is concerned with reasons or collective
rationality. Pettit (2003) has argued that a genuinely collective combination of elements of reasoning can often yield better results than is possible with an aggregate
of complete individual judgments. Judging indeed offers an instructive example.
Take a legal committee that must decide whether someone is liable for having broken a contract and whose members separately consider whether there was a valid
contract in place to begin with and whether a breach of contract has occurred. The
result may be the following distribution of premises and conclusions (Table 11.1).

Table 11.1 Individual and collective rationality in a court decision

Judge	Valid contract?	Breach?	Liability?
1	Yes	Yes	Yes
2	Yes	No	No
3	No	Yes	No

From Pettit (2003), p. 169

In this case the majority of complete individual judgments or conclusions speaks against liability (1:2)—but the sum of premises or basic judgments says the opposite (4:2 in favor of liability). So which stance is the more rational one: respecting the integral individual opinions or forming an integral collective judgment? Pettit (2003) suggests that comparable cases occur in various spheres of life and that in most cases people choose the strategy of "collectivizing reason" (p. 176). Moreover, if procedures and goals remain constant, collective agents emerge, and under Pettit's premises it really seems rational to be obliged to follow their lead. The elements of collective reason, then, are not integral individual opinions but rather observations, arguments, and other information cut out of the context of their individual processing.

The model of collective rationality, of course, does not offer a complete conception of knowledge. It offers only material for rethinking aspects of knowledge practices (affecting the element *justified* in the standard definition or, in Shera's (1970) terms, the process of filtering information; see footnote 5, above). Most important, it says little about how conclusions can be socially stabilized—Pettit (2003) only sketchily refers to the concept of the juridical person in Gierke's (1990) *Genossenschaftsrecht* (law of fellowship). Hence, a third account that explicitly introduces the notion of collective knowledge is welcome. Goldman (2004) proposed just such an account as an alternative to Pettit's (2003) collective rationality. The new aspect is the organization of epistemic competencies and epistemic authority. First, Goldman proposes to add that individual judgments may be differently weighed. (For instance, the opinion of an experienced doctor counts more than that of an apprentice.) As far as I see, this addition is compatible with (maybe even envisaged by) Pettit. What is more interesting is a second nondemocratic consideration, namely, whether an epistemic collective needs persons who are exclusively authorized to define its knowledge and draw consequences. In Goldman's (2004) view, only such an authority structure can explain sentences such as, "We learned since 9/11 that not only did we not know what we didn't know, but the F.B.I. didn't know what it did know" (p. 12).

How is it possible that the same entity, in this instance the U.S. Federal Bureau of Investigation, knew something and did not know it? Goldman's (2004) answer is that the organization's authorities did not realize the threat, so the organization could not react: "[A]t least one Bureau official with appropriate decision-making authority had to receive messages from the various agents, had to believe those messages, and had to pool or amalgamate them into a larger pattern" (p. 19).

That account may be adequate, but it confounds two different aspects: achieving knowledge and drawing practical consequences. On the one hand, one might simply ask whether knowledge of an imminent threat existed at all somewhere in the organization or even at the correct place. Such knowledge could have existed, for instance, because it would have been easy for people to combine alarming observations; because at least one agent, with or without authorization, actually brought together relevant pieces of information; or because a computerized system had switched over to flight-attack alert. On the other hand, this knowledge could have led decision-makers to draw consequences or not. In that case a fitting description would be that the FBI knew something but did not react. What remains of Goldman's (2004) account is that epistemic organizations need nodal points where information is brought together and theoretical conclusions are arrived at. But these organizations need not be so hierarchical that the persons who know and those who decide are the same individuals.

Taken together, the three accounts of social epistemic structures present an interesting range of possibilities. All may be translated into conceptions of knowledge, but into obviously one-sided ones. In Gilbert's (1994) case, keeping information available would involve dull conformity pressure, or what Durkheim (1893/1933) called "mechanical solidarity" (pp. 71–110). In Goldman's (2004) view, assembling information seems to be possible only in top echelons of a hierarchy. Even in Pettit's (2003) democratic vision constant socioepistemic unity is tied to a narrow pattern, corporate law.

Hence, two very different conclusions can be drawn. The first is that the nature of knowledge heavily depends on its social organization. Whether a collective, a person, or a set of rules decides will affect various aspects like the complexity, generality or particularity, and expandability or closure of the information kept available. Luckily, real social knowledge is circulating between different organizations and is today also structured by other patterns of social order, such as systemic codes of communication. But the claustrophobic impression conveyed by the discussed paradigms of social epistemology may also be due to another factor, their neglect of the spatial and medial externality of fixated knowledge.

More precisely, the second possible conclusion about the effect of social epistemic structures has to do with the way in which information is stored for later use. Gilbert (1994), Pettit (2003), and Goldman (2004) all aim at a seat of epistemic unity (group belief or obligation, the juridical person, and decision-making authority, respectively). However, information can be kept available for future use in spatial dispersion as well. A corporation or intelligence agency may have stored its knowledge in experts and archives and on tapes and hard drives in various locations, and may still have relatively well-organized procedures of reporting and access. Even a group of researchers may confidently rely on past publications. Recognizing such reservoirs immediately reduces social pressure in most of the given examples. Gilbert's string theorists could allow each other some free expressions of doubt at lunch time; Goldman's chief officers could leave to others some of the knowledge-generating work and concentrate on making decisions under difficult circumstances. At the level of theory, the introduction of material infrastructures helps to avoid the simplistic dichotomy of knowledge as a mere aggregation of individual views and the idea of a completely unified knowledge community.

Certainly, spatial dispersion also poses problems. In the given context they can be subsumed in a simple principle, capturing the flip side of relaxed social pressure: lack of social control. Sometimes reporting procedures fail, leaving the officers in charge little or no chance to bring the knowledge of their organization to bear. Sometimes the research group falls apart because different members draw different conclusions from collective publications. The resulting ambivalence could be a reason why spatially dispersed knowledge is not very popular in epistemology. Proponents of anarchist epistemologies like Jacques Derrida are the main (and in philosophy almost the only) ones to show a special interest in this issue.[6]

Other theoretical accounts, however, would have reason to follow, for the spatially enriched approach offers a range of systematic perspectives, not least an understanding of the way in which media- and communication-technology conditions epochs of knowledge. It undeniably helps reconstruct traditional settings in which a whole geography of knowledge centers (from Athens to Paris) and places of assembly (archives, libraries, collections, and schools) had to be mastered and in which new mechanisms of dispersion (e.g., the printing press and an expanding literary market) brought about radical change. It can even be used to analyze structural changes of knowledge in an age of ever-improving communication and information technology, where the epistemic importance of spatial distance is allegedly in decline or at least changing its character. In this context new observations concerning the density of socioepistemic control will also be possible.

Delocalized and Resituated Knowledge in the Information Age

I offer a deliberately fragmentary outlook encompassing only two schematic observations pertinent to the proposed definition and the spatial structures of knowledge. Both show changes in the organization and dispersion of epistemic practices. I first introduce my observations, then explain and discuss each in turn:

(a) As the physical location of knowledge loses importance, the social location of the agents and use of knowledge becomes increasingly relevant.
(b) As the long-standing functional division between information and knowledge becomes partly challenged by information-processing machines, the sociophysical location of stored data partly replaces the traditional geography of knowledge.

Part of assumption (a) is common sense today. An optimistic statement containing it is, "Today a child anywhere in the world who has Internet access has access

---

[6] An accessible version of Derrida's (1996/1998) theory of spatially dispersed knowledge is the partly autobiographic essay on monolingualism, where he explained what it means to learn French culture in Algeria. For a systematic reconstruction of this theory, see Quadflieg (2007).

to more knowledge than a child in the best schools of industrial countries did a quarter of a century ago" (Stiglitz, 1999, p. 318). This statement is true as far as access to textual sources of knowledge is concerned, and yet it sounds rather naïve. The reason is that Stiglitz is not speaking of the social and cognitive framework that helps one choose the right sources and make sense of them, nor does he mention possible contexts of use. Even if the child, by chance or by genius, finds the right track to develop sophisticated knowledge in genetic engineering, or investment banking, or the construction of microchips, she or he will still need other favorable conditions in order to put this knowledge to any use or even make money with it. The ensemble of such conditions—such as nationality, language background, travel opportunities, established contacts, educational credentials, and material means—is what I propose to call (with loose reference to Bourdieu, 1985) the social location of the knowledge protagonist. Of course, globalized access to knowledge sources will enable additional people to repair cars, build bombs, or engage in software programming, but in many cases the limits of their social location will replace the former effects of spatial distance.

Further reflection on the economic uses of knowledge shows that social location may even become more important than it has been in industrial capitalism. General knowledge that can be technically distributed at little more than zero cost is not well suited as a source of private wealth. Standard economic approaches show that treating it as a nonpublic good incurs general inefficiencies in both immediate consumption and the chances of creating further knowledge (Arrow, 1962; Stiglitz, 1999). Things look different, however, for the situated knowledge of experts. Tasks such as adapting software to a firm's special needs, installing new microchips in a car model's control system, finding the cheapest possible labor force where supply chains are still sufficient, and identifying the passages in U.S. patent law that keep competitors off the market involve profitable expertise. As the examples suggest, such expertise can be needed either in productive settings or in settings marked by conflicting interests, to the benefit or detriment of general welfare. In both cases, it is the unique social situation of use that determines the structure of valuable knowledge. In light of the previous discussion, this new impact of social location can also be seen as a factor that tightens social control. Instead of socially overdetermined spatial distances, mere social power relations now sort out who can successfully act as a knowledge agent.

At the same time, reduced generality, or increased sensitivity to individual capacities and specific situations, affect the concept of knowledge itself. The marginal case is that knowledge is reduced to intransparent expert reputation, or mere knowing how to do things at a certain (social) place.[7] In rather unspecific and impersonal settings, other reasons raise the question of whether knowledge is still appropriate as a name. As observation (b) suggests, the old practices of keeping information available for future use have been duplicated by a process not easily

---

[7] The examples of knowledge work discussed by Willke (1998), taken mainly from the sphere of business consulting, illustrate this aspect. What counts as knowledge in consulting is at least open to dispute.

called knowledge: storing encoded information or data for future operations. The relevant word here is *operations*, for encoded information is something that one can already find in charts, written calculations, and even books. What is new is that such information can be automatically processed without the intervention of human agents but with huge practical and epistemic effects. Examples are the instances when stock market programs buy and sell shares, police software identifies danger-ous persons, and semantic tools browse scientific data bases.

The standard definition makes it simple to distinguish the information processed from knowledge in such cases. The operations in question involve neither beliefs nor truth and justification, or do so only in the period when programs are designed. Pragmatic definitions, too, offer a clear criterion of distinction in that use or context of experience imply that human agents participate in the process. Yet I think the more interesting point is that practices of knowledge are really pervaded by pro-cesses that make it hard to draw boundaries. A semantic symptom is that the knowl-edge economy and society have always been discussed in relation to mere information.[8] That scope proves to be adequate. Human agency is only one of an increasing number of forces that keep information available and intervene in the world accordingly.

Goals and consequences are still a human and social affair. One of the most remarkable effects of the rise of information technology is that the geopolitical loca-tion of data storage is gaining new relevance. Although knowledge is spreading ever more widely across the globe, the question of whose territory data are stored on plainly matters because the answer determines who will protect them or can compel access to them. In broad theoretical terms, the duality of social control and not com-pletely controllable spatial dispersion must be complemented by a third dimension: struggles over the control of the spatial infrastructure of information. Such struggles have probably occurred ever since the first clay-tablet reports on crops were assem-bled in capital cities, and they continue in the age of the transhuman information–knowledge complex.

Conclusion

Taken together, my sketchy concluding observations convey the thrust of the pro-posed definition of knowledge. The intention is to achieve not only conceptual clar-ity but a renewed empirical view and the chance to explore hitherto unseen connections. This aim can even entail risking the stability of the definition itself or restricting its historical extension. I have highlighted an obvious, but usually omit-ted, basic function of knowledge in order to escape both restricted and unspecific

---

[8] The first paradigm was given by Machlup (1962), who simply refused to distinguish between knowledge and information (p. 8). Extensive studies of the "information economy" have followed (Porat & Rubin, 1977), and publications on the "information society" have abounded since the late 1970s.

uses of the concept. The risk stems from the fact that this very function—keeping information available for future use—is finding ever more near equivalents in the processing of information and the storing of data. In the course of the argument, however, it turned out that this hazard is not the only problem that keeps even social philosophers from leaving traditional epistemology. As soon as the spatial dispersion of knowledge looms, scholars still seem to shrink from addressing gaps in socioepistemic control and from recognizing power struggles that the mind cannot master.

References

Arrow, K. J. (1962). Economic welfare and the allocation of resources for invention. In R. R. Nelson (Ed.), *The rate and direction of inventive activity: Economic and social factors* (pp. 609–625). Princeton: Princeton University Press.

Bell, D. (1973). *The coming of post-industrial society: A venture in social forecasting*. New York: Basic Books.

Bourdieu, P. (1985). The *social space and the genesis* of groups. *Theory and Society, 14*, 723–744. doi:10.1007/BF00174048

Castells, M. (1996). *The rise of the network society. Vol. 1:The information age: Economy, society and culture*. Oxford: Blackwell Publishers.

Chisholm, R. M. (1989). *Theory of knowledge* (3rd ed.). Englewood Cliffs: Prentice Hall.

Craig, E. (1990). *Knowledge and the state of nature: An essay in conceptual synthesis*. Oxford: Clarendon Press.

Derrida, J. (1998). *Monolingualism of the other or, the prosthesis of origin* (P. Mensah, Trans.). Stanford: Stanford University Press. (Original work published 1996)

Drucker, P. F. (1969). *The age of discontinuity: Guidelines to our changing society*. London: Heinemann Verlag.

Durkheim, E. (1933). *The division of labor in society* (G. Simpson, Trans.). New York: Collier MacMillan. (Original work published 1893)

Fuchs, C. (2004). Knowledge management in self-organizing social systems. *Journal of Knowledge Management Practice, 5*. Retrieved from http://www.tlainc.com/articl61.htm

Gettier, E. L. (1963). Is justified true belief knowledge? *Analysis, 23*, 121–123. doi:10.1093/analys/23.6.121

Gierke, O. v. (1990). *Community in historical perspective: A translation of selections from* Das deutsche Genossenschaftsrecht (M. Fisher, Trans.; A. Black, Ed.). Cambridge, UK: Cambridge University Press. (Original work published 1868)

Gilbert, M. (1994). Remarks on collective belief. In F. F. Schmitt (Ed.), *Socializing epistemology: The social dimensions of knowledge* (pp. 235–256). Lanham: Rowman & Littlefield.

Goldman, A. (1999). *Knowledge in a social world*. Oxford: Oxford University Press.

Goldman, A. (2004). Group knowledge vs. group rationality: Two approaches to social epistemology. *Episteme: A Journal of Social Epistemology, 1*, 11–22. doi:10.3366/epi.2004.1.1.11

Greco, J. (2009). The value problem. In A. Haddock, A. Millar, & D. Pritchard (Eds.), *Epistemic value* (pp. 313–321). Oxford: Oxford University Press.

Machlup, F. (1962). *The production and distribution of knowledge in the United States*. Princeton: Princeton University Press.

Pettit, P. (2003). Groups with minds of their own. In F. F. Schmitt (Ed.), *Socializing metaphysics: The nature of social reality* (pp. 167–193). Lanham: Rowman & Littlefield.

Plato (1990). Meno (W. A. M. Lamb, Trans.). In *Plato in Twelve Volumes*: Vol. 2 (pp. 259–371) Cambridge, MA: Harvard University Press.

Plato (1996). Theaetetus (H. N. Fowler, Trans.). In *Plato in Twelve Volumes*: Vol. 7 (pp. 1–257). Cambridge, MA: Harvard University Press.

Porat, M. U., & Rubin, M. R. (1977). *The information economy*. 9 Volumes. Washington, DC: U.S. Department of Commerce, Office of Telecommunications.

Quadflieg, D. (2007). *Differenz und Raum: Zwischen Hegel, Wittgenstein und Derrida* [Difference and space: Between Hegel, Wittgenstein, and Derrida]. Bielefeld: Transcript.

Reich, R. B. (1991). *The work of nations: Preparing ourselves for 21st-century capitalism*. New York: Knopf.

Shera, J. H. (1970). *Sociological foundations of librarianship*. Bombay [Mumbai]: Asia Publishing House.

Stiglitz, J. (1999). Knowledge as a global public good. In I. Kaul, I. Grunberg, & M. A. Stern (Eds.), *Global public goods: International cooperation in the 21st century* (pp. 308–325). New York: Oxford University Press.

Willke, H. (1998). Organisierte Wissensarbeit [Organized knowledge work]. *Zeitschrift für Soziologie, 27*, 161–177.

Zagzebski, L. T. (1996). *The virtues of the mind: An inquiry into the nature of virtue and the ethical foundations of knowledge*. Cambridge, UK: Cambridge University Press.

Chapter 12
Semantic Knowledge, Domains of Meaning and Conceptual Spaces

Peter Gärdenfors

What Is Semantic Knowledge?

What is it that you know when you know a language? Certainly, you know many words of the language (its lexicon), and you know how to put the words together in an appropriate way (the syntax). More important, you know the *meaning* of the words (the semantics of the language). If you do not master the meaning of the words you are using, there is no point in knowing the syntax (unless you are a parrot). You can communicate in a foreign language with some success just by knowing some words and without using any grammar. In this sense semantic knowledge precedes syntactic knowledge. This chapter focuses on an aspect of semantic knowledge that has not been well studied, its organization into domains.

Children learn a language without effort and completely voluntarily. They learn new words miraculously fast. Teenagers master about 60,000 words of their mother tongue by the time they finish high school. In their speech and writing they may not actively use more than a subset of the words, but they *understand* all of them. A simple calculation reveals that they have learned an average of 9–10 words *per day* during childhood. A single example of how a word is used is often sufficient for learning its meaning. No other form of learning is so obvious or so efficient.

Nevertheless, the semantic learning mechanisms show some strong asymmetries. For instance, why is it easier to explain to a 4-year-old the meaning of the color terms *chartreuse* and *mauve* than to explain monetary terms like *inflation* or *mortgage*? The difference is not a matter of word frequency: The monetary terms are more frequent, but the 4-year-old masters the semantic domain of colors and thereby knows the meaning of many color words. Adding new color terms is just a matter of learning the mapping between the new words and the color space.

P. Gärdenfors (✉)
Department of Philosophy, Lund University Cognitive Science, Lund, Sweden
e-mail: peter.gardenfors@lucs.lu.se

© The Author(s) 2017
P. Meusburger et al. (eds.), *Knowledge and Action*, Knowledge and Space 9,
DOI 10.1007/978-3-319-44588-5_12

For example, *chartreuse* is a kind of yellowish green, and *mauve* is a pale violet. On the other hand, the child is normally not acquainted with the domain of economic transactions. To the child, money means concrete things—coins and bills—that one can exchange for other things. Abstract monetary concepts are not within a child's semantic reach. Grasping a new domain is a cognitively much more difficult step than adding new terms to an already established one. Once a domain is common to a group of potential communicators, various means (e.g., words, gestures, and icons) of referring to different regions of the domain can be developed. Conversely, if a domain is not shared, communication is hampered. The organization into domains speeds up language learning.

This chapter presents a model of such domain-oriented language learning, based on conceptual spaces. I illustrate the model with some of the semantic domains that a child acquires during the first formative years of life. I also present linguistic data supporting the hypothesis that semantics knowledge is organized into domains.

Semantics Based on Conceptual Spaces

I have proposed conceptual spaces as appropriate tools for modeling the semantics of natural language (Gärdenfors, 2000). A conceptual space is defined by a number of qualitative dimensions. Examples of perception-based qualitative dimensions are temperature, weight, brightness, and pitch, as well as the three ordinary spatial dimensions of height, width, and depth. The dimensions represent perceived similarity: The closer two points are within a space, the more similar they are judged to be. In the next section, I present a number of further dimensions that are involved in communicative processes.

I argue that properties can be represented as convex regions of conceptual spaces. For example, the color red is a convex region of the three-dimensional color space. A concept can thus be defined as a bundle of properties combined with information about how the properties are correlated (for a more precise definition see Gärdenfors, 2000, p. 105). The concept of an apple, for instance, has properties corresponding to regions of color space, shape space, taste space, nutrition space, and other spaces (see Gärdenfors, 2000, pp. 102–103, for a more detailed account of this example).

The distinction between properties and concepts is useful for analyzing the cognitive role of different word classes. In Gärdenfors (2000), I proposed that properties are typically expressed by adjectives, which describe a convex region of some domain such as color, shape, or size. Correspondingly, concepts representing a complex of properties from a number of domains are typically expressed by nouns. Gärdenfors and Warglien (2012) extended this analysis to verbs on the basis of the models of actions and events outlined in the section on Action domain, below.

Because the notion of a domain is central to my analysis, I should clarify its meaning. To do so, I draw on cognitive psychology's notions of separable and integral dimensions (see Garner, 1974; Maddox, 1992; and Melara, 1992, among others). A set of quality dimensions are said to be integral if one cannot assign an object a value in one dimension without giving it a value in one or more others. For example, an object cannot be given a hue without also giving it a brightness, and the pitch of a sound always goes along with its loudness. Dimensions that are not integral are said to be separable, as is the case with the size and hue dimensions. This distinction allows a domain to be defined as a set of integral dimensions separable from all other dimensions.

The notion of a domain has been used to some extent in cognitive linguistics (e.g., Croft, 2002; Croft & Cruse, 2004; Langacker, 1986). Langacker (1986) presented his notion of a basic domain as follows:

> It is however necessary to posit a number of "basic domains," that is, cognitively irreducible representational spaces or fields of conceptual potential. Among these basic domains are the experience of time and our capacity for dealing with two- and three-dimensional spatial configurations. There are basic domains associated with various senses: color space (an array of possible color sensations), coordinated with the extension of the visual field; the pitch scale; a range of possible temperature sensations (coordinated with positions on the body); and so on. Emotive domains must also be assumed. It is possible that certain linguistic predications are characterized solely in relation to one or more basic domains, for example, time for [BEFORE], color space for [RED], or time and the pitch scale for [BEEP]. However most expressions pertain to higher levels of conceptual organization and presuppose non-basic domains for their semantic characterization. (p. 5)

Langacker's notion of domain fits well with the one I present. Besides basic domains, Langacker also talked about abstract domains, for which identifying the underlying dimensions is more difficult. In general, though, it seems that the notion of a domain within cognitive linguistics has a broader meaning than I intend (see Gärdenfors & Löhndorf, 2013, for a narrower use). Croft and Cruse (2004, chap. 2), for example, even identified domains with frames.

Semantic Domains Involved in Children's Development

Levels of Intersubjectivity

Using conceptual spaces as my framework, I now trace the development of semantic knowledge in children by identifying and describing the domains that are required for various basic forms of communication. A central hypothesis is that many of these domains are tightly connected to the development of intersubjectivity (also called *theory of mind*). In this context, I use the term *intersubjectivity* to mean the sharing and representing of others' mentality. Following Gärdenfors (2008), I break intersubjectivity down into five capacities: representing the emotions of others (empathy), representing the attention of others, representing the desires of others, representing the intentions of others, and representing the beliefs and knowledge of others, an ordering arguably supported by phylogenetic and ontogenetic evidence (see Gärdenfors, 2003, 2008). These five components are exploited so naturally in adult human communication that their importance often escapes attention.

Emotive Domain

The ability to share others' emotions is often called *empathy* (Preston & de Waal, 2002). Bodily and vocal expressions of emotion, the most obvious signals among the social animals, communicate the agent's negative or positive experiences. Preston and de Waal argue that most, if not all, mammals are endowed with empathy (at least in a basic form) as a mechanism linking perception and action.

The importance of empathy to interaction highlights the question of how emotions are represented mentally. Several competing theories on the structure of the emotive domain exist. However, most of these theories contain two basic dimensions: a value dimension on a scale from positive to negative aspects of emotions, and an arousal dimension on a scale from calm to excited emotional states (e.g., Osgood, Suci, & Tannenbaum, 1957; Russell, 1980).[1] The Cartesian product of these two dimensions allows a spatial representation of the basic emotions (see Fig. 12.1). Distances in emotive space indicate degrees of similarity between emotions.

It is well known that emotive intersubjectivity is an important aspect of mother–infant attunement interactions (Stern, 1985). The infant learns the correlation between different emotions and the corresponding facial and vocal expressions. In other words, the child learns how to map behaviors into an emotive space. Sharing an emotion means that the participants in the exchange are in emotional states that are closely located within the same emotive space. That is, the emotions are attuned. Such coordination of emotions is arguably the most fundamental way of sharing meaning.

Visual and Physical Domains

During the first months of life, the child learns to coordinate sensory input—vision, hearing, touch and smell—with motor activities (Thelen & Smith, 1994). This process generates a narrow, egocentric space that basically maps onto her or his visual field. The subsequent role of this space in intersubjective engagement is manifested, for example, by the child's ability, as of 6 months of age, to follow the gaze of the mother if she turns her head to look at an object within the visual field of the child (D'Entremont, 2000). From 12 months of age, the child can follow the mother's gaze if the mother just turns her eyes toward the object (Butterworth & Jarret, 1991).

Representing the attention of others means that one can understand when someone is looking at some object or noticing some event. As suggested above, even very young children can understand where other people are looking. Shared attention is the result of two agents simultaneously attending to the same target. It has clearly

---

[1] Of course, a representation of more nuanced emotions may involve further dimensions.

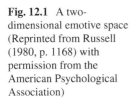

Fig. 12.1 A two-dimensional emotive space (Reprinted from Russell (1980, p. 1168) with permission from the American Psychological Association)

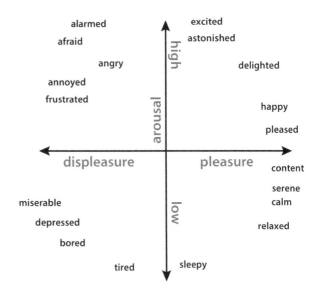

been demonstrated among the great apes (Hare, Call, Agnetta, & Tomasello, 2000). A more sophisticated version is drawing *joint* attention to an object. If I see that you are looking at an object, and you see that I see the same object, we have established joint attention.

The visual domain expands throughout the child's development. From about 18 months on, a child can follow the gaze of others even if they look at points outside its immediate visual field. This ability requires that the represented visual space extend beyond the current visual field to cover the entire physical space. The child can now comprehend references outside its visual field. It should be understood that the represented physical space is not just an extension of the visual domain but an amodal abstraction from visual, auditory, tactile, and perhaps even olfactory perceptions.

A more advanced transformation of the represented space emerges with the ability to represent an allocentric space, a space seen from the point of view of another (Piaget, 1954). This transformation involves a shift of perspective. A concrete example is the ability to direct somebody whose vision is obstructed.

More precisely, the domain of physical space should be seen as a combination of an allocentric representation of physical space and an egocentric representation provided by the visual system. This double aspect of physical space is revealed by the two linguistic codes established for referring to positions: egocentric *left* and *right*, and allocentric *west* and *east* (or *north* and *south*).

Category Domain

Objects are not only located in physical space; they are also represented in a category domain that has its own quality dimensions (Gärdenfors, 2000). If the physical
domain represents where an object is, the category domain represents *what* it is.[2]
The category domain is composed of a number of subdomains, such as color, size,
and shape.

Although communicative coordination in the emotion and physical domains can
be achieved without words, coordination in category space is, at the least, enhanced
by the use of words. The first fifty or so words acquired by children are mainly category words for perceptually identifiable concrete objects: people, food, body parts,
clothing, animals, vehicles, toys, and household objects (Fenson et al., 1994). They
are often used in situations involving the joint attention of the child and an adult.

Hurford (2007, p. 224) has written that declarative pointing communicates only
the location of an object and indicates nothing about its properties. This observation
means that pointing may function without a shared category space having been
established. Parents often scaffold children with words, in a situation of joint attention, to provide information about a category domain. As Goldin-Meadow (2007)
and others have demonstrated, children combine pointing with words long before
they rely on words alone. The words complement pointing or gaze-sharing and thus
expand the possibilities for shared meaning domains in the communicative situation. The minds of the communicators meet in two ways: in the visual domain and
in the category domain. Only later does the child learn words for abstract category
domains such as kinship relations or money.

It is not well known how category space develops in children. Some cues can be
obtained from children's ability to learn nonsense words for new things (Bloom,
2000; Smith, 2009). There seems to be a shape bias in that the shape of objects
seems to be the most important property in determining category membership for
small children (Smith & Samuelson, 2006). Children also overgeneralize concepts
(Bloom, 2000; MacWhinney, 1987).

From 18 through 24 months of age, children undergo what might be called a
naming spurt, acquiring a substantial number of nouns for representing objects.
Evidence suggests that, during this period, they also learn to extract the general
shape of objects and that this abstraction helps in category learning (Smith, 2009;
Son, Smith, & Goldstone, 2008). One interpretation is that the development of the
shape domain, as a region of the category domain, strongly facilitates the learning
of names for object categories.

---

[2] This distinction mirrors the products of the dorsal and ventral streams of visual processing in the
brain.

Value Domain

Understanding that others may not have the same desires as oneself requires a representation of value space, one that is detached from other domains. This capacity develops before the ability to represent the beliefs of others (see Flavell, Flavell, Green, & Moses, 1990; Wellman & Liu, 2004), emerging as a separable domain somewhere between 14 and 18 months of age (Repacholi & Gopnik, 1997). A reasonable hypothesis given the empirical data is that children initially consider the value of an object to be intrinsic to the object, in other words, a dimension of the category domain, such as color or size. Only later is the value domain separated from the category domain so that different individuals may be understood as assigning different values to the same object.

Whereas emotions express how an individual feels, desires express an individual's attitudes toward objects, events, and other agents. Because desires are relational, representing the desires of others is cognitively more demanding than representing their emotions is. One way to represent an individual's value domain is with a utility function that assigns values appropriately. Other representations exist. However, I do not discuss the structure of the value domain in this chapter.

Action Domain

Experiments on how one perceives the movement of persons and other objects (e.g., Giese & Lappe, 2002; Giese & Poggio, 2003; Johansson, 1973) have suggested that the kinematics of movement contain sufficient information to identify the underlying dynamic force patterns. Runeson (1994, pp. 386–387) has gone further, claiming that one can directly perceive the forces that control different kinds of motion. The process is automatic; one cannot help but see the forces. This capacity seems to develop early in infancy (White, 1995). Thus, the force domain can be understood as a shared domain for purposes of communication.

In Gärdenfors (2007b) and Gärdenfors and Warglien (2012), that analysis was extended to actions and the forces involved in generating those actions. The basic premise is that an action can be represented as a pattern of force vectors. The force pattern for running is different from the force pattern for walking; the force pattern for saluting is different from that of throwing (Vaina & Bennour, 1985). Note that forces as represented by the brain are psychological constructs and not Newton's scientific concept.

Similarities between actions should be studied in order to identify the structure of the action space. This investigation can be done with the same basic methods as those used for objects. Walking is more similar to running than it is to throwing. Little is known about the geometrical structure of action space. I make the rather weak assumption that the concept of betweenness remains meaningful. An action concept can then be characterized, like other concepts, as a convex region, in this case of force patterns. Unlike other ways of modeling action, this form of representation does not require explicit representation of the time domain. Explicit representations of time appear to develop comparatively late in childhood.

Like other basic domains, forces can be understood metaphorically. Language often describes applications of mental force, as when one person threatens or persuades another. In such cases the term *power* is often substituted for that of *force* (Gärdenfors, 2007a; Winter & Gärdenfors, 1995).

Goal Domain

Even though one can interpret another's behavior as goal-directed, doing so need not mean that one represents the other's intention. It is sufficient to represent the action's goal. Because the human cognitive system takes self-induced motion as a cue for goal-directedness, intentions to act are inferred from observed behavior. Gergely and Csibra (2003) argued that infants do not primarily interpret instrumental actions as intentional actions. Instead, they judge them by their efficiency in reaching a goal, perceiving them as a function of the physical constraints of the agent's situation, that is, as obstacles, visual conditions, and so forth. Only later do children adopt a mentalistic stance, learning to attribute intentions to the actor.

Therefore, any representation of intentions requires that goals already be represented. The goal domain is primary and must be described first. When the agent is located at a certain physical distance from a desired object, the goal domain can be read from the physical domain. Reaching the goal is reaching the location. The difference is that, in the physical domain, the locations of the agents and objects are in focus, whereas in the goal domain, the focus is on the distances between them. In this example the goal domain is the space of force vectors that extend from the initial to the desired location. When the goal is represented in this way, two principal ways of obtaining the goal arise. One is that the agent moves to the goal location and grasps the object. The other is that the agent uses imperative pointing, so that another individual brings the object to the agent.

Goal domains can be more abstract than force vectors in the physical domain. In principle, goal vectors can be defined in all kinds of semantic domains. If I want the wall to be painted purple, my goal is to change its color from the current location in the green part of the color domain to the desired location in the purple region. Goal spaces are represented as abstract spaces in economics, cognitive science, and artificial intelligence. The classic example from artificial intelligence is Newell and Simon's (1972) General Problem Solver. I suggest that these spaces are generated by metaphorical extensions from the original physical space and thus always maintain the key notion of distance. This hypothesis is supported by the pervasiveness of spatial metaphors in relation to goals, as in "he *reached* his goal," "the goal was *unattainable*," "the target was set *too high*" (see also Lakoff & Johnson, 1980).

Consider next the problem of representing intentions. The basic premise is that the intention domain can be seen as a product of the goal domain and the action domain.[3] An intention is thus a combination of a goal and a planned action conceived of as leading toward that goal. Take the difference between *blink* and *wink*. A blink is an often unintentional action, a pattern of forces exerted on the muscles around the eye. By contrast, a wink is an *intentional* action combining the action of blinking in order "to awaken the attention of or convey private intimation to [a] person" (*Concise Dictionary*, 1911).[4]

Event Domain

The most advanced test for intersubjectivity in humans or other animals is designed to find out whether they can represent what others believe or know. The most common method for evaluating this capacity is the false-belief test (e.g., Gopnik & Astington, 1988; Mitchell, 1997; Perner, Leekam, & Wimmer, 1987). It is generally accepted that this capacity develops in children during their fourth year.

Wellman and Liu (2004) have argued that children can represent other persons' diverse beliefs before they can judge false beliefs. They found that many 3-year-olds who cannot pass false-belief tests can still correctly answer a target question concerning an agent's belief that is opposite from their own; it seems they understand that people's actions are influenced by diverse beliefs. Language proficiency in children is correlated with their ability to pass the false-belief test (Astington & Jenkins, 1999). In particular, parental use of mental predicates in their child-directed speech is correlated with their children's performance in false-belief tests (de Villiers & Pyers, 1997).

What is involved semantically in representing the beliefs of others, as in knowing that somebody has a false belief? Beliefs are normally expressed as propositions. So, how is the meaning of propositions related to semantic domains?[5] One possibility is that most simple propositions express events. In Gärdenfors and Warglien (2012), we modeled an event in terms of two vectors: a force *vector*, which typically represents an action performed by an agent, and a result vector, which describes a change in the location or properties of a patient.[6] Consequently, the event domain is cognitively more complex than other domains.

Given this model, one may reasonably speculate that understanding the beliefs of others requires understanding their representation of events. If this conjecture is

---

[3] *Product* is meant in the mathematical sense. The intention domain is that product space generated from the goal domain (a vector space) and the action space (derived from the space of forces).

[4] As I show in the following section, this model of intentions is the same as the model of events— except that the action involved in an intention is only planned. This analysis fits well with Gergely and Csibra's (2003) proposal that one infers the intentions of a person from the beliefs and desires one attributes to that person.

[5] Cognitive semantics has traditionally not handled propositions well.

[6] The event domain can thus be expressed as the product space of the action domain and either the physical or the category domain (see intentions).

correct, it is no wonder that understanding the beliefs of others develops rather late in childhood. Consider Nelson (1996), who showed how the use of the word *know* develops over time in children and does not achieve its ordinary meaning until after children can pass the false-belief test.

This section has identified a number of semantic domains needed for children's communication. Several are based on the different possible levels of intersubjectivity. I have outlined how these domains can be represented with the aid of conceptual spaces. Because independent semantic evidence suggests that the domains are necessary for modeling basic meanings, their connection to intersubjectivity can be used as a stepping stone to an analysis of the development of semantic knowledge.

Some Linguistic Evidence of Semantic Domain Knowledge

A central thesis of this chapter is that the semantic domains, as structured by conceptual spaces, form an important part of semantic knowledge. In this section I present linguistic evidence that the development of semantic knowledge can appropriately be described as the development of separable semantic domains.

In the analysis of child language data, the establishment of a word in the vocabulary of children is often analyzed for the average frequency of the word's usage at a certain age.[7] Typically, the frequency of a word's usage starts at or close to zero, increases rapidly, then levels off once the word is established in the vocabulary.[8] The resulting curve thus has an *S* shape. I hereafter call the interval during which usage increases rapidly the *establishment period* for a word.

I can now formulate a general hypothesis concerning semantic domains: *If one word from a domain is learned during a certain establishment period, then other (common) words from the same domain tend to be learned during roughly the same period.* In order to test this hypothesis, I have analyzed data from the Child Language Data Exchange System (CHILDES) corpus and have used the publicly available web-based ChildFreq application, a highly efficient tool for such investigations.[9] In this chapter I can present only a few examples from my analysis.

For most of the domains discussed in the previous section, words are established during the language spurt that takes place between 12 and 24 months of age. This observation holds in particular for the different regions of the category domain. For example, consider the region of fruits, part of the category domain. Figure 12.2 shows the frequency curves for the names of several of the most common fruits: *apple*, *banana*, *pear*, *grape*, and *orange*. These words have an establishment period

---

[7] An alternative to using age as the independent variable is to consider the general linguistic competence of the children, often measured in terms of an utterance's mean length (number of words).

[8] In fact, a word's usage usually shows a slow decline, in part because the need for any particular word decreases as more words are learned.

[9] ChildFreq was developed by Rasmus Bååth. It is available at http://childfreq.sumsar.net/

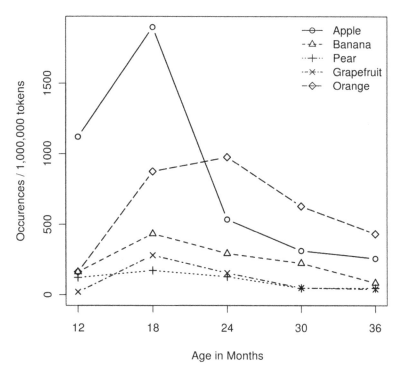

Fig. 12.2 The establishment periods for some common fruit words (Reprinted from Gärdenfors (2014, p. 67) with permission from MIT Press)

between 12 and 18 months of age. *Orange* is something of an exception, probably because it is also used within the color domain.

There are some domains for which the words are clearly established later. One such domain is that relating to life and death. Figure 12.3 shows that the establishment of the words *live*, *die*, *alive*, and *dead* occurs mostly between 30 and 42 months of age.

Another example is the domain relating to knowledge and memory. Figure 12.4 shows the frequency curves for the words *believe*, *remember*, *forget*, and *guess*. In this case the establishment period occurs between 36 and 54 months of age. Note that these words concern an individual's relation to facts and thereby relate to the event domain (see the immediately preceding section). Furthermore, the period coincides with the one during which children learn to pass the false-belief tests.

A final example from ChildFreq concerns the levels of intersubjectivity (see the section on Levels of Intersubjectivity, above). It is difficult to find a clear correspondence between these levels and the learning of particular words. However, I have chosen the verb *look* as an indicator of understanding the attention of others; and the verbs *want to* and *wanna* as indicators of understanding desires; *going to* and *gonna* as indicators of understanding intentions; and *know*, *think*, and *believe* (the latter

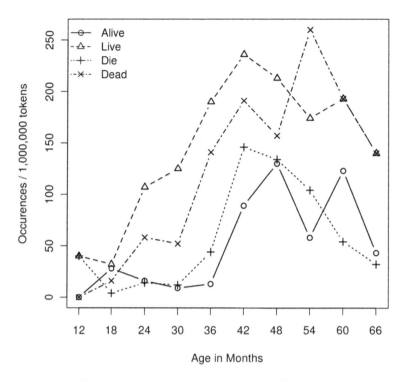

Fig. 12.3 The establishment periods for some words from the "live" domain (Reprinted from Gärdenfors (2014, p. 68) with permission from MIT Press)

two combined into one category) as indicators of understanding belief and knowledge (see Fig. 12.5).[10]

Figure 12.5 suggests that the sequence of the establishment periods conforms to the one I proposed in Gärdenfors (2008). An analysis of the uses of these words in different contexts is required in order to establish the connection with intersubjectivity more clearly than I have in this chapter. Note that *know*, *think*, and *believe* do not quite follow the usual *S* shape. Their trajectories may partly be explained by the many idiomatic uses of these words, which make their frequencies increase at a rate more constant than that of other words. Although I can present only a limited number of examples in these pages, it should be clear that my hypothesis on establishment periods is rich in empirically testable predictions. I invite corpus linguists and child development researchers to continue testing it.

Further evidence of the domain called organization of semantic knowledge is the way that metaphors do not come alone. Lakoff and Johnson (1980) convincingly argued that metaphors are organized around schemas such as "argument is war," "time is a resource," and "more is up." I have proposed that a metaphor expresses an

---

[10] It is difficult to identify any expression that corresponds to understanding emotions (empathy), for this capacity develops well before words are learned.

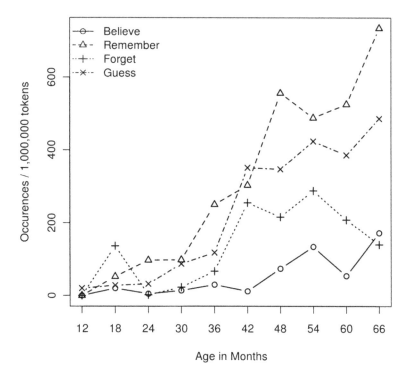

Fig. 12.4 The establishment periods for some words from the "knowledge" domain (Reprinted from Gärdenfors (2014, p. 69) with permission from MIT Press)

"identity in topological or geometrical structure between different domains" (Gärdenfors, 2000, p. 176). That is, a word that represents a particular structure in one domain can be used as a metaphor to express the same structure in another domain. Once a metaphor has established such a mapping, it can be exploited to provide other metaphors from the same domain.

An example of such a mapping is the designation of certain computer programs as *viruses*. This metaphor drawing on the biological domain has created a new way of looking at this class of programs. It has suddenly opened up possibilities for expressions like *invasive* viruses, *vaccination* programs, and hard-disk *disinfection*.

Conclusion

In the tradition of Chomskian linguistics, learning a language is learning its syntax. By the same token, one does not know a language unless one knows the meanings of the words that one uses. In this chapter I have illustrated some key aspects of how cognitive structure constrains the learning of semantic knowledge. The central

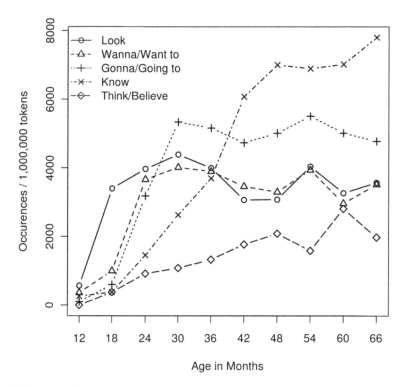

Fig. 12.5 The establishment periods for some verbs related to stages of intersubjectivity (Reprinted from Gärdenfors (2014, p. 70) with permission from MIT Press)

thesis is that semantic knowledge is structured by domains defined as sets of integral dimensions. This understanding of domains can be used to analyze semantic development in children. I have presented the central domains involved in children's cognitive development, in particular with respect to their development of intersubjectivity. I have offered some linguistic evidence supporting the hypothesis that it becomes easier to learn new words within a domain once it has been established.

Acknowledgements I gratefully acknowledge support from (a) the Vagueness, Approximation, and Granularity (VAAG) project coordinated by the Zentrum für Allgemeine Sprachwissenschaft and funded by the European Science Foundation framework LogiCCC, (b) the Swedish Research Council for support under a Senior Individual Grant, and (c) the Linnaeus environment *Thinking in Time: Cognition, Communication and Learning.*

References

Astington, J., & Jenkins, J. A. (1999). A longitudinal study of the relation between language and theory-of-mind development. *Developmental Psychology, 35,* 1311–1320. http://dx.doi.org/10.1037/0012-1649.35.5.1311

Bloom, P. (2000). *How children learn the meaning of words.* Cambridge: MIT Press.

Butterworth, G., & Jarret, N. L. M. (1991). What minds share in common is space: Spatial mechanisms serving joint visual attention in infancy. *British Journal of Developmental Psychology, 9,* 55–72. doi:10.1111/j.2044-835X.1991.tb00862.x

Concise Dictionary of Current English, The. (1911). Adapted by H. W. Fowler & F. G. Fowler. Oxford: The Clarendon Press.

Croft, W. (2002). The role of domains in the interpretation of metaphors and metonymies. In R. Dirven & R. Pörings (Eds.), *Metaphor and metonymy in comparison and contrast* (pp. 161–205). Berlin: Mouton de Gruyter.

Croft, W., & Cruse, D. A. (2004). *Cognitive linguistics.* Cambridge: Cambridge University Press.

D'Entremont, B. (2000). A perceptual-attentional explanation of gaze following in 3- and to 6-months-olds. *Developmental Science, 3,* 302–311. doi:10.1111/1467-7687.00124

de Villiers, J., & Pyers, J. (1997). Complementing cognition: The relationship between language and theory of mind. In E. Hughes, M. Hughes, & A. Greenhill (Eds.), *Proceedings of the 21st Annual Boston University Conference on Language Development* (pp. 136–147). Somerville: Cascadilla Press.

Fenson, L., Dale, P. S., Reznick, J. S., Bates, E., Thal, D. J., Pethick, S. J., Tomasello, M., Mervis, C. B., & Stiles, J. (1994). Variability in early communicative development. *Monographs of the Society for Research in Child Development, 59*(5). Retrieved from http://www.jstor.org/stable/1166092

Flavell, J. H., Flavell, E. R., Green, F. L., & Moses, L. J. (1990). Young children's understanding of fact beliefs versus value beliefs. *Child Development, 61,* 915–928. Retrieved from http://www.jstor.org/stable/1130865

Gärdenfors, P. (2000). *Conceptual spaces: The geometry of thought.* Cambridge: MIT Press.

Gärdenfors, P. (2003). *How homo became sapiens: On the evolution of thinking.* Oxford: Oxford University Press.

Gärdenfors, P. (2007a). Cognitive semantics and image schemas with embodied forces. In J. M. Krois, M. Rosengren, A. Steidele, & D. Westerkamp (Eds.), *Embodiment in cognition and culture* (pp. 57–76). Amsterdam: Benjamins.

Gärdenfors, P. (2007b). Representing actions and functional properties in conceptual spaces. In T. Ziemke, J. Zlatev, & R. M. Frank (Eds.), *Body, language and mind: Vol. 1. Embodiment* (pp. 167–195). Berlin: Mouton de Gruyter.

Gärdenfors, P. (2008). Evolutionary and developmental aspect of intersubjectivity. In H. Liljenström & P. Århem (Eds.), *Consciousness transitions: Phylogenetic, ontogenetic and physiological aspects* (pp. 281–385). Amsterdam: Elsevier.

Gärdenfors, P. (2014). *Geometry of meaning: Conceptual spaces as a basis for semantics,* Cambridge, MA: MIT Press

Gärdenfors, P., & Löhndorf, S. (2013). What is a domain? Dimensional structures versus meronymic relations. *Cognitive Linguistics, 24,* 437–456. doi:10.1515/cog-2013-0017

Gärdenfors, P., & Warglien, M. (2012). Using conceptual space to model actions and events. *Journal of Semantics, 29,* 445–486. doi:10.1093/jos/ffs007

Garner, W. R. (1974). *The processing of information and structure.* Potomac: Erlbaum.

Gergely, G., & Csibra, G. (2003). Teleological reasoning in infancy: The naive theory of rational action. *Trends in Cognitive Sciences, 7,* 287–292. doi:10.1016/S1364-6613(03)00128-1

Giese, M. A., & Lappe, M. (2002). Measurement of generalization fields for the recognition of biological motion. *Vision Research, 42,* 1847–1858. doi:10.1016/S0042-6989(02)00093-7

Giese, M. A., & Poggio, T. (2003). Neural mechanisms for the recognition of biological movements. *Nature Reviews Neuroscience, 4,* 179–192. doi:10.1038/nrn1057

Goldin-Meadow, S. (2007). Pointing sets the stage for learning language and creating language. *Child Development, 78,* 741–745. doi:10.1111/j.1467-8624.2007.01029.x

Gopnik, A., & Astington, J. W. (1988). Children's understanding of representational change and its relation to the understanding of false belief and the appearance–reality distinction. *Child Development, 59,* 26–37. Retrieved from http://www.jstor.org/stable/1130386

Hare, B., Call, J., Agnetta, B., & Tomasello, M. (2000). Chimpanzees know what conspecifics do and do not see. *Animal Behaviour, 59,* 771–785. doi:10.1006/anbe.1999.1377

Hurford, J. R. (2007). *The origins of meaning: Language in the light of evolution.* Oxford: Oxford University Press.

Johansson, G. (1973). Visual perception of biological motion and a model for its analysis. *Perception and Psychophysics, 14,* 201–211. doi:10.3758/BF03212378

Lakoff, G., & Johnson, M. (1980). *Metaphors we live by.* Chicago: University of Chicago Press.

Langacker, R. W. (1986). An introduction to cognitive grammar, *Cognitive Science, 10,* 1–40. doi:10.1207/s15516709cog1001_1

MacWhinney, B. (1987). *Mechanisms of language acquisition.* Hillsdale: Lawrence Erlbaum.

Maddox, W. T. (1992). Perceptual and decisional separability. In G. F. Ashby (Ed.), *Multidimensional models of perception and cognition* (pp. 147–180). Hillsdale: Lawrence Erlbaum.

Melara, R. D. (1992). The concept of perceptual similarity: From psychophysics to cognitive psychology. In D. Algom (Ed.), *Psychophysical approaches to cognition* (pp. 303–388). Amsterdam: Elsevier.

Mitchell, P. (1997). *Introduction to theory of mind: Children, autism and apes.* London: Arnold.

Nelson, K. (1996). *Language in cognitive development: The emergence of the mediated mind.* Cambridge: Cambridge University Press.

Newell, A., & Simon, H. (1972). *Human problem solving.* Englewood Cliffs: Prentice-Hall.

Osgood, C. E., Suci, G. J., & Tannenbaum, P. H. (1957). *The measurement of meaning.* Urbana: University of Illinois Press.

Perner, J., Leekam, S. R., & Wimmer, H. (1987). Three-year-olds' difficulty with false belief: The case for a conceptual deficit. *British Journal of Developmental Psychology, 5,* 125–137. doi:10.1111/j.2044-835X.1987.tb01048.x

Piaget, J. (1954). *The construction of reality in the child* (M. Cook, Trans.). New York: Basic Books.

Preston, S. D., & de Waal, F. B. M. (2002). Empathy: Its ultimate and proximal bases. *Behavioral and Brain Sciences, 25,* 1–20. doi:10.1017/S0140525X02000018

Repacholi, B. M., & Gopnik, A. (1997). Early reasoning about desires: Evidence from 14- and 18-month-olds. *Developmental Psychology, 33,* 12–21. doi:10.1037/0012-1649.33.1.12

Runeson, S. (1994). Perception of biological motion: The KSD-principle and the implications of a distal versus proximal approach. In G. Jansson, S. S. Bergström, W. Epstein, & G. Johansson (Eds.), *Perceiving evens and objects* (pp. 383–405). Hillsdale: Lawrence Erlbaum.

Russell, J. A. (1980). A circumplex model of affect. *Journal of Personality and Social Psychology, 39,* 1161–1178. doi:10.1037/h0077714

Smith, L. B. (2009). From fragments to geometric shape: Changes in visual object recognition between 18 and 24 months. *Current Directions in Psychological Science, 18,* 290–294. doi:10.1111/j.1467-8721.2009.01654.x

Smith, L. B., & Samuelson, L. (2006). An attentional learning account of the shape bias. *Developmental Psychology, 42,* 1339–1343. doi:10.1037/0012-1649.42.6.1339

Son, J. Y., Smith, L. B., & Goldstone, R. L. (2008). Simplicity and generalization: Short-cutting abstraction in children's object categorizations. *Cognition, 108,* 626–638. doi:10.1016/j.cognition.2008.05.002

Stern, D. N. (1985). *The interpersonal world of the infant: A view from psychoanalysis and developmental psychology.* New York: Basic Books.

Thelen, E., & Smith, L. B. (1994). *A dynamic systems approach to the development of cognition and action.* Cambridge: MIT Press.

Vaina, L., & Bennour, Y. (1985). A computational approach to visual recognition of arm movement. *Perceptual and Motor Skills, 60,* 203–228. doi:10.2466/pms.1985.60.1.203
Wellman, H. M., & Liu, D. (2004). Scaling of theory-of-mind tasks. *Child Development, 75,* 523–
   541. doi:10.1111/j.1467-8624.2004.00691.x
White, P. A. (1995). *The understanding of causation and the production of action: From infancy to
   adulthood.* Hillsdale: Lawrence Erlbaum.
Winter, S., & Gärdenfors, P. (1995). Linguistic modality as expressions of social power [Special
   issue]. *Nordic Journal of Linguistics, 18,* 137–166. doi:10.1017/S0332586500000147

Chapter 13
So What Do You Do? Experimenting with Space for Social Creativity

Ariane Berthoin Antal and Victor J. Friedman

> *Direct experience comes from nature and man interacting with each other. In this interaction, human energy gathers, is released, dammed up, frustrated and victorious. There are rhythmic beats of want and fulfillment, pulses of doing and being withheld from doing.*
>
> (Dewey, 1934/2005, p. 1)

As John Dewey (1934/2005) observed "the first great consideration is that life goes on in an environment; not merely *in* it but because of it, through interaction with it" (p. 12, italics in original). It is puzzling that although organizational scholars may agree with him, they have not agreed on how social and physical space interact. Researchers who consider it problematic that "most previous research assumes that spatial orderings of things and people are merely part of the background" (Edenius & Yakhlef, 2007, p. 207) have been exploring space in organizations from different angles. Some authors are very critical of the passive role assigned to space: "To picture space as a 'frame' or container with no other purpose than to preserve what has been put in it is an error displaying traces of Cartesian philosophy" (Kornberger & Clegg, 2004, p. 1101). However, there is a risk that analysts attempting to redress the balance sometimes attribute such great powers to space as to anthropomorphize it and thereby relegate its inhabitants to the status of pawns of masterbuilders (e.g., Kornberger & Clegg, 2004). Our contention is that a clear conceptualization of the relationship between physical and social space is critical for understanding the actions people undertake in their present setting and envisage for the future. Our

A. Berthoin Antal (✉)
Research Group Science Policy Studies, WZB Berlin Social Science Center, Berlin, Germany
e-mail: ariane.berthoin.antal@wzb.eu

V.J. Friedman
Department of Sociology and Anthropology/Department of Behavioral Sciences, Max Stern Academic College of Emek Yezreel, Jezreel Valley, Israel

© The Author(s) 2017   221
P. Meusburger et al. (eds.), *Knowledge and Action*, Knowledge and Space 9,
DOI 10.1007/978-3-319-44588-5_13

objective in this chapter is to deepen our understanding of the relationship between space and the generation of knowledge through and for action.

Theoretical Framework

Some work has been done in this direction (Baldry, 1999; Edenius & Yakhlef, 2007; Ford & Harding, 2004; Friedman, 2011; Kornberger & Clegg, 2004; Meusburger, 2009; Taylor & Spicer, 2007; Woodward & Ellison, 2010). A review of the growing literature on space in organization studies found the field fragmented but identified three principal streams, each with interesting contributions and shortcomings (Taylor & Spicer, 2007). In one stream scholars conceive of space in terms of distance and proximity between points and have convincingly demonstrated how space makes a difference for important issues at the micro-, meso-, and macrolevels. However, they are "unable to account for the ways in which actors attribute meaning and significance to a space ... [and] not able to explain the role which perceptions or experiences of distances and proximity play" (p. 329). In another stream researchers compensate for this weakness by focusing on the materialization of power—but it is questionable "whether all spaces are necessarily manifestations of power" (p. 332). Furthermore, such a focus implies a "systematic disregard of the ways that space may actually be the product of inhabitants' ongoing experience and understandings" (p. 333). Scholars in the third stream attend to this gap by exploring "how spaces are produced and manifest in the experiences of those who inhabit them" (p. 333). The inherent disadvantages are that power relations are overlooked and that the emphasis on perception undervalues the material, physical aspects of space. Logically, therefore, Taylor and Spicer argue for an integrated approach that addresses all three dimensions by building on the ideas of Lefebvre (1974/1991), who sought to bring together mental, physical, and social modalities of space (see also Ford and Harding 2004, p. 817). Although we agree that an integrated approach is needed, this particular proposal does not take some essential concepts into account.

Strikingly absent from the organizational literature on space is the work on social space by two of the twentieth century's most influential, and nonconventional, social scientists, the psychologist Kurt Lewin (1936, 1948/1997, 1951/1997) and the sociologist Pierre Bourdieu (1985, 1989, 1993, 1998; Bourdieu & Wacquant, 1992). Both placed social space as the cornerstone of their theoretical and methodological work, turning to the philosophical work of Ernst Cassirer (1923/1953, 1944, 1961), who conceived of space in rather relative terms as the positional quality of the material world. Cassirer, Lewin, and Bourdieu adopted the view that there is no empty space, only spaces that are formed by and between objects, and they applied this concept to the creation of social reality rather than to the physical world. At the heart of social space is a relational logic of social reality, which focuses neither on the individual nor the group as the unit of analysis but rather on the processes through which individuals, in interaction with others, construct their social spaces and identities (Friedman, 2011). These interactions are causal loops that link the ways people bring their thinking and feeling into the world through action, to other people's responses generated by those actions, and back again to the ways those responses are interpreted and to the ways they shape what people think, feel, and do. Cassirer (1961) depicted with special eloquence the recursive movement between thinking, feeling, and acting in space as a process of creating and experiencing possibilities: "Human action is known only in its realization; only when it is realized are we aware of its living possibilities.... [I]ndeed, its work is precisely that of seeking and creating ever new possibilities" (p. 37).

Social spaces take shape when these interactions between people are sustained and acquire patterns that differentiate them and give them distinctive configurations. Each configuration of social space can be characterized by its constituents, the positions they hold relative to each other, the "rules of the game" that govern interaction, and the shared meanings that hold the space together and facilitate sustained interaction (Friedman, 2011). Hence, social space is a creation of the mind, a construct that can be used to think relationally about the physical or the social world and thereby provide a means for making order out of any given set of elements. Both Lewin and Bourdieu applied these basic ideas to the study of society and culture at every level of aggregation.

A problem with the conceptualization of the construction of social space thus far is that it has not attended to the physical dimensions of the process: humans with bodies interacting in physical spaces that also include objects. We propose to integrate the physical environment in this construction process by seeing space and objects as *being in relation* with people rather than by allotting them a separate ontological status as containers that hold, and influence, social behavior. The relation is created by the multiple senses with which humans experience the physical environment. Whereas the importance of bodily ways of knowing has been obvious to artists and neuroscientists (Lehrer, 2007), organizational researchers misplaced corporeality for many years and have only recently begun to retrieve it by drawing on notions of aesthetics (Linstead & Höpfl, 2000, p. 3). The literature review cited above noted the emergence of this work in their third strand, though too narrowly, so we mine it further in this chapter.

Scholars seeking to bring the body back into the picture point out that "although an organization is indeed a social and collective construct…, it is not an exclusively cognitive one but derives from the knowledge-creating faculties of all the human senses" (Strati, 2000, p. 13). The aesthetic approach to studying human behavior reveals the roles the body plays in reading a context, first to make sense of it because "one of the first things a newcomer to any organization has to learn is how to navigate within this new spatial environment" (Baldry, 1999, p. 535). The newcomer makes "a prima facie aesthetic judgment" (Hein, 1976, p. 149) in defining the relational composition of a situation. People use all their senses to seek cues to make sense of and orient their behavior, and when the interaction occurs in a built physical space they orient themselves to the fixed factors (the structure, the walls, and the floor) and the semifixed factors, such as furniture and other movable objects (Rapoport, 1982). The body thereby also participates in deciding and signaling to others which rules of the game to adopt for the situation at hand. Researchers have shown "how bodily practices produce discourse in the form of rules, routines, and procedures" (Edenius & Yakhlef, 2007, p. 195).

Connecting aesthetic approaches to the analysis of the construction of social space therefore enriches the understanding of the relational processes of generating shared meaning and agreeing on how to behave in the current situation. Furthermore, the aesthetic dimension of experience plays a role in defining the scope for future social space because it has the "capacity to animate actors' imaginations and actions" (Woodward & Ellison, 2010, p. 46).

In this chapter we use this integrated relational conceptualization of social and physical space to analyze data from a series of action experiments we organized in 2009 in Israel. We invited people in small mixed groups to explore together how to envisage a future social space in the same setting. We consciously intensified attention to the aesthetic dimension of the process from the outset by choosing a fine-arts studio as the setting and by providing art materials for the participants to use there, sharing the assumption that "creative activity with portable, discrete objects allows an extension of potential space" (Woodward & Ellison, 2010, p. 50). For this chapter we have decided to apply an aesthetic approach to the data analysis by focusing only on the visual documentation in order "to avoid committing the cognitive and rational error of ignoring the bodies of the people involved in the decision process and only considering their minds" (Strati, 2000, p. 20). Our objective is, therefore, to explore how much one can learn about processes of constructing current and future social space, in which physical relations are integrated, by including aesthetic dimensions of the experience in the analysis.

The next section of the chapter describes the context in which we conducted the action experiments. It is followed by an explanation of the methodology that was used to collect and analyze the data. We then present an analysis of the sessions, in which we identify different configurations that evolved during the interactions of the participants with one another and with the physical aspects of a studio. In the final section of the chapter, we present our conclusions about how to conceptualize and analyze social and physical space in an integrated manner and suggest next steps.

Context: The Studio for Social Creativity

The stimulus for carrying out this study was the development of the Studio for Social Creativity at the Max Stern Jezreel Valley College in Israel, a college created to bring higher education to Israel's northern periphery (Friedman & Desivilya, 2010). This region is characterized by chronic socioeconomic underdevelopment and deep intergroup divisions, especially between Jews and Palestinian Arabs.[1] Victor and several other faculty members at the college were interested in

---

[1] The Israeli population is composed of approximately 80 % Jewish and 20 % Palestinian Arab citizens. This Palestinian population should be distinguished from Palestinians who live in the Occupied Territories—the West Bank (Samaria and Judea) and Gaza—and are not Israeli citizens. The Arab citizens of Israel are termed by different people in various ways, such as Arabs, Israeli Arabs, and Palestinians. Each of these terms has a political implication.

Fig. 13.1 The Studio for Social Creativity, Max Stern Jezreel Valley College, Israel (Photograph by the authors)

promoting a process in which people from the region could (a) bring up problems, ideas, and visions, (b) meet others with whom to learn and collaborate on issues of common concern, (c) work together to create innovative, viable projects and enterprises to meet human and economic needs, and (d) create and enact shared visions of regional development that promotes inclusiveness and interdependence rather than competition and divisiveness.

The original idea was to create a unique kind of incubator that would stimulate social entrepreneurship (Friedman & Sharir, 2009), a process that would also include conflict engagement because the tensions in the region severely restrict the development of social capital needed for social entrepreneurship (Friedman & Arieli, 2011; Friedman & Desivilya, 2010). The idea of bringing in the arts to support the learning process was stimulated by Ariane's research on various forms of artistic interventions as triggers for organizational learning (Berthoin Antal, 2009, 2012, 2013, 2014) and by our joint reflections on how to benefit from working with the arts in action research (Brydon-Miller, Berthoin Antal, Friedman, & Gayá Wicks, 2011).

Serendipitously, Victor discovered on the college campus a little-used fine-arts studio, which had originally been the backstage area of a theater. He immediately experienced it as a space that offered powerful creative potential and decided that the studio metaphor as the environment in which to nurture innovative social thinking and action was much more appealing than the incubator metaphor, especially if people, practices, and products from the world of the arts could be integrated into these processes. The studio's large rectangular shape (approximately 16 m long and 12 m wide, or about 52′ × 39′) offered an open, flexible space (see Fig. 13.1). A high ceiling contributed to the sense of spaciousness. The windows were set along the top of one of the long sides of the room, and the shorter sides each had a narrow balcony, accessible by narrow steep staircases. The stained linoleum floor showed signs of years of use. Water was available from a faucet in a washbasin.

Two critical questions needed to be clarified in order to launch the Studio for Social Creativity: What does it mean, in practice, to integrate processes of social entrepreneurship, conflict engagement, and the arts? How could the studio space be utilized to host and facilitate these processes? Having read the conceptual paper Victor had written with his colleague (Friedman & Desivilya, 2010), Ariane suggested interrupting the writing process to actually engage with potential stakeholders—social entrepreneurs, experts on conflict, activists, artists, college faculty, and students—in the studio. Adapting Frye's (1964) succinct definition of imagination as "the power of constructing possible models of human experience" (p. 22), we observed that the discovery of the studio on campus offered the space for experimenting with imagination in practice. The stakeholders could be invited to participate in constructing possibilities for using the space for social innovation and for strengthening the link between the college and the community.

Method: Action Experiments

The first step was to identify people in the college and in the community who we thought would be interested in participating in what we called a series of *action experiments*. By this term we meant asking participants to develop and actively try out ideas together in a given space, recording the process, then analyzing it as a basis for ensuing steps. We use the term *experiment* in this chapter only to imply an exploratory learning-by-doing—trying something out in order to see what happens. We do not mean it here in the sense of a laboratory experiment, which implies both clear predictions about what should happen and a high degree of control so as to permit a clear linkage between cause and effect. In this case the action experiments entailed bringing mixed groups to explore what the Studio for Social Creativity could be in future. Victor approached each person personally and afterward sent a brief written description of the studio and the experiment. The text also explained that the sessions were to be filmed as a basis for development of and research on the studio. We organized five sessions in June 2009, distributing the 18 volunteers so that each session included participants with experience in social entrepreneurship, conflict engagement, and the arts, as well as both Jews and Palestinian Arabs, and men and women.[2] The size of the groups varied from five to nine people, including the researchers. Although some of the participants knew each other, each mix included one or more people they did not know, so none of the sessions had groups

---

[2] We also held a sixth session but do not report on it here because it was quite different in format. It encompassed 60 students from the nursing program in the college, for whom the participants of Session 2 planned an intervention in the studio.

whose members all had experience working together. In other words, each set of participants entered what was for them a new space with a new group and a new task.

The research team consisted of three people: the two authors and the cameraman, who was a drama student and the son of one of the authors. The members of the research team did not define themselves as facilitators or observers standing outside the experiment but rather interacted with the participants and took part in the thinking and action processes that unfolded. Victor participated fully in each session. Because Ariane did not speak Hebrew, the nature of her participation varied depending on whether the session was held in Hebrew (Sessions 2 and 4) or English (Sessions 1, 3, and 5). The cameraman filmed all of the sessions in the red-nose mask from the world of theater. He felt it would greatly enhance his ability to look on the action with curiosity and openness. By definition there was no language barrier for the cameraman: The Nose does not speak; it communicates with eyes and the rest of the body. As it turned out, the Nose also became part of the studio, signaling to participants as soon as they arrived that it was an unconventional place in which playfulness was allowed.

Our hope was that the participants would generate an output that would articulate their ideas in ways that could be observed, recorded, and shared with others. We also hoped that the participants would not only interact verbally but also use the room and art materials in some process of thinking and acting together. At the same time, we wanted to leave things as open as possible rather than impose a particular process on the participants. Our intention was to maximize the probability of generating newness. As Stark (2009) pointed out, "spaces of ambiguity" (p. 3) are important when the challenge is to generate newness by integrating knowledge from different domains. Prior to the experiment, we therefore defined for ourselves a number of principles that guided our behavior as conveners and researchers.

- Allow the participants to be as self-organizing as possible in their use of the space, their interactions with each other, their use of the resources, and the topics and issues they choose to discuss.
- Bring the participants' knowledge together on as equal a footing as possible. Although we were keenly interested in seeing how art might contribute to this process, we did not privilege the artists, nor any of the other participants, by explicitly attributing to them the status of experts, facilitators, or leaders.
- Set a clear time frame (2 h maximum). Aside from practical considerations, our research on artistic interventions sensitized us to the fact that time constraints can stimulate groups to reach higher levels of performance than the participants had previously considered achievable.

By choice, we wanted to allow each group to develop its own approach, so the general principle we followed was "trust the process" (McNiff, 1998).

The studio was sparsely furnished with art equipment: easels, stools, folding chairs, a platform (probably for a model), a spotlight, and a ladder. Each time we arrived in the studio these furnishings were already distributed around the room in no given order, and we did not arrange them for our participants. The walls were bare, except in one case, where balloons had been left hanging by the previous occupants. After each of our sessions, we removed whatever work had been produced so that it would not influence the participants in the subsequent session. Building on the artful-listening approach with which Ariane had been experimenting to support reflection and expression in groups, we bought materials (e.g., oil pastels, finger paints, plasticene, scissors, glue, a bell, a beach ball, and different kinds and sizes of paper) for the participants to play with during the sessions. Experiments in seminars Ariane had conducted had shown that people often reported that their listening was enhanced when they occupied their hands with other forms of expression. We placed the materials on the low platform, which was at the middle-front of the room.[3] The participants were also invited to bring with them materials or tools they typically use in their practice. Only the musician in Session 1 took up this offer, bringing two musical instruments (an oud and a recorder).

We invited the participants in each session to meet in Victor's office and then walk together across campus to the studio so that they would begin the experiment together. The cameraman waited at the studio entrance to greet them as they arrived. Once everyone had entered the studio, we briefly explained the background to the experiment: the idea of the Studio for Social Creativity and how it had originated, the history of the space itself, the participants' task, and the guidelines. After this introduction we suggested that the participants explore the space for themselves, encouraging them to take the initiative and engage in the task without our guidance.

Data Analysis

We have undertaken several modes of analysis of the action-experiment sessions in the studio since conducting them in 2009. The first mode was simultaneous with the process—we discussed each experience intensely together and with the cameraman, exchanging thoughts and feelings about what was surprising, disappointing, or delighting us. The second was a preliminary review of the results based on transcripts we made of the recorded material, which we presented at a conference a month later (Berthoin Antal & Friedman, 2009). As interesting as that material was, however, we soon realized that we, like other colleagues, had "fallen prey to the dominant approach to studying organization, by relying on discursive material" (Edenius & Yakhlef, 2007, p. 209). We had in our hands the pictorial material those colleagues yearned for after the fact, but we had focused on the written words we had typed up! We therefore decided to write this chapter based entirely on what we could see happening in the film material. After considering different methods of analyzing these data, we decided to apply a grounded-theory approach (Glaser & Strauss, 1967) rather than use a formal coding system derived from existing theories

---

[3] Having observed in the first session that the act of unpacking the materials might have been a barrier to using them, we took them out of their packaging as of the second session, spreading out the oil pastels and paint bottles on the platform to make them more easily available.

on group dynamics or collective creativity processes that would restrict our vision to existing categories. More than a year after the experiences in the studio, we revisited the films and turned off the audio track, noting down separately what we saw people doing in the physical space—when and for how long they engaged with each other and with the fixed or semifixed physical aspects of the studio. We then compared our individual observations, jointly checking the film material again when we found we had noticed things differently. It is from this iterative process that we gained fresh insights into the integrated process of constructing social and physical space.

In the account that follows we rely as much as possible on these observations and provide visual illustrations from the video recording. Although we disciplined ourselves to base our analysis on the film material, it is difficult to exclude additional knowledge from our analysis completely, for we had jointly designed and experienced all the sessions. We include some details that are not based on the visible evidence when we feel it would be essential for the reader's understanding.

Configurations in Spaces of Social Creativity

Each of the sessions was unique in the ideas or works the participants came up with and in the ways they produced those outcomes. In observing the video recordings of the five sessions, however, we noticed patterns, or configurations, of organization and behavior. We use the term *configuration* in four senses: (a) the participants' positions in the room and relative to each other during a specific time period, (b) the observable interactions of the participants among each other and with materials in the room, (c) the observable application of behavioral rules, and (d) the creation of shared meaning (to the extent that it can be inferred from the group's observable behavior and outputs).

To illustrate these configurations and make inferences from them about the use of space for bringing together different kinds of knowledge to generate creative action, we first analyze in depth the pattern of configurations formed by participants in one of the sessions, Session 2. We then relate this pattern to those formed by participants in other sessions. We have chosen this session for presenting our analysis because it is representative in terms of the number and types of configurations and because the entire session is available on video recordings (parts of this material of two other sessions were corrupted, so we can analyze only their soundtracks).

Looking Closely at a Sample Session

As in all of the sessions, the participants in Session 2 were asked to think about how they would use this space to combine processes of social entrepreneurship, conflict engagement, and the arts in ways that would connect the college with the community and contribute to regional development. However, this session was unique

Table 13.1 The nine participants in Session 2 of the action experiment at Max Stern Yezreel Valley College in Israel

Description of participant	Reference in text
Lecturer in the college nursing faculty, Jewish woman anthropologist	Lecturer
Two Palestinian Arab women students participating in workshop on social entrepreneurship	Student 1 Student 2
Jewish woman student participant in workshop on social entrepreneurship	Student 3
Teaching assistant in a social entrepreneurship practicum, Palestinian Arab woman graduate of the college	Teaching assistant
Jewish woman artist	Artist
Action researcher, faculty member of the college, Jewish man	Researcher 1
Senior researcher in a German research institute, French-American woman	Researcher 2
Drama student filming the session, French-American man	Cameraman

Table 13.2 Session 2 of the action experiment at Max Stern Yezreel Valley College in Israel

Sequence	Configuration	Duration (in min.)
1	Orientation	15
2	Meeting mode	19
3	Expansion	25
4	Creation	10
5	Reflection	8
6	Exhibition	3
7	Rehearsal	20

because it centered on meeting an immediate need on campus for a defined target group. A class of approximately 60 nursing students, half of them Jewish and half Palestinian Arab had requested support in engaging in a real conflict they were experiencing in class. The head of the nursing program had asked Victor and a member of the nursing faculty who taught anthropology to these students whether they could help the group address the issues (see also Arieli, Friedman, & Knayzev, 2012). The two faculty members agreed to take on the challenge and decided to use a session in the studio to design it. Victor offered three students from his social entrepreneurship course the opportunity to work on the project with him as their practical assignment for the course, and he asked one of the teaching assistants in the social entrepreneurship course to help as well. The artist chosen for this session came on the recommendation of one of the students from the social entrepreneurship course. Table 13.1 provides an overview of the nine participants in Session 2.

Session 2 lasted 100 min, during which time the participants formed seven configurations in the studio space (see Table 13.2). The session was entirely in Hebrew because the students, the teaching assistant, and the artist were not comfortable using English. Researcher 2, therefore, did not speak in the session; she listened and observed but could not understand exactly what was said.

Fig. 13.2 Orientation configuration, Session 2 of the action experiment in the Studio for Social Creativity (Photograph by the authors)

The first configuration, Orientation, formed as soon as the participants entered the studio. As visible in Fig. 13.2, the participants bunched closely at the entrance to the studio (the door is invisible just to the left). Three of the participants leaned against a table, one sat on a table, and three stood (the teaching assistant had not yet arrived). At least three of the participants looked outwards into the studio space, getting a sense of the room itself. A few minutes into this configuration the video showed that the participants turned toward each other, talking, listening, gesturing, and looking at a document.[4]

In the Orientation configuration, the participants were acquiring a sense of both the space and their task in the session. Researcher 1 and the artist did most of the talking. To the extent that the participants explored the space, it was only with their eyes. The students, in particular, appeared pensive and uncomfortable with the size of the space and the uncertainty of the task itself.

The shift to a new configuration occurred a quarter of an hour into the session, shortly after the lecturer arrived. She briefly observed the situation, then found chairs, which student 3 helped her arrange in a semicircle in front of the table at which the participants were huddling. The positioning of the chairs caused a change in the positioning of the participants. Those who had been standing in front of the table sat down, facing the others, who were sitting or leaning on the table (see Fig. 13.3).

---

[4] In preparation for the intervention, the students in the nursing course had been asked to respond to a questionnaire asking them to define the kind of atmosphere they would like to create in their class, why this kind of atmosphere was important to them, and what concrete steps should be taken to create it. Researchers 1 and 3, together with the students from the course on social entrepreneurship, had analyzed the responses prior to Session 2 so as to provide a resource to the planning team.

Fig. 13.3 Meeting-mode configuration, Session 2 of the action experiment in the Studio for Social Creativity (Photograph by the authors)

The new physical arrangement signaled to the participants that they were in a meeting, hence our choice of the name Meeting Mode for this configuration. The participants looked more comfortable with the situation, into which they could bring the known rules of behavior for meetings. More of the participants spoke during this configuration than during the Orientation.

Although there was a change in the organization and physical positioning of the participants in the Meeting Mode, there was almost no change in the group's location in the room. Figure 13.3 shows that the members of the group remained closely clustered next to the door through which they had entered the studio. Researcher 2 attempted to direct attention to the availability of larger space and the art materials by walking to front-center of the room, where the art materials were located on a low platform. She began finger-painting on a large piece of flipchart paper, capturing words she picked up from the conversation. However, the other participants did not appear to pay any attention to this attempt at modeling. The ineffectiveness of this attempt may be related to the language barrier that led researcher 2 to hover around the group but never actually join in the planning process throughout the session.

The next configuration, which we termed Expansion, began after 19 min (see Fig. 13.4). Researcher 1 stood up and walked toward the middle of the room, followed quickly by the teaching assistant. The other participants began to move slowly across the room toward the art materials, with the lecturer joining them after a conversation with students 1 and 2.

Researcher 2 stopped finger-painting and picked up her sheet of flipchart paper from the pile on the platform so that others could take paper. The artist bent down

Fig. 13.4 Expansion configuration, Session 2 of the action experiment in the Studio for Social Creativity (Photograph by the authors)

and began picking up sheets of flipchart paper, spreading them on the floor in the middle of the room. Some of the participants began to look at, pick up, inspect, and handle the materials. The artist sat down on the floor, followed by researcher 1, the lecturer, and then the students and the teaching assistant. Researcher 2 carried colors, paints, clay, and other materials from the platform to various points near the group.

We called this configuration Expansion because the participants pushed back the boundaries of the space they had created for themselves. Before sitting down, the artist had taken off her shoes, and the others followed suit, signaling a shift to less formal rules of behavior in the group's new space. The video recording of Session 2 shows the participants talking in a more relaxed way than in the previous two configurations and occasionally laughing. The lecturer began writing with a marker on the paper, researcher 1 played with finger-paints, and the teaching assistant also began to draw. The Expansion configuration involved exploration and the opening up of new possibilities for the use of the physical space, the materials, behaviors, and ways participants related to each other. Laughter broke out when researcher 1 withdrew an offer he had made on a piece of paper for the group to focus on. Observing the video material, we think that this moment marks another shift in the rules of behavior because the agenda-setting power of the most senior participant and convener of the session in the studio was visibly called into question. The lecturer then began to lead a discussion, looking at the other participants and inviting them to express themselves. It lasted for 25 min, the lengthiest of all the configurations in Session 2.

Fig. 13.5 Creation configuration, Session 2 of the action experiment in the Studio for Social Creativity (Photograph by the authors)

There was a sudden transition to a new configuration in which the participants began drawing or painting on two shared sheets of paper. Everyone was leaning forward, and there was an appearance of great intensity. We term this configuration Creation (see Fig. 13.5) because a relatively cohesive group took shape and created a collective work.[5] During this Configuration the group appeared to be comfortable behaving as artists, each individual concentrating on aesthetic expression.

After 10 min of the intense Creation configuration, the participants of Session 2 stopped drawing on the paper and leaned back, looked at what they had done, and began talking again. We called this the Reflection configuration (see Fig. 13.6). The rules of the game were no longer the same as in the previous configurations that had been dominated by talking: The participants pointed to elements on the paper, asked questions, and invited others to speak. No one speaker dominated, and the material that lay in the middle of the room played a significant role. The participants remained in the same physical location and arrangement, and there was no movement through the space of the studio. However, by leaning back to consider the physical expression of their shared thinking, they appear to have expanded the space they inhabited together at that moment.

The Reflection configuration lasted 8 min, at which point all of the participants stood up, took the picture they had created, hung it on the front wall of the studio, and stepped back to look at it. We termed this configuration Exhibition (see Fig. 13.7) because it was as though the participants had transformed part of the

---

[5] The audio material reveals that at this point the group had just decided to experiment together with how they would actually envisage the intervention with the class of 60 students.

Fig. 13.6 Reflection configuration, Session 2 of the action experiment in the Studio for Social Creativity (Photograph by the authors)

Fig. 13.7 Exhibition configuration, Session 2 of the action experiment in the Studio for Social Creativity (Photograph by the authors)

Fig. 13.8 Rehearsal configuration, Session 2 of the action experiment in the Studio for Social Creativity (Photograph by the authors)

studio into an exhibition space, displaying their work as artists usually do. In this configuration the participants not only moved to a different part of the studio and used wall space for the first time, they behaved differently from all previous constellations by arranging themselves as though they were in a gallery, standing opposite a picture, observing it, and commenting to cospectators.

Figure 13.7 also documents how the participants traversed and utilized various parts of the studio space at different times. Traces of earlier configurations remain: the chairs from the Meeting Mode in the foreground, near the entrance to the studio; and the papers on the floor in the front-center of the room.

The Exhibition configuration in Session 2 lasted for only 3 min, at which point the participants re-formed into a kind of a loose circle with the picture to their backs and began talking and moving around, using a much larger part of the room. We termed this new arrangement the Rehearsal configuration (Fig. 13.8) because the video recording shows the participants physically acting something out to each other and commenting after each performance.

The audio file documents that the participants were talking about and trying out how to apply what they had learned from this process to the following week's planned session with the 60 nursing students. The Rehearsal implied expanding the space of the participants in several ways: They moved around a larger portion of the studio while acting out their presentations, they extended their space into the future, and they related to the entire studio space as they envisioned the way 60 nursing students could use it in the upcoming intervention.

Rehearsal was the final configuration we observed in this session. It lasted for 20 min—until the time for Session 2 ran out—at which point the group broke up, some participants rushed away, and others began cleaning up while talking.

Comparative Analysis Across Sessions

Having looked at Session 2 in some depth, we now compare it with the other sessions to specify the configurations and their various forms. There was a different group of participants in each session, but they were all given the same basic task. Each group used the space and the materials in a different way and came up with very different insights and products. Nevertheless, most of the configurations we observed in Session 2 recurred in the other sessions as well, though not always in the same order. A comparative analysis permits us to hypothesize that—

1. there are definable configurations of participants' positions and interactions among each other and with materials in a given place and period of time, and they change over the course of a group's engagement with social creativity;
2. some configurations are associated with greater expansion of space than others;
3. there are patterns in the flow between configurations; and
4. some patterns may be more generative of social creativity than others.

By flow, we mean the change in and order of configurations over time. Generativity in this context refers to the observable collective output.

Table 13.3 provides an overview of the configurations that took shape during all five sessions. It reveals that all the sessions started with Orientation. Sessions 3 and 4 showed the greatest similarity with the flow in Session 2, encompassing Expansion, Creation, and Exhibition. The flows in Sessions 1 and 5 were essentially the same, with a repetition of the Meeting Mode after a phase of Expansion.

A detailed comparison of the configurations in each session would exceed the scope of this chapter, but it is useful to consider some of the similarities and differences a bit more closely.

Table 13.3 Overview of the configurations in all the action experiments

Time	Basis of comparison: Session 2	Session 1	Session 3	Session 4	Session 5
	Orientation	Orientation	Orientation	Orientation	Orientation
	Meeting mode	Meeting mode	Expansion	Meeting mode	Meeting mode
	Expansion	Expansion	Creation	Expansion	Expansion
	Creation	Meeting mode	Exhibition	Creation	Meeting mode
	Reflection	Reflection	(Reflection)	Exhibition	
	Exhibition			Pseudocreation	
	Rehearsal				

Orientation

There were significant differences in the way the participants in the five sessions initially oriented themselves to the space. Whereas the Orientation configuration in Session 2 was characterized by huddling—with the participants remaining almost frozen in one spot for the whole time—the video recordings of Sessions 1, 3, and 5 show the people moving around and physically exploring the space.

Meeting Mode

In each case this configuration was initiated by someone suggesting that the participants sit or by someone bringing chairs out. The Meeting Mode seemed to be a way of reducing the size of the room and establishing a known set of behavioral rules in the undifferentiated space offered in the studio. We observed that once participants had positioned themselves in the Meeting Mode it was difficult for them to break out of that configuration and do anything besides talk. Only in Session 3 did no Meeting-Mode configuration come about.

Expansion

The Expansion configuration usually followed the Meeting Mode, but it formed in very different ways, took different amounts of time, and led to different configurations. In Session 1 Expansion began after participants had been in a Meeting Mode for over an hour. One of the participants stood up and began exploring the studio space by walking around and playing his musical instrument (a small mouth organ) at different points in the space. Researcher 1 joined in, using some of the furniture in the room for drumming. The other participants stood up, moved out of the circle of chairs, and observed what was happening. After a few minutes, however, the participants returned to the same circle of chairs, and the group appeared to revert to the Meeting Mode. There was no change in their position in the room or in their spatial relation to each other. Nor was there any sustained change in their use of the physical space. In Session 5 there was a brief Expansion when one of the participants got up from his chair and walked to the center of the room with Researcher 1 to illustrate how he would redesign the space. However, the other participants remained in their places, and everyone returned to the Meeting Mode after a few moments.

In Session 4 Expansion was quite lengthy, lasting approximately 45 min. It began with a sudden burst of movement into singing, dancing, drumming, wandering around the room, and working with the art materials. For the most part the participants carried out these actions separately—each one doing his or her own thing. After about 2 min the participants began to reconfigure themselves, interacting with each other one-on-one or wandering around the room and looking at what others were doing. Gradually, they formed into a single group around paper and materials that the researchers had placed on the floor in the center of the room. The participants then shifted into the Creation configuration, talking around the paper and starting to use the art materials. In Session 3 the participants went directly from Orientation into Expansion—sitting on the floor and playing with materials as they talked.

Creation Configuration

Creation was characterized by the participants' trying out new ways of jointly acting and expressing thoughts and feelings that led to a collective outcome. It entailed the use of the art materials provided for the session but also the use of other objects in the room and the participants' own bodies (e.g., drumming on a board or whistling to make music). In Session 2 the work was a set of pictures; in Session 3 the participants painted, danced, hummed, whistled, and engaged in pantomime; and in Session 4 they made graffiti. The Creation configuration was generally characterized by a shift from talking to doing. In Sessions 2 and 3 there was little or, for stretches of time, even no talking during Creation. In Session 4 there was an interweaving of doing and talking. The intensity and length of the configuration varied, too: Creation in Session 2 was highly intense but relatively brief (10 min). In Session 3 it was both extremely intense and lengthy (36 min). In Session 4 it lasted for almost 35 min, but at the end of that session the participants engaged in an activity that we designate as pseudocreation: They accepted the offer of one of the members to lead them in a Tai Chi exercise. Although it was a collective dance of a kind, it was highly ritualized, leaving the followers no scope for a creative response. We did not observe a Creation configuration in Sessions 1 and 5, whose participants never appeared to form as a group around a task other than talk and did not generate an observable product.

Reflection

The video recording shows evidence of Reflection in two of the sessions, and in both cases material played a focusing role. At the end of Session 1, the participants are seen holding and looking at a balloon on which the cameraman had written *satisfaction*, and they are talking while throwing it to each other. In Session 2 the participants leaned back to reflect together on their drawings. One of the factors that led us to give this configuration separate ontological status was that fact that its *absence* was conspicuous in Session 3, in which the participants had decided to communicate without speaking. The Creation configuration lasted to the end of the session, and there was no time for any other configuration. However, the participants felt such a strong need to reflect on the experience and talk about it that they spontaneously decided to meet for dinner later in the week. The experience of Creation without Reflection left the participants feeling as though something were unfinished.

Fig. 13.9 Exhibition configuration, Session 3 of the action experiment in the Studio for Social Creativity (Photograph by the authors)

Exhibition

In three sessions the participants put their work on the wall, taking the creation out of the group's realm and displaying it as artists do. There were interesting differences worth noting. In Sessions 1 and 4 the participants became observers standing opposite the work, whereas in Session 3 the participants sat under their picture and took a group photograph, capturing themselves as part of the work that they had created (Fig. 13.9).

In Session 4 the Exhibition configuration formed when the participants hung their graffiti-like outputs of the Creation configuration onto the wall at the front of the room (see Fig. 13.10). Rather than transforming that part of the studio into a gallery space, it transformed it into a kind of public wall on which one might paint or spray graffiti messages for passers-by to see.

Rehearsal

In this configuration the participants expanded the space in order to include other people in a future session. Rehearsal was most evident in the video of Session 2, when the participants tried out ways of presenting their ideas for the intervention with the nursing students. In Session 4 the Rehearsal configuration took a different form. It was an attempt to mentally enact or envision what might happen rather than a physical acting out of a future event. The Exhibition of the graffiti on the studio wall presented the participants with a vision of what their messages could look like

Fig. 13.10 Exhibition configuration, Session 4 of the action experiment in the Studio for Social Creativity (Photograph by the authors)

if displayed on walls of the college. The audio material captured a heated discussion about this scenario, revealing possible responses from students and the administration. During Rehearsal in Session 2, the participants set out the rules of behavior for themselves and the 60 nursing students, whereas Rehearsal in Session 4 involved the participants' self-projection into conditions where the rules of behavior were not under their control. In the end they decided not to pursue the idea of taking their work out of the studio.

Discussion

The goal of this chapter has been to deepen our understanding of the relationship between space and the generation of knowledge through and for action. The first thing we noticed from the analysis of the video recording was that the different groups varied widely in their use of the space, their interactions among each other, and their use of the materials. Furthermore, the groups' outputs—the ideas generated for using the space—differed significantly. The second striking outcome of our analysis was that commonalities existed across the sessions in terms of the knowledge-production processes. We identified seven distinct configurations: Orientation, Meeting Mode, Expansion, Creation, Reflection, Exhibition, and Rehearsal. These configurations differed in content, duration, and the transitions between them. However, their fundamental structural similarity allows us to formulate key insights into, or propositions about, the relationships between space, action, and knowledge generation.

Orientation in Undifferentiated Space

As illustrated in the data analysis, every group began with the Orientation configuration. The participants took some time to become acquainted with the space and to figure out where and how to situate themselves so as to engage in the task. The Orientation configuration of each group differed significantly—some stood in one spot and looked around. Others walked around, exploring the room. We recognize that this behavior was at least in part a response to our opening suggestion that the participants explore the space for themselves. But our experience of this configuration, both in the actual moment and in subsequent observation of the video, has led us to conclude that it was also a reaction to uncertainty about what to do in this space and how to do it. Kornberger and Clegg (2004) wrote that space can be conceived of in two ways, namely, "as an absence of presence, as a vast emptiness, as something that one can get lost in …[A]lternatively, it may be thought of socially" (p. 1095). By contrast, we suggest that, in practice, both conceptions can occur simultaneously because the physical and the social are interrelated in space. The participants entering the studio saw a *vast emptiness*, which led some to huddle along the wall, others to cluster close together elsewhere in the room. They perceived an absence of cues for positioning and behaving, and as a group they had no rules of their own yet for how to engage with each other in going about the task at hand in this new space.

The Orientation configuration led us to hypothesize that the uncertainty was the result of a particular relationship between features of the physical space and how the participants perceived and experienced them. The first feature was the *undifferentiated* character of the space. Kurt Lewin (1951/1997) introduced the construct of "differentiation" (pp. 218–220) to conceptualize learning as a change of sociopsychological space. In order to illustrate this notion, he drew an analogy to the process of finding one's way around an unfamiliar city without using a map. At first the city seems like a large undifferentiated mass, which a person experiences as uncertainty and in which one easily feels lost. Getting to know a city means mentally differentiating, or bounding off, distinct places and regions, seeing their location relative to other areas, and identifying ways of getting from one to another. Thus, the city becomes differentiated in the person's mind into distinct blocks, neighborhoods, and districts bounded by streets and other demarcations. Differentiation of a space also is at least partly about becoming aware of the rules governing behavior, such as knowing where one should not walk after dark.

For the participants in the experiment, the studio was, at first, highly undifferentiated, a characteristic that was influenced by both physical and social features. For them, it was a large, unfamiliar space as well as an encounter with people who came from different backgrounds and who had never worked together as a group before. Baldry (1999, p. 536) pointed out that physical environments as well as social factors (e.g., formal authority, gender) usually provide cues for behavior, so environmental cues reinforce what is socially defined as being appropriate or inappropriate. Both the structure of the room and semifixed aspects such as furniture and décor suggest what is to be done and how it should be done. To the extent that people have the prior knowledge to recognize these cues, they are likely to conform to expectations (p. 544). If we had brought the same people into a classroom, meeting room, or office, they would immediately have known where to sit and how to act because the space itself would have been perceived by the participants as full of clear cues about the rules of the game—that is, how to behave in this space. It is important to stress, however, that differentiation is not an intrinsic feature of the physical space itself but rather the way in which a person perceives that space and interacts with it.

Orientation in Unencrusted Space

The second feature that contributed to uncertainty is what we call *unencrustedness* of the space. By unencrustedness we mean that the room did not retain traces of the production of our previous sessions, that it was free of vestiges that might orient later groups in defining their task and shaping their expectations about the outcome. Unencrustedness was not a feature of the space itself but rather reflected an interaction between a decision of the convener-researchers, the physical space, and the participants. We had considered the option of leaving the products of previous groups' work in the room, of preserving changes they had made in the room's design, and/or of actually incorporating their suggestions for how the room should be used. Adopting any of those possibilities would have meant that each new group entering the studio would have been faced with evidence of the knowledge that had emerged from the previous group's engagement with the task. A group could have ignored this material or could have done something quite different, but it would still have been doing its work in the context of previous work and under its influence. Such an approach would have meant conceiving of the experiment as shaping the space through a cumulative, historical process in which each group, at least in part, interpreted and built on what earlier groups had done. We decided against this option because our guidelines called for leaving each group as much freedom as possible in determining how they would think and act in this space. Encrusting the space might have constrained the range of future possible ways of using the room. Of course, the space still had a history. Indeed, two of the participants remembered that the space had been an open stage, and its now closed structure saddened them.

Qualifying Spaces of Possibility

Our analysis confirms and extends work by scholars who have addressed the connection between space and possibility. Lewin (1951/1997, p. 268) suggested that undifferentiated space is not only full of uncertainty but full of possibilities. This assumption is also reflected in the work of contemporary scholars such as

Kornberger and Clegg (2004), who argued that "space has to contain possibilities, which might be perceived as emptiness" (p. 1106) and that organizations need "chaotic, ambiguous and incomplete space" (p. 1106) in order to generate creative problem-solving. Other scholars, too, have suggested that "spaces of ambiguity" (Stark, 2009, p. 3) and "incomplete" work environments lend themselves to the kind of collaborative inquiry that is needed to deal with problems characterized by a lack of clarity and ambiguous information (Horgen, Joroff, Porter, & Schön, 1999, p. 197). The implication is that the experience of undifferentiated space creates potential for producing new ways of thinking and acting. In an analysis of aesthetic experience with theater, Woodward and Ellison (2010) struck a similar note, describing it "as a space of imaginative elaboration, extension and perhaps even a space that afforded a type of 'reflexivity' in that it drew on existing structures as the basis for the realization of creative social action into the future" (p. 53).

The results of the experiment lead us to qualify these assumptions about undifferentiated space as spaces of possibility and to add the concept of unencrusted space. When faced with a space that generated uncertainty, almost all the groups went into the Meeting-Mode configuration. The participants sat and talked in a small circle, making no use of the open space of the room, of the artistic materials, or of other objects in the room. It appeared almost as though they created a room enclosed by invisible walls within the larger space. Thus, in a large room offering many possibilities in principle, people tended to reduce their uncertainty about how to engage with each other and the task by recreating a traditional kind of meeting space that utilized only a small fraction of the total space.

We hypothesize that the Meeting Mode provided participants with a sense of security and order in the face of uncertainty caused by a vaguely defined task and a large, strange, and undifferentiated space—and that the Meeting Mode exacts a price for this sense of security. Although we do not claim that the Meeting-Mode configuration necessarily prevents groups from thinking and acting creatively, our inference from the experiment is that the Meeting Mode is less likely to offer opportunities to experience surprise or newness. Once in the Meeting Mode, all the groups had a hard time breaking out of it and transitioning into what we called the Expansion configuration, and some of them never moved into Creation. We hypothesize that the Meeting-Mode configuration reflected a powerful norm or mental imprint that dictates how people come together to work at least in this particular organizational and cultural constellation. A theater or dance ensemble, like other groups from the art world, would most likely have perceived and used the space very differently. Future research could clarify whether mixed groups of participants who already have experience working together might be more experimental and playful than our participants were while working on a new task in the studio or whether their prior knowledge of how to work together would reduce the range of possibilities they could envision in the space.

Constructing Spaces Conducive to Newness

Our research leads us to suggest that the experience of undifferentiated and unencrusted space offers a potential source of newness—if the participants use the opportunity. This view of the relationship between physical and social space is more accurate than a claim that undifferentiated and unencrusted spaces are spaces of possibility. We hypothesize that such space provides a context conducive to experiencing *not knowing* as an opening for creating new knowledge (Berthoin Antal, 2013). However, not knowing generates a sense of uncertainty that people (other than artists) tend to experience as uncomfortable. As a consequence, this experience of spaces confronts people with a *choice* in seeking to generate new knowledge: Do they impose a familiar set of rules onto the social and physical space, or do they engage the newness of the space to experiment with unfamiliar modes of being, thinking, and interacting with each other, the space, and objects in the space?

The qualified advantages of spaces of possibility and the phenomena of the Meeting Mode illustrate how space is constructed by people through interaction with the physical space, with objects, and among themselves. This fundamental point is often obscured in the literature when authors write about physical space as though it acted, almost with a will of its own, upon the people who interact with it, independently of their perception and choices. For example, Kornberger and Clegg (2004) asserted that "space is both the medium and outcome of the actions it recursively organizes" (p. 1106) and that "such spaces are capable of transforming themselves while being (ab)used and occupied by different people only temporarily" (p. 1106). These statements tend to anthropomorphize space, attributing to it an ability to "organize" or even "transform itself" and thereby opening the door to deterministic thinking. The findings of our experiment remind us that a space becomes generative or is transformed only through the agency of people who interact with the physical space and among themselves. Our analysis of the video recordings of the action experiments we conducted in the Studio for Social Creativity illustrates how physical space comes into human perception and is then acted upon and shaped by people, becoming a part of social space.

The Relationship Between Talking and Doing[6]

Another insight from the experiments concerns the relationship between talking and doing as media for innovative thinking and action. In designing the experiment, we hoped that the participants would go beyond verbal communication and do something with the room, the materials, and each other. Our inclination to favor action

---

[6] We recognize that this duality is simplistic and even misleading because talk is also a form of action. We are using this formulation as a short form for purely cognitive verbal communication as distinct from multisensual ways of knowing, feeling, and expressing.

over talk stemmed from the assumption that *doing* would heighten the aesthetic dimensions of experience by involving the body, the senses, and movement. We assumed that this intensification would enhance the innovative thinking of the participants and ultimately increase the creativity of outputs presented as a model of aesthetic relations "centered on exchanges of emotional energy which mark out moments of intersubjectivity between people" (Woodward & Ellison, 2010, p. 52).

The familiar Meeting-Mode configuration favored talk and other engagement at the cognitive level. Even though some of this talk touched on highly interesting insights, our inference, based on our observations of the group members and our own subjective experience of this configuration, was that discussions in the Meeting Mode generated little energy. In Session 2, which we analyzed in depth, we could observe, and feel, the gradual, positive change in energy as the group moved out of the Meeting Mode into Expansion and then Creation. Our observation of the sessions revealed relationships between the engagement with objects and changes in energy levels. We confirm that "objects are manipulated and energized as products of the relations between the material, the sensual and the embodied as they play out in relation to imagination and the mind" (Woodward & Ellison, 2010, p. 46). Our observations lead us beyond corroborating this claim; they bring us to suggest that by energizing objects, people energize themselves. The bodily experience of moving and shifting position in the process of working with the objects and art materials in the room stimulated and reinforced energy at both the individual and the group levels. The engagement of multiple bodily ways of knowing heightened the aesthetic dimensions of experience in ways that were energizing. We hypothesize that this energy made it easier for the participants to engage the uncertainty and explore new possibilities for thinking and action.

In our estimation the moment of highest energy and aesthetically most powerful experience occurred in the Creation configuration in Session 3. The participants chose to stop talking entirely. For approximately 45 min they used the artistic materials and their bodies, communicating through their eyes, movements, and touch. Ironically, the experience in this configuration led us to revise our thinking about the relative value of doing and talking. The nonverbal communication lasted until the end of the session, at which point all the participants expressed a strong need to *talk* about the experience. There was a sense of incompleteness without the opportunity for shared reflection. This experience led us to see talking and doing as two crucial moments whose interplay is critical in the creative process.

Methodological Reflection

In addition to the insights gained about the relationship between social and physical space and the generation of knowledge through and for action, we offer several methodological reflections from our experience with the action experiments in the Studio for Social Creativity. We confirm the value of separating visual from verbal analysis. It has permitted us to overcome the problem of most publications in this field: that "space has mainly been associated with the aural (auditory-oral) medium, emphasizing talking and listening, overlooking other salient bodily features such as seeing, looking, gazing, glancing, contemplating, scrutinizing, gesturing and moving in specific ways" (Edenius & Yakhlef, 2007, p. 194). We benefited in at least three ways from the artistic presence of the Nose with the video camera. First, it was helpful to have an artist as part of our research team for a project that entailed exploring the possible contribution of artistic ways of knowing in social creation. He helped push us out of our comfort zone by posing questions before and after the sessions and by sharing his perspective on the experience. Second, the participants responded positively to his curious presence, reducing the camera to a playful instrument in all but one instance.[7] Third, his inquisitive, energy-seeking approach revealed in the video material spaces of possibility the groups were not (yet) using.[8]

Conclusion

The analysis of our action experiments in the Studio for Social Creativity has permitted us to formulate propositions about the interaction between social and physical space. First, we invited people to envisage how to generate new possibilities (for interaction?) and then observed how these participants engaged with each other in the social and physical space provided for their task. On this basis we identified seven distinct configurations: Orientation, Meeting Mode, Expansion, Creation, Reflection, and Rehearsal. Second, by focusing on the video material, we revealed how anxious it makes people to be in what they perceive as undifferentiated space, how quickly they try to import rules from other spaces in order to reduce their uncertainty, and how they thereby risk getting locked into established ways of thinking and behaving. Third, the visual analysis also showed that shifting from one configuration to another involved expanding into new physical space (e.g., moving to the middle of room, working on the floor, or using the wall for exhibition) and engaging creatively with art materials and other objects. Adding aesthetic ways of experiencing and communicating increased the group's social creativity. Fourth, we postulate that both undifferentiated and unencrusted space are conducive for enabling the emergence of newness by maximizing the choice participants have as to how to engage with each other and their task. We thereby underscore and clarify the significance of space for creativity while avoiding the anthropomorphization of

---

[7] Although the Nose usually greeted the participants outside the studio, in one session he was perched on a ladder and holding the camera when the participants entered the room. One of those participants did not remember having been informed about the filming of the sessions, so he addressed what he felt to be an infringement. Recording stopped while the group discussed the situation. One of the participants commented "with a cameraman like that, nothing bad can happen," and they all agreed to the filming.

[8] Sometimes participants subsequently used the space to which the Nose had turned his attention (e.g., the balcony in Session 1). We do not know whether their actions were triggered by his, or whether he sensed something earlier that they discovered a little later.

space, a conceptual trap that we encountered in the literature. Fifth, we note the need for movement between nonverbal and verbal forms of interaction in creating knowledge and sharing meaning. When people limit themselves to just talking, they tend to become stuck. Choosing not to talk during a phase of experimentation with bodily forms of knowing and communicating is generative; and verbal communication is needed once more for shared reflection.

The action experiments confirm how valuable it is for us as researchers to move out of our comfort zone when we are seeking new knowledge. We took two such steps in this project. First, we decided to participate in such an open exploratory process rather than stand back as observers or facilitators of a clearly structured workshop. Second, we chose in this chapter to focus our analysis solely on the visible evidence recorded on film. Both steps have proven highly generative. However, we recognize that the focus on the visible in our analysis did not give us access to certain important aspects. In order to explore the meaning the participants were giving to their actions, we need to listen to what they said and then connect that back to what we have observed. An analysis of the spoken words would enable us to correct or refine our configurations, for example. The other aspect we have not yet attended to are the power dynamics in the Studio for Social Creativity. Of course, they were present in the situation, for conflict in the region and tensions between groups at the college were two of the drivers for conducting the sessions in the studio. Moreover, there were differences in status among the participants (e.g., students vs. different levels of faculty; Palestinian Arab vs. Jewish backgrounds; men vs. women; and artists, academics, and practitioners). Exploring those dynamics in the construction of social space and use of physical space would require analyzing the spoken and written (e.g., graffiti) aspects along with the visible process.

Another issue that needs to be examined is the potential paradox inherent in the Studio for Social Creativity. We have posited that the undifferentiated and unencrusted nature of the space is an important condition for enabling participants to generate new ideas and ways of engaging there. How will its potential as a space of possibility be maintained for groups to return to over time? The more they use the space, the more likely it is that they will build mental models of how to use it (even if they leave it unencrusted), making it harder on their return for them to break out of an *unusual* way of having used it. We sense a need to engage more frequently and intimately with the world of the arts to stimulate our learning. Actors and musicians have experience with the paradox because they have to keep being creative on the stages they return to night after night. Fortunately, some artists are seeking inspiration precisely by moving out of the spaces they know in order to engage in learning creatively with people from other worlds, including academics (Berthoin Antal, 2015).

Acknowledgments We are grateful to the Institute for Advanced Study, Constance, for giving the first author the time and space to develop ideas for this chapter.

References

Arieli, D., Friedman, V., & Knyazev, G. (2012). Fostering cooperation while engaging conflict: An intercommunal case study. In J. Rothman (Ed.), *From identity-based conflict to identity-based cooperation* (pp. 135–156). New York: Springer.

Baldry, C. (1999). Space: The final frontier. *Sociology, 33,* 535–553. doi:10.1177/S0038038599000346

Berthoin Antal, A. (2009). *A research framework for evaluating the effects of artistic interventions in organizations.* Gothenburg: TILLT Europe. Retrieved from http://www.wzb.eu/sites/default/files/u30/researchreport.pdf

Berthoin Antal, A. (2012). Artistic intervention residencies and their intermediaries: A comparative analysis. *Organizational Aesthetics, 1,* 44–67. Retrieved from http://digitalcommons.wpi.edu/oa/vol1/iss1/5

Berthoin Antal, A. (2013). Art-based research for engaging not-knowing in organizations. *Journal of Applied Arts and Health, 4,* 67–76.

Berthoin Antal, A. (2014). When arts enter organizational spaces: Implications for organizational learning. In A. Berthoin Antal, P. Meusburger, & L. Suarsana (Eds.), *Learning organizations: Extending the field* (pp. 177–201). Knowledge and Space: Vol. 6. Dordrecht: Springer. doi:10.1007/978-94-007-7220-5

Berthoin Antal, A. (2015). Sources of newness in organizations: Sand, oil, energy, and artists. In A. Berthoin Antal, M. Hutter, & D. Stark (Eds.). *Moments of Valuation: Exploring Sites of Dissonance* (pp. 290–311). Oxford: Oxford University Press.

Berthoin Antal, A., & Friedman, V. J. (2009, July 2–4). Spaces for social creativity: Integrating social entrepreneurship, conflict engagement and the arts. Paper presented at EGOS Annual Conference, Barcelona, unpublished manuscript.

Bourdieu, P. (1985). The social space and the genesis of groups. *Theory and Society, 14,* 723–744. doi:10.1007/BF00174048

Bourdieu, P. (1989). Social space and symbolic power. *Sociological Theory, 7,* 14–25. doi:10.2307/202060

Bourdieu, P. (1993). *The field of cultural production.* Cambridge: Polity Press.

Bourdieu, P. (1998). *Practical reason: On the theory of action.* Stanford: Stanford University Press.

Bourdieu, P., & Wacquant, L. J. D. (1992). *An invitation to reflexive sociology.* Cambridge: Polity Press.

Brydon-Miller, M., Berthoin Antal, A., Friedman, V. J., & Gayá Wicks, P. (2011). The changing landscape of arts and action research [Special issue on Arts and Action Research]. *Action Research, 9,* 3–11. doi:10.1177/1476750310396405

Cassirer, E. (1953). *Substance and function and Einstein's theory of relativity* (W. C. Swabey & M. C. Swabey, Trans.). New York: Dover Press. (Original work published 1923)

Cassirer, E. (1944). *An essay on man: An introduction to a philosophy of human culture.* New Haven: Yale University Press.

Cassirer, E. (1961). *The logic of the humanities* (C. Smith Howe, Trans.). New Haven: Yale University Press.

Dewey, J. (2005). *Art as experience.* New York: Penguin. (Original work published 1934)

Edenius, M., & Yakhlef, A. (2007). Space, vision and organizational learning: The interplay of incorporating and inscribing practices. *Management Learning, 38,* 193–210. doi:10.1177/1350507607075775

Ford, J., & Harding, N. (2004). We went looking for an organization but could find only the metaphysics of its presence. *Sociology, 38,* 815–830. doi:10.1177/0038038504045866

Friedman, V. J. (2011). Revisiting social space: Relational thinking about organizational change. In A. B. (Rami) Shani, R. W. Woodman, & W. A. Pasmore (Eds.), *Annual review of research in organizational change and development: Vol. 19. Research in Organizational Change and Development* (pp. 233–257). Bingley: Emerald Group Publishing Limited. doi:10.1108/S0897-3016(2011)0000019010

Friedman, V. J., & Arieli, D. (2011). Building partnerships across cultures as negotiating reality. In H. S. Desivilya & M. Palgi (Eds.), *The paradox in partnership: The role of conflict in partnership-building* (pp. 79–92). Bentham eBooks. doi:10.2174/9781608052 1101110101

Friedman, V. J., & Desivilya, H. (2010). Integrating social entrepreneurship and conflict engagement for regional development in divided societies. *Entrepreneurship and Regional Development, 22,* 495–514. doi:10.1080/08985626.2010.488400

Friedman, V. J., & Sharir, M. (2009). Mechanisms for supporting social entrepreneurship: A case study and analysis of the Israeli incubator. In J. Robinson, J. Mair, & K. Hockerts (Eds.), *International perspectives on social entrepreneurship* (pp. 208–226). Basingstoke: Palgrave Macmillan.

Frye, N. (1964). *The educated imagination.* Bloomington: Indiana University Press.

Glaser, B. G., & Strauss, A. L. (1967). *The discovery of grounded theory: Strategies for qualitative research.* Chicago: Aldine Publishing Company.

Hein, H. (1976). Aesthetic consciousness: The ground of political experience. *The Journal of Aesthetics and Art Criticism, 35,* 143–152. Retrieved from http://www.jstor.org/stable/430372

Horgen, T. H., Joroff, M. L., Porter, W. L., & Schön, D. A. (1999). *Excellence by design: Transforming workplace and work practice.* New York: John Wiley & Sons.

Kornberger, M., & Clegg, S. R. (2004). Bringing space back in: Organizing the generative building. *Organization Studies, 25,* 1095–1114. doi:10.1177/0170840604046312

Lefebvre, H. (1991). *The production of space* (D. Nicholson-Smith, Trans.). Oxford: Blackwell. (Original work published 1974)

Lehrer, J. (2007). *Proust was a neuroscientist.* New York: Houghton-Mifflin.

Lewin, K. (1936). *Principles of topological psychology.* New York: McGraw-Hill.

Lewin, K. (1997). Resolving social conflicts: Selected papers on group dynamics. In K. Lewin (Ed.), *Resolving social conflicts and field theory in social science* (pp. 1–152). Washington, DC: American Psychological Association. (Original work published 1948)

Lewin, K. (1997). Field theory in social science: Selected theoretical papers. In K. Lewin (Ed.), *Resolving social conflicts and field theory in social science* (pp. 155–422). Washington, DC: American Psychological Association. (Original work published 1951)

Linstead, S., & Höpfl, H. (2000). Introduction. In S. Linstead & H. Höpfl (Eds.), *The aesthetics of organization* (pp. 1–11). London: Sage.

McNiff, S. (1998). *Trust the process: An artist's guide to letting go.* Boston, MA: Shambhala.

Meusburger, P. (2009). Milieus of creativity: The role of places, environments, and spatial contexts. In P. Meusburger, J. Funke, & E. Wunder (Eds.), *Milieus of creativity: An interdisciplinary approach to spatiality of creativity* (pp. 97–153). Knowledge and Space: Vol. 2. Dordrecht: Springer. doi:10.1007/978-1-4020-9877-2_7

Rapoport, A. (1982). *The meaning of the built environment: A nonverbal communication approach.* Beverly Hills: Sage.

Stark, D. (2009). *The sense of dissonance: Accounts of worth in economic life.* Princeton: Princeton University Press.

Strati, A. (2000). The aesthetic approach in organization studies. In S. Linstead & H. Höpfl (Eds.), *The aesthetics of organization* (pp. 13–34). London: Sage.

Taylor, S., & Spicer, A. (2007). Time for space: A narrative review of research on organizational spaces. *International Journal of Management Reviews, 9,* 325–346. doi:10.1111/j.1468-2370.2007.00214.x

Woodward, I., & Ellison, D. (2010). Aesthetic experience, transitional objects and the third space: The fusion of audience and aesthetic objects in the performing arts. *Thesis Eleven, 103,* 45–53. doi:10.1177/0725513610381374

Chapter 14
The Decision to Move: Being Mobile and Being Rational in Comparative Anthropological Perspective

Thomas Widlok

Small Places, Big Issues

Looking at the relationship between rationality and action in the domain of space, anthropologists first think of actions such as walking and the related decision to move or to stay. Walking may be considered the prototypical human action in a spatial setting. Correspondingly, the decision to move is the prototypical challenge to human practical reasoning in the context of moving through space. I wish to contribute to the topic of rationality and action by reviewing cases of human mobility and human orientation in space in some detail. This chapter is based on ethnographic work I have carried out with various groups of mobile hunters and gatherers over the years, particularly in southern Africa and Australia. Do these remote foragers have anything to offer to understanding decisions that matter most in the current world (regarding the current refugee and migration crisis, for instance)? I propose the following considerations with regard to this question. First, bringing in examples from far away is a key element in combating the common bias that "there is no alternative" (see Widlok, 2009a). A case study exemplifying a very different mode of engaging rationality with action underlines that alternatives always exist and that it is worthwhile to spell them out clearly and develop them creatively. Second, the forager decision to move occupies the opposite end of the spectrum of human possibilities in that it focuses on rationality and action in a basic face-to-face setting without being confounded by effects of larger institutional frameworks. Third, the major global crises always come down to numerous smaller dilemmas and questions that social agents need to solve and that preoccupy them. For most agents the

T. Widlok (✉)
African Studies Institute, University of Cologne, Cologne, Germany

Department of Anthropology and Development Studies,
Radboud University, Nijmegen, The Netherlands
e-mail: thomas.widlok@uni-koeln.de

© The Author(s) 2017
P. Meusburger et al. (eds.), *Knowledge and Action*, Knowledge and Space 9,
DOI 10.1007/978-3-319-44588-5_14

large issues become problematic only when they translate into everyday decisions such as whether or not to relocate. In this chapter I therefore adopt the general anthropological strategy of tackling big issues in small places: I study the relation between rationality and action as exemplified by foragers in the Namibian bush.

Although the decision to move may be thought of as basic, many differences between various foraging groups are ignored in this chapter for the sake of the general argument. One uniting feature of forager mobility stands out from the diversity of cases, climatic zones, and points in time: All foragers clearly have more than just ecological reasons for relocating. Granted, when social agents justify a relocation they often mention environmental factors, especially the accumulating dirt at a certain place and the anticipated ripening of a desired fruit at another, distant place, but a variety of motives can lead individuals or groups to pick up and move. Ethnographic evidence leaves no doubt that reference to environmental conditions is in fact usually a pretext to cover up either actual or imminent social conflict that people want to escape or prevent (Kent, 1989; Widlok, 1999). Moving is the main strategy for solving disputes. When ill-feelings or social tensions occur in these societies, the dominant strategy is to split up and move apart. Hence, there are many more moves than the natural environment alone necessitates. Even in situations where people are more or less settled, they move their hut within the settlement for purposes of dispute resolution, altering spatial closeness and distance in order to manage *social* closeness and distance. Out of 89 huts in a settlement that I stayed in, less than 18 % remained in the same place in the course of a single year (Widlok, 1999, p. 10). The challenge is to understand this mobility and these decisions to move, to place them in the larger framework about theories connecting rationality and action. What is the rationality behind these moves? Is it a special kind of rationality geared specifically to the action at hand? What general lessons about the social embeddedness of decision-making can be drawn?

State of the Art: Rational Choice Models of Mobility

The mobility of hunter-gatherers is not a new field, so this chapter begins with a brief review of some of the existing anthropological models so as to prepare the ground for my theoretical argument. Probably the best known anthropological model in this respect is optimal foraging theory (Martin, 1983). It is particularly interesting because its application has not been limited to living hunters and gatherers but broadened to cover human behavior more generally. For instance, this theory has served to model human behavior in western-style museum exhibitions (Rounds, 2004). The assumption is that visitors to an exhibition optimize their visit by matching elements of high-interest value with low search costs and that there are some do's and don'ts that result in rules for deciding how long and in what order one should view the items at an exhibition. These rules (search rules, attention rules, quitting rules) are aimed not at the best possible solution but at one that is satisfactory given the environment as it is (p. 404).

The original version of optimal foraging theory consists of theorems intended to explain when and how foragers move from one resource to another (see Kelly, 1995, for an overview). For example, the theorem of diminishing returns, a central feature of optimal foraging theory, holds that staying in a given patch, say a grove or a small forest of nut trees that foragers exploit, requires increasing work in the form of walking to nut trees that are ever further away within the patch. At a certain point the additional work generates ever fewer returns. The rational choice solution to the problem, namely, moving camp to another grove, is an initial extra investment, but there is a point at which that investment is compensated for by the decreasing returns of the original patch. On the basis of several assumptions about caloric requirements and caloric expenditure (Kelly, 1995, pp. 133–134), the optimal foraging theory predicts that hunter-gatherers will make a move to another patch when a one-way foraging distance reaches 3 km (1.9 miles) on average. This calculation matches what many reports say about the way in which foragers move. Foragers do not stay in a forest until the last nut has been consumed. They walk off much earlier, and the model can show that this strategy complies with rationality in terms of getting the best deal given a number of available patches. When the gathering of the same amount of nuts requires ever more effort, the point at which foragers will leave a given patch of resources will be earlier than the point at which approaching starvation would necessitate a move. Optimal foraging theory also goes beyond this scenario, for it takes into account more complicated ones as well. Indeed it must because many factors are involved (e.g., the number of foragers, the size of a group that shares foraging returns, the variety of storage possibilities, increases or decreases in the desired quantity to forage, and the nature of what is foraged). One could even say that it will eventually be very difficult to disentangle causes and effects in such a model. What appears to be a given patch may turn out to be the variable outcomes of a combined set of practices.

According to optimal foraging theory, forager movements are rational because they follow calculable thresholds. Of course, foragers do not perform this calculation abstractly with graphs. Instead, they are driven by the logic inherent in the environmental conditions and the ways in which human exploitation interacts with these conditions. Other proximate reasons, such as social tensions, may also be considered, but they are thought to boil down to the *ultimate* causes inherent in the logic of resource exploitation (Kelly, 1995, p. 140). In other words, in this model rationality (as exhibited in the way foragers use scarce resources) is completely contained in the environmental action and ultimately dictated by environmental conditions. It is still a sort of rationality but one that mandates certain cultural practices by ecological necessity instead of being mandated by cultural rules.

Nonetheless, caution is needed to avoid succumbing to the "fallacy of the rule" (Bourdieu, 1977, p. 29), which establishes a likely outcome and reinstills it in the minds of the agents as something that has caused the outcome. Optimal foraging theory exemplifies a strongly deductive notion of rationality. It is usually seen as adhering a strict, nomothetic, deductive approach. The conditions of a patch and the characteristics of the forager group exploiting it (e.g., the number of people and their caloric intake) are defined as premises allowing one to derive what the rational behavior in that situation will be, for that behavior necessarily follows. If real-life foragers depart from what is predicted, either they are mistaken (and will eventually die out from maladaptation) or the observers are mistaken in their premises and need to adapt the formula (the values making up the graph), but the deductive logic of the model at large is not questioned. However, optimal foraging theory may be more productive in combination with abductive reasoning (see below). After all, the assumption that foragers move (or shall move) after three days *because of* the inherent rationality of patch depletion holds only until there are alternative explanations that are more plausible.

A need for alternative explanations seems evident from a close examination of the ethnographic record that describes the life of foraging groups. As formulated in a study on Canadian Unuk (Eskimo) hunter-gatherers,

> In the spring…the spirit of impermanence seemed to infect people, so that, from my point of view, they seemed to make the maximum rather than the minimum necessary number of moves. When the flooding river forced us uphill, the retreat was always made foot by foot as the river rose. For several days we moved camp at least once a day and sometimes oftener, and always when the water had arrived within inches of our doorsteps....It sometimes seemed as though moving—rearranging the environment—were a form of play for the Eskimos, a pleasure in itself. Whatever the explanation, I never completely shared the Eskimo spirit....Moves were a nuisance that disrupted my work and, worse, shifted my world as a kaleidoscope shifts its bits of glass, making me uncomfortably aware of the pattern's fragility. (Briggs, 1970, p. 32)

This account is but one of the many that have shed doubt on the universal applicability of optimal foraging theory. As pointed out above, residential moves are not guided only by subsistence efficiency. The acquisition of other raw materials or the attraction of other places may also be important (e.g., for finding a spouse or for joining a ritual). A place's adverse conditions (e.g., a plague of insects) may be a crucial factor, too. All these aspects are possible social motivations for residential moves (Kelly, 1995, p. 147). The model of diminishing returns is not a *law* of diminishing returns. One cannot assume (or deduce) that moves are *ultimately* due to foraging efficiency. It is possible only to abduct that this foraging efficiency for food resources is a factor that is part of the rationality at work, more in some cases and less in others. The implication is not, however, that the aforementioned Unuk Eskimos (and the other known groups) are acting irrationally. Should one assume instead that they have a kind of primitive rationality, now politically more correctly called a forager mode of thought? What else may lie behind formulations such as "spirit of impermanence" or "the Eskimo spirit" in the quotation above?

State of the Art: Decision-Making Probability

Most anthropologists studying hunter-gatherers have explored this relativistic alternative by trying to come as close as possible to achieving what is usually called the *emic* view. It is the approach of basing descriptions of the decision-making process on locally defined criteria, taking the decision-makers to be the experts, and allowing that the rationality of the agents may be very different from that of the observer.

One can try to systematically adopt the emic view by drawing on ethnographic decision tree modeling (Gladwin, 1989). The textbook example for this theory is not one of foragers but rather of American college students and the question of whether or not they go to have lunch at McDonald's. The technique is that one tries through interviews to elicit as many criteria as possible that are said to be relevant for this decision to go or not to go (criteria such as whether one likes the food, likes the service, knows where a McDonald's is). Then the criteria are sorted according to a decision-making tree, which is subsequently tested against the decisions that the college students actually report when being asked where they have lunch. That is, the model should account for most of the decisions observable in real life. Failure to do so would indicate that a criterion is either missing from or misplaced in the decision-making tree. As a product of inductive reasoning, the tree makes predictions on the basis of probability and takes account of local values and decision-making criteria. If some of the decision-making tree's underlying criteria and values are subject to change (e.g., with age), decision-making trees will likely differ from one cultural or subcultural group to the next. One can thereby test and substantiate a relativistic hypothesis through the inductive reasoning of probability.

Again, this model of ethnographic decision trees works well in some instances. It apparently holds in particular for small-scale farmers and their choices of which crop to grow and when. Stated differently, it seems to work in settings of small homogeneous groups with decisions of seasonal regularity. It does not work as nicely with foragers, however, as I found when trying to employ this method with San ("Bushmen") in Namibia. The individuals there are not homogenous in their responses, and it seems that the decision to move camp is not considered an instance that can be looked at through the lens of probability but rather only in personal terms as it were. The question that I asked in my field research was not about going to McDonald's (Namibia being one of the world's few countries without McDonald's). Instead, I asked what locals thought about attending secondary school, which for them means moving away from home, attending boarding school, or staying with distant family. There was no problem in eliciting an ethnographic decision tree. Everyone agreed that secondary education was important and that children should take this opportunity if they had found someone to pay their fees, buy them a school uniform, and offer them a place to stay. There was also agreement that discrimination by teachers or fellow students, food shortage at the place one was staying, or similar problems should not be permitted to make the children quit school. Despite this consensus, however, individuals constantly, and often for highly idiosyncratic reasons, deviated from the outcome predicted by the model.

It emerged in this research that the social agents concerned refused to see major personal choices (such as moving away from home to attend school) as decisions to be taken from a perspective of nowhere in particular. The agent was not regarded as replaceable by anyone else. There was no notion of "all things being equal," which would have allowed for a neutral weighing of alternatives. This personalization of decisions applied to the manner in which the agent is perceived, the fact that a decision is seen to be analogue rather than digital, and the degree to which individual decisions are seen as incongruent with those of others. In the following paragraphs I examine these aspects in more detail.

First, the San place a high social premium on allowing individuals to make their own decisions, and this applies to children from an early age. Parents leave it to their children to choose whether or not to go to school. The teachers, who are exclusively from other ethnic groups with a farming background, tend to be outraged about this practice and shake their heads. When they go to see the parents to ask them why a child has run away from school or did not attend, the parents would usually respond, "Go and ask the child. She [He] is sitting right here." Whereas the teachers feel that the parents have a duty to make their children go to school (and that the children have a duty to obey their parents), San parents and children see it as a matter of personal autonomy for the pupil to decide. Even if one is generally in favor of schooling, this preference is trumped by the self-determination of the individual for his or her own life.

Second, San parents and children alike strongly emphasize the need to be able to revise decisions. Decisions are made as one goes; they are not thought of as on/off switches or inexorable if-then mechanisms. This characteristic, too, clearly surfaces in intercultural contact when understanding breaks down. Employers (and anthropologists for that matter) who think they have struck a medium- or long-term agreement that, for example, obliges local people to produce tools in exchange for money or to attend school for an extended period are constantly frustrated. The local people often decide to abandon the plan or their cooperation halfway through, even if it means that they do not receive the money or diploma they had originally envisioned. This frustration by outsiders has been translated into a stereotype casting San people as unreliable and unstable. From a San perspective, however, it is a consequence of avoiding decisions that cannot be revised in the light of new information and events. They do not wish to make a decision once and for all at the beginning of an action but rather only once the action has been completed.

Third, social agents in the San cultural settings seem to be aware at all stages of the decision-making process that they are living only that one life and that decisions such as splitting up or joining up again are not repetitions of one another, although they may occur frequently. In discussions of past or future decisions, there is a preoccupation with particulars. Even if everyone has agreed in principle on the criteria for a sound decision on schooling, for instance, the underlying assumption is that one small thing can be sufficient to allow the shared hierarchy of criteria to topple. A minor thing of this sort could be, for instance, a brief exchange of words with a teacher or another student, some insult, or some minor problem with food. What seem to be excuses to the outside, such as the fact that one had no soap with which to wash, no shoes to wear, or no decent food that morning, are acceptable contingencies that distinguish one decision from another. Just as personal lives are ultimately unique because they are subject to particular differences, so are individual decision-making processes (see, Widlok, 2009b, for a discussion of moral decision-making). Decisions may be faulty with respect to principles but comprehensible and justifiable in terms of the particulars.

Given the high premium on individual autonomy, a stance representing a probabilistic model of reasoning becomes inimical to understanding the personal and
situational aspects of the decisions in this ethnographic case. Arguably, the decision
to move is felt to be a personal, not a rational, one if the term *rational decision* is
understood to mean a choice arrived at from no particular perspective that allows
one to weigh aims and means in a detached manner. By contrast, the default assumption is that the decision to move is made at a particular time by a particular person
in a particular evolving setting. I thus realized that there would always be cases
unaccounted for by any of these decision-making trees despite a degree of agreement on the criteria for the decision to move from one location to another. In practice the predictive value of these tree models is precarious: Because of everyday
life's imponderabilia, decision-makers in these settings are ready to reconsider their
decision at any time. These decisions are seen as uniquely affecting personal lives,
so people refuse to judge them aloofly as being instances of a general type. Instead,
they highlight the personal, ultimately unique setting. A calculus of probability does
not work, for the underlying presupposition of such a calculus is that one such decision is interchangeable with other decisions of the same type and that the two alternatives can be weighed against each another. However, one should be cautious to
treat this observation as evidence of the rare or exotic nature of decision-making in
this particular group of foragers. In fact, many observations in modern western settings also fit the description of personalized decisions (Fuchs, 2008, p. 342), especially when considering fundamental, irreversible decisions of one's life that do not
comply with ideas of stock-taking (Spaemann, 1996, p. 126).

The Pragmatics of Decision-Making

At this juncture I take the opportunity to recapitulate the two models presented so
far for understanding forager mobility. Optimal foraging theory is generally used as
a deductive model that underlines the necessity to move, that is, the assumed exi-
gencies that ultimately dictate the decisions that foragers make. Ethnographic decision tree modeling, by contrast, has been employed primarily to generate inductively
whatever local models of decision-making may exist to offer agents (and observers)
probable outcomes and probable criteria that constitute a decision-making process.
Optimal foraging theory, one could say, links all rationality to outcomes, whereas
ethnographic decision trees separate out different rationalities and their resulting
actions. I have suggested that neither of these models can fully account for the ethnographic evidence of forager mobility. There appear to be patterns in the ethnography, but the arguments involved are neither those of necessity nor of probability but
rather of *plausibility*.

The need is for a less problematic model that links rationality and action in a
procedural view of rationality. I suggest going beyond the traditional models of
strict deductive or inductive logic, strict in the sense that they claim truth outside the
conversations and interactions that unfold in the social context of the reasoning in

question. As a first step it is important to have an idea of what the social context looks like in this case.

Decision-making in a forager group such as the San of Namibia does not follow quasi-legal or rigid procedures. Instead, participants and observers alike can derive decisions only from the continuous discourse that allows them to make decisions based on plausibility. Their conversational and interactional style is a particular one of repetitions, overlaps, and echoing in everyday talk. Consensus is achieved as the interlocutors repeat and echo some opinions or arguments and leave out others. This kind of exchange enables people to make intelligent guesses about what they and others will be doing next. The strategy requires that everyone be allowed to join in the conversation while avoiding prominence (and exposure) as an individual voice of authority. Similar strategies for achieving consensus have been observed else-where, as in Aboriginal Australia (Liberman, 1985, p. 104). Taken together, they differ not only from the dominant western-style conversation and interaction but also from the aggressive and self-assertive style found in many societies, including "Big Man societies" in Melanesia or segmentary systems in sub-Saharan Africa.

The following excerpt is one of the best known examples from the !Kung San, who are neighbors of the Hai//om San with whom I have worked and who have a similar interactional practice of overlapping and echoing talk: "'Yesterday,' 'eh,' 'at Deboragu,' 'eh,' 'I saw old/Gaishay.' 'You saw old/Gaishay.' 'eh, eh.' 'He said that he had seen the great python under the bank.' 'EH!' 'The python!' 'He wants us,' 'eh, eh, eh,' 'to help him catch it'" (Marshall, 1976, p. 290).

Among the San, people often talk in parallel, and there is no formal conclusion to this talk. Instead, it is made up largely of "topographical gossip" which invokes places and movements but without any formal decisions (Widlok, 1997, p. 321). Apart from this feature of particular conversational forms, the reasoning involved allows for unpredictable events in that nonhuman and apparently nonanimate fea-tures of the environment are expected to come in as well, influencing the direction that a decision may take. When people in this community refrain from long-term planning, it is not that they are incapable of doing so but rather that they allow the state of the environment or of other persons to prompt or trigger their decisions at certain stages of the process. Detailed studies on the process of tracking animals have shown that anticipating and predicting the movement of an animal that one is pursuing involves a continuous creation of new hypotheses in the light of new infor-mation added to the incomplete picture of tracks and other signs on the ground. This activity also involves a constant dialogue between trackers who are allowed to maintain their diverging views as events unfold (Liebenberg, 1990, p. 108). Making decisions about moving (or indeed any other decision) entails a similar process of encouraging heterodoxy in views, keeping the decision open until very late in the process and ultimately always allowing individuals to maintain their own diverging view. In residential mobility this tolerance of diverging views is facilitated by the fact that packing up one's belongings is easy; it allows for fast and flexible reactions either to join a party that leaves or simply stay put.

Having briefly described the mode of reasoning ethnographically, one may now ask whether there is a more general model that can help reintegrate these observations into a comparative theory on rationality and action. It turns out that the plausibility mode of decision-making that has been observed in field research with foragers appears to have its counterpart in current strands of the theory of reasoning. More specifically, the philosophy of science has a growing body of literature by scholars seeking to define rationality not as a narrow logical concept based on necessity (deductive inference) or probability (inductive inference) but rather as reasoning based on plausibility, or what is called abductive inference (see Flach & Kakas, 2000; Josephson & Josephson, 1994; Walton, 2004). In other words, there is at least a third form of reasoning that is both widespread in everyday decision-making and capable of accounting for the complexity of decision-making among mobile people.

Abduction is the generation of hypotheses based on the evaluation of alternatives (Walton, 2004). People witnessing a surprising event (e.g., the light going out, foragers relocating yet again) creatively seek an explanation that would make sense of it, would make it appear to be a matter of course. When the light goes out, one works backward as it were, usually first suspecting that the bulb is burned out. If *all* light bulbs are observed to have gone out, one may plausibly infer that a fuse has blown. If the lights are out not just in one's own house but in all the houses on the block, then one may suspect a wider power failure as the cause, and so on. None of these inferences is necessary, deductively valid, or probable in a strict sense. There are many possible reasons for the light bulb(s) having gone out, and some may have the same estimated probability (e.g., burned-out bulbs and blown fuses). What people do when reasoning abductively is tap into their background knowledge and select the most plausible explanation in a procedural fashion. Given the premium that the San place on personal autonomy, a forager of that community is constantly prompted to make sense of the sometimes erratic movements of other elements in the environment, whether fellow foragers, game animals, or erratic rainfall. The decision by the forager to move or stay rests on the background knowledge of persons and places that he or she has encountered. It is a type of reasoning that does not follow strict rules of necessity, the regularities of majority rule, or predictable seasonality but emerges by deleting the less plausible alternatives in the course of protracted social decision-making. Abduction is a way of generating an emerging certainty (not truth) that identifies the least defective alternative given the group's incomplete knowledge.

Abduction is, of course, a prevalent form of reasoning. When making sense of actions, humans usually combine deductive, inductive, and abductive arguments—each type of logic having its distinct function (Walton, 2004, p. 86). They all feature in scientific explanation, including that in the natural sciences (see Agar, 2013). But unlike deduction and induction, abduction reminds one that explanation and knowledge formation as a whole are dialogical and procedural. Processes of knowledge formation do not follow a fixed set of linear rules. Selection of the most plausible hypothesis is a process of dialogue with both objects that play a role (e.g., bulbs and natural processes) but also with other humans with whom one is engaged and who may support or doubt one's hypotheses.

For a long time, abduction was taken to be a defective form of deductive reasoning, for it was frequently defined as a case of affirming the consequent (e.g., where there is smoke, there must be fire). The idea of abductive reasoning seems to have been marginalized together with everyday cognition (Lave, 1988) as exemplified by the reasoning of foragers (Liebenberg, 1990). But the strength of abductive inference is evidently not in an isolated statement (a syllogism) but rather in a creative and explanatory mode of logical reasoning that establishes the best available hypothesis at a certain point in an open, explanatory dialogue that invites additional testing and evaluation. In other words, this strength is less likely to show up in experimental isolation than in ethnographic cases. Understanding reasoning in processes means recognizing that it matters where actors are in a complex decision-making process. Abduction is a plausible short-cut, especially in the early stages of trying to make sense of a situation or an action. But there may be situations (e.g., the tracking of animals) in which it is useful to cultivate this mode of reasoning for as long as possible in the problem-solving process. Similarly, I argue that this mode of reasoning is important *throughout* many decision-making processes, not just in their initial, creative stages.

Trying to explain why someone has moved is, I suggest, very much an abductive dialogical exercise that entails observation of natural givens (e.g., the distribution of resources and the number of people involved) but also interaction with other agents with whom one is in constant communication (and whose motivations one may abduct if they are not made explicit). Moreover, I suggest that making a rational decision on when to move is also a form of abductive reasoning. Determination of the best time to move (and the best destination to move to) is typically *not* based on necessity or probabilistic calculus but rather on broad background knowledge, informed guesses as it were, in dialogue with others, and not only fellow human beings. Moreover, I suggest that abductive inference can provide an account that links reasoning and action into a coherent whole that can also explain cultural variation. The recognition of cultural variation in abductive reasoning is the final point of this chapter.

Variation in Reasoning

The case material presented in this chapter can enhance a general model of abductive inference pertaining to dialogical knowledge formation as it emerges in contemporary philosophy and logic. An explanation of variation surfaces when one realizes that both the type of dialogue through which reasoning takes place and the partners with whom it takes place are likely to vary across situations. The prototypical forms that the dialogue of explanation takes in the philosophical literature are those between teacher and student, between judge or prosecutor and witness, and, more recently, between a user and an expert system of artificial intelligence through an interface (Walton, 2004, p. 88). None of these three examples resembles that of a group of foragers determining whether they should move or not.

- Forager decision-making on any matter (as exemplified by the San ethnography) differs greatly from the typical teacher–student relationship. As Hoymann (2010) reported, asking inquisitive questions is not encouraged among foragers. Young people are expected to learn by observing and trying or by being told at the appropriate moment, not by prompting adults as in a typical teacher–learner situation.
- Communal talk among foragers is also very different from the hierarchical setting of court proceedings in that communal talk among foragers has no fixed leadership roles and no clearly delimited sequences or groups of speakers. Indeed, their communication makes heterodoxy possible and sometimes even encourages it. People in these settings may stick to their decisions and explanations. Because they are supported by others, they also have "the freedom to be wrong at times" (Liebenberg, 1990, p. 162). When hunting, for instance, individuals may maintain rather different views as to what the tracked animal is likely to do next. When it comes to moving camp, anyone may decide not to go with the majority, but there are other options, such as being on one's own or splitting up the group.
- Expert systems today commonly take the form of multiple digital circuits of yes/no decisions. Research specifically on questions established that San speakers have a preference for not posing yes/no questions (Hoymann, 2010). In contrast to speakers of many other languages, they do not seem not to use requests for confirmation that would press the interlocutor to use yes/no. In contradiction to the most typical form of questioning used in expert systems (Widlok, 2008), they avoid cornering their interlocutors and seem to take care not to infringe the autonomy of others. When they draw on the knowledge of others, it seems very unlike the process of consulting an expert machine.

What the forager cases suggest is that the dialogic nature of reasoning is compatible with a variety of equally competent forms of dialogue: inquisitive, circumspect, digital, open, bilateral, multilateral, unilinear, and multistrand. In fact, I argue that the different practices of dialogue may produce different forms of reasoning and a spectrum of rational outcomes. It is neither one rationality only nor anything goes but rather a limited spectrum of possibilities describable in terms of the dialogical practices in which reasoning takes place.

The form of dialogue is not the only entity that may be broader than what the philosophical literature usually covers; the dialoging partners, too, may have a wider range. Reasoning is usually thought to take place either in an experimental mode between individuals and nature (as in much of the research on infants) or among investigating humans pursuing their own individual decision-making strategies. The aforementioned example of light bulbs that had gone out could include interaction with objects (e.g., shaking the bulb, checking the fuses) or interaction with other subjects (e.g., the neighbors, people in the room, or the electric utilities company). The peculiarity of the case about foragers on the move is that the boundary between nature and other persons is drawn in a particular way and differently from what nonforagers may expect. Personalization does not necessarily mean that natural objects are treated as persons, although such anthropomorphization occurs as well. In many Australian examples, Aborigines do not just talk about the land and its features but may address it directly, as when expressing their respect or even their pity when the land has not been cared for properly. In Aboriginal Australia, a typical indication of a country[1] that has not been cared for is that no one has set fire to it and that it should be visited (see Rose, 1995). Cases differ as to what is subject to person-alization. It could be animals, various supernatural beings, sacred places or—most commonly—a combination thereof (as in the Australian case of totemic Dreaming beings that involve animals, superhuman creative beings, and places). The main and more general point is not that a certain set of beings (animate or inanimate) can fea-ture as personalized subjects, as partners with whom one may reason. Rather, it seems that anything can become personalized if it is treated as a person, by which I mean that this *some-thing* is taken not as a thing, an instance of a category, but rather as a unique subject with which one interacts. By contrast, many phases of decision making in present day economics, for instance, entail processes of depersonalization and isola-tion. The procedures of reasoning are regarded not as a dialogue between persons but either as the interaction between users and computational systems or as abstract sys-temic processes devoid of personal relations, aspirations, and apprehensions.

Therefore, both the style of the dialogue and the partners in the dialogue may be much more variable than is apparent. Beyond this case of foragers on the move, it may be wise to consider procedural rationality broadly enough to allow inclusion of variations in how procedures unfold as particular forms of dialogue and how part-ners in this dialogue are personalized or depersonalized. Rationality would thereby cease to be a purely mental phenomenon. Instead, it would reside partially in forms of social communication and interaction as well as in features of the environment that western philosophy and science tend to discount as irrelevant but that can be important triggers or partners in the procedure of reasoning. Why does abductive reasoning describe my ethnographic cases so aptly? I do not think its capacity to do so is coincidental. Rather, it is because this mode of inference is not a stand-alone mode but one that is tied closely to the interacting, corporeal, and relational social beings that we humans are.

References

Agar, M. (2013). *The Lively Science: Remodeling Human Social Research*. Minneapolis: Publish Green.

Bourdieu, P. (1977). *Outline of a theory of practice*. Cambridge: Cambridge University Press.

Briggs, J. L. (1970). *Never in anger: Portrait of an Eskimo family*. Cambridge: Harvard University Press.

Flach, P. A., & Kakas, A. C. (2000). On the relation between abduction and inductive learning. In D. M. Gabbay & R. Kruse (Eds.), *Handbook of defeasible reasoning and uncertainty manage-ment systems* (pp. 5–36). Abductive reasoning and learning, Vol. 4. Dordrecht: Kluwer.

Fuchs, T. (2008). *Das Gehirn—ein Beziehungsorgan: Eine phänomenologisch-ökologische Konzeption* [The brain as a relational organ: A phenomenological-ecological conception]. Stuttgart: Kohlhammer.

---

[1] This term is used in Australia to refer to the land belonging to a specific Aboriginal group.

Gladwin, C. H. (1989). *Ethnographic decision tree modeling*. Qualitative Research Methods Series: Vol. 19. Newbury Park: Sage.

Hoymann, G. (2010). Questions and responses in ≠Akhoe Hai//om. *Journal of Pragmatics, 42*, 2726–2740.

Josephson, J. R., & Josephson, S. G. (1994). *Abductive inference: Computation, philosophy, technology*. Cambridge, UK: Cambridge University Press.

Kelly, R. L. (1995). *The foraging spectrum: Diversity in hunter-gatherer lifeways*. Washington, DC: Smithsonian Institution Press.

Kent, S. (1989). *Farmers as hunters: The implications of sedentism*. Cambridge, UK: Cambridge University Press.

Lave, J. (1988). *Cognition in practice: Mind, mathematics and culture in everyday life*. Cambridge, UK: Cambridge University Press.

Liberman, K. (1985). *Understanding interaction in central Australia: An ethnomethodological study of Australian Aboriginal people*. London: Routledge.

Liebenberg, L. (1990). *The art of tracking: The origin of science*. Claremont: David Philip.

Marshall, L. (1976). *The !Kung of Nyae Nyae*. Cambridge, MA: Harvard University Press.

Martin, J. F. (1983). Optimal foraging theory: A review of some models and their applications. *American Anthropologist, 85*, 612–629. doi:10.1525/aa.1983.85.3.02a00060

Rose, D. B. (1995). *Country in flames: Proceedings of the 1994 Symposium on Biodiversity and Fire in North Australia*. Canberra: North Australia Research Unit, Australian National University.

Rounds, J. (2004). Strategies for the curiosity-driven museum visitor. *Curator, 47*, 389–412. doi:10.1111/j.2151-6952.2004.tb00135.x

Spaemann, R. (1996). *Personen: Versuche über den Unterschied zwischen "etwas" und "jemand"* [Persons: Experiments on the difference between "something" and "somebody"]. Stuttgart: Klett-Cotta.

Walton, D. (2004). *Abductive reasoning*. Tuscaloosa: University of Alabama Press.

Widlok, T. (1997). Orientation in the wild: The shared cognition of Hai//om Bushpeople. *Journal of the Royal Anthropological Institute, 3*, 317–332. http://www.jstor.org/stable/3035022

Widlok, T. (1999). *Living on Mangetti: "Bushman" autonomy and Namibian independence*. Oxford: Oxford University Press.

Widlok, T. (2008). Local experts—expert locals: A comparative perspective on biodiversity and environmental knowledge systems in Australia and Namibia. In M. J. Casimir (Ed.), *Culture and the changing environment: Uncertainty, cognition and risk management in cross-cultural perspective* (pp. 351–382). New York: Berghahn.

Widlok, T. (2009a). *Van veraf naar dichtbij: The standing of the antipodes in a flat world*. Inaugural lecture, Radboud University Nijmegen. Retrieved from http://repository.ubn.ru.nl/handle/2066/77162

Widlok, T. (2009b). Norm and spontaneity: Elicitation with moral dilemma scenarios. In M. Heintz (Ed.), *The anthropology of moralities* (pp. 20–45). New York: Berghahn.

Chapter 15
Continuity and Change in Older Adults' Out-of-Home Mobility Over Ten Years: A Qualitative-Quantitative Approach

Heidrun Mollenkopf, Annette Hieber, and Hans-Werner Wahl

Both the ability and the opportunity to move about constitute essential requisites to older adults' independent living and societal participation. The ability–that is the fundamental physical capacity–to move is a basic human need and essential to personal health (e.g., Heikkinen et al., 1992; U.S. Department of Transportation, 2003). In that sense, declining mobility has been understood predominantly as a physical health and geriatric issue. For decades, a broad range of research has been conducted to understand, among other things, the increasing decline in mobility performance, including decrements in sensory abilities and sensorimotor integration, loss of motor control and voluntary strength, slowing motor action and speed of processing. shrinking range of motion and flexibility, and decreasing ability to stabilize posture (e.g., Fozard, 2003; Fozard & Gordon-Salant, 2001; Ketcham & Stelmach, 2001; O'Neill & Dobbs, 2004; Owsley, 2004; Spirduso, 1995).

The ability to move about—and by extension to travel—is required to navigate from point A to point B, to seek out places of subjective interest or that are essential to meeting daily material needs, to participate in cultural and recreational activities, and to maintain social relations, familiar habits, and life styles—in short, to live an autonomous life for as long as one's mental and physical capacities permit one to participate actively in society (Schaie, 2003). At the same time, age-related changes such as physical, cognitive, and/or sensory impairments and social losses may limit older adults' possibilities of ambulating and venturing out.

A multitude of studies in transportation research have provided rich statistical data on older adults' actual travel behavior, usually defined as a movement in time

H. Mollenkopf • A. Hieber
German Center for Research on Aging, Heidelberg University, Heidelberg, Germany

H.-W. Wahl (✉)
Institute of Psychology, Heidelberg University, Heidelberg, Germany
e-mail: hans-werner.wahl@psychologie.uni-heidelberg.de

© The Author(s) 2017
P. Meusburger et al. (eds.), *Knowledge and Action*, Knowledge and Space 9,
DOI 10.1007/978-3-319-44588-5_15

and space, measured in terms of trips or journeys and reported in standardized diary forms (e.g., Centre d'études sur les réseaux, les transports, l'urbanisme et les constructions publiques [CERTU], 2001; Clarke & Sawyers, 2004; European Conference of Ministers of Transport [ECMT], 2000; Organisation for Economic Co-operation and Development, 2001; Rosenbloom, 2001; Schaie & Pietrucha, 2000; Transportation Research Board [TRB], 1988). It is true that findings differ depending on national peculiarities, but general tendencies and structures correspond in some salient aspects: In general, travel of older adults has clearly increased for about two decades. However, the older individuals are, the less they tend to travel, mainly due to declining health and sensory impairments. Older individuals with a driver's license and access to a private automobile travel more than those with no car at their disposal. Because the current generation of older women has less education, a lower income, and less likelihood of having a driver's license than men of the same age, it is not surprising that they use public transportation more than men do, whereas older men use the car more often, take more trips, and travel more miles than older women (see e.g., Banister & Bowling, 2004; ECMT, 2000; Marottoli et al., 1997; Mollenkopf et al., 2002; Owsley, 2002; Rosenbloom, 2004).

Despite the abundant information available from these research strands, the functional approaches to mobility often neglect the key mobility concerns of older adults (Alsnih & Hensher, 2003; Banister & Bowling, 2004; Gabriel & Bowling, 2004; Hildebrand, 2003; Mollenkopf, Marcellini, Ruoppila, & Tacken, 2004a; Schlag & Schade, 2007; Siren & Hakamies-Blomqvist, 2004). The meaning individuals attribute to mobility and their experiences when venturing out are only scarcely assessed. However, mobility can be for its own sake and not just as a derived demand (Mokhtarian, 2005). Case studies conducted in four European cities showed that mobility means much more to older adults than the mere covering of distance (Mollenkopf et al., 2004a). In this context the attraction or deterrence of the natural, social, and built environment can play a crucial role (Banister & Bowling, 2004; Holland et al., 2005). Motivational, cognitive, or personality aspects also play an important role in their decisions to go out. Moreover, in modern society, mobility is associated with highly appreciated goals like freedom, autonomy, and flexibility (Cobb & Coughlin, 2004; Handy, Weston, & Mokhtarian, 2005; Lash & Urry, 1994; Mollenkopf, Marcellini, Ruoppila, Széman, & Tacken, 2005; Rammler, 2001). Older adults are members of current societies and therefore are affected by these societies' Zeitgeist, values, and expectations.

Only in recent years has the focus shifted to more subjective and motivational aspects of travel and driving behavior. A series of recent studies showed that older adults' ability to move about and to pursue outdoor leisure activities contributes significantly to their autonomy, social participation, and subjective quality of life (Banister & Bowling, 2004; Cvitkovich & Wister, 2001; Fernández-Ballesteros, Zamarrón, & Ruíz, 2001; Marottoli et al., 1997; Mollenkopf et al., 2004a; Mollenkopf, Baas, Kaspar, Oswald, & Wahl, 2006; Owsley, 2002; Pochet, 2003). Satisfaction with one's ability to get around, to pursue leisure activities and to travel were significant determinants of quality of life in a study comparing the impact of subjective appraisal of different life domains on satisfaction with life in general (Mollenkopf et al., 2006). In a study focusing on elderly people's own definitions of quality of life, Farquhar (1995) found that the ability to go out more was cited as improving quality of life, whereas being housebound detracted from quality of life. Similar findings were reported by Coughlin (2001) with respect to the significance of transportation, albeit mostly related to being able to drive a car. Banister and Bowling (2004) found that a sense of optimism and positive expectations of life constitute a main building block for the transport dimension of older adults' perceptions of quality of life. Psychological variables such as control beliefs and the individual importance attributed to being out also played a role in characterizing groups of older adults who differed in their out-of-home mobility patterns (Mollenkopf et al., 2004b).

Altogether, these findings offer some evidence that functional necessities, on the one hand, and modern values and individual needs on the other, strongly complement one other. In this chapter we wish to further pursue a comprehensive understanding of older adults' out-of-home mobility by taking up and integrating the diverging concepts of mobility in an environmental gerontology perspective (Wahl, Mollenkopf, Oswald, & Claus, 2007; Wahl & Oswald, 2010). Proceeding from this approach, which asserts that an individual's well-being is influenced by how well environmental resources match personal needs, we propose that mobility and related appraisals are determined by personal (health-related and psychological) and socioeconomic factors as well as by environmental (structural) conditions and features of the person-environment interaction. Findings of the European MOBILATE project largely confirmed this fundamental view of mobility in cross-sectional as well as longitudinal analyses over the 5-year observation period from 1995 to 2000 (Mollenkopf et al., 2005).

This chapter presents data based on an extended observational period up to 2005, for a total observation time of 10 years. We assume that during that time the men and women who had participated in the 1995 study might have experienced age-related health impairments, critical social life events (e.g., death of a spouse), and changes in their local environments, all of which can seriously jeopardize the outdoor mobility of the older individual.

The goals of our work are threefold. First, we describe 10-year trajectories in terms of stability and change of various key qualifiers (e.g., satisfaction) of out-of-home mobility such as out-of-home mobility in general, public transportation, out-of-home leisure activities, and travel. Second, we link and undergird these trajectories with the explicit consideration of meaning imposed on mobility, perceived changes in mobility and perceived reasons for change, as well as satisfaction with life in general. Third, we will explore interindividual differences in stability and change. We strongly believe that only a mix of methods, in other words, qualitative and quantitative, allows these goals to be addressed in a comprehensive manner.

Method

Study Design

This study started with an initial inquiry on older adults' out-of-home mobility carried out in four European cities in 1995 (Mollenkopf et al. 2004a). The German parts of the investigation—on which the present study is based—were carried out in the cities of Mannheim (western Germany) and Chemnitz (eastern Germany). Both of them are middle-sized industrial cities with diversified settlement structures and public transportation (tram and bus lines) as well as rail connections and national roads. The quantitative part of the study included $N = 804$ persons aged 55 years or older, which resulted from a randomly drawn sample of addresses from the population registers of the Municipality Registration Offices of Chemnitz and Mannheim. Thirty-five of the participants were selected for additional in-depth interviews because they showed a particularly low or high degree of mobility. Five years later (2000), 271 respondents from the original sample could be reassessed in an initial follow-up as part of the project entitled "Mobilate: Enhancing Outdoor Mobility in Later Life" funded by the European Commission in the Fifth Framework Programme (Programme Area no. 6.3, Project QLRT-1999-02236). The comparative findings of this international and interdisciplinary project, including data from Finland, Germany, Hungary, Italy, and the Netherlands, have been published elsewhere (e.g., Mollenkopf et al., 2003, 2005, 2006; Mollenkopf, Ruoppila, & Marcellini, 2007). Another 5 years later (2005), a third assessment took place in the German cities and resulted in $N = 82$ participants, or approximately 30 % from the first follow-up and 11 % from the original sample. Hence, the present study covers these participants over a 10-year period.

Well-trained interviewers from the USUMA research institute (Berlin) conducted the German interviews in 1995 and 2000. The 2005 Chemnitz interviews were also conducted by USUMA interviewers, and the interviews in Mannheim were conducted by the project staff.

Sample Description and Drop-Out

The original German sample of $N = 804$ participants was disproportionately stratified by age and sex, resulting in almost equal subcategories of men and women (50 % each) and two age groups (51.2 % respondents aged 55–74 years and 48.8 % aged 75 years or older). The composition of the age groups changed from the first assessment in 1995 to the second in 2000 (61.3 % aged 55–74 years and 38.7 % aged 75 years or older) and even more dramatically from the second to the third assessment in 2005 (84.2 % aged 55–74 years and 15.8 % aged 75 years or older). By shifting the age group limit by 10 years and drawing on the participants' actual age in 2005, we again obtained two groups of the same size (50 % each of respondents 65–74 years old and 75 years old or older).

The reasons for dropping out of the sample were documented in standardized protocols. Because of the long period of time, the most frequent reasons were the death of the former participants or a deterioration in their health (almost 20 % each). Other dropouts were due to refusals to continue participation and failure to locate or gain access to them. Logistic regression analysis based on data from the 2000 study indicated that age $(OR = .94*)$,[1] education $(OR = 1.59*)$, and the number of transport modes used in 2000 $(OR = 1.27**)$ seemed to influence participation in 2005. Probability of participation increased with younger age, higher education, and greater variety of transport modes used. The level of education among the participants can be regarded as relatively high, with almost half of them having earned a standard or advanced degree.

As Table 15.1 shows, the average age of the 82 individuals who could be assessed over the 10-year interval was 75.2 years at T3, with 50 % of these participants belonging to the younger age group (65–74 years old) and 50 % to the higher age group (75 years old or older). Women and men were almost equally represented in the sample (48 % and 52 %, respectively). Most of the participants were married (66 %) and living in multiperson households (68 %). Approximately one in four (24 %) had lost their spouse. Satisfaction with their financial situation decreased on average from $M = 7.7$ in 1995 to $M = 7.0$ in 2005. Similarly, albeit at a lower level, subjective health was rated less positively 5 and 10 years after the first assessment ($M = 6.9$ and 6.7, respectively, compared to $M = 7.3$ in 1995).

Instruments

In order to guarantee the comparability of the answers from all assessments, each follow-up retained main aspects of the instruments used in the first wave of data collection, that is, the standardized Outdoor Mobility Survey 1995 and the semi-structured interview guidelines for the in-depth 1996 interviews (Mollenkopf et al., 2003, 2004a). Both of the instruments included questions on objective factors as well as subjective ratings concerning important prerequisites for mobility such as health and socioeconomic status (individual factors), social networks, and the physical environment (environmental factors). The survey questionnaire was partially based on methods used in previous studies, such as the Finnish Evergreen project (Heikkinen, 1998), the Nordic Research on Ageing (NORA) study (Avlund, Kreiner, & Schultz-Larsen, 1993; Heikkinen, Berg, Schroll, Steen, & Viidik, 1997), and the German Welfare Survey (Zapf & Habich, 1996). Satisfaction with mobility, with the ability and opportunity to pursue leisure and other important life activities, and with

---

[1] Odds Ratio is a way to quantify how strongly the presence of a variable A increases or reduces the risk that another variable B is present or absent. Risk is calibrated in this analysis such that 1.0 means no change in the risk of B appearing when A is present. An OR of .94* means in our case that being younger significantly reduced the risk that a participant in our study would drop out. * = significant at the .05 level; ** = significant at the .10 level (tentatively significant).

Table 15.1 Older adults' out-of-home mobility in two German cities: Description of the sample ($N = 82$)

Characteristics	Year					
	1995		2000		2005	
Mean age (years)	62.2		–		75.2	
	Size of household					
	n	%	n	%	n	%
Living alone	13	15.9	19	23.2	26	31.7
Living with others	69	84.1	63	76.8	56	68.3
	Marital status[a]					
	n	%	n	%	n	%
Married, living with a partner	66	80.5	61	74.4	54	65.9
Widowed	8	9.8	13	15.9	20	24.4
	Satisfaction with the financial situation of the household[b]					
	M	SD	M	SD	M	SD
	7.7	1.8	7.6	2.0	7.0	2.4
	Satisfaction with health[b]					
	M	SD	M	SD	M	SD
	7.3	2.1	6.9	2.4	6.7	2.5
	Changes in health					
	n	%	n	%	n	%
Became better			6	7.3	3	3.6
Became worse			35	42.7	45	54.9
Remained the same			41	50.0	34	41.5

[a]The analyses also included the characteristics married, living separately ($n = 1$), divorced ($n = 3$), and never married ($n = 4$), which comprised 10 % of each assessment.[b]Satisfaction was assessed on an 11-point scale ranging from 0 (*lowest satisfaction*) to 10 (*highest satisfaction*)
Design by authors

life in general was assessed on an 11-point Likert-type scale ranging from 0 (*lowest satisfaction*) to 10 (*highest satisfaction*) (see Veenhoven, 1996; Zapf & Habich, 1996), which was also used in the German Welfare Survey and the German Socio-Economic Panel (SOEP).

The focus of the semistructured interview, representing the qualitative part of the assessment, was on the aging adults' personal experiences and the subjective meanings they attributed to their out-of-home mobility options. In the second and third wave of assessment, additional questions were posed concerning changes between 1995 and 2000 and between 2000 and 2005 with respect to factors possibly affecting mobility.

Data Analyses

All interviews of the third assessment were tape recorded. After transcription of the qualitative portions of the interviews, content analysis (Mayring, 2003) was used to extract the main aspects and to group them into conceptually meaningful categories.

The statements quoted in the results section represent especially characteristic and meaningful examples from the extensive amount of material. All names were changed to comply with data protection acts.

Quantitative data records were analyzed using the SAS statistical package (SAS Institute, Inc.), and the analysis was kept simple because of the rather small sample size. Statistical testing consisted mostly of t-tests and chi-square tests, with the usual levels of $p < .05*$ applying.

In this study we focus particularly on finding ways to combine quantitative and qualitative data so that each data-analytic component complements the other.

Results

Overview

We start with findings addressing the subjective meaning of mobility over time, followed by perceived changes in mobility and perceived reasons for change. We then report on trajectories of satisfaction with key areas of outdoor mobility as well as the course of satisfaction with life in general. Finally, we explore the interindividual variability over time based on case analyses selected to underscore some of the extremes inherent in the data. Results presented in the first step are completely qualitative, whereas quantitative and qualitative data analyses are interwoven in the remaining steps.

Subjective Meaning of Out-of-Home Mobility Over Time

The terms in which our participants in 2005 expressed what out-of-home mobility meant to them were nearly the same as those they had used 10 years earlier (see Table 15.2). As in our earlier studies (Mollenkopf & Flaschenträger, 2001; Mollenkopf et al., 2004a), we were able to categorize the elicited semantic material into seven categories: out-of-home mobility as a basic emotional experience; physical movement as a basic human need; mobility as movement and participation in the natural environment; mobility as a social need; mobility as an expression of personal autonomy and freedom; mobility as a source of stimulation and diversion; and mobility as a reflective expression of one's life force. For most of the respondents, mobility included more than one aspect, and some of the various facets are tightly interwoven, reflecting the multidimensional meaning of mobility. Taken all together, it seems that out-of-home mobility has maintained more or less the same bandwidth and richness of meaning over the 10-year observational period.

Table 15.2 The meaning of out-of-home mobility: Main categories in sample verbal citations

Year	Category
	The overarching meaning of mobility as a basic emotional experience, as essential for the quality of life or for life itself
1995	"Joy!"; "It's everything, it's life!"
2005	"A part of quality of life—yes, that's a really considerable part of quality of life!"
	"Really, it's getting out that makes up life, isn't it? When you stay at home you can watch TV, but that's not life, that's dying slowly."
	Physical movement as a basic human need
1995	"A person has to move! I want to move and feel good when I do."
2005	"Moving about outdoors is very important for me. I use every opportunity to get out into the open air."
	Mobility as movement and participation in the natural environment
1995	"I have to get out, have to know what is going on in nature!"
2005	"That's worth a lot....Of course, getting out, open air, movement, and other environments and other people and nature—all this has to be worth a lot to everybody."
	Moving around as a social need, as a desire for social integration and participation
1995	"Still being able to take part in social life." "So that I don't get lonely."
2005	"Getting out of one's home—this means meeting friends and acquaintances, socializing, participating in culture, broadening one's horizons, and a lot more."
	The possibility to move about as an expression of personal autonomy and freedom
1995	"Being able to go out any time I want!" "Not being locked in!"
2005	"A wonderful step to freedom....It has always been like this, the desire to go out into the open and the ability to do so—that's simply beautiful. Being able to do so is important, very important."
	Mobility as a source of stimulation and diversion
1995	"Sometimes seeing something other than the four walls you live in!"; "So that I don't go crazy up here!"
2005	"This means a great deal to me. Freedom of movement – and you have to see what's new, the celebrations, meet other people and enjoy things a bit – that's what you need in old age."
	The ability to move about as a reflective expression of one's remaining life force—A typical topic of old age
1995	"The last bit of freedom!" "Proof that I'm still a human being like anyone else."
2005	"This I can say: I'm still well—I am happy that I am still able to go out and move about on my own."

Design by authors

Perceived Changes in Out-of-Home Mobility Over Time and Perceived Reasons for Such Change

Comparing the older adults' subjectively perceived changes in their out-of-home mobility over the 10-year interval gives a clear picture of continuity and change in this domain: About two thirds of the study's participants said in both follow-up assessments (2000 and 2005) that their mobility had not changed (Table 15.3). About one third (27 % in 2000 and 34 % in 2005) reported a decline each time.

Table 15.3 Perceived changes in out-of-home mobility: Two German cities

	Year			
Change	2000		2005	
	Total sample ($N = 82$)			
	n	%	n	%
Better	3	3.7	0	0.0
Worse	22	26.8	28	34.2
The same	57	69.5	54	65.8
	Age group (in years)			
	65–74 ($n = 41$)		75 and older ($n = 41$)		65–74 ($n = 41$)		75 and older ($n = 41$)	
	n	%	n	%	n	%	n	%
Better	3	7.3	0	0.0	0	0.0	0	0.0
Worse	10	24.4	12	29.3	8	19.5	20	48.8
The same	28	68.3	29	70.7	33	80.5	21	51.2
	Gender							
	Female ($n = 39$)		Male ($n = 43$)		Female ($n = 39$)		Male ($n = 43$)	
	n	%	n	%	n	%	n	%
Better	1	2.6	2	4.6	0	0.0	0	0.0
Worse	11	28.2	11	25.6	14	35.9	14	32.6
The same	27	69.2	30	69.8	25	64.1	29	67.4

Design by authors

Whereas 4 % of the participants still stated an improvement in mobility in 2000, no one in 2005 reported an improvement. When age is applied as the distinguishing factor, it becomes evident that mobility worsens mainly after the 75th year of life. Almost 30 % of the older age group stated a decline in 2000 compared to just 24.4 % of the younger age group. Five years later, the proportions differed even more starkly (50 % and 20 %, respectively). Men and women showed only minor differences in this regard.

The perceived reasons for change in mobility can be attributed to both personal and environmental circumstances and are centered mostly on the theme of loss and deterioration. Declining health, in particular, but also financial constraints; the necessity of caring for a family member; difficulties with using a bicycle, car, or public transport and with coping with traffic conditions in general; and barriers in the built environment tend to result in mobility restrictions. The following quotations illustrate how older people experience their declining mobility and what impacts it has on their daily life.

> I can no longer move about in the open countryside the way I used to. Five years ago I still went fishing, but I can't any more. If I go to the river, I risk being alone. And if I were to pass out, maybe I wouldn't fall into the water, but I might lay there a long time. (Mr. Nolte, 88 years old)

Despite the prosthesis I feel pain, and this restricts my walking. And when I come home—not in winter, but in the spring and summer—I have to undress, and my wife gives me a shower. (Mr. Walter, 86 years old)

I don't have a car anymore and have to go everywhere on foot. There are only public modes of transport like the tram. But I have no further options. I would have to ask my son to take me somewhere. (Mr. Ober, 77 years old)

Well, as I said, I can no longer use my bike and I need some help for heavy household tasks more often nowadays. (Mrs. Diffler, 68 years old)

Of course, my whole situation has changed because of this task [caring for her husband, who suffers from dementia]. I myself, if I were independent, if I did not have to care for someone, I could walk, I could travel, and I could do anything I want. (Mrs. Hansen, 75 years old)

Satisfaction with Key Areas of Mobility and Satisfaction with Life in General Over Time

Out-of-Home Mobility

The appraisal of one's possibilities for mobility—assessed on an 11-point scale ranging from 0 (not *satisfied at all*) to 10 (very *satisfied*)—included all means of getting where one wants to go, either on foot, by bicycle, by car as a driver or passenger, or by public transport. In general, the older adults' satisfaction with their mobility options over the 10-year interval was high (Table 15.4). Toward the third assessment, however, it decreased from an average rating of $M = 8.4$ (T1) to $M = 8.3$ (T2) and $M = 7.8$ (T3). This tendency was true of male participants in particular. Men and women aged 75 years or older also expressed less satisfaction with their mobility options than did younger elders (65–74 years old). As expected, older adults who reported a decline in their mobility options in the second and/or third assessment were significantly less satisfied with their mobility in general than people whose mobility had not changed.

Public Transport

Average satisfaction with public transport increased over the 10-year interval among the people who used it ($M = 7.2$ in 1995 to $M = 8.1$ in 2000 and $M = 8.2$ in 2005; see Table 15.5). Women were less satisfied than men in all assessments. When respondents with mobility impairments were distinguished from respondents without such limitations, satisfaction of the impaired decreased only slightly between the second and third assessment (from $M = 7.9$–7.2). Older adults who had not reported mobility restrictions showed a remarkable increase in their appraisal of public transport.

Table 15.4 Satisfaction with mobility possibilities: Two German cities

Characteristics of the sample	Year					
	1995		2000		2005	
	M	SD	M	SD	M	SD
N = 82	8.4	1.9	8.3	1.9	7.8	2.1
	Age group (in years)					
65–74 (n = 41)	8.3	2.0	8.4	2.0	8.2	1.8
75 and older (n = 41)	8.5	1.8	8.1	1.9	7.4	2.3[b]
	Gender					
Female (n = 39)	7.9	2.1	7.8	2.4	7.6	2.5
Male (n = 43)	8.8	1.6	8.7	1.4	8.0	1.8[b]
	Perceived changes in mobility 2005					
Became worse (n = 28)	8.6	1.6	7.8	2.3[a]	5.8	2.4[b]
Remained the same (n = 54)	8.3	2.1	8.5	1.7	8.7	1.2

Note. Satisfaction was assessed on an 11-point scale ranging from 0 (not *satisfied at all*) to 10 (very *satisfied*)
[a]Significant differences between 2000 and 2005.[b]Significant differences between 1995 and 2005
Design by authors

Table 15.5 Satisfaction with public transportation in two German cities

Characteristics of the sample	Year					
	1995		2000		2005	
	M	SD	M	SD	M	SD
n = 53 (users only)	7.2	2.8	8.1	1.7	8.2	1.7[b]
	Age group (in years)					
65–74 (n = 28)	7.2	3.0	8.3	1.9	8.1	1.7
75 and older (n = 25)	7.3	2.5	7.8	1.4	8.3	1.7
	Gender					
Female (n = 27)	6.	2.8	7.8	2.0	8.0	1.9
Male (n = 26)	7.7	2.7	8.3	1.3	8.4	1.4
	Perceived changes in mobility 2005					
Became worse (n = 14)	7.9	1.9	7.9	1.6	7.2	2.3
Remained the same (n = 39)	7.0	3.0[a]	8.1	1.7	8.5	1.3[c]

Note. Satisfaction was assessed on an 11-point scale ranging from 0 (not *satisfied at all*) to 10 (very *satisfied*)
[a]Significant differences between 1995 and 2000.[b]Significant differences between 1995 and 2005
Design by authors

Out-of-Home Leisure Activities and Travel

Just as everyday activities require at least a minimum of physical mobility, so do leisure activities and travel. Hence, it is no surprise that changes in these domains eventually occurred most in people who reported mobility restrictions (61 % in both domains compared to 33 % change in leisure and 49 % change in travel among the nonimpaired). The main reasons for decreasing activities were the same as for

Table 15.6 Satisfaction with possibilities of pursuing out-of-home leisure activities: Two German cities

Characteristics of the sample	Year					
	1995		2000		2005	
	M	SD	M	SD	M	SD
N = 82	8.1	2.0	7.9	2.4	7.5	2.3
	Age group (in years)					
65–74 (n = 41)	8.0	2.0	7.7	2.7	7.8	2.1
75 and older (n = 41)	8.2	2.1	8.0	2.1[a]	7.1	2.5[b]
	Gender					
Female (n = 39)	8.1	2.0	7.6	2.7	7.6	2.3
Male (n = 43)	8.1	2.0	8.1	2.1	7.4	2.4
	Perceived changes in mobility 2005					
Became worse (n = 28)	8.1	2.1	7.4	2.7	6.3	2.5[b]
Remained the same (n = 54)	8.1	2.0	8.1	2.2	8.0	2.1

Note. Satisfaction was assessed on an 11-point scale ranging from 0 (not *satisfied at all*) to 10 (very *satisfied*)
[a]Significant differences between 2000 and 2005.[b]Significant differences between 1995 and 2005
Design by authors

decreasing mobility: declining health, lack of money, the necessity of caring for a family member, the absence of a companion, difficulties with using transport modes, and environmental barriers.

About a quarter of all respondents and about half of the respondents with mobility impairments do not travel at all. This means, however, that half of older adults with impairments still travel, albeit to less distant destinations and for a shorter period than previously.

With regard to satisfaction with one's opportunities to pursue leisure activities and travel, the evident tendency was similar to that pertaining to satisfaction with mobility options. On average, and by subgroups, there was a significant decrease within the 10-year interval. Satisfaction with leisure activities decreased from $M = 8.1$ in 1995 to $M = 7.9$ in 2000 and $M = 7.5$ in 2005 (Table 15.6). The figures for satisfaction with travel were $M = 8.5$ (1995), $M = 7.9$ (2000), and $M = 7.0$ (2005) (see Table 15.7). The drops occurred mainly between the second and third assessment and among people who reported impaired mobility.

Life in General

The diverging individual developments in older adults' mobility and the respective impact on domain-specific satisfaction can be examined further in terms of satisfaction with life in general (Table 15.8). In the course of the follow-up investigations, overall satisfaction with life remained almost the same among the older adults who participated in all three assessments. On average it was rated $M = 8.2$ in 1995, $M = 8.2$ in 2000, and $M = 8.0$ in the year 2005. The slight decrease toward the third

Table 15.7 Satisfaction with possibilities for travel: Two German cities

Characteristics of the sample	Year					
	1995		2000		2005	
	M	SD	M	SD	M	SD
N = 82	8.5	2.0	7.9	2.7[b]	7.0	2.8[c]
	Age group (in years)					
65–74 (n = 41)	8.1	2.3	8.2	2.4[b]	7.1	2.6[c]
75 and older (n = 41)	8.8	1.6[a]	7.5	3.0	6.8	3.1[c]
	Gender					
Female (n = 39)	8.3	2.2	7.6	3.1	6.9	3.0[c]
Male (n = 43)	8.7	2.0	8.1	2.3[b]	7.0	2.7[c]
	Perceived changes in mobility 2005					
Became worse (n = 28)	8.5	2.6	7.3	3.1	6.7	2.5
Remained the same (n = 54)	8.5	1.7	8.1	2.5[b]	7.0	2.9[c]

Note. Satisfaction was assessed on an 11-point scale ranging from 0 (not *satisfied at all*) to 10 (very *satisfied*)
[a]Significant differences between 1995 and 2000.[b]Significant differences between 2000 and 2005.[c]Significant differences between 1995 and 2005
Design by authors

Table 15.8 Satisfaction with life in general: Two German cities

Characteristics of the sample	Year					
	1995		2000		2005	
	M	SD	M	SD	M	SD
Sample (N = 82)	8.2	1.6	8.2	1.5	8.0	1.8
	Age group (in years)					
65–74 (n = 41)	8.0	1.5	8.2	1.3	8.1	1.8
75 and older (n = 41)	8.3	1.7	8.1	1.6	8.0	1.8
	Gender					
Female (n = 39)	7.9	1.7	8.1	1.6	7.8	2.0
Male (n = 43)	8.5	1.4	8.2	1.3	8.2	1.6
	Perceived changes in mobility 2005					
Became worse (n = 28)	8.6	1.7[a]	7.5	1.7	7.1	1.9[b]
Remained the same (n = 54)	7.9	1.5	8.5	1.2	8.5	1.5

Note. Satisfaction was assessed on an 11-point scale ranging from 0 (not *satisfied at all*) to 10 (very *satisfied*)
[a]Significant differences between 1995 and 2000.[b]Significant differences between 1995 and 2005
Design by authors

assessment point is not statistically significant. Women were somewhat less satisfied than men in all assessments, but again the decrease in satisfaction did not reach statistical significance. There was almost no difference between the younger and older age groups. However, when individuals with and without mobility impairments were distinguished, differences that support the notion of a close relationship between mobility and quality of life became obvious. Whereas satisfaction of older adults without mobility limitations even increased over time (1995: $M = 7.9$; 2000: $M = 8.5$; 2005: $M = 8.5$), life satisfaction of mobility-impaired individuals dropped significantly between both the first and second assessment and over the 10-year interval (1995: $M = 8.6$; 2000: $M = 7.5$; 2005: $M = 7.1$).

Exploration of Interindividual Variability Over Time in a Case Contrast Approach

In this section we again examine the key areas of out-of-home mobility from the above perspective and contrast selected extreme cases in their divergent trajectories. We use the total sample as a platform for overall comparison and provide background material and quotations, and figures to improve understanding of this diversity. In addition, Fig. 15.1 provides an illustration of interindividual differences in mobility as people age.

In comparison with changes in satisfaction of the total sample, the changes in satisfaction of Mr. Lechner (80 years old) and Mrs. Dahlmann (87 years old) mirror characteristic developments over the 10-year interval (Fig. 15.1, panel a). Mr. Lechner's satisfaction with his out-of-home mobility options had decreased between the years 1995 ($M = 10.0$) and 2000 ($M = 9.0$) because of a severe illness. He recovered between the second and the third assessment and was happy about his new freedom: "Thanks to my recovery it is possible to put more strain on my body, and I make the most of it for trips, hiking, and long-distance trips."

Together with his wife he walks at least five to six kilometers every day and does all his shopping and errands on foot or by public transport because they have no car available. He is still able to actively pursue his hobbies—cooking, painting, and forming wood and other materials—and because he experiences no impairments he said, "Hence, I can be quite satisfied" ($M = 9.0$).

The course that Mrs. Dahlmann's satisfaction took was quite different. Her mobility-related satisfaction had increased between 1995 ($M = 7.0$) and 2000 ($M = 9.00$). However, she suffered from late effects of a cancer surgery and had to undergo operations on her veins and hip joint between the second and third assessment. Because the latter surgery was not completely successful, her mobility is severely restricted. She can still reach shops and services in the neighborhood on foot. However, longer trips are no longer possible: She gave up driving and is not yet accustomed to using public transport.

> Inside activities are only a little limited—of course, my range is not large and that makes a big difference. But outdoor mobility and out-of-home activities are restricted....Actually, because of pain I walk with the aid of a cane anyway, and I feel extremely unsure as a result....The movability of my feet has decreased, and when I step down a curb or something similar I have to pay careful attention....In the past I loved hiking, even in high mountain areas—but this is no longer possible. My activities are limited to what I have to do: shopping and what is necessary for daily living.

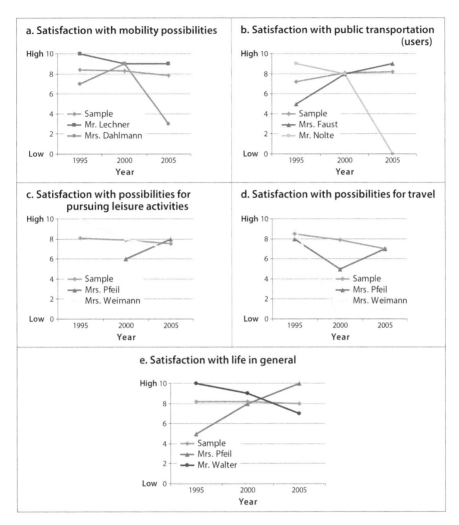

Fig. 15.1 Case examples to illustrate inter-individual differences in intra-individual changes in mobility-related indicators and general life satisfaction (Note: Satisfaction was assessed on an 11-point scale ranging from 0 (not *satisfied at all*) to 10 (very *satisfied*). Design by authors)

Against this background, Mrs. Dahlmann's satisfaction with her possibilities of moving about decreased sharply in the third measurement ($M = 3.0$). Together, the two examples point to large individual differences behind the general tendencies (Fig. 15.1).

The diverging individual conditions and experiences and the resulting evaluations regarding satisfaction with public transportation are again underscored with two examples (Fig. 15.1, panel b). Mrs. Faust, 77 years old, has taken daily care of her husband, who has been living in a nursing home. Her limited possibilities of moving about were reflected by a rather low satisfaction with public transport

(1995: $M = 5.0$). When her husband passed away between the second and third assessment, she was able to recover from this difficult life event mainly by pursuing out-of-home activities. Because she never obtained a driver's license, she has taken most of her trips on foot or by public transport. Because of her severe visual impairment, she has difficulties orientating herself when moving about on foot. For several years now public transport modes have therefore grown in significance to her because they allow her to maintain her activities (2000: $M = 8.0$; 2005: $M = 9.0$). "Everything by bus or tram," she said. "Except to the baker's. I walk there because of my visual impairment and—well, indeed, you are no longer entirely agile with advancing age."

Mr. Nolte is 88 years old and seriously impaired in his physical mobility. Nonetheless, in the first and second assessments he was still quite satisfied with public transport (1995: $M = 9.0$; 2000: $M = 8.0$). However, between the second and third assessment, his state of health worsened to the extent that he has depended ever since on help to be able to leave the house, so his satisfaction dropped to zero ($M = 0.0$). He complained:

> My problem is that I no longer have the strength to walk to the tram stop by myself... because I am physically handicapped. I am no longer satisfied with the tram because I cannot use it anymore!

Satisfaction with one's possibilities for travel decreased significantly over time even among nonimpaired elders, whereas satisfaction with leisure opportunities stayed almost the same in the respective intervals. There were again great individual differences, however, as seen in the examples of Mrs. Pfeil and Mrs. Weimann (Fig. 15.1, panels c and d).

The options for leisure activities and travel for 72-year-old Mrs. Pfeil had improved substantially in the last several years before the third assessment, not because of her health but because of changes in her social network. Caring for her almost 100-year-old mother required a great deal of time and energy and made other activities almost impossible. The situation changed when her mother passed away in 2002. "Since retiring…, I often take short trips, short cultural trips. Longer travel was not possible as long as my mother was living. I always went to see her. This has improved a lot now." Mrs. Pfeil was able to slowly resume her previous hobbies and traveling.

> Well, I occupy myself with my computer, with my video recorder. I have been doing this for some time and have built up a little video library. I read—there just isn't time enough! I listen to music, actually everything beautiful....I watch TV, especially cultural programs.... Moreover, I visit the museum. In fact, outside the home I exercise, bowl, attend the theater and concerts, major events such as the one in the park recently.

Her wide range of activities contributes substantially to both her satisfaction with possibilities of pursuing outdoor leisure activities (2000: $M = 6.0$; 2005: $M = 8.0$) and travel (2000: $M = 5.0$; 2005: $M = 7.0$).

Mrs. Weimann, 85 years old, is experiencing quite the opposite. Her husband's stroke has so severely restricted his mobility and reactions that she has to support him in almost all his activities of daily living. This situation heavily impacts her own and shared activities.

> Leisure—I am rather satisfied in this regard....I still can go out with the dog; and at home, of course, I can do cooking, baking, gardening. Elsewhere, I play golf and bridge—but the latter is more in winter....What is hard is that I can no longer play golf with my husband, that we can no longer take bicycle tours together, and that we cannot go on holiday anymore....I cannot take him with me. Even if he had a wheelchair, he would not be able to move around.

Consequently, her satisfaction with leisure activities, which had the highest rating ($M = 10$) in 1995, fell to $M = 8.0$ in 2000 and to $M = 7.0$ in 2005. Regarding satisfaction with travel, the decline was even worse (1995: $M = 9.0$; 2000: 0.0; 2005: 1.0).

With respect to individual differences in general life satisfaction (Fig. 15.1, panel e), we refer again to Mrs. Pfeil, whose satisfaction with outdoor activities and travel rose remarkably when she no longer needed to care for her mother, a task that had prevented her from pursuing desired activities. The same holds true for her satisfaction with life in general. Starting from a very low rating ($M = 5.0$) in the first assessment in 1995, her subjective quality of life also increased when her radius of action widened again (2000: $M = 8.0$; 2005: $M = 10$).

> Well, as long as I worried about my mother—I mean, even though she was very old she was still my mother. You are so worried, it was like a cloud hovering over you. We watched her decline for four years, and we did a lot of grieving. Meanwhile, I have gotten over it and can say, "This has changed." And this burden—it is a burden, whether you want to admit it or not—this has changed.

Hence, the positive changes in Mrs. Pfeil's out-of-home options and her related domain-specific satisfaction and subjective quality of life are due to changes in her social commitments.

By comparison, the example of 86-year-old Mr. Walter represents those men and women whose satisfaction with life in general decreased with advancing age, particularly because of health and mobility impairments. Although Mr. Walter was completely satisfied with his life in the first assessment ($M = 10$) and almost equally satisfied 5 years later ($M = 9.0$), this appraisal decreased in the third assessment ($M = 7.0$), although he did not suffer from severe impairments. Instead, he reported a general decline that most aging people have to cope with: "Because movability has diminished and sensitivity to pain has increased—thus we are somewhat less satisfied, I would say."

At the same time he is an example of the strength and adaptability older people develop in order to meet everyday hardships and to maintain satisfying activities despite mobility restrictions. "But yes, we struggle through, there is no whining and sniveling.... When the weather is reasonable we sit outside in the garden, and mostly we are four to five more people; that's fun."

Discussion

The longitudinal investigation of aging adults' out-of-home mobility, carried out in two German cities over an observation interval of 10 years, provided the opportunity to assess and describe how individual, social, and environmental changes affect older men's and women's options of moving about and what effect these changes have on their satisfaction in different mobility-related domains.

One initial key finding is that out-of-home mobility—the opportunity and ability to move about outside one's home and get to places one wants or needs to go— keeps its remarkable significance as one grows older. Individual statements and the correlation between mobility and subjective evaluations indicate the manifold meanings of out-of-home mobility and, in particular, its positive quality. The meanings include aspects as basic as zest for life, autonomy and freedom, the sense of belonging, and just the pleasure of moving. These results are in line with findings reported in previous research (Banister & Bowling, 2004; Coughlin, 2001; Fernández-Ballesteros et al., 2001; Holland et al., 2005; Mollenkopf et al., 2006), demonstrating that being able to go out, be active, and meet other people can result in positive feelings. Consequently, we agree with Banister and Bowling (2004), whose view on older people's travel and quality-of-life issues is wider than that conventionally found in transport research.

The results of the follow-up assessments also correspond with the well-documented risk of declining health and movability with advancing age (Fozard & Gordon-Salant, 2001; Heikkinen et al., 1997; Ketcham & Stelmach, 2001; Spirduso, 1995), conditions that lead to decreasing out-of-home mobility (CERTU, 2001; Marottoli et al., 2000; OECD, 2001; O'Neill & Dobbs, 2004). Study participants reported decreasing mobility and activities in all related domains. The decline in mobility finds expression in the older adults' subjective evaluation of their possibilities of getting out and about. In general, their satisfaction with possibilities for general mobility and with their opportunities to pursue leisure activities and travel over the 10-year interval is high, albeit with substantial individual differences. Moreover, subjective evaluations decreased in the total group among the persons aged 75 years or older, and in particular among individuals with mobility impairments in the third assessment. Women showed slightly lower satisfaction scores than men with respect to most of the domain-specific aspects of mobility, perhaps because of the fact that, among the present generations of older people, basic preconditions of mobility are generally more favorable for the "young" old and for men (e.g., Banister & Bowling, 2004; ECMT, 2000; Rosenbloom, 2004; Siren & Hakamies-Blomqvist, 2004). However, the general decline of out-of-home mobility over the 10-year interval was similar.

The development of satisfaction with public transport differs from this general pattern—it increases among all subgroups except for the users whose mobility had become worse between the second and third assessment. This positive appraisal can be explained in part by real improvements in the local transport systems of the cities under study. Moreover, if the nearest stop is within easy reach, the vehicles are easily accessible, and the connections are reliable and cheap, the public modes of transportation can be used as an alternative once previously used modes such as driving a car are no longer possible.

Apart from health decrements, environmental circumstances, including technological deterrents, taxing traffic conditions, and obligations such as caring for a family member, were found to interfere severely with the older adults' options of venturing out. The effect of such restrictions actually extends over all activities outside the home, so it is no surprise that mobility limitations affected the respondents' subjective quality of life as well. Although average life satisfaction of the total group remained almost the same over the 10-year interval, individuals whose mobility had worsened over time were not only markedly less satisfied than their nonimpaired contemporaries with their possibilities of being mobile and active but were also less satisfied with life in general. Together with the differential courses of domain-specific satisfaction among individuals whose venturing out was limited due to family obligations, these findings suggest a strong relationship between out-of-home mobility and overall life satisfaction. They also support our view that older adults' quality of life is largely affected by mobility aspects that promote self-determination, flexibility, and the freedom to get where one wants and to do what one wants to do.

The results of our previous European studies (Mollenkopf et al., 2005, 2006) back up this supposition. The most important variable in almost all domain-specific appraisals and satisfaction with life in general was the ability to move about. Moreover, participation in a great diversity of outdoor activities and/or the satisfaction with one's opportunities to move about and pursue desired activities contributed substantially to both satisfaction with life in general and emotional well-being. Similarly, English studies found that poor morale became increasingly prevalent among older individuals with worsening mobility (Holland et al., 2005).

In addition, the findings can partly qualify the so-called satisfaction paradox, according to which high adaptability of older individuals allows them to maintain a high level of well-being despite unfavorable or aggravating life conditions (Staudinger, 2000). Obviously, such adaptability no longer has this effect if fundamental needs such as the need to be mobile and active are concerned. Means and average numbers are apt to obscure remarkable individual developments and related evaluations. Hence, only a differentiated view that considers the various conditions of older adults' living circumstances allows for valid statements about their out-of-home mobility. In this respect, the longitudinal perspective of our study and its combination of qualitative and quantitative methods proved particularly useful.

In terms of limitations of this study, it should be stressed that the individuals who were still able and willing to participate in this research after 10 years are a positive selection. Another limitation of this study is that we cannot distinguish the extent to which the findings are attributable to regional conditions. Studies comparing regional differences (e.g., Holland et al., 2005; Mollenkopf et al., 2005, 2006) suggest that a range of mobility factors play an equally important role in older adults' quality of life under diverging national and regional conditions. At the same time some mobility components showed differential significance depending on the area under observation. This observation points to the necessity of considering regional peculiarities as well as individual aspects in order to fully understand the respective relation between mobility options and quality of life.

The findings confirm what is known from our basic environmental gerontology approach (Wahl & Oswald, 2010; Wahl et al., 2007), that an older individual's physical, social, and technical resources, as well as the structural resources provided by a region or locality, constitute basic prerequisites for moving about. The strong impact that the ability to pursue fulfilling activities has on the satisfaction with life reflects the importance that a congruence between personal and environmental resources has for an individual's well-being. At the same time, the respective circumstances seem to be mediated by the subjective evaluation of one's own possibilities and prevailing environmental conditions.

We believe that our findings have relevance for policy measures and further research alike. On the one hand, more detailed knowledge is necessary to improve the understanding of the nature, meaning, and significance of specific aspects of out-of-home mobility for older adults' quality of life. In this respect, compiling sociological, behavioral, and transportation approaches could provide further insights. On the other hand, the available data already show how crucial it is to promote the mobility of older adults as a means of enabling them to take part in meaningful activities at locations outside their homes through various structural, technological, and social measures of prevention and support in order to maintain their quality of life and well-being.

Acknowledgment We thank the Eugen-Otto-Butz Foundation, Germany (www.butz-stiftung. de), which was kind enough to provide the funding for the second follow-up in 2005 and, hence, the long-term perspective of this study.

References

Alsnih, R., & Hensher, D. A. (2003). The mobility and accessibility expectations of seniors in an ageing population. *Transportation Research, Part A: Policy and Practice, 37,* 903–916. doi:10.1016/S0965-8564(03)00073-9

Avlund, K., Kreiner, S., & Schultz-Larsen, K. (1993). Construct validation and the Rasch model: Functional ability of healthy elderly people. *Scandinavian Journal of Public Health, 21,* 233–246. doi:10.1177/140349489302100403

Banister, D., & Bowling, A. (2004). Quality of life for the elderly: The transport dimension. *Transport Policy, 11,* 105–115. doi:10.1016/S0967-070X(03)00052-0

Centre d'études sur les réseaux, les transports, l'urbanisme et les constructions publiques [CERTU] (2001). *La mobilité des personnes âgées—Analyse des enquêtes ménages déplacements* [Mobility of older adults: Analysis of survey of household mobility]. Lyon: Rapport d'étude.

Clarke, A. J., & Sawyers, K. M. (Eds.). (2004). *Transportation in an aging society: A decade of experience.* Transportation Research Board (TRB) Conference Proceedings: Vol. 27. Washington, DC: TRB.

Cobb, R. W., & Coughlin, J. F. (2004). Transportation policy for an aging society: Keeping older Americans on the move. In A. J. Clarke & K. M. Sawyers (Eds.), *Transportation in an aging society: A decade of experience* (pp. 275–289). Transportation Research Board (TRB) Conference Proceedings: Vol. 27. Washington, DC: TRB.

Coughlin, J. (2001). *Transportation and older persons: Perceptions and preferences*. Washington, DC: Public Policy Institute. Retrieved from http://assets.aarp.org/rgcenter/il/2001_05_transport.pdf

Cvitkovich, Y., & Wister, A. (2001). The importance of transportation and prioritization of environmental needs to sustain well-being among older adults. *Environment and Behavior, 33*, 809–829. doi:10.1177/00139160121973250

European Conference of Ministers of Transport [ECMT]. (2000). *Transport and aging of the population: Report of the 112th round table on transport economics*, Paris, 19–20 November 1998. Paris: OECD.

Farquhar, M. (1995). Elderly people's definitions of quality of life. *Social Science & Medicine, 41*, 1439–1446. http://dx.doi.org/10.1016/0277-9536(95)00117-P

Fernández-Ballesteros, R., Zamarrón, M. D., & Ruíz, M. A. (2001). The contribution of socio-demographic and psychosocial factors to life satisfaction. *Ageing and Society, 21*, 25–43. doi:10.1017/S0144686X01008078

Fozard, J. L. (2003). Enabling environments for physical aging: A balance of preventive and compensatory interventions. In K. W. Schaie, H.-W. Wahl, M. Mollenkopf, & F. Oswald (Eds.), *Aging independently: Living arrangements and mobility* (pp. 31–45). New York: Springer.

Fozard, J. L., & Gordon-Salant, S. (2001). Sensory and perceptual changes with aging. In J. E. Birren & K. W. Schaie (Eds.), *Handbook of the psychology of aging* (5th ed.) (pp. 31–45). San Diego: Academic Press.

Gabriel, Z., & Bowling, A. (2004). Quality of life from the perspectives of older people. *Ageing and Society, 24*, 675–691. doi:10.1017/S0144686X03001582

Handy, S., Weston, L., & Mokhtarian, P. L. (2005). Driving by choice or necessity? *Transportation Research, Part A: Policy and Practice, 39*, 183–203. doi:10.1016/j.tra.2004.09.002

Heikkinen, E. (1998). Background, design and methods of the Evergreen Project. *Journal of Aging and Physical Activity, 6*, 106–120.

Heikkinen, E., Berg, S., Schroll, M., Steen, B., & Viidik, A. (Eds.). (1997). *Functional status, health and aging: The Nora Study. Facts, research and interventions in geriatrics 1997*. Paris: Serdi.

Heikkinen, E., Era, P., Jokela, J., Jylhä, M., Lyra, A., & Pohjolainen, P. (1992). Socio-economic and life-style factors as modulators of health and functional capacity with age. In J. J. F. Schroots (Ed.), *Ageing, health and competence* (pp. 65–86). Amsterdam: Elsevier Science.

Hildebrand, E. D. (2003). Dimensions in elderly travel behaviour: A simplified activity-based model using lifestyle clusters. *Transportation, 30*, 285–306. doi:10.1023/A:1023949330747

Holland, C., Kellaher, L., Peace, S., Scharf, T., Breeze, E., Gow, J., & Gilhooly, M. (2005). Getting out and about. In A. Walker (Ed.), *Understanding quality of life in old age* (pp. 49–63). Berkshire: Open University Press.

Ketcham, C. J., & Stelmach, G. E. (2001). Age-related declines in motor control. In J. E. Birren & K. W. Schaie (Eds.), *Handbook of the psychology of aging* (5th ed.) (pp. 313–348). San Diego: Academic Press.

Lash, S., & Urry, J. (1994). *Economies of signs and space*. London: Sage.

Marottoli, R. A., Mendes de Leon, C. F., Glass, T. A., Williams, C. S., Cooney, L. M., & Berkman, L. F. (2000). Consequences of driving cessation: Decreased out-of-home activity levels. *Journal of Gerontology: Social Sciences, 55B*, S334–S340. doi:10.1093/geronb/55.6.S334

Marottoli, R., Mendes de Leon, C. F., Glass, T. A., Williams, C. S., Cooney, L. M., Berkman, L., & Tinetti, M. E. (1997). Driving cessation and increased depressive symptoms: Prospective evidence from the New Haven EPESE. *Journal of the American Geriatrics Society, 45*, 202–206. doi:10.1111/j.1532-5415.1997.tb04508.x

Mayring, P. (2003). *Qualitative Inhaltsanalyse. Grundlagen und Techniken* [Qualitative content analysis: Principles and methods] (8th ed.). Weinheim: Beltz.

Mokhtarian, P. L. (2005). Travel as a desired end, not just a means. *Transportation Research, Part A: Policy and Practice, 39*, 93–96. doi:10.1016/j.tra.2004.09.005

Mollenkopf, H., & Flaschenträger, P. (2001). *Erhaltung von Mobilität im Alter* [Maintaining mobility in old age]. Schriftenreihe des Bundesministeriums für Familie, Senioren, Frauen und Jugend: Vol. 197. Stuttgart: Kohlhammer.

Mollenkopf, H., Baas, S., Kaspar, R., Oswald, F., & Wahl, H.-W. (2006). Outdoor mobility in late life: Persons, environments and society. In H.-W. Wahl, H. Brenner, H. Mollenkopf, D. Rothenbacher, & C. Rott, (Eds.), *The many faces of health, competence and well-being in old age: Integrating epidemiological, psychological and social perspectives* (pp. 33–45). Dordrecht: Springer.

Mollenkopf, H., Marcellini, F., Ruoppila, I., Baas, S., Ciarrocchi, S., Hirsiaho, N., Kohan, D., & Principi, A. (2003). *The MOBILATE follow-up study 1995–2000. Enhancing outdoor mobility in later life: Personal coping, environmental resources, and technical support.* DZFA Research Report: Vol. 14. Heidelberg: German Centre for Research on Ageing [DZFA].

Mollenkopf, H., Marcellini, F., Ruoppila, I., Széman, Z., & Tacken, M. (Eds.). (2005). *Enhancing mobility in later life—Personal coping, environmental resources, and technical support. The out-of-home mobility of older adults in urban and rural regions of five European countries.* Amsterdam: IOS Press.

Mollenkopf, H., Marcellini, F., Ruoppila, I., Széman, Z., Tacken, M., Kaspar, R., & Wahl, H.-W. (2002). The role of driving in maintaining mobility in later life: A European view. *Gerontechnology, 1,* 231–250. doi:10.4017/gt.2002.01.04.003.00

Mollenkopf, H., Marcellini, F., Ruoppila, I., & Tacken, M. (Eds.). (2004a). *Ageing and outdoor mobility: A European study.* Amsterdam: IOS Press.

Mollenkopf, H., Marcellini, F., Ruoppila, I., Széman, Z., Tacken, M., & Wahl, H.-W. (2004b). Social and behavioral science perspectives on out-of-home mobility in later life: Findings from the European project MOBILATE. *European Journal of Ageing, 1,* 45–53. doi:10.1007/s10433-004-0004-3

Mollenkopf, H., Ruoppila, I., & Marcellini, F. (2007). Always on the go? Older people's outdoor mobility today and tomorrow: Findings from three European countries. In H.-W. Wahl, C. Tesch-Römer & A. Hoff (Eds.), *New dynamics in old age: Individual, environmental and societal perspectives* (pp. 175–198). Amityville: Baywood.

O'Neill, D., & Dobbs, B. (2004). Age-related disease, mobility, and driving. In A. J. Clarke & K. M. Sawyers (Eds.), *Transportation in an aging society: A decade of experience* (pp. 56–66). Transportation Research Board (TRB) Conference Proceedings: Vol. 27. Washington, DC: TRB.

Organization for Economic Co-operation and Development (OECD). (2001). *Ageing and transport: Mobility needs and safety issues.* Retrieved January 10, 2015, from http://www.ocs.polito.it/biblioteca/mobilita/OECDAgeing.pdf

Owsley, C. (2002). Driving mobility, older adults, and quality of life. *Gerontechnology, 1,* 220–230. doi:10.4017/gt.2002.01.04.002.00

Owsley, C. (2004). Driver capabilities. In A. J. Clarke & K. M. Sawyers (Eds.), *Transportation in an aging society: A decade of experience* (pp. 44–55). Transportation Research Board (TRB) Conference Proceedings: Vol. 27. Washington, DC: TRB.

Pochet, P. (2003). Travel practices and access to the car among the elderly. Current developments and issues. *Recherche Transport Sécurité, 79/80,* 93–106. doi:10.1016/S0761-8980(03)00009-8

Rammler, S. (2001). *Mobilität in der Moderne. Geschichte und Theorie der Verkehrssoziologie* [Mobility in modern society: History and theory of traffic sociology]. Berlin: edition sigma.

Rosenbloom, S. (2001). Sustainability and automobility among the elderly: An international assessment. *Transportation, 28,* 375–408. doi:10.1023/A:1011802707259

Rosenbloom, S. (2004). Mobility of the elderly: Good news and bad news. In A. J. Clarke & K. M. Sawyers (Eds.), *Transportation in an aging society: A decade of experience* (pp. 3–21). Transportation Research Board (TRB) Conference Proceedings: Vol. 27. Washington, DC: TRB.

Schaie, K. W. (2003). Mobility for what? In K. W. Schaie, H.-W. Wahl, H. Mollenkopf, & F. Oswald (Eds.), *Aging independently: Living arrangements and mobility* (pp. 18–27). New York: Springer.

Schaie, K. W., & Pietrucha, M. (Eds.). (2000). *Mobility and transportation in the elderly.* New York: Springer.

Schlag, B., & Schade, J. (2007). Psychologie des Mobilitätsverhaltens [Psychology of mobility behavior]. *Aus Politik und Zeitgeschichte, 29/30,* 27–32. Retrieved from http://www.bpb.de/system/files/pdf/0R4AHM.pdf

Siren, A., & Hakamies-Blomqvist, L. (2004). Private car as the grand equaliser? Demographic factors and mobility in Finnish men and women aged 65+. *Transportation Research Part F: Traffic Psychology and Behaviour, 7,* 107–118. doi:10.1016/j.trf.2004.02.003

Spirduso, W. W. (1995). *Physical dimensions of aging.* Champaign: Human Kinetics.

Staudinger, U. M. (2000). Viele Gründe sprechen dagegen, und trotzdem geht es vielen Menschen gut: Das Paradox des subjektiven Wohlbefindens [There are many reasons against it, but many people still feel well: The paradox of subjective well-being]. *Psychologische Rundschau, 51,* 185–197. doi:10.1026//0033-3042.51.4.185

Transportation Research Board, National Research Council (1988). *Transportation in an aging society: Improving mobility and safety for older persons* [Special report 218]. Washington, DC: Transportation Research Board.

U.S. Department of Transportation (2003). *Safe mobility for a maturing society: Challenges and opportunities.* Washington, DC: U.S. Department of Transportation.

Veenhoven, R. (1996). Developments in satisfaction-research. *Social Indicators Research, 37,* 1–46. doi:10.1007/BF00300268

Wahl, H.-W., Mollenkopf, H., Oswald, F., & Claus, C. (2007). Environmental aspects of quality of life in old age: Conceptual and empirical issues. In H. Mollenkopf & A. Walker (Eds.), *Quality of life in old age—International and multidisciplinary perspectives* (pp. 101–122). Dordrecht: Springer.

Wahl, H.-W., & Oswald, F. (2010). Environmental perspectives on aging. In D. Dannefer & C. Phillipson (Eds.), *International handbook of social gerontology* (pp. 111–124). London: Sage.

Zapf, W., & Habich, R. (Eds.). (1996). *Wohlfahrtsentwicklung im vereinten Deutschland* [Welfare development in the united Germany]. Berlin: edition sigma.

The Klaus Tschira Stiftung

In 1995 physicist Dr. h.c. Dr.-Ing. E. h. Klaus Tschira (1940–2015) created the German foundation known as the Klaus Tschira Stiftung. This organization is one of Europe's largest privately funded non-profit foundations. It promotes the advancement of natural sciences, mathematics, and computer science and strives to enhance the understanding of these fields. The focal points of the foundation are "Natural Science–Right from the Beginning," "Research," and "Science Communication." The involvement of the Klaus Tschira Stiftung begins in kindergartens and continues in primary and secondary schools, universities, and research facilities. The foundation champions new methods in the transfer of scientific knowledge, and supports both the development and intelligible presentation of research findings. The Klaus Tschira Stiftung pursues its objectives by conducting projects of its own but also awards subsidies after approval of applications. To foster and sustain work on selected topics, the Stiftung has also founded its own affiliates. Klaus Tschira's commitment to this objective was honored in 1999 with the "Deutscher Stifterpreis," the award conferred by the National Association of German Foundations.

The Klaus Tschira Stiftung is located in Heidelberg and has its head office in the Villa Bosch (Fig. 1), once the residence of Carl Bosch, a Nobel laureate in chemistry. www.klaus-tschira-stiftung.de

© The Author(s) 2017

P. Meusburger et al. (eds.), *Knowledge and Action*, Knowledge and Space 9,
DOI 10.1007/978-3-319-44588-5

Fig. 1 The Villa Bosch (Photo: Peter Meusburger)

Participants of the symposium "Knowledge and Action" at the studio of the Villa Bosch in Heidelberg (Photo: Thomas Bonn, Heidelberg)

Index

A

Abductive reasoning, 23, 256, 262, 264
Action
    control, 169–179
    duality of, 19
    experiment, 22, 224, 226–228, 230–237,
        240, 241, 245–248
    theory, 3–5, 8, 16, 23, 24, 45, 58–60, 100
Action-in-thought, 67–86
Action-theoretic approach, 57–60
Aesthetic(s), 2, 22, 58, 223, 224, 234, 244,
    246, 247
Ageing, 272, 283, 284
Agency, 3, 16, 59, 60, 94, 196, 199, 245
Anthropological constant, 18, 118
Anthropology, 58, 60, 230
Artful listening approach, 228
Artist, 22, 74, 223, 226, 227, 230–234, 236,
    240, 245, 247, 248
Artistic interventions, 21, 225, 227
Arts studio, 22, 224, 225
Associative
    learning model, 136–138
    processing, 149, 152
Asymmetric
    information, 119–120
    knowledge, 119–120
Asymmetries of knowledge, 18
Attitude, 19, 61, 72, 76, 85, 102–105, 120,
    146, 148, 155–158, 209
Australia, 23, 253, 260, 264
Autarky of knowledge, 122
Authoritative resources, 44
Authority, 14, 23, 35, 37, 63, 73, 76, 121, 139,
    195, 196, 242, 260

B

Barnes Foundation, 70
Behavior, 1, 2, 9, 17, 19, 20, 22, 32, 59, 78,
    100–106, 109, 117, 120, 121, 128, 130,
    132, 134, 139, 140, 146–150, 154–161,
    170, 172, 176, 178, 179, 206, 210,
    223, 227, 229, 232, 233, 241, 242,
    255, 267, 268
Behavioral
    control, 103, 146, 157–158
    decision research, 127, 128, 130, 136, 140
    intention, 20, 147, 170, 179
    schemata, 20, 154, 155, 161, 162
Belief, 8, 9, 16, 21, 61, 69, 71, 76, 79, 85, 95,
    100, 133, 146, 150, 155, 188–194, 196,
    199, 205, 209, 211, 212, 214, 269
Biologistic reduction, 37, 38
Black swans, 127
Bounded knowledge, 100, 122
Bounded rationality, 6, 8, 100, 102
Brazil, 95
Brundtland report, 4, 34, 52

C

Canadian Unuk, 256
Cartographic reason, 83, 85
Central place theory, 17, 73, 86
Chemnitz, 270
Children, 73, 74, 77, 82, 92, 96, 147, 203,
    205–213, 216, 257, 258
China, 95
Choice, 9, 19, 58, 69, 128–133, 136, 137, 153,
    170, 227, 232, 245, 247, 257, 259
Chorography, 36

P. Meusburger et al. (eds.), *Knowledge and Action*, Knowledge and Space 9,
DOI 10.1007/978-3-319-44588-5

CPSIA information can be obtained
at www.ICGtesting.com
Printed in the USA
LVHW080022061218
599431LV00003B/15/P